THUNDER ON THE DNEPR

THUNDER ON THE DNEPR

Zhukov-Stalin and the Defeat of Hitler's Blitzkrieg

Bryan I. Fugate and Lev Dvoretsky

PRESIDIO

This edition printed 2001

Copyright © 1997 by Bryan I. Fugate and Lev Dvoretsky

Published by Presidio Press
505 B San Marin Drive, Suite 160
Novato, CA 94945-1340

Library of Congress Cataloging-in-Publication Data

Fugate, Bryan I., 1943–
    Thunder on the Dnepr : Zhukov-Stalin and the defeat of Hitler's Blitzkrieg / by Brian I. Fugate and Lev Dvoretsky.
    p.   cm.
    Includes bibliographical references.
    ISBN 0-89141-529-7 (hardcover)
    ISBN 0-89141-731-1 (paperback)
    1. World War, 1939–1945—Soviet union. 2. World War, 1939–1945—Campaigns—Eastern Front. 3. Zhukov, Georgii Konstantinovich), 1896–1974. 4. Stalin, Joseph, 1879–1953. I. Dvoretsky, L. S. (Lev Semenovich) II. Title.
    D764.F845   1997
    940.54'2177—dc21   96-51177
                                     CIP

Index courtesy of J&B Imaging Services
Printed in the United States of America

Thus, those skilled at making the enemy move do so by creating a situation to which he must conform; they entice him with something he is certain to take, and with lures of ostensible profit they await him in strength.

—Sun Tzu, *The Art of War,*
translated by Samuel B. Griffith

From the expectations which preceded more than a score of wars since 1700, a curious parallel emerges. Nations confident of victory in a forthcoming war were usually confident that victory would come quickly. Nations which entered a war reluctantly, hoping to avoid defeat rather than snatch victory, were more inclined to believe that they were embarking on a long struggle. The kinds of arguments and intuitions which encouraged leaders to expect a victorious war strongly influenced their belief that the war would also be swift. The belief in a short war was mainly the overflow from the reservoir of conscious superiority.

Wars can only occur when two nations decide that they can gain more by fighting than by negotiating. War can only begin and can only continue with the consent of at least two nations.

—Geoffrey Blainey, *The Causes of War*

CONTENTS

LIST OF ABBREVIATIONS

German

Abwehr—Counter-intelligence department of the OKW

Dulag—Transit camp for prisoners of war

OKH—Army high command

OKW—Armed forces high command

SS—Elite military organization commanded by Heinrich Himmler. SS units such as *"Das Reich"* fought alongside regular army units in Russia

Russian

Commissar—Political officers with rank and authority equal to military commanders

KGB—Post-Stalin successor organization to the NKVD

NKVD—Stalin's secret police organization, headed by Beria

OSOVIAKHIM—General Society in Aiding Antiaircraft and Chemical Defenses

Politburo—Political bureau of the Central Committee of the Communist Party

STAVKA—General headquarters of the supreme command with Stalin as head

LIST OF IMPORTANT PEOPLE

(Rank as of June 22, 1941)

German

Bock, Field Marshal Fedor von—Commander of Army Group Center

Brauchitsch, Field Marshal Walter von—Commander in chief of the army

Göring, Reichs Marshal Hermann—Head of the Luftwaffe and one of the top leaders of the Nazi Party

Guderian, Gen. Heinz—Commander of Panzer Group 2

Halder, Gen. Franz—Chief of the General Staff

Heusinger, Gen. Alfred—Chief of operations of the General Staff, Halder's deputy

Hitler, Adolf—Head of state, supreme dictator

Hoth, Gen. Hermann—Commander of Panzer Group 3

Jodl, Gen. Alfred—Head of the OKW operations department

Keitel, Field Marshal Wilhelm—Head of the OKW

Kesselring, Field Marshal Albert—Commander of Luftwaffe Air Fleet Two

Kluge, Field Marshal Gunther von—Commander of Fourth Army

Paulus Gen. Friedrich—Staff Officer (Chief Operations Officer) of OKH, working for Halder

Schweppenburg, Gen. Leo Geyr von—Commander of XXIV Panzer Corps during Barbarossa

Warlimont, Gen. Walter—Head of Department "L" of the OKW

Weichs, Gen. Maximillian von—Commander of Second Army

Russian

Bagramian, Gen. I. Kh.—Head of the operations staff of the Southwestern Front

Budenny, Marshal S. M.—Civil War hero and commander of the Southwestern Direction at the time of the Kiev encirclement

Eremenko, Gen. A. I.—Commander of the Briansk Front

Khrushchev, N. S.—Commissar of the Southwestern Direction, succeeded Stalin as head of state and supreme dictator in the mid-1950s

Kirponos, M. P.—Commander of the Southwestern Front, killed in the Kiev encirclement

Konev, Gen. I. S.—Commander of Nineteenth Army at the battle of Smolensk, commander of the Western Front in September 1941, commander of the Kalinin Front during the battle of Moscow

Kuznetsov, Gen. F. I.—Participant in the February war game, commander of the Northwestern Front at the start of the war, commander of Twenty-first Army during counterattacks on the southern flank of Army Group Center in July 1941, commander of the Central Front in late July 1941

Meretskov, Gen. K. A.—Chief of the general staff during the January war games, executed on Stalin's orders after the destruction of the Bialystok salient

Pavlov, Gen. D. G.—Commander of the Western Front at the start of the war, executed on Stalin's orders after the destruction of the Bialystok salient

Rokossovsky, Gen. K. K.—Cavalryman, commander of Sixteenth Army during Barbarossa

Shaposhnikov, Marshal B. M.—Chief of the general staff at the time of the Kiev encirclement

Stalin, Joseph—Head of state, supreme dictator

Timoshenko, Marshal S. K.—Head of defense commissariat at the start of the war, replaced Budenny as commander of the Soutwestern Direction at the end of the Kiev encirclement

Zhukov, Gen. G. K.—Chief of the general staff at the start of the war, commander of the Reserve Front at Yelnia, commander of the Western Front during the battle of Moscow

Vasilevskii, Gen. A. H.—First deputy chief of operations at STAVKA, 1939–May 1940; head of operations directorate after 23 June 1941; trouble shooter for Stalin for remainder of 1941 going from front to front; replaced Shoposhnikov as chief of the General Staff in June 1942.

PREFACE

It is an enduring myth of the twentieth century that the German invasion of the Soviet Union in June 1941 caught Stalin and the Red Army totally by surprise. According to the legend, Stalin was so afraid of provoking Hitler that he purposefully took steps to ensure that the U.S.S.R. was woefully unprepared for war. There are stories about Russian officers wailing in anguish, "the enemy is firing on us, what shall we do?" Other tales are told about how easily the German panzer groups and mechanized forces cut through the ill-prepared border defenses and advanced rapidly for hundreds of kilometers into enemy territory.

The opening days and weeks of the campaign in the east named Operation Barbarossa by the Germans and "The Great Patriotic War" by the Russians, fulfilled all of the desires of the German General Staff. According to their plans, once the concentrations of the Red Army along the western frontier had been destroyed and the first (and only) defensive echelon had been decisively pierced, then nothing barred the way into the broad interior of the country including the rich granaries of Ukraine and the oil fields of the Caucasus. With these resources at their disposal, the German Wehrmacht would bestride the world like a colossus, impervious to defeat by any imaginable coalition of enemies. In short, by July 1941 the war was over for all practical purposes. All the necessary goals for a complete German victory had been achieved. Or, at least this should have been so if conventional wisdom about the disposition and preparedness for defense by the Red Army had held true.

But the war was not over. Events occurred in the period from July to September 1941which forever changed the course of the war. Instead of triumphs, the German Army experienced a series of delays and reversals culminating in a strategic defeat at the hands of Georgii Zhukov at the very gates of Moscow in December 1941.

It is the purpose of this book to focus not only on the crucial July-December period but to explore as well how the stage was set for the Soviet victory in the Great Patriotic War.

The thesis of this book is that Stalin and the Soviet High Command were not caught off guard by the German invasion but in fact had developed a skillful, innovative, and highly secret plan to oppose it. This plan was not conceived by one man in a unique flash of genius. Neither was the plan agreed to and carried out with the full cooperation of all the important participants, nor was the actual implementation of the plan accomplished without serious mistakes. Yet, it worked.

The reason the plan worked was its basic simplicity. The plan also took good advantage of both the enemy's weaknesses as well as the intrinsic strengths of Stalin's Soviet Union, its resources, manpower, and overall capabilities. It was, under the circumstances, probably the only plan that could save the country from suffering a total and ignominious defeat.

The first part of the book examines the state of military planning and preparedness in the Soviet Union during the time after the rapid German defeat of France in 1940 up to the January-February 1941 period when the final defense strategy was formulated. This strategy would ensure the nation's ability not only to survive the biggest and most violent invasion in history but indeed to prevail over it. The key elements of the strategic plan were developed during three vitally important war games in January and February. The first two of these were held at the Kremlin in early January under Stalin's personal direction.

Although both war games in January were highly significant in terms of their influence on Soviet planning, it was the third game, the one in February, that gave final form to what would become the Soviet Union's strategy for winning the war.

It should be mentioned here that the last two of these war games have never been discussed in Western sources. The two games in January have been openly written about in Soviet publications, but the third, the one in February, has never been reported anywhere.

Because the official records of the first two games were made available to the authors, their play and significance is examined in some detail.

The facts the authors have been able to gather about the third war game are less certain in some respects but, nevertheless, we have assembled considerable evidence to show what happened at the game and we present a compelling analysis about what effect the game had on the overall outcome of the war on the Eastern Front.

In brief, the two games in January convinced Stalin and his high command that concentrating the bulk of the Red Army close to the western frontier was a recipe for disaster. This was particularly true of the forces located within the so-called Bialystok salient which jutted far to the west and could easily be cut off and its defenders surrounded and annihilated. The third and most secret war game played out the final strategy for winning the war.

We now come to the title of this book, *Thunder on the Dnepr*. The reader will discover what the "thunder" was and how it came to be positioned on the southern flank of German Army Group Center along the upper Dnepr and its tributaries, such as the Sozh.

The second part of the book deals with the actions of the combat forces as they encountered each other in the vast theater of operations in the Soviet Union. The maneuvers of the opposing forces are explained in the context of the strategies that were in place. The halt of the Army Group Center at Smolensk and along the upper Dnepr in July-August and the deflection of part of its force, Guderian's Panzer Group 2, to the south, eventually reaching all the way to east of Kiev, were truly major turning points in the course of the war. After this turn to the south, the Wehrmacht had no hope of crushing the Red Army before the onset of winter. The Wehrmacht was caught in the open as it neared Moscow by the powerful blows of Zhukov's well-prepared counteroffensive.

The fateful turn to the south is usually explained as a blunder by Hitler who refused to listen to his generals. The evidence we present here, however, shows that the problems on the southern flank of Army Group Center were brought about by Russian forces positioned opportunely to assault the advancing Germans at the moment of their maximum vulnerability. This moment occurred as the Wehrmacht pushed north and east of the screening Pripyat Marshes. All of this had been envisioned in the February war game.

The third and final portion of the book sums up all of the results which flowed from the flaws and mistakes in strategy on both sides as well as the successes. It was at Yelnia on the upper Dnepr in July and August that the Wehrmacht suffered its first real setback on the Eastern Front. The strategy and tactics used at Yelnia by the Russians were honed and fine-tuned by Zhukov until he perfected them on an enormous scale around Moscow in December.

After Moscow, Germany had no hope of winning the war on the Eastern Front. The concentration of the Red Army in the north led to a spectacular victory over the frozen Germans, ill-equipped for a winter war. The continued success of the Wehrmacht in the weakened south only lasted until the most visible turn of the tide at Stalingrad in late 1942-early 1943. But, Stalingrad was merely an inevitability. The war was essentially won in 1941 along the upper Dnepr and at Moscow, much in the same way that Germany's fate was sealed after the "miracle of the Marne" in 1914 turned the powerful German right wing away from an envelopment of Paris as had been envisioned in the Schlieffen Plan.

In my earlier book, *Operation Barbarossa: Strategy and Tactics on the Eastern Front, 1941*, (Presidio Press, 1984) I presented the idea that Soviet strategic planning on the eve of the German invasion was not as backward as commonly believed. The book postulated that the Soviet supreme command had developed a brilliant, though desperate, strategy for dealing with the Barbarossa plan. The evidence we present here based on Soviet documents discovered by co-author and retired Russian colonel and eminent historian, Lev Dvoretsky and made public for the first time, shows convincingly that the failure of the German blitzkrieg in Russia was not an accident nor a blunder on anyone's part, other than a general error in not perceiving the enemy's strategy and countering it effectively. Rather, the defeat of Barbarossa was much more due to the strategic vision of two remarkable men, Zhukov and Timoshenko. Without them, unquestionably the war would have had a much different ending. Their success during the January war games in demonstrating to Stalin the disaster that would flow from a forward strategy in the west was crucial beyond all estimation. Their ability to get the go-ahead from Stalin to implement the new in-depth strategy after conclusively proving its effectiveness in the February war game was absolutely vital.

But, no strategy, however far-seeing and effective, can work unless the adversary conducts his operations in conformity with the basic scenario—in the case of the Zhukov/ Timoshenko strategy it was assumed that the Germans would place Moscow above all other objectives. If this had not been so, had the German high command been more flexible, as Halder and Jodl attempted to be, and shifted the thrust of the attack further to the south at the expense of Army Group Center, then the carefully laid Soviet strategy might have come to naught.

It is not exaggeration to say that that Germany could have won the war on the Eastern Front had they forgone the assault on fortress Moscow in December 1941 and not placed Army Group Center in extreme peril from Zhukov's skillfully positioned strategic reserve.

Why and how all of these fateful decisions were made and what the influences were of the key personalities on both sides is the story of this book.

In such ways are the fates of nations decided.

ACKNOWLEDGMENTS

The author's wish to thank the Staff of AMSCORT International in Moscow amd Dr. Jonathan Carson in Austin, Texas, for their invaluable help in creating this book.

Susan Fugate and Katherine Fugate also made the work possible.

INTRODUCTION

The Origins of Russian Military Doctrine

In the realm of military doctrine, Russia and the Soviet Union had been remarkably consistent in their basic world outlook since the time of the earlier tsarist imperialism. The primary concern in this introduction will not be with the details of doctrinal development or with the lives of the various individuals who contributed so greatly to its evolution (for example, Suvorov, Kutuzov, Trotsky, Frunze, Tukhachevsky, and Zhukov). Rather, it will be with those organic characteristics of Russia, and the Soviet state, that created an environment allowing these doctrinal elements to flourish.

Traditionally, the transformation of Russia into a major European and military power is said to have occurred during the reign of Peter I ("the Great," 1682–1725). Certainly, however, there was a history of fighting spirit and doctrinal coherency dating back much earlier, to the time of the Tatar occupation and the rise of the Muscovite principality. These struggles in Russia's infancy were, for the most part, absorptive in nature.

The shock of the Tatar invasion under Batu and Subudai in the mid-thirteenth century could not have been withstood by any force that Kievan Russia could muster. The nature of the Tatar occupation was such, however, that it gave the Russian people a chance to survive as a separate entity; they were not submerged and incorporated as a nation into the corpus of the Golden Horde. There were two main reasons for this: (1) the Tatars did not try to move into the forests and towns in the north, choosing instead to remain in the south feeding their herds on the rich grasslands, and (2) the Tatars, nomadic by nature, did not develop the urban productive base,

1

including metalworking and weapons manufacture, that would allow them to keep pace with advancing technology. Economically, the Russians were able to maintain a system isolated from the Tatars, who were content merely to enforce the payment of tribute. In the long run, the relationship of economic and political forces was such that the Tatar rule would wither away, which it did, in fact, during the reign of Ivan III (1462–1505).

From the military standpoint, the Russian people learned several things from the Tatar occupation. The first lesson was that barriers had to be erected in the east and south to prevent a repetition of those events. Initially, this was done in the reign of Ivan IV ("the Terrible," 1533–84) by conquering centers of Tatar power in Kazan and Astrakhan and later by erecting fortress cities such as Orel for "island defense" and hiring Cossack troops as mercenary guards. Ivan's aggressive liquidation of the Tatar and Turkish menace continued under Peter I and Catherine II ("the Great," 1762–96). Another lesson the Russians took to heart was the importance of developing a military caste. This process was first begun during the reign of Ivan III with the creation of the *pomestie* system, whereby land grants could be obtained by the nobles from the Moscow government only on the condition that they help raise armies and pay for them. This system of land tenure forced the nobles to tie the peasants to the land as much as possible and keep them from leaving. According to one respected Russian historian, the wide use of the *pomestie* system was one of the prime factors in the spread of serfdom throughout Russia.[1] The danger from outside invasion and depredation was much worse than the danger of losing freedom to a crushing system of serfdom that, in many ways, was harsher than the treatment meted out to slaves in the Western world.

In Russia, the vestiges of serfdom were not eliminated until 1917, for the threat of the Tatars was quickly replaced by that of other powers with predatory interests, particularly in the rich and bountiful farming area that had supported the old Kievan state, the Ukraine. The military caste and the *pomestie* warrior-estate system provided a practical means for repelling these threats, now from the west from Poland-Lithuania and from Sweden. The ascendency of the Principality of Moscow, the neutralization of the Turko-Tatar threat, the ending of the expansionist aims of Poland-Lithuania, and the institutionalization of serfdom and the military caste were all logically connected and formed the basis for the next stage of military development—the creation of a large national standing army and navy under Peter the Great and the other Romanovs.

Much has been written about the military reforms of Peter the Great, so no attempt will be made here to recount his achievements in detail. Suffice it to say that after the defeat of the Swedish king Charles XII at Poltava and the Treaty of Nystad in 1721, Russia emerged as a major European power. Although Peter had gleaned his ideas about military reform from his extensive travels in the West and from numerous western military advisors imported into Russia, such as the Dutch Franz Timmermann, the Scot Patrick Gordon, and the Swiss François Lefort, among others, the shape of the new army and its methods of warfare had some uniquely Russian characteristics.

In terms of strategy, Peter did not choose to meet Charles on unfavorable territory. Peter was content to allow the Swedish king to become mired first in a seemingly endless war in Poland. Then, when Charles did strike directly at Russia, the tsar did not try to blunt the offensive too soon but instead allowed the invading army to spend its energy overcoming the countless difficulties in maneuvering across great distances and over inhospitable terrain. Peter had learned scorched earth tactics from the Tatars and used them against the Swedes, denying them the use of crops and fodder. Finally, when Charles's offensive force was spent, a relatively easy victory was gained at Poltava at a small cost to Russia.

The commanders of Peter's army were initially drawn from the old nobility (*dvoriane*), which had been expected to serve as the officer caste as well as to staff the ranks of the newly created civil administrations. Since there were no military colleges, the upper-class youth trained in one of the three guards regiments—the Semenovskii, the Preobrazhenskii, and the "Life Regiment" (later the Horse Guards). The growing need for military and civilian officers, however, soon outstripped the supply of hereditary nobles. An attempt to remedy this was the enoblement of bright young men who succeeded in making their way upward in the hierarchy. Finally, in 1722, a "Table of

Ranks" was instituted, which, among other things, granted the title of hereditary noble to every military man who achieved the lowest officer grade. This Table of Ranks remained in use substantially without change in Russia until 1917. Despite the fact that a certain "democratization" was admitted in the opening of a path into noble status, the older aristocracy maintained a firm grip on the higher military posts. The traditional gap between nobles and nonnobles in the military continued to exist, but after 1722 it existed in official bureaucratic form. One of the "outsider" representatives of the new military caste, Alexander Suvorov (1730–1800), became the spiritual father of Russian military doctrine and still is paid high homage by modern Russia in the form of a coveted military decoration that is named for him. In many ways, the privileged officer caste was perpetuated in the USSR, with officers' families intermarrying and attending special schools. The Russian officer even today is a breed apart from the "nonnoble" lesser ranks and civilians.

In the career of Suvorov can be seen many of the elements that pointed the way toward Russia's future greatness as a military power. The essence of the great general's teachings can be found in his book *The Science of Victory*: (1) The offensive is the main weapon of war. (2) Achieve rapidity in attack; use the bayonet. (3) Do not lapse into methodical routine; use objective observation. (4) Full power to the supreme command. (5) Fight in the field, not in fortifications; confuse the enemy. (6) Sieges are wasteful; open assault is best. (7) Do not waste forces in occupation of points; bypass the enemy if possible.

Russia sought to play a major role in European affairs for the first time in its history through Suvorov's Italian campaign in 1799, where he astonished some of the best French generals, such as Joubert and Moreau, by long forced marches and rapid deployment for the attack. It was Suvorov's plan never to defend a location for long but always attack whenever the opportunity arose. It was also his plan never to assault a fortress simply for the sake of occupying it; rather, his goal was always "to destroy the enemy's life force and his ability to make war." Suvorov became known as a practitioner of combined-arms tactics; that is, no one branch of arms, such as cavalry or artillery, was given favored treatment or allowed to operate autonomously from the other armed branches. Suvorov's phased and integrated attacks utilizing all forms of combat, including lavish artillery (so loved by Peter) and the bayonet, earned him a fearsome reputation, especially after the assault of the Turkish fortress of Izmail in 1790. Suvorov's emphasis on training for the battlefield and cultivation of morale, plus his unique methods of march, deployment, and attack, established a theme for the future progress of the Russian national army. As great as Suvorov's legacy was, however, it remained to be seen whether the graft of his genius had actually taken hold on the roots left by Peter's reforms. Had the army been annealed in the campaign of 1799 to withstand an onslaught of the largest European army ever raised, led by one of the most outstanding commanders of all time, Napoleon?

The course of events leading up to Napoleon's invasion of Russia in June 1812 should not concern us here. The outcome of the war and its general pattern are also well known. From the doctrinal standpoint, however, several interesting features need to be mentioned.

In the first place, the Russian general Barclay de Tolly's decision to allow Napoleon's Grand Armée to enter Russia without a serious attempt at resistance caused an enormous political problem, both at court and with Russia's chief ally, Britain. It is important to bear in mind, however, that it is the oldest maxim in war "never to do what your enemy wants you to do" and that Napoleon would quickly have blown the Russian army into chaff had he been challenged close to the frontier. It should be remembered also that Kutuzov (1745–1813), Suvorov's disciple, continued de Tolly's retreat after he became supreme commander. The point is this: the Russian army had to rely on a strategy of retreat and scorched earth despite all the political and economic liabilities of such a strategy. To have done otherwise would have invited complete disaster. In this respect, Joseph Stalin's position was not much different from Tsar Alexander's.

There is another interesting parallel between Alexander's and Stalin's wars: the peasant factor. In both cases, the peasantry remained loyal to the regime and gave their lives in vast numbers to repel the invaders. One might wonder why this was so, considering that conditions for them, both in serfdom and later on collective farms, were so harsh and degrading. Answering this question provides an insight into what has made the heart of Russia beat with a singular will to live.

Before Napoleon's great adventure in 1812, there had been much talk in Russia about what the French emperor might do if he succeeded in unfurling his flag above the Kremlin. There seemed to be a widespread hope among the peasants (and fear among the nobility) that Napoleon would abolish feudalism and serfdom in Russia and encourage the emergence of a small-holder class of farmers, similar to what had emerged in France during the revolution. It is not precisely certain what the origins of this rumor were, but anyone familiar with Napoleon's attitude toward the land question in Poland would have expressed extreme reservations about liberation of the serfs in Russia by the French. Polish peasants were "liberated" in name only in 1807, but no move was made really to free them. The Polish nobles rallied to Napoleon's cause in 1812 because he pointedly refused to liberate the serfs in White Russia and in Lithuania. Napoleon also used French troops to put down peasant revolts in White Russia at the request of Polish landowners. Once the war began and Napoleon failed to issue an edict freeing the serfs in Russia, the peasantry rallied to the Tsarist cause with a vengeance.

Kutuzov's strategy of retreat without giving battle was, until the fateful confrontation at Borodino, forced by necessity, as in fact most Russian strategic decisions have been. What was unique about Kutuzov was his refusal to destroy the Grand Armée in November 1812 en route back to Poland. The reason for Kutuzov's "parallel pursuit" of the demoralized Grand Armée could be that the French were being destroyed through exposure and starvation anyway, and although it is true that an attempt was made to keep them from crossing the Berezina River, another explanation could be that Kutuzov simply did not consider that ridding Europe of Napoleon was truly in Russia's best interest at that particular point. Russia had not yet reached the stage when massive intervention in European affairs was an all-consuming objective; this characteristic of Russian foreign policy would appear later.

After the Congress of Vienna and the final defeat of Napoleon in 1815, Russia, under Nicholas I and Alexander II, began a long and steady decline in military preparedness. Whereas in 1812 the average Russian army unit was equipped with more cannon than its counterpart in the French army, during the period after 1815 virtually no improvements were made in Russian artillery. This lack of progress became painfully evident during the Crimean War (1854–56).

The events in the Balkans that preceded the Crimean War are of peripheral importance here. The key points to observe are that Russia by 1854 was interested in obtaining world power status by commanding the Bosporus and the Dardanelles and that a joint operation by two major powers, Britain and France, albeit with limited tactical objectives, was just sufficient to hold the Russian bear in check. The fourth major European power, Prussia, maintained a strained silence; nevertheless, Russia could not overlook the possibility of a threat either from the west or from the north against Saint Petersburg. Russian military doctrine had accounted for the difficulties that might be encountered in a two- or even three-front war, but not against major opponents. The other European powers had coped with this problem many times before, notably Prussia during the Seven Years' War and Britain in its war against Napoleon and against America in 1812, but for Russia the problems seemed especially grievous considering the vast distances involved and the poverty of its transportation resources. These problems in fighting multifront wars remained essentially unsolved by Russia in the nineteenth century, and at the same time became ever more important because of the continuous expansion of colonization in Asia—in Turkestan and Siberia. The dangers inherent in such rapid expansion became all too real when Japanese torpedo boats sank the Russian fleet at Port Arthur in late 1904.

In the war against the Japanese, despite the twin catastrophes on land at Mukden and at sea at Tsushima, the army held together and did not crack, even though the homeland seethed with unrest, culminating in the abortive Revolution of 1905. The reasons for the steadfastness of the army under these conditions are instructive, especially when its behavior is contrasted with the inward collapse that occurred in 1917.

First, the Japanese war objectives were clearly limited in scope, and all of the fighting took place on foreign soil, in China and Korea.

The point is that the Japanese made no attempt to take what was per-
ceived to be Russian territory proper, nor did they have a political
philosophy that they cared to promulgate among the Russian people. Second, the war was a short one, lasting only a few months. Had
it turned into a protracted conflict, the unrest at home would have
worked as a poison among the ranks of soldiers. However, in 1917,
by contrast: (1) a political philosophy hostile to the regime was
spread through the army by a well-organized group within Russia;
(2) the First World War was a protracted conflict, and the heavy losses
on the battlefield, coupled with the hope of positive good coming
from a change in the regime, resulted in a devastating moral collapse
in the military.

Russian military doctrine on the eve of World War I in 1914 had
become a virtual prisoner of Allied planning. France, in particular,
had been given a full claim in Russia's stake in strategic and tactical
theory. Probably never in history has a major power so completely
prostrated itself to the goals of its allies. The reasons for this utter
abandonment of independent thought are complex, but the point
needs to be made that by August 1914, Russian military doctrine had
become a mere extension of French revanchist dreams. Aside from
vague musings about Pan-Slavist causes, which few Russians could
ever understand, in the beginning Russia had no publicly voiced
strategic objectives in the war. Beneath the surface there were objectives that, in the past, had caused Britain's adamant and undying
opposition: the breakup of the Austro-Hungarian Empire and the
seizure of the Straits from Turkey, Germany's ally. The seizure of the
Straits would have transformed Russia immediately into a world
power and would have put it squarely into the arena of competition
with Britain from Suez to India. In March 1915, Britain formally
agreed that Russia could annex the Straits and Constantinople, but
after the failure of the British Dardanelles campaign in that year, this
seemed to be a moot point. As it was, the agreements with the Allies
concerning the Straits were kept secret until December 1916, but by
then the overall military situation had deteriorated to the point that
the announcement failed to stir any public support whatsoever.

Russia's supporting role in the war, as determined by French requirements, called for it to take up the offensive into East Prussia

soon after the commencement of hostilities, a mission for which the army was tragically ill equipped. The inertia of Russia's mobilization schedule alone (and early mobilization itself would have been tantamount to a declaration of war) should have predicated against such a foolhardy scheme as tramping directly into the lair of the strongest enemy. Had Russia waited until the proper moment for full mobilization of its steamroller, and had the army been used properly against Austria-Hungary, an opponent more nearly equal to Russia in fighting capacity in 1914, then good results might have been achieved. As it was, however, the outcome was virtually predestined. As the sun set over the bloody battlefield of Tannenberg, so it set over Russia's hopes for a quick victory. Once the war ground on into an interminable struggle, new forces came into play that brought about the eventual disintegration of the armed forces. The lack of objectives or any sense of moral cause in the war, in addition to the windrows of casualties, themselves probably would not have caused the collapse of the army. The injection, however, of a political "virus"—Bolshevism—into Russia by the German enemy created conditions favorable for the development of a revolutionary fever.

The Bolsheviks—Lenin, Trotsky, Stalin, and the others—were astute enough to realize that their chances for success in toppling the regime were directly related to Russia's continued participation in the war. The war provided the catalyst for change, and when the provisional government decided not only to stay in the conflict but indeed even to increase the effort, the roof began to cave in on the Russian army.

Russia had given a good account of itself in the war, especially against the Austrians. A. A. Brusilov's offensive into Galicia in the summer of 1916 was a significant success and showed what the army could do when it was given a good plan and was well led against forces more or less its equal. But the army's record against German forces was dismal, even disastrous. This failure is tied to economic developments: industrialization in Russia in 1914 was still in its infancy, and the country had certainly not kept pace with Germany in any area of manufacture, let alone armaments. In 1913 Germany produced 29.1 million tons of iron and steel and 191.5 million tons of coal; in the same year Russia produced 4.43 million tons of iron and steel and 39.85 million tons of coal. The Russian transportation system was weak and the methods of supply heartbreakingly slow, this in a country that had undertaken the invasion of East Prussia as its first act in the war. In October 1914, the Russian army needed four weeks to move ten army corps a distance of about 325 km. from western Galicia to the middle Vistula. The entire month of May 1915 was needed to deploy an army in Bukovina, and even after a successful offensive operation was concluded, the army had to pull back because of supply problems. By way of comparison, in March 1918 the French were able to concentrate twelve divisions to defend Amiens within only four days. The Germans needed only a week to pull eight divisions into the Gorlice-Tarnow area in May 1915—a force that was increased to thirty divisions in another two weeks to block a Rumanian intervention and ward off an expected Russian offensive. The Russians themselves calculated that it required two weeks to move one army corps of two divisions from the northern to the southern part of the front. It is clear that the strategic role assigned to Russia by its allies was not in its best interests. But finally, it must be said that the external enemy was not what overcame the army; instead, the forces of adhesion in its ranks began to loosen due to internal propaganda.

The First World War differed from Napoleon's invasion in 1812 in its effect on the Russian people and the army. As has been mentioned, the Russian people felt that they had nothing to gain from a Napoleonic victory in 1812. On the contrary, the peasants felt they had potentially a great deal to lose from the French alliance with the Polish nobility. During World War I, however, the army gradually came to perceive that the survival of the tsarist regime would be a greater evil than revolution at home and a humiliating peace with the enemy. This gradual change in mood came about because the country's war aims, at least publicly, were dictated by the Allies and had little or nothing to do with Russia's interests as a nation or those of the people. The whole way the war was conducted, at both the strategic and the tactical levels, demonstrated eventually even to the lowest private that the army was literally being used up for the Allies' cause, not Russia's. Finally, an ingredient was added in 1917 that had been missing during the earlier invasion of Russia; an internal political movement at home promised something definitely better if the soldiers would turn their guns against the regime instead of the enemy.

The partisan movement, which has existed in Russia at least since the time of Pugachev's rebellion under Catherine the Great, is illustrative of this point. Soviet commentators lauded the usefulness of the partisans who operated behind German lines in World War II, but they failed to mention that large bands of partisans, such as the one led by Taras Borovets, fought against the Red Army. Some of the Ukrainian nationalist groups, Stepan Bandera's, for example, were particularly troublesome to both the Germans and the Soviets and attempted to organize a resistance against both sides in the war. Other disaffected army men and peasants joined the so-called Russian Liberation Army (ROA) headed by General Vlasov, a former Soviet hero who lent his services to the Nazis. In addition, one only has to recall the fierce struggle of collectivization in 1929–33, which led to the wholesale slaughter of livestock by the peasants, to realize how potentially devastating such disaffection can be.

We now turn to the immediate pre–World War II period in the USSR and examine the events leading up to the crisis in strategic planning that was brought to the surface in the war games of early 1941.

Strategy in the Early Soviet Period

Much of the debate about strategy in the 1920s and 1930s and in the period immediately prior to the war took place behind closed doors, and many of the works associated with strategic issues have never been publicly aired either in the West or in the East. The reasons why this has been so until the present day are not hard to understand. Basically, the elements of the debate revolved around (1) the inevitability of a life-and-death struggle between socialism and capitalism, and (2) the necessity of a first-strike strategy in order to achieve victory over the enemies of socialism. The final stage of the pre-war debate took a bizarre turn when, after the hard evidence of a German invasion became irrefutably apparent, the first-strike strategy had to be hurriedly and incompletely improvised for a strategic defense.

The effort to develop military doctrine in the Soviet Union in the 1920s was multifaceted. The nature of future war was considered from the political and military as well as the economic and technological points of view. The core principle of Soviet military theory concerning the political nature of future war was as follows: it would be a fight to the death between capitalism and socialism—this was the legacy of Lenin and Trotsky's theory of "Permanent Revolution."

In the 1920s a group of theoreticians in the Red Army headquarters headed by M. N. Tukhachevsky along with Ia. M. Zhigurat, A. N. Nikonov, and Ia. K. Bersin produced a work entitled *Future War,* in which it was supposed that an attack against the Soviet Union might take the form of an intervention by a military coalition comprising six groups: (1) adventurers and bankers financing the venture, (2) organizers of a military and economic anti-Soviet armed front, (3) suppliers of manpower ("cannon fodder") for this front, (4) instigators and disseminators of hostile political propaganda, (5) hostile capitalist interests who wanted an economic blockade against the USSR, and (6) so-called "observers" who would maintain a "neutrality" favorable to the enemies of the USSR. It was believed that there were some countries that had suffered at the hands of western imperialism, China perhaps, that would take a favorable position toward the USSR.

Great hopes were placed on support from the international proletariat guided by the various national Communist Parties in the advanced capitalist countries—England, Germany, France, and the United States. Tukhachevsky and the others believed that the proletariat (the "toiling masses") would rally to the side of the Soviet Union in its just fight in repelling blatant capitalist aggression. The battles of the Red Army, then, would be supplemented by rebellions and civil wars in the enemy's rear. At the same time it was stressed that assistance on the part of the proletariat of the countries conducting aggression would hardly become decisive very quickly. As was stated in *Future War,* "without serious effort—and victories of the Red Army—there would be no demoralization of our enemies great enough to transform a war against the USSR into a civil war, a revolution." In other words, after paying homage to the hearthstone of Communist ideology—that the industrial nations of the world were on the brink of a socialist revolution—the Soviet Union's best military minds had concluded that in the event of war with any combination of major capitalist powers the country was essentially on its own and had to provide itself with whatever means necessary for defense with no view toward any meaningful outside help.

In 1928 the headquarters of the Red Army conditionally divided all main countries of the world into four groups as follows:[2]

- States obviously hostile to the USSR and making up the anti-Soviet front
- States capable under certain conditions of joining this front
- States not interested in war with the Soviet Union because of geographic, economic, and political factors
- States friendly to the USSR

After careful analysis of the potentially hostile forces arrayed against the USSR, scenarios were developed for how a war might begin. In these scenarios the basic assumption was that war could begin with little or no warning. The niceties of diplomatic ultimatums and formal declarations of war were artifacts of the past. Once this reality was accepted, it followed then that the Soviet Union had no choice but to embark on a rearmament and reorganization plan to massively build up the armed forces in the shortest possible period of time. The baseline assumption in all scenarios was that until the country could arm itself and achieve parity or superiority vis-à-vis its likely opponents, the Soviet Union would be vulnerable to attack by an enemy willing and able to launch a first strike. Particular strategic concern was given to the situation along the western borders, the age-old avenues of attack by Teutonic knights, kings of Sweden, Polish nobles, and emperors of France. Translating theory into fact, the armed forces headquarters staffs began the work of delineating defensive zones, defining operational boundaries between fronts, and setting forth tactical guidelines. Defense, although first in the minds of the planners during the country's vulnerable phase, was always considered to be a prelude to counterattack. It was believed that eventually the Soviet Union would be able to carry the war back into enemy territory and that the enemy states would then crumble from within as the proletariat rose up to strike down the ruling class, as the workers had done in Berlin in 1918.

In this outlining of a defense strategy against attack from the west, considerable attention was devoted to an area known in Eastern Europe as Polesia or more widely in the West as the Pripyat Marshes, a vast area of thousands of square kilometers along the drainage area of the Pripyat River as it meanders through Bielorussia and empties into the Dnepr River. These impassable marshes provided a natural defensive barrier that served the purpose of dividing the zone of combat on the Western Front into northern and southern zones. As will be seen later, the Russians managed to use the marshes to their benefit, whereas the Germans were never able to cope successfully with coordinating their armies on both sides of them. In a critical maneuver in August and September 1941, the German high command had to divert a significant part of Army Group Center to the south of the Pripyat to aid in the encirclement of Kiev. This diversion and the way it was handled had vital consequences for the outcome of the war on the Eastern Front that are impossible to overestimate.

The most important political aspect of Soviet military doctrine during the vulnerable period in the 1920s was to prevent immediate war. After ending the war with Poland in 1921 and concluding the Treaty of Rapallo with Germany in 1922, thus stabilizing the situation on the Western Front for a time, serious work was begun on mobilizing the state-controlled economy for war and revamping the military to take advantage of new situations and new technologies. The assessments and forecasts of what was needed and the directions all of these new efforts should go were undertaken by several remarkable and gifted theoreticians, perhaps the best in the world, including M. V. Frunze, M. N. Tukhachevsky, N. E. Varfolomeev, A. N. Lapohinsky, V. A. Molikov, A. A. Shilovsky, A. A. Svechin, V. K. Triandafilov, and D. M. Karbyshev. Much of their collective philosophy was embodied in the Red Army *Field Manual* of 1929 (PU-29).

Taking into consideration the potential power and resources of possible belligerents in a future war as well as their weaknesses, Soviet military theoreticians came to the conclusion that the ultimate conflict would be conducted by highly mechanized mass armies equipped with the most modern weapons. It was always a fundamental assumption in Soviet military planning that the next war would be waged by combined-arms elements comprising infantry, mechanized infantry, armor, artillery, airpower, and, where applicable, naval forces. Never, except for a brief period of aberration, did the Soviet leadership elevate any one single element of the combined-arms matrix above all others. The one time when Stalin listened to his armored commanders to the exclusion of the others and became convinced that tanks could rapidly wipe out the enemy along the Western Front in a Soviet first strike, it nearly cost the country its existence. When Zhukov and Timoshenko finally exposed the fallacies of a first-strike strategy in the January 1941 war games and convinced Stalin of the folly of this approach, the situation was righted, but by then a terrible price had to be exacted for repairing a colossal blunder, the sacrifice of the armies of the Western Front.

V. A. Melnikov wrote the following to substantiate the need to view war in a combined-arms context: "The immense scope of contemporary war, which will be conducted by the most powerful armed coalitions comprising millions of soldiers and many thousands of modern weapons, can be victoriously resolved only by skillful use of all three armed services operating on land, in the air and at sea."

Soviet military theoreticians reasoned that the decisive role in the future war would be played by the army supported with artillery, tanks, and aircraft. In accordance with these views, they continually shifted the balance between the different armed services and arms to meet the requirements of the newly emerging military science. The rear of the country was considered to be a direct participant in the war as wide employment of aviation, especially bombers and air defense forces (PVO), led to the further obliteration of the distinction between front and rear. For the first time, planners had to consider that civilian losses could equal or exceed those of the military.

Taking into account the coalition nature of war, the availability in advanced countries of well-equipped armies comprising millions of soldiers, mass mechanization, and motorization of troops, Soviet military theoreticians accepted the idea that combat would be highly dynamic and maneuverable and the breadth and depth of warfare would occur on an unprecedented scale. But at the same time theoreticians did not ignore traditional forms of combat, and continued emphasis was placed upon the development and implementation of fortified zones of defense. Thus, M. V. Frunze stated that "no war, be it highly maneuverable, would ever be waged without fortified zones. The very carrying out of maneuver requires to some extent the existence of fortified zones that can be used as a base of operations. Therefore, it is urgently necessary for all Red commanders to acquaint the Red Army with the new techniques of battle."

The above-mentioned theoretical views provided the basis for Soviet military doctrine during the post–Civil War period (1921–34). However, many of the principles of warfare were subjected to serious alteration during this period because of the impact of the technological revolution in the economy and within the armed forces. Taking into account these changes, two stages in the development of Soviet military doctrine can be defined: (1) from 1921 to 1929, and (2) from 1930 to January 1934. The first period was characterized by a linear concept of warfare, which was based on the capability of troops to influence the enemy only along the line of immediate contact with his forward units to the depth of the effective range of artillery fire. All this was reflected in the theory of successive operations and the theory of "successive neutralization of separate elements of the enemy's formations."[3]

The second stage was characterized by a transition to the development of deep ("spatial") formations engaged in combat with mass employment of tanks, aviation, artillery, and airborne forces coordinated to defeat enemy groupings in the complete depth of their disposition and the rapid achievement of strategic as well as operational and tactical superiority. This new concept later was referred to as the theory of "deep battle and operations," the main outlines of which were developed before the beginning of Barbarossa and were reflected in the "Regulation on Deep Battle" (1933, 1934, 1935) and in the *Field Manuals* of 1936, 1939, and 1941. It was on the basis of the theory of deep operations that Zhukov and Timoshenko laid down their plans for an in-depth echeloned defense of the country in February 1941.

Emphasis in military science was also placed upon the increased role of logistics and the economic factors of modern war.

In 1926 a group of officers at the Red Army headquarters headed by M. N. Tukhachevsky wrote a "Thesis for Militarization of the Country," which called for mobilizing the economy and the civilian population to a level never before achieved. The need was foreseen to provide a schedule for mobilizing trained manpower for the armed forces as well as personnel for all vital industries. Specific needs were also identified in the areas of security, both against external and internal threats, education, health, and civilian defense. These measures as they were eventually elaborated had the aim of repelling aggression and made it possible to solve the most important task of the peaceful respite—the preparation of the country's strategic rear for future war. The concept of a "strategic rear" (*strategicheskii tyl*) became more advanced in the Soviet Union than in any other country. It was intended that in the event of war every element of civilian society would be integrated into the vast machinery of the military state. The psychological aspects of this integration were not ignored. The propaganda machinery of the Party and the state was finely tuned to make each citizen aware of his and her duties to combat the enemies of the Soviet Union, both from without and from within. There were also ample demonstrations of what happened to traitors and saboteurs who did not conform.

The most important task of the strategic rear was forming combat reserves. According to Soviet military theory, it was believed that the exceptionally intense nature of future war, with the general deployment of automatic weapons and other weapons of large-scale destruction, would lead to considerable human and material losses, which could be compensated for only by a continuous supply of trained reserves. To solve this problem, the Soviet government and military provided for a transition from the *levée en masse* principle of manning the armed forces to a professional concept, which would make it possible to gradually increase the strength of the armed forces and prepare a considerable number of trained reserves. There was developed a system for training personnel eligible for military service and new rules for their participation in the reserves. This system provided for rapid mobilization and deployment of the army, the air force, and the navy. The new rules created a wide network of higher and secondary military educational establishments for training officers, including staff and battlefield commanders as well as political commissars. Emphasis was also placed on recruiting and training combat engineering personnel and enhancing the education of reservists who had been specialists in active service. The government also organized military training for the civilian population, which in the period between two world wars was conducted on a huge scale especially through paramilitary organizations such as parachute and flying clubs and OSOVIAKHIM (the acronym stands for *Obshchestvo sodeistviia oborone, aviatsionnomu i khimecheskomu stroitel'stvu*, or General Society in Aiding Antiaircraft and Chemical Defenses).

Soviet military theoreticians believed that a war of aggression against the Soviet Union would be a protracted conflict, that victory would not be instantaneous due to the capabilities of modern states to rapidly replenish their armed forces even after heavy losses. The theorists were sure that the USSR would have inherent advantages in mobilizing the total population of the nation to gain victory because of its ability to centrally plan, control, and direct all resources within the country. In retrospect it can be said that in this they were largely correct. Nothing like the Soviet Union's ability to organize an entire nation of millions of people and apply them to the singular purpose of achieving victory in war had ever been seen before and it is unlikely that it will be again. Stalin and his political and military leaders had succeeded in outdistancing even Sparta in this respect. The other model of a dictatorial state, Nazi Germany, by comparison was woefully deficient in its ability to shift totally to a wartime economy. Albert Speer, Hitler's minister of armaments, in his memoirs laments that Germany was not able to transition fully to a wartime state of production in its key industrial areas until 1943, but by then Allied bombing had already begun to take its toll.

Strategy in the Period Leading Up to Barbarossa
The pre-war years in the mid- to late 1930s were a period of advancement and transformation in Soviet military strategy. Its greatest founders were the Soviet military scientists B. M. Shaposhnikov, A. M. Zaionchkovsky, A. A. Svechin, A. D. Shimansky, A. A. Neznamov, G. S. Isserson, M. V. Frunze, M. N. Tukhachevsky, and a number of others. Many of their works were made public dozens of years later,

and others are only now being accessed by Soviet military historians. One such treatise by B. M. Shaposhnikov is titled *Outline of Modern Strategy*, written as a critical analysis of A. M. Zaionchkovsky's lectures on strategy. This work highlighted the main issues in the ongoing debate on strategy. Shaposhnikov as well as Zaionchkovsky believed that the process of preparing for war should be logically organized into a "state strategy" and a "command strategy," with the emphasis being that preparation for war is the responsibility of the state in its entirety with no element of the nation's economy and society being omitted from the equation. Shaposhnikov criticized the views of Zaionchkovsky regarding the supposed superiority of offensive over defensive operations. Zaionchkovsky believed that "offensive strategy is a natural form of military art as it corresponds more to the nature of war." But, he also admitted there could be neither purely offensive nor purely defensive operations. Shaposhnikov picked up on this point in his criticism and stressed that "in war, attack and defense are intertwined and to recommend attack as a sole form of combat is not only forbidden but also harmful." He shared the view of Svechin that "defense is the most effective form of waging war."

Both Shaposhnikov and Svechin agreed that a future war would be a war of coalitions and that the USSR could gain victory only by the offensive. But their ideas of the purpose of the offensive were different. For example, Svechin believed that "the mission of Red strategy in the initial period of war is to strike the weakest link in the enemy's front, to consolidate successes, and to rapidly regain freedom of maneuver for the main operational forces after the initial shock of battle." The main enemy attacking forces should be engaged and stopped by the defenses, and after the enemy has been exhausted and attrited, the initiative should be seized and maintained. At that point the Red Army should assume the offensive and finally defeat the enemy. In contradicting this, Shaposhnikov stated that "war should begin with defeating the strongest and the most potent enemy forces and not be carried away by successes over a weak enemy, leaving a stronger enemy at one's back." The example of World War I was clear; it did little good for the Russian forces to defeat Austria in the field while being unable to cope with the much more powerful Germans. The arguments of B. M. Shaposhnikov contain political as well as purely military considerations. He wrote: "One should not forget that to win a war not only are military successes important, but one should also gain the political success necessary to win a victory over a significant enemy. . . . Otherwise we'll have to resume the war with the enemy later, only this time for a longer and more difficult period." In other words the idea was not merely to defeat militarily a nation such as Germany and leave it able to rebuild its armies and become a threat again, as was the case after Versailles, but rather to bring about pro-Soviet political changes such as a socialist revolution, which would result in a permanent solution to the problem. This was the plan that was implemented in the areas of Eastern and Central Europe that fell under Soviet occupation after the end of World War II.

A considerable contribution to Soviet military strategy was made by Soviet military theoretician A. A. Neznamov.[4] In his investigation of the impact of new technology on the military, he stressed that "the appearance of a new weapon changes people's roles, and when combined with other new tactical possibilities, it requires a serious reform sometimes in areas not directly connected to the new weapon." In speaking about the strategic importance of weapons, Neznamov especially stressed that "weapons are capable of increasing to a great degree the combat effectiveness of a human being but without him cannot provide any benefit." In this connection, it was his opinion that to achieve a strategic success, particular attention must be paid to how weapons are used in various situations, and only a trained specialist can define how that should be done.

Neznamov offered his definition of strategic surprise as "surprise against which there are no means whatsoever for sufficient counteraction in a short period of time. To organize such counteraction, significant time is required during which the initiative would be transferred to the enemy." In his opinion, one of the secrets of the art of achieving strategic surprise was in the timely identification and adoption of technological innovations.

In an article by Lyamin titled "Destruction and Attrition," published in the *Army and Revolution* magazine (No. 1 of 1926), a detailed analysis is given of the views of military experts during the sixteenth to nineteenth centuries on the forms and techniques of warfare. The author pointed out two leading trends: "wars of destruction" and "wars of attrition."

Tracing back through history, the author notes successive changes in the forms of waging wars either by destroying or exhausting the enemy. The author draws conclusions similar to Clausewitz's based on the "fog of war concept":

> The strategy of modern war has become more and more flexible, more dialectical, more changeable. During wartime a form of waging war does not remain unchanged but is subjected to transformations that are noticeable between separate campaigns and even in the process of conducting separate operations. The question of whether to wage war by methods of destruction or by exhausting (attriting) the enemy has a serious practical importance. Measures to organize the armed forces, to develop industry and the railroad network, to train the army—all these depend on correctly solving this question in good time prior to the beginning of a war. All strategy, tactics, and calculations concerning these two methods of waging war are quite different. Due to the above-mentioned causes, it would be absurd to base planning of an entire war on a single one of these methods. It is clear that the most far seeing politician and strategist will not be able to foresee the whole course of war. He can make calculations for only the first period of war, on the conditions most likely to exist immediately after the beginning of a war.

In his article "Strategic Reserves," A. D. Shimansky considered important questions concerning strategy and its peculiarities in wars waged by coalitions. In analyzing the experience of World War I he came to the conclusion that strategy for future wars should necessarily take into account the multinational and international composition of belligerents. In the opinion of Shimansky, the strategy of modern war represented for the state and its army a multiplicity of strategies within a coalition grouping—in his words, a "strategy of internal operational lines" and a strategy of fighting against a coalition, that is, a "strategy of external operational lines."

It is interesting to note that Shimansky thought it necessary to mobilize all forces of a state even against a weak enemy. In his view of strategy a state must mobilize at once the "forces prepared by politics" and deploy them in a theater of war. Otherwise, as he said, "these forces will have to be strengthened by waves of reinforcements."

Shimansky placed much emphasis on strategic reserves, a problem generally not well elaborated in the 1920s. His presumption was that strategy must be designed "to allocate forces to fronts and their operations not equally but in a certain proportion according to their relative importance." He also stressed the necessity of creating strategic reserves, or "reserves common for all fronts," which, as he put it, "shouldn't be late, shouldn't be idle, and shouldn't make unnecessary maneuvers."

In his work Shimansky also placed emphasis on the combat mission of the strategic reserve and the forms of its maneuver in strategic and defensive operations. Speaking of the composition of strategic reserves, the author pointed to two of their components. He believed they should include (1) "all combat resources of the state not raised yet or deployed in a theater of war, and which are capable within a certain period of time of occupying their position as strategic reserves" and (2) "the part of forces deployed in a theater of war left at the disposal of strategy . . ." As to the composition of the strategic reserve, it is defined "by the purpose, direction, and urgency of the developing operation."

The ideas of Shimansky about the necessity of having a strategic reserve available for several fronts were fully justified, as will be seen later in this book.

In 1934, Tukhachevsky wrote an article entitled "The Character of Border Operations" in which he stated that the traditional method of moving mass armies up to the border areas by rail was now outmoded due to the danger of disruption by air attack. According to Tukhachevsky, the previously planned character of battles along the frontier no longer conformed with actual conditions. The only tactic that could succeed would be that of preparing a defense in depth, leading to a protracted conflict with broad fronts and deep operations. The initial struggle along the frontiers would be important but would by no means decide the issue. The new form of deep battle would allow the enemy to be destroyed by a series of actions in a given strategic direction, not just by defending the borders. In this respect, Tukhachevsky remained true to the philosophy of Lenin, who believed that wars between states that had the capability of mobilizing their entire productive and population resources would always be protracted conflicts.

Tukhachevsky went on to say in the article that, because of the danger of concentrating mass armies in the border sectors, it would be best to place there forward armies only strong enough to be considered the first operational echelon of the main force. In his opinion, the main force armies were to be concentrated secretly in areas that were most likely to be on the flanks of the advancing enemy. He attached much significance to fortified zones positioned along the border, which would serve as the shield, absorbing the initial shock of the enemy's offensive and covering the concentration of second echelon armies—the sword—which would deliver blows to the enemy's flanks. The fortified regions were to offer more than just passive resistance. In Tukhachevsky's plan they were to be organically connected with the maneuvers of the field army and act as support for its carrying out a general offensive operation.

It is necessary here to emphasize the importance of these conclusions; it was on the basis of them that Zhukov and Timoshenko implemented a plan for defense against Germany in 1941.

On the use of armor, Tukhachevsky's ideas followed Triandafilov's to a certain extent as he attempted to describe specific ways in which independent tank operations could be carried out. Tukhachevsky proposed that armored units be divided into different categories depending upon the operational characteristics of the tank and the specific combat mission that was to be carried out. Essentially, there should be three echelons of tanks: (1) tanks for close support of infantry (NPP), which could be slower models of relatively limited range; (2) tanks for distant support of infantry (DPP), which could move faster and farther; and (3) independent long-range striking armor (DD). In the period before the infantry attack in the offensive operation, artillery and air cover should be used to support the tanks in their initial breakthrough of the enemy lines. Here, Tukhachevsky tried to bridge the gap between a combined-arms philosophy and a new tactic based on independent armored operations. The general tenor of this plan, as one future chief of the general staff would put it, was "to assign a mistaken importance and priority to the tanks." As will be seen, however, events leading up to the German invasion of 1941 compelled Stalin and the then chief of the general staff, Zhukov, to reject this concept and to rely almost totally on close infantry-armor cooperation. It should be mentioned also that a parallel attempt was being made in the early 1930s to come to grips with the use of independent strategic airpower, the virtues of which had been extolled by the Italian general Douhet. Triandafilov and B. M. Feldmann had written an article entitled "Characteristics of New Tendencies in the Military Sphere" in which they advocated the creation of a strategic air arm. This approach was roundly criticized by R. P. Eideman, Tukhachevsky's successor as head of the Frunze Military Academy, who believed that the air force's major role should be to support the army.

After some degree of debate and study, in December 1934 the defense commissariat decided that the "deep battle" scenario proposed by Tukhachevsky was not merely a type of tactic but a wholly new and different strategy that included many tactical variants. During a meeting that month, Voroshilov declared that this new theory should be put into practical use at once. Egorov agreed, saying that tanks were to be considered "core units" in the "deep battle" concept. These theories were, in fact, embodied in Field Regulations of 1936 (PU-36). However one might try to apply the new ideas of using armor, the reality was that Russia still lacked the industrial base to mechanize the Red Army as fully as its potential opponents in the West. Germany had already begun its program of full-scale rearmament in 1934, and there were other ominous clouds on the horizon: the Spanish Civil War was being waged in full fury by the summer of 1936, and both Russia and Germany would become progressively more involved in this conflict. A more chilling portent for the future was also visible in 1936; in August the trials began for the so-called Trotsky-Zinoviev center, events that proved to be preludes to the massive purges in the Party, in the NKVD state security apparatus itself, and finally, in the military.

PU-36 fully reflected the main ideas about deep battle worked out by Tukhachevsky and his colleagues. PU-36 stated, in part, that "the enemy is to be paralyzed in the entire depth of his deployment, surrounded and destroyed." PU-36 seemed in tune with the rest of the world when Heinz Guderian's book *Achtung Panzer* was published early the next year. In the offensive operations, tanks were to be employed on a mass scale in echelons, as Tukhachevsky had already proposed. Taking a leaf from the books of the western theorists, PU-36 called for aviation to be used also on a large scale, "concentrating the forces according to the times and targets which have the greatest tactical importance." The new field regulations assigned a leading role to artillery in achieving tactical breakthroughs of enemy defenses.

The day of the "artillery offensive" so effectively employed by the Red Army had not yet arrived, but still, PU-36 attempted to come to grips with the problem of the spatial gaps that would widen between fast-moving armored groups and slower artillery units. The Germans tried to get around this problem by using the Ju-87 Stuka dive-bomber in a close support role in cooperation with the tanks. The Russian planners, too, favored this approach for their aviation, but the distances in Russia proved too great for the air force (VVS) to manage. The fact is, neither side had enough aircraft to make up for the lack of self-propelled artillery support for long-distance drives by armored spearheads. The Germans found this out to their sorrow after penetrating to the Dnepr line in July 1941. The Germans paid their price in blood for this lesson and, after the reverses in the Army Group Center area in December 1941, were not able to recoup their offensive posture on this strategic front.

In summarizing the currents of strategy theory during the 1920s and 1930s, one should note first of all their practicality as well as their originality. The pioneering nature of many of the theoretical works discussed here determined the direction of Soviet military strategy for years to come and provided a solid basis for winning the war.

A comment is also necessary about the atmosphere of freedom and independence in military thought that prevailed during the 1920s and early to mid-1930s. These were halcyon days in which highly intelligent individuals' thoughts and opinions could flower. These days could, however, not last for long, as the shadow of Stalin's paranoia began to darken the land.

During the second half of the 1930s the development of Soviet military theory and particularly strategic theory fell victim to the purges by Stalin of the Party, military, and state security organizations. Stalin's cult of personality seriously injured the defense posture of the country by inhibiting objective analysis of real-world conditions. This proved to be a near-fatal error on the eve of Barbarossa, and had not the first-strike strategy of Stalin's and his armor expert, General D. G. Pavlov, been dumped literally at the last minute, defeat would have followed almost as a matter of course.

Questions of strategy became ever more the prerogative of the highest leadership, personified by Stalin. The slightest hint as to the necessity of investigating strategic defense was met by a blank wall. The purges of 1936–38 stopped the development of strategic theory for the time being. Many interesting conceptual principles elaborated in the 1920s and the beginning of the 1930s were declared hostile to the state and branded as treason or sabotage. In the words of Isserson:

> We were limited by certain declarative principles about the offensive nature of waging war, that our army would be the attacking army, that we would carry the hostilities to the enemy, and so on. These proposals were directed from the upper spheres, as indisputable directives for our military policy and were made the basis of military thinking for all command personnel without questioning. During the period of Stalin's cult of personality they assumed the importance of law and were not even to be discussed in theory.[5]

The superiority of attack over defense imposed on the military by Stalin turned out to be an insurmountable barrier for continuing the development of a realistic and comprehensive strategy on a rational basis. Although the necessity of balancing defensive and offensive operations was admitted in private conversations behind closed doors, it was not voiced in public. Isserson wrote: "One can be a philosophical adherent of the offensive doctrine and have a theoretically well-elaborated defense. Or one can actually try to apply the offensive doctrine which would mean ignoring a thorough elaboration of defense on an operational scale."

By contrast, the emerging concepts of maneuver warfare elaborated by western theorists such as Liddell Hart and Heinz Guderian did not contradict in any way the feasibility of conducting both offensive and defensive operations. It was assumed by western theorists that defense could have both fluid and positional characteristics. An open discussion of these trends in the West and a true analysis of their possible meaning and implications for the Soviet Union were prohibited under Stalin.

Stalin's system in the late 1930s crippled Russia's ability to defend itself by consistently underestimating the emerging foreign trends of strategy and tactics while imposing strategic views from the top, with no dissent tolerated. In addition, broad layers of military theorists and experts were denied participation in the elaboration of strategic theory. All of this could not fail to have disastrous consequences when the threat of war proved to be a reality. The root of all the trouble that was to follow was the mistaken importance given to strategic offense as opposed to strategic defense. It was only through the efforts of a small group of high-ranking officers and theorists who continued to focus on strategic defense issues in secret that the nation was spared destruction.

Retribution for Contrary Thinking
It must be remembered that for a long period of time the lives of the Soviet people and the indoctrination and discipline of the armed forces were dictated by Communist dogma. The particular interpretations put on this dogma by Stalin negatively affected the formulation of military strategy as well as many operations and campaigns of World War II. One example of a negative dogma was the idea of world revolution.

From the very beginning, the highest leaders of the Soviet state supposed that the victorious revolution in Russia would be a base for world revolution. G. B. Zinoviev, commenting on the period before the revolution, said, "We in the Central Committee for many hours discussed the development of events in Germany and Austria. We thought that if we took power tomorrow, it would contribute to the cause of revolution in other countries." Although the attempt in 1920 to bring revolution to Poland on the bayonets of the Red Army failed, the Soviet leadership continued to try to export revolution for more than sixty years.

Even though many senior military leaders did not accept the idea of world revolution, the so-called "proletarian" military leaders tried to follow this idea. For instance, M. N. Tukhachevsky wrote in one of his earlier works, "An offensive of the revolutionary army of the working class against neighboring bourgeois states can overthrow the bourgeois power and put dictatorship into the hands of the proletariat." Recalling the march of the Red Army to the Vistula in 1920, he stated that if only the Red Army had succeeded in defeating the Poles, then the fire of revolution would not be limited to Poland: "Like a swollen torrent it would spread across the rest of Europe." At that time M. V. Frunze made similar statements. He said, "Soviet Russia as a strong point of the world revolution is not only able to survive until the moment of revolutionary explosion, but also can help bring the revolution to other countries . . ." These kinds of essentially extremist views adversely affected the development of military science. Because of the pernicious influence among the ruling Party elite of ideas concerning immediate assistance to the revolutions in western countries, only a small number of strategists were able to openly investigate the problems associated with preparing the country for defense. A defensive strategy was not suited to aiding the world proletarian revolution.

In the mid-1920s the classic work of Professor A. A. Svechin, *Strategy*, was published. Due to its wealth of content and depth of analysis, this work must be regarded as belonging to the first rank of military theory. Svechin's ideas on the problems of defense are extremely valuable, but the military and political leadership paid it scant attention at the time. Some critics even accused Svechin of wanting to repeat the strategy of Kutuzov, the victor over Napoleon, by permitting the enemy to reach Moscow. This charge later provided one of the reasons for Svechin's arrest and subsequent execution. Toward the end of the 1920s Svechin made a final attempt to save himself by sending a letter to defense commissar Voroshilov. Svechin pointed out that a future war would be characterized by flexibility: troops on some sectors of the front would have to shift to defense while other sectors would be able to launch an offensive. He also wrote that the lack of respect for defensive operations in the Red Army was based on a misunderstanding of the underlying connection between offense and defense. "He who cannot conduct defensive operations also cannot carry out an offensive."

The chief of the general staff of the Red Army, B. M. Shaposhnikov, in accordance with instructions from Voroshilov, wrote an answer to Svechin. Shaposhnikov agreed with some of the professor's remarks, but he also said, "It's no secret that it's a slow and evolutionary process to equate defensive and offensive operations in their relative importance. Defense is a more difficult kind of military action and our units are rather bad at that."[6] He also stressed that revolutionary armies in world history always waged offense better than defense; that's why "it is necessary to take into account the character of the Red Army and not to deprive it of its offensive spirit." Shaposhnikov surely knew the views on defense of not only Voroshilov but also Stalin. That is why he used covering phrases such as "slow and evolutionary" to describe defense and the "offensive spirit of the Red Army" to avoid giving a meaningful reply to Svechin.

It is true that the Red Army leadership in general and Voroshilov in particular suppressed real work on defensive strategy, but it should also be said that this was not their determination—it was Stalin's.

Since ancient times the quality of personnel of any army has been determined first of all by the professional level of the commissioned staff. Although there is no exact definition of professionalism, no country can afford to have military cadres that are inferior to those of its potential enemies.

The military buildup in the USSR shows that, even under the best system of military education, no less than fifteen to twenty years are necessary to train excellent senior field-grade officers, and junior officers require five to ten years. Senior staff officers require ten to fifteen years of training. High-ranking commanders need fifteen to twenty or more years. During the Civil War in Russia the needs of the Red Army for senior and high-ranking commanders were met by inducting officers of the former Russian army. Some of them joined the Red Army voluntarily, some were drafted, and still others deserted from the White Army. Many of these officers had been educated in the military colleges and various schools in the old tsarist system. By 1920–21 the Red Army had between 150,000 and 180,000 officers, out of which 70,000 to 75,000 had come from the old officer corps. Of these, 10,000 were officer cadets and 60,000 to 65,000 were commissioned officers who had received their training in the years of World War I.

According to Trotsky, the first commander in chief of the Red Army, there were insufficient numbers of noncommissioned officers because former noncommissioned officers had been taken from the tsarist army and given commands of companies, battalions, and even regiments. Until the end of the Civil War, more than 43 percent of the officers in the Red Army lacked any formal military education. The percentage of noncommissioned officers lacking formal training was 13 percent, and about 34 percent of the officers taken from the Imperial Army had no military schooling whatsoever. All newly formed units lacked junior commanders, which is why more than 200,000 noncommissioned officers from the Imperial Army were called up for service in the Red Army.

The highest command billets in the Red Army (front and army commanders and chiefs of staffs) in the period of the Civil War usually were occupied by generals and senior officers of the former Russian army. For example, out of twenty front commanders seventeen were former tsarist generals and officers as well as all twenty-two chiefs of staff of the various fronts. Out of a hundred army commanders, eighty-two were former Imperial officers, as were seventy-seven out of ninety-three army chiefs of staff. Officer cadets of the Russian army I. I. Vatsetis and S. S. Kamenev at different times occupied the post of commander in chief of the Red Army.

Higher-ranking officers in the Red Army were under double and even triple control. Many political commissars were attached to senior officers as "representatives of the Party," a situation that was bound to create friction. The higher ranks were also under the watch of the NKVD, which caused them to fear arrest and death for any deviations, real or imagined, from the Party line. In general, the independence of senior officers was greatly hampered by interference from the political and the security apparatus.

In the summer of 1919 commander in chief of the Red Army I. I. Vatsetis, chief of the field staff F. V. Kostyaev, and some of their close collaborators were arrested. Some months later the trumped-up cases against them were halted and the Presidium of the All Union Central executive committee passed a resolution stating that there were no reasons "to suspect the former commander-in-chief being involved in direct counterrevolutionary activities." Such events were remembered and had a braking effect on the individual initiative and risk taking of senior commanders.

Although the service of former Russian officers in the Red Army was extremely difficult, most of them loyally performed their duties. Cases of treason, sabotage, and desertion were rare among the former officers of the Russian army. The valuable work of these officers in training command cadres as well as in organizing the Red Army and guiding its development was highly appreciated by the Soviet government. But eventually, the rewards they earned were paid back in a form that was not expected. Many high-ranking and senior officers were driven out of the army during the reforms of the mid-1920s. By the end of the 1920s and the early period of the 1930s, a purge was carried out against the former officers of the Russian army. According to Voroshilov, 47,000 commanders were discharged from the Red Army, the bulk of them being specialists and officers of the old Russian army. This purge was, of course, a minor prelude to the great bloodletting of 1937–38.

Isserson said that Stalin's "cult of personality" was responsible for the gap in defense planning, but clearly the problem was a great deal larger than that. Stalin had not yet grasped firm hold over the military, nor had he succeeded in finding people he could trust who would give him objective advice about the whole direction of military strategy, let alone tactics. Voroshilov turned out to be a plodder and a yes-man, as the 1939 war against Finland would show, and Tukhachevsky proved to be a gadfly, constantly flirting with his contacts in the West. Eventually, these contacts were used by Reinhard Heydrich of the Nazi SS secret police to fabricate false evidence against Tukhachevsky and show him guilty of treason. Whether

Stalin actually believed the counterfeit documents prepared by Heydrich or not is immaterial; Stalin came to believe that Tukhachevsky had become too immersed in the West and was no longer to be trusted. When the old Bolshevik Karl Radek was brought to trial in January 1937, a collective shudder went down the spine of the officer corps at the mention of Tukhachevsky's name in connection with certain evidence bearing on treasonable activities. The end could not be long in coming. By the summer of that year Tukhachevsky had been arrested and shot, and by the end of the year a dreadful blood purge of the officer corps was taking place. The instrumentality for this purge was the NKVD security apparatus then headed by N. I. Yezhov, known as the "bloodthirsty dwarf" (he stood only five feet tall), whose reign of terror is called the "Yezhovshchina" in Russia. By the end of 1937 Stalin ruled the military with an iron hand through the person of Lev Mekhlis, the head of the military main political administration (PUR).

The Great Purges reduced the number of commanding officers in the armed forces by about 10 to 15 percent. The senior ranks were, however, particularly devastated. By 1938, only 20 to 25 percent of them remained at their posts, and the most able and intellectual officers had perished. Out of some 75,000 former tsarist officers, only a few hundred remained in uniform. This tiny group was used as a reserve for replacements in the posts of chief of the general staff and front commanders in the years of the war, but usually those tsarist officers who remained in the army after the purges were promoted to higher ranks very slowly. Class and party considerations meant more than talent in the way promotions were handed out for a period of almost twenty years. Many students of the General Staff Academy were subjected to investigations and denunciations. For instance, A. M. Vasilevskii suffered from political suspicion as the son of a clergyman, I. Kh. Bagramian suffered as a "former *dashnak*" (member of Deshnaksutun Armenian Nationalist Party), and L. A. Govorov was denounced as a "former soldier of the Kolchak army" (meaning the White Army during the Russian Civil War).

But like the phoenix from the ashes, the officer corps rose again from the ruins of the former organization. The new group of men owed their careers and even their lives to Stalin. Those who had been spared the purge, such as G. K. Zhukov, S. K. Timoshenko, and

B. M. Shaposhnikov, were able to move up swiftly in rank, provided they had the natural instincts and abilities to survive in this tough environment. The Red Army had not been battle tested on a large scale since the war with Poland and the abortive advance on Warsaw in 1920, but this peaceful lull was soon to be sharply broken. Russia's old enemy, Japan, had been increasing its forces rapidly in China since 1934, and now it was ready to test the sinews of the Red Army in a place where its supply lines were stretched thinnest: in Mongolia, which had become a Soviet satellite in 1922. First at Lake Khasan in the summer of 1938 and then at Khalkhin-Gol in the spring of 1939, the Japanese strove mightily with infantry, armor, artillery, and airpower to push the Red Army back into the Soviet Union proper, but these attempts failed.

The Japanese attack at Lake Khasan was thwarted by Marshal Blukher, a curious man who may have wished to become potentate of Siberia—until he was cut down by Yezhov's henchmen virtually on the morrow of his victory in Mongolia. The Japanese assault at Khalkhin-Gol, by contrast, was broken by a man who received high awards from Stalin and was much trusted by him, Georgii Zhukov. Zhukov was probably successful under Stalin first of all because, at least in his early years, he was unassuming and unpretentious. Zhukov also had two other characteristics that the dictator valued: he had the habit of telling the blunt truth when asked (as we shall see he did in 1941) and of being right.

At Khalkhin-Gol, Zhukov used a combined-arms counteroffensive to sweep the enemy from the battlefield. It has been said that here he demonstrated the effectiveness of an independent armored thrust, but this is not really true. There was a freewheeling armored encirclement of some Japanese units, but this was carried out on a narrow front with limited range and depth, hardly to be compared with the great German panzer "cauldrons" of 1941. After Khalkhin-Gol, Zhukov was definitely a comer. He gained more experience in Finland and Bessarabia in 1940. Finally, Stalin relied upon him to pull Russia out of the worst crisis it had faced since the seventeenth century.

As a result of Zhukov's experiences against the Japanese and the tank commander D. G. Pavlov's difficulties in Spain, in November 1939 the order went out to disband the tank corps, which had been first created in 1932 (then called mechanized corps), and use the tanks in close cooperation with the infantry. Pavlov's attempts to employ armor independently had come to grief in Esquivas, south of Madrid, where tanks operating inside a town with narrow streets without infantry support had proven to be quite ineffective. But the controversy regarding tanks was far from over, especially after the failure of the Red Army to achieve a decisive victory in Finland in the Winter War of 1939–40 and after Guderian's rapid blitzkrieg defeat of France in May–June 1940. The debate was stirred anew in an article by I. P. Sukhov entitled "Tanks in Contemporary War," published soon after the fall of France. Sukhov was a senior lecturer, and later head, of the Military Academy for the Motorization and Mechanization of the Red Army in Moscow. He denied that tanks operating in the depths of the enemy's forces, either on his flanks or in his rear, were risking disaster. Also, he discounted the potentially disastrous supply problems that armored units might face operating far from their own bases. All of these difficulties could be overcome, he said, by creating masses of motorized infantry that would ride tracked vehicles and would be capable of keeping up with the advancing armor. Motorized artillery also would be necessary, but here the proper use of support aviation would make up for deficiencies in long-range firepower. Sukhov's article is interesting for several reasons. First of all, this was precisely the theory that the Wehrmacht attempted to put into practice in Russia a year later. Second, although the Red Army undertook a rapid about-face and tried to implement some of these ideas, precious little time was allowed to acquire the necessary level of motorization for the Red Army. Third, this theory is what modern armies practice today.

Prior to Barbarossa, defensive operations on a tactical scale utilizing fortified zones were studied in the Frunze Military Academy. As for mobile (elastic) defense, the professors at Frunze, deferring to Voroshilov, said that this kind of defense was advocated by enemies of the people in order to more easily yield Soviet territory to an advancing enemy. Since everyone knew what happened to "enemies of the people" who were denounced to the NKVD, there were few officer candidates who spent much time thinking about in-depth elastic defenses.

After Timoshenko replaced Voroshilov as commissar of defense in May 1940 following the debacle of the war in Finland, the negligent attitude toward the problem of defense remained. Based on the experience of the Winter War in Finland, the military leadership, at Stalin's direction, concentrated on breakthroughs of fortified enemy lines as the most likely form of battle in a future war. Offensive operations were analyzed as front-scale operations, but the analysis of defensive operations was limited to the army level. Within this framework it was impossible to examine questions of organizing and waging strategic defense, including such issues as how to launch counterattacks with front strategic reserves, how to carry out strategic withdrawal under attack, how to avoid encirclement from the flanks, and how to launch counteroffensives. These problems became real in the first few days of war with Germany, and Soviet commanders' inexperience in solving them contributed directly to the severe losses on the Western Front.

The Foundations of Soviet Wartime Strategy

Both Soviet and Western historiography abound in stereotypical interpretations of the course and outcome of the Soviet-German war of 1941–45.[7] This is especially true about Operation Barbarossa and the Red Army campaign in the winter of 1941–42. What is the essence of these interpretations?

Stalin's desire not to give Hitler a pretext for starting an aggressive war against the Soviet Union and Stalin's and the general staff's disbelief that the Germans were preparing for an invasion are considered to be the major reasons why the Soviet military leadership failed to issue orders putting on alert the Soviet troops guarding the western frontier on the eve of Barbarossa.

The idea also persists that the main reason for the defeat of the Nazi troops on the Eastern Front, including their failure at Moscow, was mistakes made mainly by Hitler and, to a lesser extent, by his commanders and not because of anything that was done right by their opponents.

Both these interpretations suggest that the Red Army was unprepared and that the general staff and the Soviet supreme command failed to coordinate an in-depth defense strategy before Barbarossa.

However, an analysis of the recently opened defense ministry archives as well as of newly published memoirs and correspondence (Zhukov's in particular, which are included in the second volume of his book *Memoirs and Reflection,* published in 1990) demonstrates that these interpretations are at variance with facts. Moreover, the familiar picture of the most important events of the Barbarossa campaign must be revised in light of new information.

Victory or defeat in war greatly depends on the outcome of the quiet and unheralded work done by strategists. It is the main mission of generals in the field to foresee what solutions may lead to success and at what stages they should be applied, taking into account the overarching strategic vision. This was the task of Soviet military leaders who had the responsibility of defending the nation and its people on the eve of Barbarossa. Some Soviet generals, primarily G. K. Zhukov and S. K. Timoshenko, expanded and modernized the theoretical views of Triandafilov, Tukhachevsky, and other Russian military theorists. They created a concept of modern war that at its foundation inseparably joined both offensive and defensive strategies in a holistic (using a modern term), all-encompassing, synergistic pattern that was dictated by the rhythm and flow of battle. Some historians do not recognize this duality of Zhukov's strategy and, therefore, underestimate his true role.

Long before the war began, Zhukov came to the conclusion that Soviet military strategy was one sided. It was dictated by the omnipotent Stalin that an aggressor could be defeated only through offensive actions. Although Zhukov in the early stages of his career never openly called this article of faith into question, at the same time he advocated the study of meeting engagements, forced withdrawal, fighting in encirclement, night operations, and other primarily defensive maneuvers. He strenuously opposed ignoring active defense or relegating it to a lesser status. "In studying operational-tactical problems," recalls Zhukov, "I came to the conclusion that the defense of such a huge country as ours has many serious drawbacks."

In a discussion of the development of Soviet military art in the prewar years, and in particular the importance of strategic defense plans, the contemporary political and economic situation of the country should not be overlooked. Zhukov, Timoshenko, and other military leaders, taking into consideration the threat presented by Germany, went out of their way to prepare the army for defensive and offensive operations, whereas Stalin up until the January war games refused even to talk about strategic defense, believing that it was absolutely irrelevant to the character and role of the Red Army. This largely explains the restraint that the higher command, Zhukov and Timoshenko in particular, demonstrated in December 1940 at the Kremlin high-level staff conference held immediately prior to the war games. It is a credit to the generals, however, that what would happen if strategic defense continued to be ignored was made abundantly and devastatingly clear to Stalin in the first game in January when Zhukov systematically took apart Pavlov's position in the Bialystok salient. Zhukov's play in the game showed with startling clarity how the sword and the shield could be struck from Stalin's hands, leaving him powerless and at the mercy of a rapacious enemy. The lessons taught by Zhukov that day were not lost on a dictator whose paranoia had no bounds.

Was Stalin aware of the underground plans for defense? Probably so. Stubborn as he was, Stalin could not give up the idea of offensive initiative. At the same time, deep inside, he must have understood the insight of his military leaders, yet he would not openly acknowledge that they were correct. He did, however, come close to publicly admitting the truth when at the discussion of the January 1941 war games he savaged Pavlov's poorly organized defense and commended Zhukov for his expert actions both in defense and attack.

As noted earlier, the February 1941 war game, which excluded Pavlov and his supporters, consolidated the idea of an echeloned strategic defense deep within Soviet territory. But, despite receiving Stalin's reluctant approval for the plan, Zhukov and Timoshenko were prevented from implementing it fully due to their leader's fear of detection and provoking Hitler. It can be said, however, that the partial implementation of the plan was better than none and that Zhukov's and Timoshenko's execution of it in practice, even without all of the resources that they had requested, proved skillful enough to defeat the enemy, albeit at a much more terrible price than would have been the case had an effective defense plan been implemented earlier.

Thus, the blame for Stalin's unpreparedness for war has been misplaced in historical writings up until now. The fault was not in ignoring the threats of war and being caught off guard by the German onslaught. The fault was in Stalin's adherence too long on a first-strike or offensive war strategy for the Red Army plus his failure to allow the February 1941 defense plan to be implemented fully to the extent demanded by his ablest leaders.

From this point of view, the sacrifice at Bialystok could not have been prevented given the February late start and improvisations in making an offensive springboard useful in an in-depth strategic defense. The later chapters of this book will focus on the actual execution of the plan and reveal its workings, not only in the maneuvers of the Red Army but in how it affected the Germans and their leadership and strategy. Specifically, the January war games showed that a German onslaught could be stopped only by an echeloned defense organized in depths of hundreds of kilometers east of the border areas. Any attempt to adapt the Bialystok salient for defense would be foolhardy and doomed to failure. These lessons were taken to heart by Stalin, as proved by his appointment of Zhukov as chief of the general staff in January 1941, and they provided the basis for the February war game. The echeloned defense plan tested on the map boards in February was, in fact, the plan that was carried out.

·1·
THE WAR GAMES OF EARLY 1941

Background

There is ample evidence to show that during the war games of January 1941 Stalin became a convert to the Zhukov-Timoshenko point of view: that the Bialystok salient should not be fortified any further, despite the growing German threat, but rather used as a Trojan horse, a gift, the acceptance of which would lead to dire consequences for the attackers. The disaster suffered by the Red Army at Bialystok was not fatal. On the contrary, Bialystok provided cover for a carefully staged counteroffensive by the Red Army along the Smolensk-Dnepr line. The accounts of the January and the February war games presented in this chapter provide substance for this interpretation.

One of the most significant new discoveries among Timoshenko's and Zhukov's private papers concerns a highly secret war game held in February 1941, soon after the January event. Until this discovery it could only be postulated that a February war game had taken place. The occurrence of the February war game is proof that a secret defense plan was being tested. Not only was the plan worked out in theory, it was carried out in fact. The war diaries of the German units on the southern flank of Army Group Center, including Guderian's Panzer Group 2, testify to the effectiveness of the Timoshenko-Zhukov echeloned defense strategy.

In order to understand the setting for the momentous war games of January and February 1941, it is necessary to turn back to events that occurred in 1939. In August of that year, Hitler and Stalin agreed to the infamous nonaggression pact. As is now known, there was a secret protocol attached to that agreement leading to the partition of Poland in September and to the later occupation of the Baltic states by the Red Army. After some adjustments were made in the zones of control, the Red Army occupied territory known as the Bialystok salient, an area around Bialystok (now in the eastern part of Poland) that jutted approximately 240 km. on a side deeply into German-controlled territory.

Stalin intended to occupy this indefensible position to use it as a springboard for a future offensive against Germany after Hitler had become bogged down on the Western Front against France and Britain, much as had happened in 1914. Then, as an ally of the old resurrected *Entente,* the Soviet Union could assume the role that Russia had played in World War I as a combatant against Germany. This time, however, the Red Army would be victorious; it would occupy a defeated Germany, opening the gates for Soviet power to conquer all of Europe. If in light of today's events such a scenario seems laughable, in those days and times it was all too real. It is easy to forget how close the Red Army came to overrunning all of Germany in 1945, not merely the eastern half of it.

Stalin's fundamental error in judgment was that he misunderstood the transformation that Hitler had wrought in Germany and how helpless France and Britain would be in the face of it. In May 1940, Stalin's springboard offensive strategy was shattered after the Wehrmacht made short work of the army of the French Third Republic. The newsreels of goose-stepping German soldiers beneath the Arc de Triomphe affected Stalin like a panic attack. The resulting paralysis of decision brought about a profound and heated discussion in the highest Soviet political and military circles. The debate eventually turned into a mortal struggle. Why was the Soviet leadership divided? What were the issues that caused such a deep rift within the highest ranks of the Red Army?

The heart of the debate was whether the Red Army should fortify the Bialystok salient in the hope of making it an impregnable barrier that would break the back of any army that tried to attack it, much in the way the French had done with Verdun in World War I. Or should it be abandoned, concentrating instead on reinforcing the fortified zones along the pre-1939 frontier? Stalin's reliance on an offensive strategy had been a high-risk one, one that was now in extreme jeopardy. What should be done? It turned out that in the January 1941 war games, the true pivotal turning point of Soviet strategy, the dictator's sudden flash of insight led him to go along with a defense plan that Zhukov, Timoshenko, and others had developed in the strictest secrecy, without Stalin's knowledge or approval. In so doing the decision was made simultaneously to sacrifice Pavlov, the commander of the Western Front.

After September 1940, Timoshenko, the commissar for defense, began to develop the broad outlines of a conservative strategy, that to try to defend Bialystok would be a suicidal mistake. Later, two other key generals joined Timoshenko's side: Zhukov, head of the Kiev Special Military District, and Voroshilov. On the opposite side was General Pavlov, the tank expert who had won international attention during the Spanish Civil War. Along with Pavlov were Generals Kulik, defense commissariat deputy for armaments, and Meretskov, who had been chief of the general staff since July 1940. Pavlov's position as commander of the forces within the Bialystok salient gave him a particular reason for fashioning a dual-use strategy.

Pavlov contended that Bialystok could be successfully adapted for defense so that it would wreak great harm on an attacking enemy. It could also serve its springboard role after the enemy was repulsed. The Red Army would still be in a position for Pavlov to lead a vast surge of tanks into the heart of Germany. From what is known of Soviet plans against NATO in the post-war environment, Pavlov's plans did not seem all that unreasonable, and Stalin was not prone to dismiss them, despite the obvious dangers.

Part of the problem that western historians have had in dealing with these issues is that they assume a discontinuity between Stalin's pre-war strategy and that of his successors during the cold war. They understand how aggressive Soviet strategy was after World War II but fail to see a similar threat prior to the war. It may have been that the Allies needed Stalin during the war but were freer to characterize his post-war successors as dangerous aggressors. It would be impossible to explain the reasons for the events that unfolded during Operation Barbarossa without understanding the debate over offensive versus defensive strategies that so sharply divided the Soviet military leadership in late 1940 to early 1941.

Interestingly, the Russians today are grappling with these issues and trying to decide what interpretation to put on them. A partial answer to their problem would be to say that the Communist Party and its expansionist ideology forced the military always to adopt an aggressive doctrine that put a premium on the offensive and rewarded the most offensive-minded officers. That continued to be a matter of state policy until very recently.

Zhukov, as head of the Kiev Special Military District, was notified at the end of September 1940 to prepare a report entitled "The Nature of Modern Offensive Operations" for a Kremlin conference scheduled in late December. It is not likely that Zhukov was assigned this topic accidentally, for his reputation as a leader of offensive operations had already been well established at Khalkhin-Gol against the Japanese in 1939, and he had gained more experience in the summer of 1940 when the Soviet Union occupied northern Bukovina and Bessarabia. While reporting his ideas about achieving goals in an attack, Zhukov emphasized that the success of an offensive operation was largely predetermined by its planning. It involved not only good supply and sophisticated weapons and equipment, but the ability to foresee various options of combat in the course of the attack, including switching to defense, harassing the enemy, and counterattacking.

His report was constrained within the limits of his assigned theme. This is why he could not dwell upon the importance of modern strategic defense, which he greatly regretted afterward. Zhukov was very critical of General I. V. Tulenev's report "The Character of the Modern Defensive Operation," also presented at the session, though he realized that Tulenev, being limited by his own assignment, could not discuss all the facets of modern strategic defense.

The character of Zhukov's assignment also reveals the importance the Kremlin attached to the area south of the Pripyat Marshes as an area for a future offensive. This was why the premier commander of offensive operations in the Red Army had been appointed to head the Kiev Special Military District. The concentrations of troops gathered in the Western and Kiev Military Districts in 1940 were committed to an offensive mission. Soviet sources, of course, do not say that the USSR would have begun the war with an act of aggression; nevertheless, they make it clear that the forces in the Lvov and Bialystok salients had an offensive purpose. In assembling a powerful force in Ukraine, Stalin hoped to be able to deprive Germany of 90 percent of its oil at once, if war came suddenly, or to intimidate Rumania for as long as possible, if war were to be delayed. Playing a double game such as this so close to the demarcation line with Germany was, however, playing with fire, for although the Bialystok and Lvov salients were good to occupy in strength from an offensive point of view, from the standpoint of defense these positions were a distinct liability.

At the late December conference much attention was given to Pavlov's report on the employment of mechanized corps in the offensive. Pavlov forcefully argued that modern tank and mechanized corps, with their high mobility and lesser vulnerability to artillery and air strikes, as opposed to slower-moving, unprotected infantry, would be able to maneuver around well-prepared defenses and destroy an enemy force in its depth.

Following Timoshenko's summation report at the Kremlin conference, on December 30 Stalin called together a group of generals and began to query them about the war game scheduled for the next day. Although Zhukov, who was present, mentions this meeting, he does not explain why Stalin convened it, but there can be no doubt about the reason. The intelligence information made available to Stalin by this time shows that by the final week of December 1940, there was complete information regarding German intentions to invade the Soviet Union in the spring of 1941. Statements in a Soviet historical journal claim that the Soviet military attaché in Berlin came into possession of either a detailed document describing the Barbarossa Directive, which was signed by Hitler on December 18, 1940, or a draft copy of the plan itself.[1] Although no copy of it has been found anywhere in the Russian archives, it is probable that such a document did in fact exist. What probably happened was that the Soviet dictator called together his closest military and security advisors after the conference and told them in general terms what he knew, not revealing the exact German timetable. Then he asked them for their opinions on what to do.

Giving Stalin a direct answer for a question such as this was not easy. Zhukov and Timoshenko no doubt restated their objections to the forward strategy and pointed out the Bialystok salient's unsuitability for defense, but still Stalin would not give up his cherished offensive plan. Zhukov and Timoshenko, probably acting out of sheer frustration, offered a compromise—put the current situation on a map board and play it out with the Germans beating the Red Army to the punch. By now it was obvious to Stalin that this was the only way he could ever know if the strategy needed to be revised. The chief of the general staff, Meretskov, agreed. At this time Meretskov and Pavlov were allies, and it is likely that the foregoing discussion took place in a heated, even angry, manner, with caustic verbal exchanges ensuing between the opposing Meretskov/Pavlov and Timoshenko/Zhukov camps.

Then, with a nod of his head, Stalin ordered Meretskov to revise the game plan and assemble the necessary people. In the back of his mind, Stalin already knew that Pavlov would command the Russian side defending the Bialystok salient and Zhukov would play the German aggressor. What better choice? The advocate of the springboard and the armored warfare expert, Pavlov, would play against the premier commander of offensive operations, Zhukov.

The victor in the war games, determined by crushing blows both on the offensive and defensive sides of the board, was Zhukov, and it was his views that succeeded in winning over Stalin. The loser, Pavlov, was sacrificed almost in a ritualistic manner.

The Atmosphere Surrounding the War Games

Before discussing the January war games, it is important to note that war-gaming in the Soviet military was considered the ultimate form of strategic planning. The same has not often been true in the West. During the planning stage of Barbarossa by the German General Staff and the Wehrmacht high command (OKW), several studies were commissioned and one highly significant war game was held under General Paulus, then the quartermaster general of the army and later the commander of the Sixth Army, which surrendered at Stalingrad in early 1943.[2] In the Paulus game it was shown that the Wehrmacht would not have the strength and the logistics support it needed to defeat the Red Army and conquer the Soviet Union in one short blitzkrieg campaign. The German high command chose, however, to ignore the lessons of the Paulus exercise, and they explained away its results in a superficial way. The Red Army supreme command did not make this mistake—they took to heart the lessons learned in their war games and acted upon them competently.

There are no personal eyewitness accounts of the games other than the official transcripts, but the atmosphere in the Kremlin must have hung heavy with death and intrigue. The blood of the many officers killed in the purges of 1938 still stained Stalin's hands. In the January war games the fate of an entire nation and its people swayed in the balance. If the wrong decision had been made, the outcome of World War II might have been very different.

The aura that surrounded the war games is an important element in evaluating their significance. Stalin's very presence equaled tremendous pressure. A westerner has difficulty in grasping the effect the Soviet leader had on those around him. The Soviet/American movie *The Inner Circle* provides some insight into the awesome power the man had over others. There is a scene, allegedly a true story, in which the Kremlin film projectionist makes an offhanded deprecatory remark in Stalin's presence about the projector. The Soviet projector was a copy of a German model, but the Soviet version had a defective part. Stalin turns and with a quiet and innocent voice speaks to the minister and asks if this is so and doesn't he think it is important that the thousands of movie theaters in the Soviet Union be equipped with machines that work? The crowd of people in the screening room visibly shrink back from the minister and leave him standing alone to answer Stalin's question.

Reprimanding his subordinates was Stalin's customary behavior. For those who worked in close proximity to the dictator, it was almost impossible to avoid his rage or at least his sharp criticism. Stalin totally disregarded the feelings of everyone, even those he had to rely on and trust. One of his favorite techniques was to sit at the head of a conference table and ask the views of everybody, one by one around the table, about some important issue. Stalin, of course, would not render his opinion until the very last, seeing who would disagree with him. Sooner or later those who did would feel the dictator's unbridled wrath.

Stalin would arrange senseless command changes in the heat of combat operations when stability and coordination were needed.

One of his closest comrades in the Civil War had been Kliment Voroshilov, and even he was not spared. Stalin summoned him away from the front on a pretext and then dismissed him. The charges against Voroshilov were drafted by Stalin but disguised as a decision of the Politburo. In this document Stalin characterized Voroshilov as a shallow and worthless commander, starting with the Finnish campaign of 1939 when Voroshilov was the commissar of defense. In conclusion Stalin wrote:

> First, we should acknowledge that comrade Voroshilov's work at the front has been without merit.
> Second, comrade Voroshilov should be sent to work in the rear.
> Signed: Secretary of the Central Committee of the All-Union Communist Party (Bolsheviks), Stalin

For Voroshilov, who some time before had been Stalin's right-hand man and the apparent number two man in the country, this was a crushing blow.

Usually when removing a commander, Stalin relied on no outside advice and made the decision alone. On February 27, 1943, while reading routine reports from the Western Front, he noticed that the Sixteenth Army had failed in its attack in the direction of Briansk. Stalin immediately, without finding out the details, dictated STAVKA order N0045, in which he relieved the commander of the Western Front, Col. Gen. I. S. Konev. The reason given was that Konev had allegedly failed to accomplish his assigned mission. Konev was one of the lucky ones. He was summoned to the STAVKA and later given another post. Usually removal from command entailed severe consequences, as can be seen from the following telegram sent by Stalin:

> To the Commander of Cavalry Front comrade Koslov:
> . . . Maj. Gen. Dashichev, acting temporarily as the Commander of the Forty-Fourth Army, should be relieved of his command and immediately arrested and sent to Moscow. You should immediately take the steps necessary to restore order to the troops of the Forty-Fourth Army. . .

Stalin would unexpectedly summon a commander from the front and "talk" to him face-to-face, believing that the man in front of him was able to know everything and be ready to answer all questions that Stalin considered important. Although he himself was excused from knowing all the answers, Stalin considered it absolutely intolerable that his subordinates could fail to answer a question that he considered vital. If an "invited" person failed to answer some of Stalin's questions and tried to gloss over a few details, then, as Zhukov recalled, "Stalin's look turned heavy and cruel. I didn't know many people who could withstand Stalin's rage and keep from cowering in fear."

Zhukov was one of those rare individuals whom Stalin absolutely needed and therefore tolerated. The reason was that Zhukov knew the truth and was not afraid to speak it.

Stalin's ability to rally the military and the country at large to throw back the invader relied mainly on fear and intimidation. The Soviet dictator was aided enormously by Hitler's ideology that called for the German colonization of the Soviet Union and the enslavement of its peoples. For this reason, despite Stalin's mistreatment of them, the Soviet peoples were willing to sacrifice their lives in large numbers to save their country from depredation and enslavement. Thus, in a crude way, it can be said that Hitler was Stalin's greatest ally.

Despite the deafening silence from the dictator until his radio address to the nation on July 3 (included in full in Appendix A), there was a national upwelling of hatred for the enemy, without which the Red Army could not have survived beyond the first few weeks of the war. Stalin's propaganda was much less effective than the word-of-mouth reports about atrocities committed by the Germans. Hitler, like Napoleon, had ignored even the bare necessities of waging a political war that would appeal to the Russian people to rise up against the Bolsheviks. The problem was that the Nazis had become the victims of their own propaganda, and they could not realize the truth about Russia even when it confronted them in a real and irrefutable way. The Russian people were fighting to save their land from occupation; the fact that their leaders were oppressing them mattered little compared to the urgency to defeat the traditional foreign enemy from the west. Stalin had cleverly played upon this primitive part of

the national consciousness when in 1938 he commissioned the famous Eisenstein movie *Alexander Nevsky*. The most compelling scene
in the movie is when the charging Teutonic knights are shown sink-
ing beneath the cracking ice of Lake Peipus. No one who has seen
that film can deny its powerful imagery. Stalin also was unabashed
in using religious icons such as the 500-year-old "Kazan Mother of
God" to whip up religious and patriotic fervor during the war, although earlier he had personally ordered the magnificent Cathedral
of Christ the Savior in Moscow dynamited as well as many others
throughout the land.

There is also another factor to consider. As brutal despots have
learned throughout the centuries, and as Machiavelli counseled,
Stalin could show himself to be a caring, even benevolent father figure. Pavel Sudoplatov, himself an agent who had been personally ordered by Stalin to callously murder a Ukrainian separatist leader, recalls in his book *Special Tasks: The Memoirs of an Unwanted Witness, a
Soviet Spymaster* a scene at a Kremlin banquet in 1945 celebrating the
end of the war. Stalin came over to a table where there was a veteran
who had lost a leg and could not stand to drink a toast. Stalin warmly
thanked the man and apologized for the great damage the Fascists
did to the people and to the country. Sudoplatov remarked on the
open display of emotion and tears of gratitude for Stalin. Everyone
at the table felt that they were Stalin's children and that he had sin-
gle-handedly saved the nation from ruin.

Even today, among some older Russians a strong nostalgia persists
for "Uncle Joseph," a kindly, all-seeing, and all-caring man who never
really existed but lives on that way in the myths that still surround
him. The use of skillful propaganda alone cannot account for Stalin's
public image. His power over others was truly transcendent.

Despite everything that has been written about Stalin, the man remains an enigma to this day. Above all, his ability to act in an effective way depended solely on the effect he had on others around him.
Such was the atmosphere of dread and paranoia that prevailed in the
Kremlin in late 1940 and early 1941. From the accounts of people
who were in the court of Ivan the Terrible in the sixteenth century,
the feeling then was much the same. Understanding Stalin's power

over others is the only way to understand the context for all that happened at the highest levels of the Soviet government and its military in the time leading up to the greatest peril the nation had ever experienced, the invasion of the German Wehrmacht on June 22, 1941.

The January War Games

Under the supervision of the Soviet defense commissar, Marshal S. K. Timoshenko, the largest map exercises ever staged by the Red Army were held in January 1941. Their announced objective was to simulate "front offensive operations concerned with penetrating fortified areas." The real reason was that D. G. Pavlov's theories about the Bialystok salient's being adaptable for defense and then counteroffense were about to be tested. The district and army commanders, chiefs of staff, operational section commanders, air force commanders, artillery commanders, tank and armored unit commanders, and many others were involved in the games.

Two games were played: the first from January 2 to January 6, 1941, the second from January 7 to January 11.

In the first game, Pavlov played the eastern (Russian) side commanding the Northwestern Front. His chief of staff was V. E. Klimovskikh. The western (German) side was played by Zhukov commanding the Northeastern Front. His chief of staff was Gen. M. A. Purkaev. The names and sides here are very confusing. Zhukov's command was the Northeastern Front, but he was playing the west, whereas Pavlov was on the east playing the commander of the Northwestern Front. These directions make sense only if the reader views the map board from the respective sides of the "German" and "Russian" armies.

The forces of the participating parties were as follows:

- The eastern five armies had sixty-four divisions, including ten tank and motorized divisions, with 8,811 tanks and 5,652 aircraft.
- The western armies had sixteen divisions, including four tank and one motorized division, with 3,516 tanks and 3,336 aircraft.

The initial length of the front line in the map layout was about 650 km. The concept was that military operations of both sides should include offensive and defensive maneuvers. The ultimate goal of the western side was to occupy a part of Bielorussia and the Baltic region with an advance to the line of Baranovichi-Dvinsk-Riga. The goal of the eastern side was to stop the German attack near the border. Then the goal was to crush the Southeastern Front of the western side, destroy the enemy's well-prepared defenses in East Prussia, occupy East Prussia, and advance as far as the Vistula River. The assignments and the defense commissariat's directions emphasized the necessity to master not only offensive operations but defensive ones as well. In particular, point four of the assignment read, "The parties should familiarize themselves with the basics of defensive operations, particularly in regard to the fortified area (the Bialystok salient)." Gen. N. F. Vatutin (deputy chief of staff of the Red Army) added in his own hand the word "modern," which means that the game was intended among other things to improve the methods of modern defensive operations.

General Zhukov's Directive No.1 as commander of the Northeastern Front also stressed the importance of the defense, though at the first stage of the game he took the offensive. Zhukov's defensive role, as it turned out, was more active than passive. Thus, he assigned the Tenth Army the mission of blocking the eastern units advancing toward Aris and Lützen. Instead of digging in, he insisted on launching a counterattack from the Mishinetz region toward Kolno and Bialla. In another aggressive maneuver the Ninth Army was ordered to strike a sharp blow and force the enemy back behind the August channel.

Later, Zhukov created a tank group, two to three brigades strong, in the region of Krasnopol. The commanders of these units were to prepare a counteroffensive in the direction of Mariashpol and Suvalki.

It was characteristic of Zhukov that even when preparing for an offensive or counteroffensive, he never underestimated the need to devise a fallback defense strategy in case it was needed. Zhukov's tactical genius was that he always appreciated the necessity of wearing down the enemy, draining him of energy, and letting him extend beyond his sources of supply, and then following with well-coordinated and supported counterattacks. The idea of combining offensive and defensive operations runs through all the operational documents of the armies and corps under Zhukov's command in the games and became a trademark of his operational art throughout the war.

Events in the first game took the following course: the eastern side repelled the enemy attack in the border battle and limited its penetration to the depth of 15–20 km. They then launched a number of counterattacks and developed an all-out offensive. Pavlov envisaged a deep enveloping maneuver by the front's left wing, two armies and a mobile group (a cavalry-mechanized army) in the direction of Deutsch-Ilau and Marienburg. The aim was to outflank the East Prussian enemy group from the west, thus ensuring the encirclement of Zhukov's main forces in the region of the Masurian Lakes by meeting engagements in the direction of Allenstein. Pavlov's operation was strikingly similar to the future Red Army East Prussian operation carried out by the forces of three fronts in 1945.

Pavlov tried to bypass the enemy's fortifications in an end-around, which was expected. But, Zhukov knew that his opponent lacked sufficient forces to bring the operation to a successful conclusion. A longer front line demanded strong support for the enveloping group from the left, which it did not have.

Zhukov decided to stop the advance of the eastern forces by entangling them in his fortified lines, including tank traps, wire, trenches, and minefields, channeling the attackers into killing zones covered by interlocking fields of fire while concentrating his reserves for an attack. He decided to set up a strike force using his left wing in East Prussia to support an assault in the direction of Riga-Dvinsk. After this attack succeeded in punching through Pavlov's defenses north of the Bialystok salient through Grodno toward Lida, the referees halted the game and awarded the advantage to the western side.

The significance of this war game has never been fully appreciated, but it should not be underestimated because it had a profound effect on Stalin, who reacted with extreme displeasure when he was informed of the result. The impact on the Soviet dictator was as shattering as the news had been that the Germans had broken through

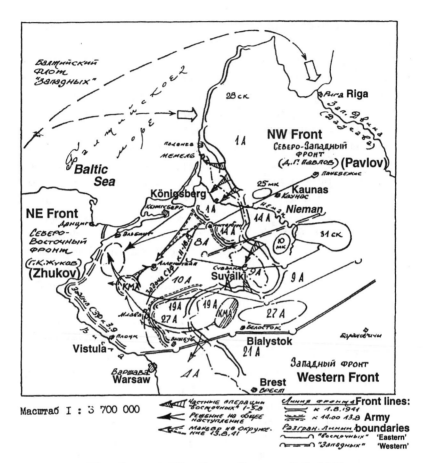

Масштаб I : 3 700 000

Частные операции "Восточных" 1-5.8

Решение на общее наступление

Манёвр на окруже-ние 13.8.41

Линия фронта Front lines:
к 1.8.1941
к 14.00 13.8 Army boundaries
Разгран. линия "Восточных"   'Eastern'
"Западных"   'Western'

First Strategic War Game, January 2–6, 1941

the Ardennes and routed the French army in May 1940. With startling clarity Zhukov had exposed the dangers of Pavlov's forward strategy of adapting the salient for defense while using it as a springboard for an offensive into the heart of Germany. He had succeeded in dispelling the illusion that the Red Army could easily carry the banner of victory into Central Europe without a fundamental reexamination of the basic precepts of the Soviet Union's forward defensive-offensive strategy.

The problem was a real one. If Stalin had finally come to grips with the awful truth of what Zhukov and Timoshenko had been telling him, what could be done? In point of fact, "fixing" a mistake in strategy is not easy. By this time Stalin knew the details of the German "Barbarossa" directive, and he knew that the date was set for May 15, 1941 (after the Balkan campaign in March, the date was changed by Hitler to June 22). If Stalin considered this information authentic, this could have been the basis for his instructions to Zhukov on his role as a German aggressor in the war games.

In the second game, which probably was the only one originally scheduled, Zhukov and Pavlov switched sides. Zhukov headed the eastern side, Pavlov the western. It should be noted here that Zhukov does not mention the second game at all, saying in his memoirs that he was invited to play the "blues," clearly referring to the first game. It can be surmised that he was instructed not to mention the second game because its conclusion left the Red Army in control of a substantial portion of southeastern Europe.

Judging by the operational-strategic situation, the second game was much more complicated than the first (see following map). The exercise was focused on the southern zone, from the Pripyat Marshes to the Black Sea.

Pavlov's western side had two fronts—the southeastern and southern, with nine armies; 94 divisions, including 5 tank and motorized; 8,000 guns and mortars; 5,500 tanks; and 4,500 combat aircraft. Pavlov took direct operational control over the Southeastern Front; the Southern Front was commanded by F. I. Kuznetsov.

On the eastern side of the board, Zhukov commanded the Southwestern Front, which had seven armies; one cavalry-mechanized army; 101 divisions, including 14 tank and mechanized; 16,000 guns and mortars; 8,800 tanks; and 5,800 combat aircraft.

The frontage lengths in the map layout were as follows: southwestern, 900 km.; southeastern, 510 km.; southern, 450 km.

The idea of the game was to engage both sides in vigorous operations. The western side was to launch attacks by its two fronts in the direction of Shepetovka and to encircle the main forces of the Southwestern Front in the region of Lvov. It was the assignment of the eastern side to repel the enemy's attacks and to launch an all-out counteroffensive at the first opportune moment.

The initial situation, compared with that of the first game, was much more tense. The enemy was supposed to have deeply penetrated in the Proskurov direction, where the troops of the Southern Front of the west advanced up to 130 km. within six days, thus threatening to collapse the eastern defenses.

Under these circumstances, the eastern commander launched a series of attacks at the flanks of the western group penetrating in the direction of Lipkai and Botashani. This eventually led to the encirclement of the western penetrating group in the region of Kamenetz-Podolsk.

In the next stage of the play, Zhukov organized counterattacks in the directions of Budapest and Bucharest with the aim of reaching the line Krakow-Budapest-Kraiova and crushing the German allies, Hungary and Rumania. Zhukov directed part of his force to strike from the region of Krakow at Czestochowa in the rear of the main force of the Southeastern Front. To achieve his goal he concentrated a strike group (two strike armies and a cavalry-mechanized army; thirty-two divisions in all, including six tank and motorized) in the area around Tarnuv and Sanok. This strike group was deployed along a 120-km. front, which amounted to more than 8 percent of the entire front and represented about one third of the total force, including 43 percent of all tank and mechanized units.

Along other parts of the front, Zhukov was engaged in stubborn defensive battles, counterattacking the penetrating enemy, outflanking him, and reaching the rear of his main strike groups. In the course of reaching Budapest, Zhukov planned and successfully executed an encirclement of the right wing of the west's Southeastern Front in Transcarpathia with one of his cavalry-mechanized armies and an airborne group. It was clear that the forces under Zhukov's command had once again butchered those led by Pavlov.

It is interesting to look at the assumed losses in the course of the strategic war games. The Red Army forecasted losses before the start of the games not to exceed 5 to 6 percent of total manpower. Should the manpower of the army be at the 1.3 million level, the casualties were expected to be 65,000 to 78,000 personnel a month. The number of others incapacitated could be as high as 51,000 a month. Thus, the total monthly losses were expected to average around 120,000.

However, the war of 1941–45 proved these assumptions seriously wrong; the Red Army suffered much greater losses. Zhukov himself was never guilty of underestimating the enemy by downplaying projected losses in the event of war. He refused to agree to the casualties assessed by the umpires in the January war games, and they were not given in the final report.[3] Already the man had an unclouded vision of the way things were going to be once the dogs of war were set loose. The unenviable trap that Stalin had built for them in Bialystok had only one, very bloody, way out.

An important feature of the document that set forth the rules of the war games is that it assumes that the start of hostilities with the

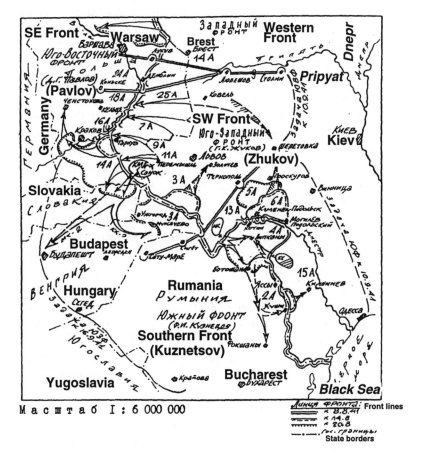

Second Strategic War Game, January 7–11, 1941

enemy (Germany) would begin on August 1, 1941. This date is curious since it is known that Stalin had in his possession the details of the Barbarossa Directive soon after December 25, 1940. Why then would a start date of August 1, 1941, be chosen? The answer is that he wanted to keep this intelligence to himself, sharing it with only those he trusted. Stalin chose to keep the real date secret because he no longer believed in Pavlov's solution to the Bialystok problem.

This document, plus other information contained in the January war games that will be discussed later, supports the idea that the fundamental agreement about an echeloned strategic defense was made between Zhukov and Timoshenko before the play of the war game. Stalin's conversion to this strategy could be seen by the events after the games were called to a halt.

The accounts of the discussion that followed the war games from Zhukov as well as Khrushchevian sources reveal the true impact that the exercises had on Stalin.

In his explanation to Stalin of the method of the "red" counteroffensive operation carried out in the critical first exercise, Meretskov displayed a hypothetical map showing a situation in which sixty to sixty-five Soviet divisions overwhelmed a defending German force of fifty-five divisions. In reply to Stalin's question about how victory could be achieved with such a slight advantage in strength, Meretskov answered that the Red Army did not have a general superiority in manpower and firepower, but a local superiority could be gained in the main direction of an offensive by pulling in units from quiet sectors. Stalin contradicted this and said that the Germans had enough mechanized forces to maneuver rapidly and redress a temporary unfavorable balance of strength to their favor. He also advised Meretskov to dispense with hypothesis and get down to specifics, asking him, "Who won, the reds?" The chief of the general staff avoided giving a direct answer, however, saying only that the "blues" were very strong in tanks and aircraft. Stalin then sealed Meretskov's fate by dismissing his claims of qualitative superiority for Soviet divisions, particularly the rifle divisions, as being "the stuff for agitators, not realists."

For his part, Pavlov tried to explain the reds' failures in the first war game by making a small joke about how things such as unexpected defeat often happen in map exercises, but Stalin was a deadly serious man and his sense of humor was lacking when it came time to decide grave issues. Pavlov would pay the ultimate price for his inability to understand this.

After some additional inconclusive or muddled reports by Timoshenko, G. I. Kulik, and others, in what must have been a state of utter frustration, Stalin then asked if anyone else wished to speak. It was Zhukov who answered. The commander of the Kiev district pointed out, quite correctly, that the Bialystok fortified region, crammed far to the west into an indefensible salient, was virtually indefensible.

"The way I see it," said Zhukov, "the fortified regions in Bielorussia are being built too close to the border and are at a disadvantage in terms of operational configuration, especially in the area of the Bialystok salient. This may allow the enemy to strike from Brest and Suvalki in the rear of our whole Bialystok group. Besides, our forces are unlikely to hold out long as the depth of the fortified region is insufficient, allowing the entire depth of the salient to be reached by artillery. I think fortified regions should have been built somewhere deeper, farther behind the state border."

General Pavlov was quite angry at the criticism and responded: "And in Ukraine [Zhukov's area of command], the forward regions there, are they being organized correctly?"

Zhukov replied: "It was not I who chose the locations for the fortified regions in Ukraine; however, I think they also should be built farther from the border." It was his earnest recommendation that the first main line of defense be constructed no closer than 100 km. from the border.

The importance Stalin attached to these recommendations may be judged by the fact that on the day following the final reports on the war games, January 14, 1941, Stalin announced the Politburo's decision to replace Meretskov with Zhukov as chief of the general staff.

In securing Zhukov's new appointment, Stalin was, in essence, preparing to abandon his plans for the deployment of the Red Army's offensive forces in the exposed regions far to the west. The evidence regarding German intentions in 1941 had been mounting with increasing reliability as spring drew closer, and after early March no thought would be given to massing more men and materiel up close to the demarcation line. The objective now would be to concentrate wholly on means of repelling the imminent invasion. After the war, Stalin, and later Zhukov, came under sharp criticism for failing to position enough strength along the state border to repel the invaders as soon as they set foot on Soviet soil. According to the interpretation put forth by Khrushchev at the Twentieth Party Congress in 1956, Stalin was afraid to heed the warnings of the impending attack and neglected to fortify the border properly because he was reluctant to do anything that might provoke the Germans into aggression. In answer to this charge, Zhukov has argued as follows:

> In recent years it has become common practice to blame the General Headquarters for not having ordered the pulling up of our main force from the interior zone in order to repulse the enemy. I would not venture to guess in retrospect the probable outcome of such an action. . . . It is quite possible, however, that being under equipped with antitank and antiaircraft facilities and possessing lesser mobility than the enemy forces, our troops might have failed to withstand the powerful thrusts of the enemy panzer forces and might, therefore, have found themselves in as grave a predicament as some of the armies of the frontier zone. Nor is it clear what situation might then have developed in the future on the approaches to Moscow and Leningrad and in the southern areas of the country.

Here Zhukov has eloquently refuted the contention that the Red Army could have stopped the Wehrmacht on the frontier in 1941. It is plain to see that Zhukov never intended to place the main body of the Red Army close to the initial shock of the onslaught, depriving it of the ability to maneuver while leaving it in a position highly vulnerable to being cut off and then annihilated. Zhukov knew that the German armored thrusts would have to be continually drained of energy by successive echelons of defense located deep within Russia. After a period of active defense, of absorbing and blunting the enemy's momentum, conditions would become favorable for the launching of a counteroffensive by the last echelon, the strategic reserve. Such a plan, of course, would mean that terrible disaster would befall the forces of the first echelon, which would have to stand their ground while the German armor flowed around them.

Western historians have never made any mention of the fact that Zhukov's appointment as chief of the general staff indicated that Stalin had become a convert to his ideas. In point of fact, Zhukov's victory in the first war game, coupled with the startling demonstration of his skill in the second, left no doubt in Stalin's mind that his horse was the one that would have to be ridden.

Background to the February War Game

The most immediate problem that Zhukov had to face after becoming chief of the general staff was that a way had to be found to make the best use of the troop concentrations already in the Bialystok salient for defense. Since no force on earth could have saved the Red Army units there from being cut off and surrounded soon after the war began, this would mean that they would have to be sacrificed. If handled properly, however, this sacrifice could be expected to pay big dividends later on, much in the way a "poisoned pawn" is offered up as a victim in a chess game. The loss of a small piece is relatively unimportant if the opponent can be placed in a difficult strategic posture. It would require no small amount of skill, planning, and deception in order to ensure that the sacrifice would cost the Germans a maximum amount while still remaining rather "cheap" for the Soviet side.

Although Stalin was now convinced that the Pavlov-Meretskov forward strategy would have to be abandoned, there was still much to be done to create a new strategy based on an active defense. Zhukov believed that an active defense could be turned into an effective counteroffensive that would not only sweep the invader from Soviet territory but destroy the core of his army.

Sometime within days after the January games, Zhukov, Timoshenko, and Stalin came to an understanding that in order to test the deep-echelon theory of defense using real force ratios as Soviet intelligence had revealed them to be, there had to be held yet a third war game. Probably at no earlier time in history has a major belligerent in a soon-to-start war ever had more complete intelligence about the strength of the opponent and the disposition and capabilities of his forces as did the USSR in early 1941. Based on such detailed reports, Zhukov and Timoshenko were able to engage in a thorough analysis of precisely what would have to be done to repel the invasion.

The third war game in February was the outcome of this analysis.

Taking the "deep battle" theory of Tukhachevsky as a starting point, the forces along the western frontier, including Bialystok, could be considered the first, or tactical, echelon of defense. A second, or operational, echelon should be positioned some 300–500 km. behind the first. The third, or strategic, echelon should be a mobile reserve positioned to reinforce the most vital and threatened sectors of the front, most probably on the flanks of the enemy along the most direct route to Moscow.

In looking at the maps of the areas that were certain to become the theater of operations once the war started, there were several obvious and compelling conclusions that could be drawn. The map that follows shows that a natural funnel exists on the route to Moscow from the west.

An invading army would certainly have to pass north of the impenetrable Pripyat Marshes. Taking that as a given, the map shows that the route to Moscow compels an invader to cross the so-called "land bridge" formed by the uplands between the headwaters of the Western Dvina River, which flows north into the Baltic Sea, and the headwaters of the upper Dnepr River, which flows south into the Black Sea. It was the control of this critical territory, in reality the only approach to Moscow from the west, that would determine the outcome of the war. This obvious geographical feature was not a secret; rather, it was well known to Napoleon's generals. The following is a quote from a U.S. Military Academy publication.

> The Smolensk-Moscow Upland played a key role during Napoleon's invasion of Russia in 1812 as the upland's east-west, high-ground approach made it a logical choice for Napoleon's axis of advance upon Moscow. However, the hilly nature of the upland was also ideally suited to the delaying tactics adopted by the Russian Army.[4]

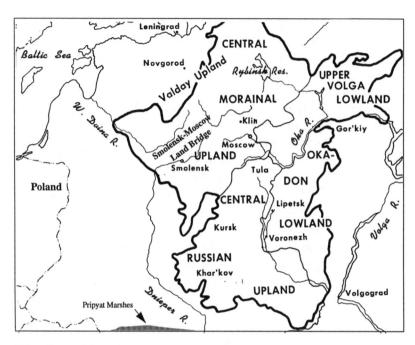

The Central Russian Plain and the Smolensk-Moscow Land Bridge

It should be noted here that although several German studies prior to Barbarossa and the only serious war game played by the Germans testing the Barbarossa scenario featured the "land bridge" as an important area to control, none of them dwelled on the criticality of it. Although the "land bridge" dominated the Timoshenko-Zhukov February war game, it was treated by the Germans almost as a passing thought. Why, one might ask, should such an obvious feature on the map be so lightly regarded by the Germans? It was the most likely (and perhaps only) place where a Soviet counteroffensive could occur.

The answer is that the German General Staff believed that the surprise of the invasion and the swiftness of the advancing panzers would prevent the Red Army from assembling the necessary reserves around the "land bridge" to offer any effective resistance so deep in the interior of the country. This in and of itself was probably the single bad assumption that cost Germany any chance of winning the war on the Eastern Front. In early 1941 no one on the German General Staff had ever heard of a village called Yelnia located in the hilly area south of the upper Dnepr near the headwaters of the Desna River—but they would.

In addition to knowing the strength and disposition of his enemy, Zhukov possessed an intimate knowledge of the geography of the coming battleground. The Soviet general was born and raised in a village in Kaluga province, some 200 km. due east and south of Smolensk and southwest of Moscow.

In regard to the capabilities of the opponent, there was much information available about the effectiveness of the Wehrmacht's blitzkrieg campaigns in France and in Poland. The Soviet general staff had very accurate information about the speed of movement and general maneuverability of the various components of the German army. In general, German infantry could keep up a sustained march of no more than 18–20 km. per day. A mechanized unit such as a Panzer division was capable of moving no more than 120 km. per day over hard-surfaced roads. But these numbers were considered valid only for the opening days or weeks of a campaign. Once fatigue set in and the logistics trains were lengthened, the offensive would begin to run out of steam. The wear and tear on equipment was also considered to have a telling effect on a sustained offensive drive, especially over terrain like that of central Russia. Good roads there are few and far between, and the dust and mud are legendary at different times of the year.

As Zhukov and Timoshenko continued their analysis of how to stop a German blitzkrieg operation from overrunning their country, one outstanding opportunity began to emerge. As the Wehrmacht plunged farther and farther east, a natural separation between the slow-moving infantry and the fast-racing mechanized units would occur. In close-bounded theaters of operation such as France and Poland, this had not caused the Germans much of a problem. There, the opponent's armies had been deployed relatively tightly, and they could be surrounded and annihilated by close infantry-armor coordination. In the Soviet Union, however, a wholly different scale of operations was in the offing, and new rules would apply that the Germans had not yet encountered.

The fact that German tanks could rapidly race around large pockets of Soviet soldiers, as at Bialystok, was no guarantee that the pockets themselves could be quickly or effectively reduced. On the contrary, it was considered plausible that weeks of delays would be encountered by the Germans as their infantry grappled with cut-off Red Army units around Bialystok and Minsk. It was also believed that the mechanized forces would have to turn back to the west to contain the pockets (*Kessel*, or "Cauldron," in German) and prevent Russian soldiers from breaking out to the east and re-forming effective combat units.

The problem of containing the surrounded pockets of Soviet soldiers was not solved by the German commanders as the war developed. The German reliance on blitzkrieg tactics, more rationally tailored for Western and Central European theaters of operation, was an important element in the Zhukov-Timoshenko plan for defeating the enemy.

Another aspect of the defense plan needs consideration at this point—that is, the nationality question. As noted in the Introduction, it was always problematic whether or not the minority peoples of the Russian Empire and later the Soviet Union would fight an invader or instead turn and fight the regime. Since Stalin's harsh collectivization of the farms in the early 1930s, there was even some doubt about the loyalty of the Russian peasantry, the backbone of the Russian army. There can be no doubt that the nationality and peasant factors seriously influenced the Zhukov-Timoshenko defense plan.

It might be wondered how a military strategy could be countenanced that would concede so much territory and place the populations of the occupied zones under such extreme danger. The Jews, in particular, among the Soviet minority nationalities, many of whom lived in White Russia and in the western Ukraine, could be expected to suffer greatly from a Nazi occupation. There is evidence to support the belief that Stalin's general attitude toward the Jews was not much different from that of the Nazis. In August 1939, at the time of the negotiations over the German-Soviet "Treaty of Friendship," which led to the dismemberment of Poland, Stalin told Ribbentrop, Hitler's foreign minister, that the Jews were tolerated in Russia only because there was no native Russian intelligentsia and that, when such a class developed in the Soviet Union, "the Jews could be disposed of." With regard to the other nationalities, there may have been other than purely military reasons for Stalin's preoccupation with the defense of Ukraine. In his secret speech to the Twentieth Party Congress in 1956, Khrushchev remarked that Stalin would have relocated the Ukrainians, the largest non–Great Russian minority in the USSR, as he had done some of the smaller peoples (such as the Kalmyks and the Chechin-Ingush) during the war, but that "there were too many of them and there was no place to which to deport them." Stalin's concern about the loyalty of the Ukrainians to the Soviet regime was justified, as the civilian population there was, in general, well disposed toward Germany. Harsh German occupation policies such as the maintenance of the collective farms and the transportation of forced labor to the Reich, however, quickly used up the reservoir of goodwill.

Stalin, then, counted on the minority nationalities to fight the Nazis because he believed that the treatment the Germans would mete out to them would cause resentment and fear. In this respect, Hitler made the same mistake as Napoleon, discounting the need for winning a political war in Russia as well as a military one. How could Stalin assume that Hitler and the Nazis would be so stupid as to play right into his hands in such a manner? The answer is that the Nazi leadership had already given evidence in Poland of how it would treat the Slavic and Jewish people, and Hitler had already set down in writing an official policy toward Russia that left little doubt about what kind of occupation would be carried out there. According to P. K. Ponomarenko, head of the partisans in Bielorussia, Stalin told him in December 1941 that the spontaneous upsurge of guerrilla activity in the summer of 1941 against the Nazis was a complete surprise both to himself personally and to the Party. Only later did the NKVD bring the partisans under organizational control.

In summarizing the forces at work prior to the February war game, Zhukov and Timoshenko were compelled to position the second or operational echelon for an active defense in the area of the upper Dnepr to the north and south of Smolensk. As we have seen, the logic of geography could not be escaped. The potential areas of unrest in the Soviet Union were the non–Great Russian territories that had been colonized by Moscow during the previous 400 years. Certainly Ukraine was high up on this list of possibilities, as were the Caucasus, Bessarabia, and Bielorussia with its large Polish minority. The active defense/counteroffensive had to be planned for the land bridge within the western part of Great Russia. It could be said that this was almost a preordained condition if the in-depth strategy was to have any real chance of success.

The February War Game

The February war game and the resulting in-depth echeloned defense plan calling for coordinated counterattacks against the flanks of German Army Group Center as it debouched into Russia proper north of the Pripyat Marshes closely modeled the actual strategy that was executed after the war began.

The attendees of the February 1941 war game were Timoshenko, Zhukov, M. Kazakov, A. Eremenko, I. Tulenev (the future commander of the Southern Front), Ia. Cherevichenko (the future commander of the Southwestern Front), P. Bodin (the future chief of staff of the Southwestern Front), Lieutenant General Kuznetsov (the commander of the key Twenty-first Army), and major general of aviation Kopets. The future commands of the participants are noted to lend weight to the contention that these were the handpicked select few who were destined to play vital roles in saving the nation.

The leader of the war game was Timoshenko, who, along with Zhukov, had a personal hand in crafting a strategy for stopping the advance of German Army Group Center along the key axis of attack aimed directly at Moscow.

A copy of the original attendance list along with Timoshenko's signature across the top of it follows. Not one of Pavlov's group of supporters—Kulik, Meretskov, or Klimovskikh—is included, further direct evidence that this war game was concealed from them.

The final proof that this war game was of decisive significance in laying down Soviet defense strategy before the war is that until now no one even suspected its existence. This document and all others making reference to the February 1941 war game have been hidden for the past fifty-six years. Some notations found in private papers made reference to "grave consequences" should this information become widely known. It is likely that once the mechanism was put in place to cover up the existence of the war game, it was never discovered by anyone else. The participants themselves never disclosed publicly what happened, either; they remained silent to the ends of their lives. In his secret speech to the Twentieth Congress of the Communist Party in 1956, Khrushchev denounced Stalin's failure to heed the warnings about the German invasion in order to explain

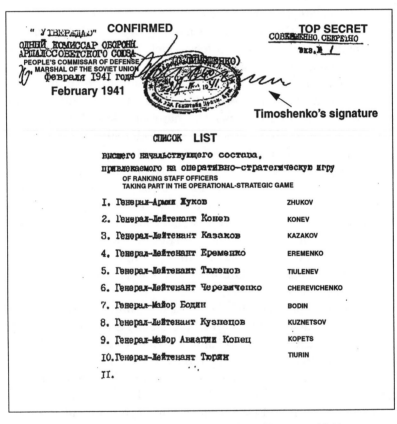

Invitation List to the Clandestine February 1941 Defensive War Game

the debacle on the Western Front. Khrushchev's interpretation was, of course, the one that most historians from the West picked up and never seriously questioned.

Although no maps used in the February war game could be found, it is possible to construct a map of the echeloned defense plan that was agreed upon by the participants of the February event. This map, based on orders found in the archive detailing the mobilizations of various units, shows with startling clarity what the general staff was preparing to do to blunt the German offensive. The effectiveness of this strategy may be evaluated based on commentaries taken from the original German unit war diaries, presented later in this book, that clearly demonstrate the problems the German commanders had in dealing with these counterattacks.

The desired goal of the counterattacks in the upper Dnepr region envisioned in the February war game was to force Hitler and the German high command to deal with the situation on the southern flank of Army Group Center before resuming the offensive in the direction of Moscow. The ultimate purpose of the Dnepr defense was to gain time for Timoshenko and Zhukov to mass reserves around Moscow and position them for a much bigger assault on the flanks of Army Group Center later as it approached the gates of the capital. These attacks, as planned, would fall on Army Group Center's exposed flanks after the onset of the Russian winter.

But, everything hinged on how much of a delay in the German offensive could be caused by the second operational echelon of defense along the Dnepr. Although the records of the February war game are no longer in existence, the evidence is that the game proved the Zhukov-Timoshenko supposition—that is, properly handled, a defense of the upper Dnepr, the keystone of which was a powerful counterattack against the southern flank of Army Group Center as it crossed to the north of the Pripyat Marshes, would offer the best possible opportunity for not only checking the enemy's advance but causing him to halt his movement in the direction of Moscow for a considerable time. The plan's chances for success were enhanced due to the shielding effect of the Pripyat Marshes, making the forces assembled for the counterattack invulnerable to attack directly from the westerly direction. Effective camouflage and con-

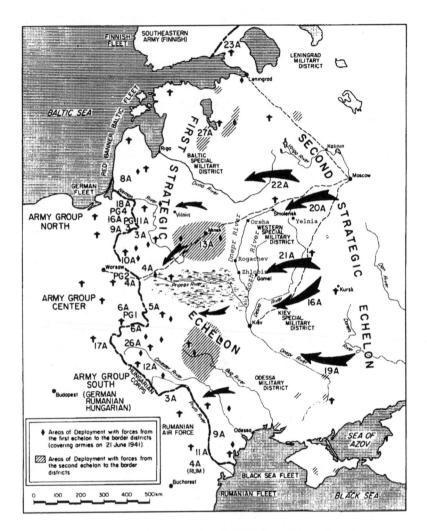

**Zones of Deployment for the Zhukov–Timoshenko
Deeply Echeloned Defense**

cealing movements by night would, it was hoped, keep the counterattacking forces from being detected by high-altitude Luftwaffe reconnaissance patrols.

Another important element of the counterattacks was to create a large separation between the rapidly advancing German motorized units and the slower moving infantry. Timoshenko and Zhukov demonstrated in the war game that the Germans would be ineffective in forming tight rings around surrounded Soviet units if coordination between the German armor and infantry was disrupted.

The map following has a history of some controversy. The first mention of this map can be found in the War Diary (*Kriegstagebuch* or KTB) of Guderian's Panzer Group 2. On July 8 the XXIV Panzer Corps operating near the Dnepr River near Stary Bykhov captured a Russian map showing that the powerful forces of the Red Army around Rogachev-Zhlobin were part of a general counterattack being launched from the area of Gomel. The commander of the XXIV Panzer Corps, Gen. Geyr von Schweppenburg, found this map so convincing that he recommended that the crossing of the Dnepr be postponed until either the German infantry was able to support him or he received other immediate reinforcements. Another map, probably the same or a similar one, was found on July 15 by the LIII Army Corps concealed within a Komsomol (Communist Youth Group) house on the Bobruisk-Rogachev road. This map was described as "a high command war game exercise organized by Marshal Timoshenko" and was dated February 1941. A rendering of this map from memory by an unnamed German officer who saw it was printed in a U.S. Department of the Army pamphlet in 1949. It is possible that the German officer in question was Guderian, since the XXIV Panzer Corps was part of his Panzer Group 2 when the map was found, and he is known to have been debriefed by the U.S. Army at the Karlsruhe barracks.

The map is included here because evidence from three separate sources testifies, at least indirectly, that it was a map either used at the February war game or drafted as a result of that war game. First, it is known that the war game took place; the attendance list and references to it in Zhukov's and Timoshenko's private papers are proof of this. Second, the war diaries of at least two German units make references to such a map. Third, the U.S. Department of the Army published the map after the war.

Finally, a comment is in order about a curious remark that Zhukov made to Stalin at the close of the January war games.

> Noting the considerable value of such games for raising the strategic and operational skills of high-ranking commanders, I suggested they should be held more often despite the complexities involved in organizing them.[5]

This statement seems to be a thinly veiled reference to the future February war game. There is no other obvious reason why Zhukov should have thought it important enough to put in his memoirs.

The map, if it is assumed to be authentic, reflects the actual plan by Timoshenko and Zhukov to assault the southern flank of German Army Group Center. It is probable that this was the basis for the February war game. It is also likely that the game was held somewhere in western Russia, not the Kremlin.

There are several interesting features and aspects of this map that deserve discussion.

One should note that the boundaries of the map are very strange from the standpoint of it being a defensive war game against an invasion from the west. The westernmost position on this map is more than 400 km. away from the closest German entry point into Soviet-controlled territory. In other words, the map is entirely focused on the secondary echelon along the upper Dnepr and seems to make the assumption that the entire Western Front, including all the forces in the Bialystok salient and around Minsk, have already been swallowed up.

Thus, the very setup for a war game of this nature in February 1941 would have been shocking and alarming for anyone charged with the defense of the western border. The big question is, what effect did the map have on Stalin?

A scene can be imagined in which Zhukov and Timoshenko present to Stalin a map that obviously features the destruction of all of the country's western defenses and shows the invader already advanced more than 600 km. into Soviet territory along the direct route to Moscow. Probably there has been no parallel to this scene in all of history. Before a shot was fired, months before the start of the war,

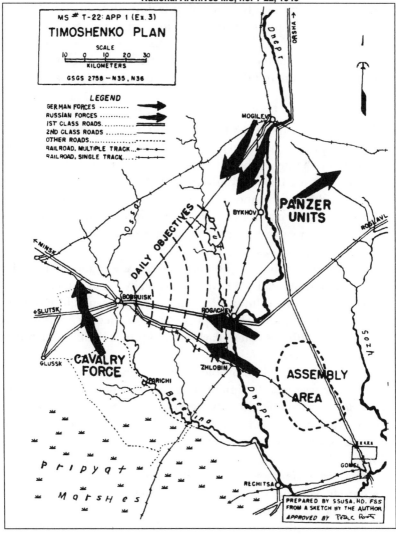

Map Computer Imaged from "Peculiarities of Russian Warfare"
Unpublished study by Office of Chief of Military History,
National Archives MS, no. T-22, 1949

Map of the February 1941 War Game

Stalin was painted a scenario of such crushing loss and defeat that it would have to be considered a near total collapse of all defenses. From what we know about Stalin, it is startling that he not only examined the map without having his "defeatist" generals summarily executed, but gave it his approval. It is difficult to imagine the personal conviction and bravery of the men who handed that map to Stalin.

This was a clear demonstration of how desperate the situation had become for Stalin and the nation as a whole in early 1941.

The Delusion
Why would it be necessary for Stalin and his inner circle of military leaders to purposefully and tragically delude their key frontline commander in charge of the forces along the border of the most important axis of attack—straight toward Moscow?

The evidence is compelling that Pavlov played the role of a pawn. He could not be made aware of the true strategic defense plan, for no general on earth could be expected to react any way but negatively to being used as a sacrifice.

It would seem that a deliberate attempt was made after the January war games to delude Pavlov, specifically about the key facts regarding the German timetable, which were known before the time the war games began. This impression is fortified by a report of an intelligence officer's visit to Pavlov dated June 20 published in Pavel Sudoplatov's book.

Pavlov anticipated no problems and believed that even if the enemy at first seized the initiative on the border, he had enough *strength in reserve* (meaning the reserves promised to him by Stalin) to counter any major breakthrough. He saw no necessity for subversive operations to cause disorganization among the attacking force.

From what he knew of the mobilization schedule, Pavlov had a right to feel confident. The reserves, however, were not intended to save his position in the Bialystok salient, and they never arrived.

By consistently using later dates in all the intelligence reports released to the commanding generals in the field, Zhukov and Timoshenko could further delay Pavlov in pressing harder for more forces to be brought into the Bialystok salient without unduly alarming him. After all, there was no point in having a man play a role unless he was absolutely convinced that it was an honest one and that a major effort would be made to reinforce him. There is another factor to consider in this scenario as well. In order to make the role complete, Pavlov had to be executed after his armies were defeated. Only then would the Germans be likely to believe that Stalin was caught off guard and was using Pavlov as a scapegoat. That Pavlov had been involved in a general's conspiracy made the decision to liquidate him all that much easier. Pavlov and his friends had been discussing ways in which the power of the NKVD security apparatus over the military could be limited.

Not only was Pavlov and his command to be used as a deliberate sacrifice, there can be little doubt that the general's life was part of the ruse to make it more believable. From the time of the war games on, then, a skillful and successful campaign was under way to deceive both Pavlov and the Germans while carrying out a mobilization plan and positioning the new forces in such a way that they could be used to maximum effectiveness to support the real strategic defense plan. The mobilization plan had to have a cover story to justify not bringing the new forces immediately into the Bialystok salient. The cover story involved not only a false schedule for the German attack but also an artful construct about where the Germans were positioning their troops, as will be seen in the next chapter.

The Fateful Impasse

After the collapse of the Western Front in the first days of the war, Pavlov and his closest allies, Kulik and Meretskov, were arrested by the NKVD and shot. They were made the most visible scapegoats of a failed strategy.

However tragic the deaths of these men might have been, it is true that their fate was preordained. Despite all their involvement in what Stalin regarded as a general's conspiracy, none of this would have spelled their doom had it not been for those fateful days in January during the war games. It was here that their advocated forward strategy for dealing with the coming German invasion was exposed with all of its fallacies readily apparent. Had these men been in possession of the insight and vision of Zhukov and Timoshenko, there can be little doubt that they would have adjusted their views accordingly and lived on to serve their country nobly. Yet this was not to be.

· 2 ·
SOVIET PREPARATION FOR WAR

USSR Defense Posture and Strategy on the Eve of Barbarossa
Given the fact that the Soviet Union had declared itself to be the implacable enemy of capitalism, the likelihood of attack from the west was always regarded as high. The assumption that there would be war between the Soviet Union and its potentially hostile neighbors, Germany and Japan in particular, affected Soviet policy in every area: social, economic, political, foreign, and military. "We have finished one period of wars," Lenin pointed out after the end of the Civil War in 1921, "we must prepare ourselves. We do not know when it will start, but if it does start we should be ready for it." Moreover, "A preparation for a war takes a long time," he said. "It should be started with improving the country's economic performance."[1] The resolution of the Fifteenth Congress of the Communist Party in 1926 in outlining the first five-year plan for Soviet economic development read, "Taking into consideration a possible military aggression on the part of the capitalist countries against the proletarian state, it is necessary that maximum effort be directed to a speedy development of the branches of the economy that will secure defense and economic stability in wartime." The same requirements were included in the second five-year plan.

The defense industrial sector in the pre-war years supplied the Soviet armed forces with ample quantities of military materiel. However, much of the military equipment grew obsolete by the late 1930s. Under the threat of German rearmament it was recognized that more sophisticated weapons would have to be designed and mass produced. Soviet design bureaus came up with a variety of innovative weapons—tanks, aircraft, guns, mortars, and other equipment. However, new weapons were slow to be designed and adopted. The unique armored Il-2 attack aircraft was designed by the Ilyushin bureau and rolled out in 1939. It was tested in the battles at Khalkhin-Gol but started coming into the armed forces no sooner than 1941. It soon acquired the nickname "Sturmovik" and gained the reputation as a fearsome tank buster. The Yak-1 fighter, designed by A. S. Yakovlev, had a top speed of 572 km. per hour. The plane went into mass production early in 1940, but only sixty-four fighters were produced during that year. Things were practically the same with the MiG fighters designed by A. I. Mikoyan and M. I. Gurevitch and with the Pe-2 dive-bomber by V. M. Petlyakov. The capabilities and tactical characteristics of the old planes were greatly inferior to German aircraft. To make matters worse, the Soviet air force was far behind the German Luftwaffe in rigging its units with radios, radio navigation, and radio location equipment. Only squadron commanders' planes were equipped with radios capable of receiving and transmitting, seriously impairing command and control.

Communications in the Red Army did not meet western standards, as there were few radios in the hands of the troops in the field. For example, the Western Military District had only 27 percent of its *shtat* (authorized number) of transmitters. The corps and divisions were only 7 percent properly equipped. Radios were not at first enthusiastically accepted, as this kind of communication had been underrated in value. But the war in the west clearly demonstrated the indispensability of radio as a major means to command troops in mobile warfare. The December meeting of the Red Army commanders in 1940 suggested that a decisive turn toward radio communication should be taken without delay. But on the eve of the invasion practically all communications equipment except for radio was obsolete. Many officers and generals had not been trained to command by radio, and, because radio was difficult to handle and tended to be unreliable, many commanders preferred to make use of wired signals.

The tank industry was one of the bright spots. In the years 1936–39 Soviet designers created the T-34 tank (designed by M. I. Koshkin, A. A. Morozov, and N. A. Kucherenko) and the KV (the chief designer was L. Y. Kotin), considered the best in the world. These tanks possessed formidable battle characteristics, including strong armor, powerful guns, great maneuverability, high speed, and cross-country ability. This is how German general Erich Schneider described the T-34 tank: "The T-34 has caused a sensation!"[2] This twenty-six-ton Russian tank was equipped with a 76mm gun whose shells could pierce the armor of German tanks at a distance of 1,500 to 2,000 meters, whereas German tanks could penetrate the Russians at a distance of not more than 500 meters and then only when the shells hit the tank's hull from the side or rear. A German tank's frontal armor was 40mm, hull side, 14mm. The Russian T-34 had frontal armor of 70mm and hull side armor of 45mm with sharply tilted armor plates, causing direct hits to be deflected. The attempt to create a tank on the pattern of the Russian T-34, after it had been carefully examined by German designers, appeared unrealizable. This superb tank was adopted late in 1939. It was planned to produce 600 tanks in 1940; however, only 115 tanks actually rolled off the assembly lines.

Steps were taken to improve the performance of industry in order to satisfy the growing needs of the military. A defense industry economic council was set up to oversee military production. An outstanding Soviet economist, N. A. Voznesensky, was appointed its chairman.

By mid-1940 tangible increases in production had been achieved. Before June 1941 the tank industry had produced 300 units per month. In the second half of the year 1,684 tanks rolled off the assembly lines, with 1,500 of these being the newer model T-34s and KVs. Unfortunately not all of these tanks were delivered to the troops, and many of those delivered were lost due to improper handling.

The Moisin rifle model 1891/30 was the main infantry weapon. There were no handheld automatic weapons. This omission was a result of flagrant errors and blunders in small-arms production. Obsolete models were being withdrawn and modern ones were too slow in delivery. The production of antitank rifles, which were essential in stopping enemy tanks, was halted as newer models were brought on-line. The PTRD (single shot, bolt action) and PTRS (magazine fed) 14.5mm antitank rifles, as Nazi general Schneider admitted, "caused the German tanks much trouble." These rifles were not issued to the troops, however, until August 1941 and then only in a trickle.

Much effort in the 1930s was spent in the improvement of artillery. As with other types of weaponry, upgrading artillery depended on the introduction of new technology. The 76mm division gun, model 1939, designed by V. G. Grabin was a first-class weapon in every respect. The 122mm howitzer, model 1938, and the 152mm howitzer, model 1937, were excellent weapons as well. The 45mm antitank gun was also quite effective.

Nevertheless, by the beginning of the war the Red Army lacked sufficient numbers of the latest model antitank weapons. Early in 1941 the chief of the Main Artillery Command (MAC), marshal of the Soviet Union G. I. Kulik, informed the armaments commissar, B. L. Vannikov, that the German army was rapidly rearming its troops with more powerful tanks and that the Soviet 45mm and 76mm artillery would prove ineffective against them. He suggested that the production of these guns be stopped. The production facilities that would then become available could be switched to manufacturing 107mm antitank guns. Vannikov, however, rejected this recommendation, saying that it was too risky to withdraw the older models from production on the eve of war. Finally, the argument was brought before Stalin, who rendered his judgment as follows: "Those [older] guns are very good. I remember using them during the Civil War." In this way, the introduction of the new models was seriously delayed.

Another weak point in Soviet artillery was in the lack of good-quality tractor-haulers. All the army had in 1940 were low-speed tractors, but even they were in short supply. The defense industry did much on the eve of the war, but it was unable to satisfy the demands of a bigger army. Stalin's dictatorship and abuse of power dramatically affected the performance of the defense industry. Arrests of designers and engineers on false charges and frequent changes of the key staff brought about chaos, fear, and instability, killed initiative, and greatly slowed down the pace of work. As an example of this, the chief designer of the 82mm and 120mm mortars was accused of sabotage and disrupting production. Vannikov tried to defend the man, but he too was arrested in early June 1941. After several delays, the new mortars finally did go into mass production shortly before the German invasion.

The improvement of the country's defenses included civil defense. To serve the goal of making the civilian population ready for the rigors of war, military departments were created in every district, city, and region throughout the country. These departments supervised the activities of OSOVIAKHIM, which in 1940 numbered 13 million people. The organization arranged military-physical training activities and local antiaircraft defense and helped the military in recruiting. The Soviet people, especially the youth, learned the art of war in these public organizations.

The propaganda campaigns unleashed in the pre-war years played an important role in boosting the morale of the Soviet people. Some of this had a negative effect, however, in that there was a widespread assumption that victory would be swiftly and easily won. This false propaganda did a lot of harm in preparing the Soviet people to cope with the hardships of war. The press carried boasts from political and military leaders saying, "Should the enemy strike, our retaliation would be three times as strong; a war would be fought in the enemy's territory and won with few casualties on our part." Defense commissar Marshal Voroshilov's speech at an officers' meeting on March 23, 1939, is a good example of the widespread complacency: "The Germans won't dare to attack us anytime soon," he said, "but if they do, they would get what they deserve. We shall easily beat them, about this I am certain."

The Soviet-Finnish Winter War provided a shock to the leadership. Marshal Timoshenko wrote at the time he took over the defense commissariat from the unfortunate Voroshilov, "Mistakes in training and educating the troops have been in underestimating the hardships a war might bring about . . . Soldiers lack physical fitness and endurance, there is no mindset to implicitly, quickly and precisely obey orders. Also they have not been taught to improvise. Instead, false democratism often undermines a commander's prestige and ability to lead."[3]

Political and military leaders on the eve of the war failed to give a realistic assessment of the enemy's likely resilience. They believed that Germany would soon be in a state of revolution in case of a war against the socialist Soviet Union. The power of Nazi propaganda in indoctrinating the army and the civilian population of Germany in the spirit of militarism was totally underestimated. It is interesting to note that German propaganda, too, gave the impression that the Soviet Bolshevik state would collapse like a house of cards as soon as war broke out. The German leaders had no way to imagine the kind of "loyalty" Stalin had instilled in the Soviet peoples, nor could they imagine how fiercely they would rise up to repel an outside invader.

Much effort was directed to the development of tanks, airborne troops, and aviation, as well as air defense formations, all of which were vital in the support of ground operations. The credit here goes to M. N. Tukhachevsky, who persisted in creating new service branches. In his work *The New Challenges of War,* published in 1932, he wrote, "While the neglect of artillery before the imperialist war [World War I] caused nearly all participating parties severe difficulties at the front, the disregard of new possibilities in aircraft, tanks, chemical weapons, radio communication, etc. may mean still bigger troubles and defeat in a future war."

Marshal Tukhachevsky and his supporters had to overcome the resistance of K. E. Voroshilov and S. M. Budenny, who idealized the experience of the Civil War and the cavalry in particular. A few days before his arrest and subsequent execution in 1937 as part of Stalin's blood purge, Tukhachevsky wrote, "We were confronted with the theory of the 'exceptional' mobility of the Red Army, a theory founded not on a careful study and estimation of new weapons either in the hands of our possible enemies or in the hands of the Soviet soldier, but on the lessons of the Civil War, on the notions evoked by the heroic spirit of the Civil War rather than grounded on the growing might, heavy industry, and culture of the socialist state. Neither is it grounded on the realities of the military buildup among our possible enemies in the capitalist camp."[4]

In 1932, much earlier than in Germany, the first large tank units were formed in the Soviet Union. There were two mechanized corps with two more added a couple of years later. However, defense commissar Voroshilov, instead of improving the methods of using tanks and designing new tactics for the new formations, came out against large tank units. He declared at the Seventeenth Party Congress in

1934, "It is essential that we once and for all do away with the harmful 'theories' of substituting the vehicle for the horse, of the horse's dying off." Somewhat later, at a session of the Military Council, he expanded on this viewpoint: "It is self-evident that such large units as tank corps are unmanageable in principle and we'll have to, in all probability, reject them." The formation of new mechanized corps, which in 1938 were renamed "tank corps," was stopped largely because of a misunderstanding of lessons learned in the Spanish Civil War.

Despite the boost in new military equipment and weapons, Voroshilov and his supporters still downplayed the importance of large tank units and insisted on the major role of cavalry. "The cavalry," Voroshilov said in 1938, "in all armies of the world is undergoing, to be more precise, has undergone a crisis; in many armies it has practically disappeared . . . We have a different point of view . . . We are convinced that our valiant Red cavalry will continue to be victorious. The Red cavalry still is a vigorous and shattering military force which can and will fulfill major tasks on all battlefields."

By order of the Chief Military Council of the Red Army on November 21, 1939, the tank corps were disbanded. This proved to be a serious error in the pre-war buildup of the Red Army. The words of the chief of the Frunze Military Academy, R. P. Eideman, eventually turned out to be prophetic. In 1931 he said: "It would be disastrous for an army if this or that senior officer's love of a certain type of combat dictated the central elements of military training for this or that unit, this or that school, this or that arm of the service."

The German experience in using large mechanized formations in Western Europe proved that Soviet military leaders were right in creating large tank units and correctly appraised their role in future combat. Tank units came into existence in the Red Army once again. But their revival had to wait for a new leader of the defense commissariat; S. K. Timoshenko succeeded Voroshilov on May 8, 1940. In June and July the new commissar ordered the formation of eight mechanized corps and one more later in the year. They were, however, not fully manned. In February–March 1941 another twenty mechanized corps, composed of two tank and one motorized division each, were put into service. The outbreak of war found them in the process of training and being equipped.

Along with tank units, considerable attention was given to the development of the air force. Air force exercises in 1936 demonstrated that "it was impossible to fight the Luftwaffe, which had longer range of action and better mobility along the width and depth of a front." Better cooperation between the fronts and aviation support was clearly needed. Coordination of aviation support on a frontal scale should have been organized by the supreme command rather than at the front level, although this was not immediately realized.

The air force was soon united into three air armies, but frontal aviation for all practical purposes was organized into air corps. The air corps organizational structure was designed to win air superiority, carry out raids against operational and strategic reserves in the enemy's rear, cooperate with ground forces along the main line of resistance (MLR), and secure airdrops of supplies, fuel, munitions, and airborne troops. Unfortunately, however, the air corps were not capable of achieving all that was expected of them. The air corps organization, however it was intended, inevitably scattered the aviation support forces and failed to ensure their effectiveness in winning air supremacy. Marshal Timoshenko, who was a vigorous advocate of Red Army reform and better training, made a mistake in not giving control over the air force a better focus. At the December 1940 meeting, he said that the contest for air supremacy should be waged within frontal operational areas.

In another serious setback in 1939, the air force suffered the same fate as the tank corps. The air force's armies of long-range bombers were disbanded, depriving the country of a strategic weapon capable of hitting targets deep in the enemy's rear, much less his homeland.

Airborne troops were regarded as one of the most promising new innovations. The first paratroop units took part in Red Army exercises as early as 1930. Airborne troops were used more widely during maneuvers in Ukraine in 1935. Transport aircraft dropped 1,200 paratroops near Kiev. Then aircraft flying in from another direction dropped another 2,500. An eyewitness of the exercise, the British general (later a field marshal) Wavell, informed his government, "Had I not been an eyewitness of this, I would have never believed that such an operation was at all possible." In 1936 an even bigger airborne drop was featured as part of the Bielorussian Military District's spring exercises.

During the period 1937–39, airborne forces in the Soviet Union made little headway. Advocates of airborne operations were men such as Tukhachevsky, I. E. Yakir, I. P. Uborevich, and other military leaders who then were in the process of being purged. Thus, airborne exercises were halted temporarily but were revived in 1940. There were five airborne corps by the beginning of the war. Each one was authorized 10,419 personnel, but like the tank units they too were understaffed and not up to minimum training and leadership standards.

It is noteworthy that the Wehrmacht used Soviet experience widely, and those Soviet military leaders who advocated disbanding the tank corps paid dearly for their mistake. Pavlov, based on his disastrous experience in Spain, together with G. I. Kulik, L. Z. Mekhlis, and E. A. Shadenko, had earlier supported disbanding the tank corps. But the Russian tank general admitted at the December 1941 Kremlin meeting that the idea of setting up large tank units proved to be correct; the effectiveness of the large independent German tank formations had been clearly demonstrated. "The Germans had not created anything new, they borrowed what we used to have."

By the beginning of the war the Soviet military structure consisted of four armed services: army (SA), air force (VVS), navy (VMF), and air defense force (PVO). This organization finally took shape in the fall of 1941. On the eve of Barbarossa the armed forces contained a total of over 5 million soldiers, sailors, and airmen. The army was the backbone of the military, though the air force and navy also played important roles in their respective areas of activity.

The defense commissariat and the general staff headed the armed forces excluding the navy. Marshal of the Soviet Union B. M. Shaposhnikov held the post of the chief of the general staff until August 1940. He was succeeded by General of the Army K. A. Meretskov, but on January 15, 1941, General of the Army G. K. Zhukov took over the post.

In 1938 the People's Commissariat of the Navy was established. Admiral N. G. Kuznetsov was appointed commissar of the navy, and

Admiral I. S. Tsakov was appointed commander of the navy general staff.

It was the infantry, however, which was called "the queen of fields," that was the major arm. The infantry equaled 50 percent of the Red Army, with the infantry division the primary combined-arms tactical unit. During wartime the *shtat* of a Soviet infantry division was 14,483 men, 294 guns and mortars, 16 light tanks, 13 armored vehicles, 558 vehicles, and 99 tractors. During peacetime, the Western Border Districts' divisions were staffed at about 8,000 to 12,000 personnel, whereas home front divisions numbered 6,000.

Tank and mechanized units were the striking forces of the army. The responsibility for manning, training, and equipping the tank forces was in the hands of the chief of the Mobile-Armored Command, Lt. Gen. Y. N. Fedorenko, who succeeded Pavlov.

The proportion of the cavalry in the army noticeably diminished on the eve of the war and amounted to just 2.5 percent of total strength. In terms of organization it consisted of thirteen divisions, with eight of them integrated into four cavalry corps.

Artillery provided the major firepower support of the infantry. At a Kremlin reception in honor of military academy graduates on May 5, 1941, Stalin described artillery as the "God of war." Organizationally Soviet artillery was based on the following principles: first, artillery units were to fire in support of the infantry and tanks at the full depth of their mission; second, artillery was to be massively used in support of units maneuvering from one sector of the front to another as well as in the immediate front area. Depending on its designation, artillery was divided into army artillery and Chief Command Reserve (CCR) artillery. The CCR artillery was under the command of the Chief Artillery Command (CAC) headed by deputy defense commissar Marshal Kulik.

Late in April 1941 the supreme command began the formation of antitank brigades under the CCR. They consisted of two artillery regiments, one engineer–mine-laying battalion, and one vehicular transport battalion. The plans for these units were drawn from studying the German panzer operations during the war in Western Europe. According to the *shtat,* a brigade was to be armed with 120 antitank guns, 28 antiaircraft machine guns, 4,800 antitank mines, and 1,000 antipersonnel mines. If such brigades had been established earlier, they would have been a powerful force to disrupt the enemy's tank attacks.

The Red Army engineer troops were under the command of the engineering department. Although engineer units had lots of heavy equipment, most of it was not very mobile, thus not fit for war of rapid movement. This fact motivated the design and production of lighter types of road and excavating machines. The first deliveries of the new equipment were received on the eve of the war. The troops were short of mine detection and mine-laying equipment, especially for antitank mines. This may be explained by the fact that the old leadership of the defense commissariat kept underestimating defense, and the new one had insufficient time to rectify the situation.

The air force consisted of two air services, bombers and fighters. The number of personnel and the equipment of the fighter arm exceeded the bombers by about 10 percent. The Soviet air force, though quite large on the eve of the war, had precious few of the newer models; they were no more than 17 percent of the total.

The experience of previous wars clearly demonstrated the role the home front could be expected to play in securing a continuous flow of materiel and personnel to the fronts. It had become quite evident that the success of an operation largely depended on a well-organized home front (strategic rear).

By the beginning of the war the Red Army had rich stores of materiel. The stocks of ammunition, fueling, and food at army warehouses were enough to last through 2 to 3 months of combat. Half of the stock was located in the western border districts, mainly in Bielorussia and Ukraine. General of the Army A. V. Hrulev, a former home front commander, recalled, "Back in 1940 the government discussed the question of where to locate the mobilization stockpiles. The military suggested that they be stored behind the Volga, but Mekhlis vetoed the idea. He insisted on stockpiling our military stores close to the border areas where the enemy could capture or destroy them. Mekhlis saw sabotage in any contradiction with his views . . ." Mekhlis managed to convince Stalin to support his position. "Later on," pointed out Hrulev, "we had to pay a hard price.

Much of the stockpiles were either destroyed by our retreating troops or captured by the enemy."[5]

On the whole, by the summer of 1941 the structure of the Soviet armed forces answered to the demands of modern warfare. Its fighting efficiency was affected, however, by the incompleteness of rearmament and reorganization.

The process of modernizing the army and navy required more well-trained and skilled specialists. The number of military schools and academies continuously grew. Whereas in 1937 there were 13 academies and 75 military colleges and schools, the number of academies grew to 18, and colleges and schools to 255 by 1941.

These academies and schools supplied the army and navy with a considerable number of military specialists: 79.6 percent of all military personnel had secondary and higher education by 1937. In tank and mechanized forces the percentage of military school and academy graduates reached 96.9 percent, in the air force 98.9 percent, and in the navy 98.2 percent.

In 1938 the number of students in the military schools doubled, civilian colleges arranged training for commanding personnel, and numerous junior-grade courses for lieutenants were established. More than a third of the 1939 and 1940 wave of recruits had secondary and higher educations. As a result of the tremendous work in personnel training, the cadre deficiency in the army was reduced to 15 percent.

Before 1939 military education was largely based on the experience of the Civil War and World War I, with little effort being made to teach modern strategy and tactics. This was also true for the lesser ranks, including basic training for the troops.

The new defense commissariat leadership under Marshal Timoshenko implemented drastic changes in the entire system of military training. A week after Timoshenko took over the post of the defense commissar on May 8, 1940, he issued Order No. 120, which set aggressive goals for the summer training period. He made it clear that routine training should be brought nearer to combat reality. He demanded that the "troops should be taught only the things needed in a war, the way they should be done in a war."

Intensive round-the-clock military exercises started in the spring of 1940. Troops were placed on an accelerated program of learning all about the new models of weapons and equipment. The battles against the Japanese at Lake Hasan and Khalkhin-Gol, the Soviet-Finnish war, and the unfolding world war in Western Europe provided new scenarios for these intensive exercises.

The summer of 1940 was a crucial period for training. The defense commissar informed the district commanders on July 25 that he intended to supervise the August–September division maneuvers. He demanded that the incoming exercises correspond to battlefield conditions to the maximum degree possible: "The exercises must include defensive installations and entanglements; infantry units [must] attack and break through the enemy's defenses in cooperation with the artillery and air forces."

Late in September 1940 demonstration maneuvers were held at the Kiev Military District's Yavorovsky training range by the 99th Infantry Division. The mission of the exercise was "a breakthrough of an enemy fortified line." Coordinated artillery and air support were featured in the demonstration. In cooperation with tanks and artillery the infantry successfully broke through the enemy's defenses in their full tactical depth. Timoshenko personally observed the action and assessed the skills of the 99th Division as high. Defense commissariat representatives attended similar maneuvers in other military districts. Preparation for war was definitely in high gear.

But other exercises and inspections revealed major drawbacks in unit preparedness. Although much was known by the fall of 1940 about German battlefield tactics, there was an imperfect transmission of this knowledge to the training commands. Exercises, for example, usually did not employ large tank formations on either side of the front. Nor was attention paid to fighting defensively, especially in battles of encirclement. Thus, neither the troops nor their commanders were adequately prepared for the reality of combat in the early phases of the war.

New tank parks, firing ranges, and training grounds were constructed in record time. Accelerated maneuvers and firing exercises continued right up to the start of the war. Artillery training was based on experience gained in Spain and Finland. The breakthrough of the Mannerheim Line demonstrated the importance of massed fires and shelling with specialized ammunition designed to defeat different kinds of targets, such as tanks, bunkers, and infantry. Timoshenko ordered the artillery to practice intensive saturation fires and better organize cooperation with the infantry, tank, and air forces. Night firing exercises based on grid coordinates were also ordered.

In the spring of 1941 many newly formed artillery units and antitank brigades were just starting their training. Most of them, including antiaircraft units, were directed to participate in district exercises on the eve of the war. Artillery units were, in general, well trained, but not the antiaircraft artillery. The science of tracking enemy aircraft and alerting the appropriate antiaircraft positions in time for them to respond effectively was still in its infancy in June 1941.

The air force was also engaged in intensive training. Although new aircraft models were rapidly coming into service, their integration into combat units proceeded slowly. Pilots were trained in air-to-air combat as well as in bombing troop concentrations and other ground targets. Despite the drawbacks in training, Soviet pilots were able to hold their own against the more experienced Luftwaffe. In the beginning of the war, however, ground support missions generally were not carried out successfully. In this respect the Red Air Force was well behind its opponent.

The training of the navy concentrated on better coordination with the air force, army, and coastal defenses. Beginning in the summer of 1940, training for ship crews and coastal defense units was continuous. Firing exercises by ships and coastal artillery were held as well as practice torpedo runs and mine laying. Before the war the navy had been fully brought up to a state of combat readiness to a greater extent than the other armed forces.

It is regrettable that the principles of organizing and conducting operations and the views on the character of a future war were being worked out anew, although they had been elaborated much earlier. Soviet military leaders and theorists had been trying to foresee the character of a future war, particularly its early stages, since the late 1920s. Their studies determined the composition of the armed services and the nature of combat and strategical training.

In 1931 the journal *Voina i Revolutziia* (*War and Revolution*) offered for discussion an article by R. P. Eideman, "On the Issue of the Character of the Early Stage of a War." The article read, "It is only natural that military theorists on all sides are trying to model the early stages of a future war. . . . A study of the differences between the armies of 1930 and those of 1914 will undoubtedly bring about a new understanding of the way a war will begin. Should this study and analysis be neglected, severe repercussions will not be long in coming." Later in the same article he came to a prophetical conclusion: positional defensive tactics in the early stages of modern war will be murderously foolish. Such tactics will inevitably make the defenders suffer heavy losses in their mobile air and tank forces, as they would have to be scattered along the entire defensive line, since it might not be obvious where the enemy would launch his main thrust.

The Party newspaper *Pravda* published an article by a brigade commander, S. N. Krasilnikov, on May 20, 1936, under the title "The Early Period of a Future War." In estimating the challenges of a future war and its early period in particular, he maintained that the military-technical base of modern mass armies had undergone dramatic changes compared to World War I. New offensive weapons such as bombers and tanks massed in large independent units would profoundly change the character of initial operations. In analyzing western military thought, Krasilnikov stressed that the main capitalist armies attached particular importance to strategic surprise—that is, a first strike—which offered great advantages to the attacking party: "bursting bombs and the rumble of tanks will be the only declaration of war we will see."

In the mid-1930s Soviet military science accepted the conclusion that a future war would start as a surprise attack. Thus, from the very start operations would be intensive, with the engagement of large tank and air units. Although their influence on the outcome of World War I was only minor, armor and aviation were expected to greatly influence the course of developments. The purges and the crisis in leadership caused the Soviet armed forces to lose their initial lead in armor and aviation. Due to Stalin's mistaken view of strategy, realistic plans for defense against massive deployments of enemy aviation and armor along concentrated avenues of attack were not permitted until February 1941.

The western Soviet border area was fortified to protect the front-line troops and to allow time for deployment of the main forces to launch an all-out counteroffensive as the enemy moved east into the depths of the country. The first fortified zones were constructed along the state border in 1929–35. These fortifications were a line of permanent fire emplacements deployed at a depth of 1–2 km. They were mainly equipped with machine guns. There were only a few installations capable of offering protection against artillery barrages. In 1938 more artillery was brought forward, and a refurbishment of the pillboxes was begun, but the work was never finished. In 1939 the defensive works were completely stopped. The fortifications were mothballed and many of them were buried under earth. It was only after the war in Poland started in September that measures were taken to make them combat ready. Late in 1939 the decision was made to build a fortified zone along the new state border, which resulted from the entry of the Red Army into Poland two weeks after the Wehrmacht had started the destruction of that country. Old Russian fortresses such as Ivangorod, Osovetz, and Brest were included in the system of organized defense. The mistake that Pavlov and others made when setting up the depth of deployment from the border was that they thought the enemy could be stopped relatively close in. Zhukov showed how false this sense of security was during the January war games.

The government allocated significant resources to the construction of defenses. To illustrate the scale of work under way in the spring of 1941, about 58,000 people worked daily at construction sites in the Baltic District, nearly 35,000 in the Western District, and 43,000 in the Kiev District. A great number of trucks and tractors attached to artillery units were directed to transport building materials and heavy equipment.

Although there were enough transport vehicles available, building materials and construction equipment were in rather short supply. Soviet industry was unable to produce all the necessary material, including concrete, bricks, wood, and structural steel, as well as equipment and armament for the pillboxes and other installations, including artillery emplacements. Out of 2,300 pillboxes built by the spring of 1941, fewer than 1,000 were fully equipped; the rest had only swivel-mounted machine guns. In order to improve this bad situation, the district military councils with the defense commissar's approval had some weaponry moved to the new zones from the fortifications along the pre-1939 state border. This process was stopped after Zhukov became chief of the general staff.

By order of the deputy defense commissar, Marshal B. M. Shaposhnikov, who exercised general command of defense construction, fortified positions, mainly between the strongpoints, for infantry were to be built in the Bialystok salient and other forward zones. To speed up the construction of trenches and other works, the defense commissariat ordered one battalion per regiment on a rotating basis to engage in construction. By the beginning of the war, construction was in full swing.

One of the weak points of the border areas defense was the lack of minefields, which could be laid only during a mobilization period by the order of the defense commissar. But, the border areas did employ a variety of other obstacles. In compliance with previously given orders, engineering and construction units deployed nonexplosive obstacles such as antitank ditches and traps, escarpments and counter scarps, wire entanglements, and others.

Engineer support of the navy and air force, along with that of the army, was of great significance in the overall system of defense in the western theater of operations. The Baltic district started in February 1941 to construct coastal fortifications on the islands of Saaremaa (Ösel), Hiiumaa (Dago), and Moon and also in the Vindav and Liban fortified zones along the Baltic coast. These defenses were meant to secure protection for the most important Baltic positions both from sea and land. The construction was not finished by the beginning of the war. However, the fortifications that had been built played an important role in the defense of the islands of Saaremaa and Hiuma.

Large-scale construction of a wide network of strategic airfields and concrete runways got under way in the spring of 1941. Pavlov and others wanted to bring air units closer to the new border and disperse them as widely as possible. Specialized construction units were created to build new airfields, and the civilian population was involved as well. However, it was impossible to widen the airfield network on such short notice. As a result, the existing airfields were crammed with aircraft, and their usability was limited by unfinished runways and heaps of construction materials. Some of the existing airfields had to be shut down entirely. The Kiev District air force had no emergency airfields available on the eve of the war. To make matters worse, the neglect of camouflage during the construction led to early discovery of airfield locations by the Germans. The Luftwaffe conducted regular reconnaissance flights over Soviet territory without challenge from the Red Air Force.

Much importance was attached to the construction of railways and highways as well as various warehouses and communications in the western theater of operations. The carrying capacity of the railways in the Baltic area, western Bielorussia, and western Ukraine was poor. No matter how intensive the railway construction was in 1941, it failed to achieve much, because the work required such a huge investment in men and materiel. The main railway junctions were inadequate to handle the increased traffic, and many lines were not double tracked. Since rail sidings were often too short, they were unable to accommodate long trains for passing. All this impeded troop concentration and deployment in the early stages of the war.

On the eve of the war much effort was spent building reliable communications vital for uninterrupted command and control of forces under attack. Installation of both under- and aboveground wire communications in the fortified areas was given top priority.

Despite the herculean labor on the large-scale engineering works in the western border area under way on the eve of Barbarossa, few were completed by the time the German invasion started in the early morning hours of June 22, 1941.

The Soviet general staff assumed that Nazi Germany could advance up to 170 divisions against the Soviet Union, that Germany's allies could provide about 70 divisions, and that 50 Japanese divisions in the Soviet far east were expected to attack the USSR. Soviet leadership expected the German command to deploy its main forces in East Prussia to direct the main attack against Riga, Kaunas, then Polotsk, Vilnius, and Minsk. A secondary blow was expected to come from the Brest region toward Baranovichi and Minsk. Simultaneously with the main attack from East Prussia, an advance of the Wehrmacht south of the Pripyat Marshes toward Dubno and Brodi was considered likely. On the northern part of the front, the Finnish army was expected to attack Leningrad, while on the southern part Rumanian and German troops would attack Zhmerinka. The possibility of the main attack being directed south of the Pripyat Marshes in the direction of Kiev was not ruled out by the general staff. However, the first option was looked at as the most probable. Attacking the naval installations at Vladivostok was thought to be the first strategic aim of Japan.

Estimating the intentions of the likely enemies and defining the main fronts of a future war, the defense commissar and the chief of the general staff prepared a report for Stalin in September 1940 outlining their ideas for the Soviet armed forces' basic strategic deployment in the west and the far east for 1941. The main force, about 170 divisions strong, was supposed to be deployed on the western border; 34 divisions were to be deployed in the east and 17 in the south. (In reality, by the beginning of the war with Germany, the Soviet Union kept 31 divisions in the far east, and 25 divisions at the southern borders because of troubles with Turkey and Iran.) The general staff developed and presented for the political leadership's approval two options for the Soviet armed forces' retaliation against an invasion from the west with a corresponding strategic deployment of the forces. According to the first option, the main force was to be deployed north of the Pripyat to repel aggression, defeat the enemy's East Prussian group, and carry combat operations into enemy territory. The second option called for the main force to be deployed south of the Pripyat. In case of aggression it was to break the enemy offensive, then crush him by a powerful strike in the direction of Lublin and Breslau. On reviewing these two options, Stalin demanded that the main group of forces launch the key counteroffensive against German Army Group Center and be attached to the Kiev Military District. Stalin's demand was met, and from late in 1940 the preparation for a retaliatory strike was being carried out in compliance with the second option. Some changes, prompted by developments on the western border and fresh information on the Nazi command's intentions, were introduced into the plan. However, the document, which bore the title "The Plan of the State Borders' Defense, 1941," reached the commanders and staffs of the border districts only early in May 1941.

According to the defense plan, the border areas' troops were ordered to stop any intrusion into Soviet territory; to protect through stubborn defense the mobilization, concentration, and deployment of the army, to win air supremacy through active air operations, and to use air units to attack bridges and railway junctions to disrupt hostile troop concentrations and deployment, thus creating favorable conditions for an all-out counteroffensive. The contents of the defense plan largely reflected the official view of the early stage of war and said nothing about the secret defense plan. Under the official plan the troops in the western border areas were to engage and hold the enemy long enough for the operational troops and the reserves to be brought up for the counteroffensive.

Should the enemy succeed in its advance into the depth of the rear, he was to be stopped by the obstacles and special antitank brigades being formed for the purpose. Pavlov's mechanized corps, shielded by these brigades and in conjunction with special air units, were to destroy the penetrating enemy. The western defenses were expected to hold out for fifteen days. This was the time necessary for the mobilization, concentration, and deployment of the Red Army main forces and the reserves for the hammer blow of the counteroffensive.

Pavlov's plan looked good on paper, and the high command approved it. Zhukov, however, had different plans of his own.

The Leningrad, Baltic, and Odessa Military Districts were to cooperate respectively with the Northern, Baltic, and Black Sea Fleets. The ships and the air units of the fleets had the task of stopping the enemy advancement from the sea, protecting the naval bases from capture, and not allowing any seaborne landings. The Baltic Fleet had the vital mission of barring hostile ships from the coasts of Finland and Latvia.

By the defense commissar's directive, district defense plans were to be made by May 25, but this was not done. These plans were ready only in June. Protection of the army was the core of the district defense plans. One can see what these plans were by looking at the defense plan of the Sixth Army of the Kiev District, defending Lvov.[6] This army, including the VI Rifle Corps and the IV and XV Mechanized Corps, had the mission of protecting the deployment and concentration of troops and checking any enemy intrusion into Soviet territory. The army's front extended 165 km. The Sumilovsky and Rava-Russka fortified areas were defense lines that had a large number of permanent fire emplacements and were its main pillars of support. Border defense was to be organized in the following way. Two border guard detachments, the 91st and 92d, were to establish reliable communication lines with support units from the first-echelon divisions (all in all there were eight units in the army's zone, each attached to a reinforced infantry battalion). In case of an attack the frontier guard teams were to call the support units and together with them destroy the enemy in front of their fortifications. In the meantime, the main forces of the first echelon were to take their positions together with the regular garrison troops of the fortified areas (the 21st, 36th, 44th, 140th, and 141st Machine Gun Battalions). "Defense readiness," the plan read, "was to be achieved within two hours after war is declared." Such plans were indeed fanciful and proved totally unworkable in the chaos and shock of the invasion.

According to the "Plan of the State Borders Defense, 1941," the defense of the Soviet western borders, some 4,500 km. long, was entrusted to the forces of five military districts.[7] There were 170 divisions and 2 brigades in the western border military districts. The first echelon totaled 63 divisions and 2 brigades the second echelon had 53 divisions. An additional 45 divisions were in reserve under the district commanders' control, and 11 divisions were placed under the control of the supreme command. These forces, according to the official plan, constituted the first strategic echelon of the Soviet armed forces. They were facing the challenge to rebuff the enemy's first strike and secure the mobilization, concentration, and deployment of the Red Army main forces.

The withdrawal of the troops from their regular deployment zones to the newly prepared fortified zones was to be ordered by an alert from the supreme command. Detailed marching orders were worked out to ensure a rapid fulfillment of the order. It was expected that the frontier forces would have from two to sixteen hours to take up their positions, whereas the divisions deployed 100–150 km. farther east had a few days.

In analyzing the official defense plan, the one issued by the supreme command and the one by which Pavlov and the other commanders in the border areas were preparing to live—and die—one cannot avoid the conclusion that the plan was insufficient to stop the

German advance. This was true even if the operational and strategic reserves had been committed immediately to the battle to launch a counteroffensive according to the plan, as Pavlov expected. Zhukov and Timoshenko knew this. They were struggling with turning a very bad situation into a makeshift strategy that would save the army and the country from a total disaster.

Once Stalin made the most momentous decision of his life in agreeing to the Zhukov-Timoshenko secret plan, the dictator went out of his way to buy time and prevent the war between the USSR and Germany in 1941 for as long as possible. A delay would give the mobilization, training, and equipment modernization programs more time to be brought to completion. He persistently demanded that the diplomats and the military avoid the slightest provocation for war. The fact that the western border regions were not brought up to full readiness for war despite all that was known about German intentions is still a sore spot for the Russian military. Zhukov and Timoshenko had no choice but to do what they did. It is true that they were in an extremely awkward and disadvantageous situation, but that was Stalin's fault, not theirs.

The chief of the general staff, Zhukov, issued a directive on May 13 to start a redisposition of troops from the rear districts to the Western Dvina and the Dnepr Rivers. The Twenty-first Army was to play a key role in inflicting heavy damage on the southern flank of German Army Group Center along the upper Dnepr–Sozh Rivers. It was no accident that this was where it was deployed. The unit war diary of the Twenty-first Army records that mobilization orders were received on May 13 from the headquarters of the Volga Military District. But the army did not receive orders to move until June 26, fully four days after the start of the war, when it was directed to the area around Gomel on the Sozh east of the Dnepr. The army was not ordered into action until July 13, when it hit the southern flank of German Army Group Center, retook Rogachev and Zhlobin, and threatened Bobruisk. It did not abandon its position around Gomel until August 20, five weeks later.[8]

The orders given to the Twenty-first Army remove any doubt that it was intended all along to be in the second echelon of defense and was never meant to be part of the defense of the state border. It was positioned by Zhukov and Timoshenko where it would do the most good according to the secret defense plan. In this respect it admirably fulfilled its mission. Later in this book more time will be devoted to what happened on the southern flank of Army Group Center and how the threat to the flank forced the German high command to make major changes in its entire strategy on the Eastern Front.

The districts' military councils took a series of steps to upgrade the troops' combat readiness. However, when Moscow learned about these measures they were stopped and characterized as provocations. Strict warnings were issued not to let anything of the kind happen again. For example, the military council of the Kiev District made a decision early in June to advance some troops of the rear garrisons to the border zones to help bring the field emplacements up to combat readiness. On June 10 Col. Gen. M. P. Kirponos, the Kiev District commander, was ordered to cancel this order and report back that he had done so. That same day Zhukov and Timoshenko issued orders for the districts not to move any additional forces into the western border areas unless given explicit instructions to do so. At the same time they ordered the districts to make plans to move border units into fortified areas on short notice.

Because of the mounting and obvious German threat, on June 12 the defense commissar, with Stalin's permission, ordered the military councils of the border districts to start advancing the troops closer to the state border. The commissar's directive to the military council of Kiev District read that for the purpose of upgrading the troops' combat readiness, all the rearward divisions, the corps commands, and units must be located closer to the state border in the new facilities by July 1. Note that this date ensured that these forces would never actually be close to the border when the war started. The rear divisions were told to remain in their old positions, meaning that their advance to the border could be started only by a special order of the defense commissar. No written orders to the infantry corps and divisions of the Western District to advance troops from the rear closer to the border could be found. Some unit commanders, however, did receive oral instructions from district chief of staff Maj. Gen. V. E. Klimovskikh. These troops took all their training equipment with them. The soldiers were told they were scheduled to participate in large-scale exercises.

In compliance with these seemingly tardy directives, only four divisions in all the border districts had time to take up positions in the new zones farthest to the west; the remaining thirty-eight were still on the march when the war broke out. This is how the Zhukov-Timoshenko plan was working in practice. The plan had to give the threatened border forces assurance that they would be supported. Surrender en masse of the border forces would jeopardize the forces being positioned farther east intended to stop the Germans along the Dnepr and the Sozh Rivers.

Four fronts were to be formed along the western border: the Northern, Northwestern, Western, and Southwestern Fronts. The commands of the fronts were to be based on the commands of the Leningrad, Baltic, Western, and Kiev Military Districts.

On June 19 the commanders of the Leningrad, Baltic, and Odessa Military Districts received an order from the defense commissar to coordinate anticipated operations with the Baltic and the Black Sea Fleets in compliance with their district defense plans.

On June 21, the day before Barbarossa, Timoshenko and Zhukov secured Stalin's approval to put the troops of the Western Border Districts on alert.

The coded directive was sent from Moscow at 0030 on June 22. The military districts got it in an hour, and it was sent to army headquarters later, after 0200. Many units never got the directive. Since several district and army commanders felt threatened by the numerous demands "not to provoke war," they transmitted it to their troops with the remark, "In case of German provocations do not open fire. If German aircraft fly over our territory, remain hidden, do not open fire until they start hostilities."

Thus, by the time of the German attack against the Soviet Union, these deficits still remained. The Red Army was still undergoing restructuring. Rearmament was not finished, the theaters of operations were not ready, and the troops of the border districts were not put on alert in a timely fashion. The first-echelon infantry divisions were inadequate to stop the enemy invasion, and nothing could be done to save them. The mechanized corps, tank, and motorized divisions were intended to launch powerful counterattacks against the enemy's panzer groups, but they, for reasons explained later, were not able to carry out their mission effectively. The air force also was unable to retaliate effectively.

All these facts put the Soviet Union at an extreme disadvantage at the early stage of the war and made it difficult for the Red Army to fight against a strong, experienced enemy, especially since the frontier troops and commanders had been left in the dark about what was in store for them.

Final Preparation

Knowing in advance that two panzer groups would lead the main thrust of the German offensive north of the Pripyat Marshes in closing off the Bialystok salient, Zhukov decided to allow these armored spearheads to pass around the main body of Soviet infantry relatively unimpeded. Nothing could be done anyway to stop the panzer groups along the border; they would have to be dealt with later by specially constructed antitank strongpoints and detached tank brigades in the second echelon. The combined-arms units in the salient, however, could be expected to hold their ground and fight effectively against the German infantry coming in from the west, while at the same time acting as a threat to the rearward areas and supply lines of the rapidly advancing panzer groups. Zhukov's tactics were to allow the German armor to separate itself as much as possible from the following infantry and then deal with each group, armor and infantry, separately. Later, the larger combined-arms units would begin to disintegrate under intense pressure, and smaller formations of infantry and cavalry could be expected to take to the forests and continue to operate in groups as partisans. In fact, the Germans were never able to seal off the large pockets of Soviet troops, and many formations eventually managed to escape almost intact to the east. The phenomenon of the "floating pockets" that drifted steadily toward the east and south would cause the Germans no end of trouble in 1941, and they constantly acted as a bone caught in the throat of the armored jaws, which could snap shut but could not chew or swallow. Surrounded units or groups of units were thus intended to continue to function as organic entities of the tactical echelon and play an important part in checking the German advance. The composition of forces in the Bialystok salient would, therefore, have to contain just the proper balance of tanks, artillery, and infantry if the desired result were to be achieved economically and effectively.

One of the more important questions to be considered in deciding what to do with the Bialystok salient concerned the construction of fortifications in the west, which had been continuing since the occupation of eastern Poland in September 1939. By June 22, 1941, some 2,500 fortified points had been built; however, all but a thousand of them were equipped only with machine guns. The Mobilization Plan (MP-41) approved in February called for accelerating the new construction, but this was not enough to suit some individuals who still believed that the German invasion could be checked at the border. In late February–early March, the Supreme Military Council of the Red Army met in Moscow, and G. I. Kulik, deputy commissar for armaments, B. M. Shaposhnikov, deputy commissar for fortified areas, and Politburo member A. A. Zhdanov argued for stripping the fortifications along the old pre-1939 frontier and sending the material to the recently built defense line farther west. Zhukov and defense commissar Timoshenko vigorously opposed this action, insisting that the old fortifications could still be useful. The key element of contention was the artillery, which could not be moved easily once it was put into position.

Although Zhukov did not specifically say that he was trying to keep all but the minimum amount of artillery and hauling equipment out of the Bialystok salient, it is evident that this was his intention. Stalin wavered on this question temporarily and then sided with his chief of the general staff. The question of the artillery was, therefore, partially resolved in favor of the pre-1939 fortifications. This so-called Stalin line of defense proved to be of little use after the war began, but some of the artillery, at any rate, was saved from certain destruction. As for the artillery already in the salient, much of it was pulled back a considerable distance eastward under the pretext of the need for "firing practice." In addition to artillery pieces and tractor-haulers, most of the engineers and the pontoon bridge battalions of the tank divisions were also sent rearward for "training missions." It is true that many of the big guns and artillerymen were not in frontline positions on June 22, but this had nothing to do with Stalin's failure to heed the warnings of the imminence of war. Stalin would make several mistakes during the course of 1941, but leaving masses of artillery in the Bialystok salient was not one of them.

In Appendix A of this book a document is presented, "Report on the Antiaircraft Defense of Troops Located on the Southwestern Front," found in the Timoshenko private archive, which shows the level of planning that took place during the February war game. It is clear from this document that in late February 1941 serious attention was being given to the antiaircraft defense of strategic locations deep within the country.

Also in Appendix A is a document entitled "Plan for the Strategic Deployment of the Armed Forces of the Soviet Union," dated March 11, 1941, signed by Zhukov and Timoshenko, which was a situation report to the defense commissariat. This document purports to show that the main threat from the Germans was in the south, that is, against Ukraine and Kiev, not along the Moscow axis through Bialystok, a direction of attack that could only be reassuring to Pavlov.

A curious feature of this document is the words "there is no documented information available to the general staff concerning the operational plans of probable enemies in the west and in the east." It may be inferred from this that the strategic analysis being put forward here was presented as based on hard, verbal intelligence information. In other words, the military commanders except Zhukov and Timoshenko would not have any other way of knowing the true nature of the German plans. Since German deployment in the east had not yet progressed, this strategic analysis could not be independently verified from any intelligence source that Stalin did not have under his direct control. During his interrogation after his arrest, Pavlov made reference to his belief that the main German threat was to be from the south. His impression that this was true was no doubt enhanced by the German invasion of Yugoslavia and the Balkans in March.

The following sentence in the document also had a purpose: "The deployment of the main body of the Red Army in the west, including the major forces grouped against East Prussia in the direction of Warsaw, arouses grave concern that the armed struggle on this front might entail prolonged hostilities."

This shows that publicly, at least, Zhukov was still being critical of Pavlov's strategy of positioning troops forward in the Bialystok salient for later use in an offensive. That is what Pavlov expected him to say, and he continued to say it in order not to arouse the tank general's suspicions.

The following document shows the ultimate lengths to which Zhukov and Timoshenko were prepared to go in order to keep Pavlov quiet and in place to perform his role. By May 15, 1941, it was obvious to all that the enormous German buildup and the positioning of two panzer groups, one on each of the two sides of the Bialystok salient, could have but one intent—that is, the Bialystok salient was going to be cut off, and the main German thrust was going to be carried out along the Smolensk-Moscow axis.

Due to its extreme importance and the controversy surrounding it, the document is presented here in its entirety.

To the Chairman of the Soviet of Peoples Commissars:
15 May 1941

Considerations on the plan of strategic deployment of the Armed Forces of the Soviet Union in the event of war with Germany and its allies.

I. According to the latest intelligence information from the Red Army, Germany has 230 infantry, 22 tank, 20 motorized, 8 airborne, and 4 cavalry divisions—altogether a total of 284 divisions.

On the borders of the Soviet Union as of 15 May 1941 were concentrated 86 infantry, 13 tank, 12 motorized, and 1 cavalry division—altogether 112 divisions.

The Germans plan to deploy against the USSR 137 infantry, 19 tank, 15 motorized, 4 cavalry, and 5 airborne divisions, altogether 180 divisions.

The main striking force consists of 73 infantry, 11 tank, 8 motorized, 3 cavalry, 5 airborne divisions—100 divisions altogether—which will strike on both sides of Brest.

Considering that Germany has its army mobilized and is developing its logistics and supply, it is possible they will anticipate our moves and launch an attack without warning. In order to prevent this, I consider it vital to deprive the German command of the initiative, to pre-empt [underlined in the original] the enemy and attack them in deployment and deny them the possibility of organizing a front capable of cohesive action.

The first strategic goal of the Red Army should be to destroy the main strength of the German Army, which is deployed south of Brest-Demblin, and by day +30 move to north of the line Ostrolenka-River Narev-Lovich-Lodz-Kreizburg-Opeln-Olmutz.

The next strategic goal will be to advance from the area of Katowicz to a northern or northwesterly direction and destroy the strong central and northern wings of the German front and seize control of the territory of former Poland and East Prussia.

The immediate mission is to defeat the German Army east of the River Vistula and in the direction of Krakow advance to the line River Narev–Vistula and seize control of the Katowicz region. In order to accomplish this, we must:

A) Strike a main blow by the Southwestern Front toward Krakow-Katowicz thereby isolating Germany from its southern allies;

B) Launch a supporting attack by the left wing of the Western Front towards Warsaw-Demblin with the goal of pinning down the Warsaw group (of the enemy) and capture Warsaw as well as coordinate with the Southwestern Front to destroy the enemy forces around Lublin;

C) Conduct an active defense against Finland, East Prussia, Hungary, and Rumania and be prepared to invade Rumania when conditions become favorable.

In this scenario the Red Army would begin the attack from the front of Chizhev-Liudovleno with a force of 152 divisions against 100 German. Along the other sectors of the state border an active defense would be conducted.

SIGNED:

COMMISSAR OF DEFENSE, MARSHAL OF THE SOVIET UNION

S. K. TIMOSHENKO

CHIEF OF THE GENERAL STAFF OF THE RED ARMY

GENERAL OF THE ARMY, G. ZHUKOV
RECORDED BY: MAJOR GENERAL VASILEVSKII
(CADD, 16-A/2591, vol. 239, p. 4)

This document, handwritten in its original form, was found in the Central Archive in very poor condition. A sample of the official type-written version follows.

This document is sensational in and of its own right apart from any interpretation that could be given it. After examining it, there can be no doubt that the Soviet leadership was aware of the size and nature of the German buildup. The figures that Zhukov gives about the size of the German forces and his precise positioning of them is fatal to any interpretation of the early phase of the war that maintains that Stalin and the Soviet army were caught off guard by a surprise attack. It is clear from this document that the Soviet high command had precise, detailed information of exactly what was going to happen. The emphasis Zhukov places on the necessity for a pre-emptive strike against the Germans from the direction of Bialystok is extremely hard to square with reality unless it is accepted that Zhukov's real plan was to hit the Germans deep within the interior of the Soviet Union.

It is a remarkable fact that there is no date associated with the pre-emptive strike and that they were still working with August 1, 1941, as being the most likely time for the German assault.

The outstanding feature of this document is that it is a skillful confusion of the true and the untrue. What Zhukov and Timoshenko (and now Vasilevskii, who had been brought into the inner circle) desperately wanted to do was convince Pavlov that the German buildup would not be complete before August 1 and, therefore, there would be time enough to move the mobilizing forces into position to hit the Germans before they were ready. In actuality, the mobilizing forces were being positioned along the Velikie Luki-Smolensk-Yelnia-Dnepr line and there was no intent to move them farther westward. The purpose of this document, then, was to provide a rationale to Pavlov that he could accept. It is curious to note that until the last hours before the war, Pavlov did not put his forces on alert and that he clearly expected immediate reinforcements to be brought westward as soon as the German attack started, but this was not to be.

Document CADD, 16-A/2591, vol. 239, p.4

ПРЕДСЕДАТЕЛЬ СОВЕТА НАРОДНЫХ КОМИССАРОВ от 15 мая 1941 г.

СООБРАЖЕНИЯ ПО ПЛАНУ СТРАТЕГИЧЕСКОГО РАЗВЕРТЫВАНИЯ ВООРУЖЕННЫХ СИЛ СОВЕТСКОГО СОЮЗА НА СЛУЧАЙ ВОЙНЫ С ГЕРМАНИЕЙ И ЕЕ СОЮЗНИКАМИ

I. В настоящее время Германия по данным разведывательного управления КА имеет 230 пехотных, 22 танковых, 20 моторизованных, 8 воздушно-десантных и 4 кавалерийских дивизии, Всего 284 дивизии.

На границе Советского Союза по состоянию на 15.5.41 г. сосредоточено 86 пехотных, 13 танковых, 12 моторизованных и 1 кавалерийская дивизия, всего 120.

Чтобы предотвратить это, считаю необходимым ни в коем случае не давать инициативы действий Германскому командованию, упредить противника в развертывании и атаковать германскую армию в тот момент когда она будет находится в стадии развертывания и не успеет еще организовать фронт и взаимодействие родов войск.

8

Maj.Gen.
ГЕНЕРАЛ-МАЙОР

А. ВАСИЛЕВСКИЙ   **A. Vasilevskii**

chief of the general staff
НАЧАЛЬНИК ГЕНЕРАЛЬНОГО ШТАБ

Исполнял **Confirming**   ГЕНЕРАЛ-АРМИИ
People's Commissar of Defense   **Gen. of the Army**
НАРКОМ ОБОРОНЫ
МАРШАЛ СОВЕТСКОГО СОЮЗА   Г.К. ЖУКОВ
Marshal of the U.S.S.R.   **G.K. Zhukov**
С.К. ТИМОШЕНКО
S.M. Timoshenko

Considerations on the Plan of Strategic Deployment,
May 15, 1941

It is likely that a German agent obtained Zhukov's report of May 15, 1941, advocating a first strike against Germany. The report was sent to the center of collection of information in Prague in June 1941.[9] The agent stated that, according to new information coming into his possession, the plan of the general staff of the Red Army to strike against concentrations of German troops, using tank units and the air forces, was rejected by Stalin. It could be that this information was deliberately planted in the German spy's hands to make Hitler and his General Staff more confident, in that they knew they had two to three weeks' lead time to get the jump on the enemy and therefore would be less inclined to look for the real plan of strategic defense of the Soviet Union, which had been in place since the February war game. At present this can be only conjecture. This judgment makes even more sense, however, when it is considered that throughout the war German intelligence generally failed to come up with meaningful, accurate, and timely reports, especially dealing with strategic issues. None of the pre-war mobilization directives were picked up, nor were large-scale operations such as the Moscow counteroffensive in December 1941 detected in advance.

As noted earlier, it was decided in the aftermath of the February war game to keep all but the minimal amount of artillery out of the exposed western areas, particularly the Bialystok salient. But even though the problem of the artillery was met and solved to a more or less satisfactory degree, the question of what to do with all the armor in the salient still remained. For several reasons it was impossible to shift tanks out of the Western District's forward zone. To do this would be to arouse unnecessarily the suspicions of the Germans, who would be sure to discover the redeployment by means of their continuing overflights of Soviet territory. A significant removal of tanks from the salient could also be expected to cause undue panic among the infantry units there by making the officers and men feel as if they were about to be abandoned to fend for themselves, without sufficient artillery or armor to give support in case of a German attack. The three armies in the salient—the Third, Tenth, and Fourth—had to be left with their armor intact if the soldiers there were to be expected to stand and fight, not flee or surrender en masse. According to the official standards set by the State of Military Readiness decree issued in April 1941, each Soviet combined-arms rifle division was supposed to have 16 light tanks and 13 armored vehicles. A Soviet mechanized corps nominally consisted of two tank divisions, each with 375 tanks, and one motorized infantry division with an additional 275 light tanks.

It was Pavlov, the tank expert, unaware of the true nature of the defense plan being put into effect by Zhukov and Stalin, who unwittingly provided the solution to Zhukov's problem. Pavlov, still convinced that it was Stalin's plan to stop the Germans along the border, proposed that three of the four operational mechanized corps be concentrated on the flanks of the two German panzer groups that were to operate against the salient. The plan was substantially the same one Pavlov had used against Zhukov in the January war game, and Zhukov must have known full well what its outcome would be. Nevertheless, Pavlov's proposal suited Zhukov, even though any chance for success it might have had in rolling back the German panzer groups was small.

Pavlov believed that three of his mechanized corps—the VI and the XI in the north around Grodno and the XIV near Kobrin in the south—positioned to threaten the flanks of Hermann Hoth's Panzer Group 3 debouching from Suvalki and Guderian's Panzer Group 2 advancing from the direction of Brest Litovsk, would be sufficient to halt the German drive until reinforcements could arrive from the operational echelon and the strategic reserve, if need be, to set up a stable front and drive the invaders back. Zhukov was willing to accept Pavlov's plan for his own reasons, for he had reckoned that the three mechanized corps used in this fashion would cause the Germans some trouble and retard the speed of their armored spearheads, but he had no intention of committing the operational echelon, much less the strategic reserve, to the battle for the Bialystok salient. He was prepared to expend armor so abundantly during the early stage of war because the large mechanized corps, with their many obsolete BT and T-26 tanks, were not intended to be the backbone of the Red Army's armored force. The new T-34 and KV model tanks that were being produced would outclass anything the Germans had in the field at the time, so it was decided to reserve them in order to stiffen the back of the operational echelon along the

Dnepr-Dvina line and to provide the cutting edge for the eventual counteroffensive by the strategic reserve whenever an opportune moment should arise. Western historians have chided the Russians for not immediately forming the new tanks into proper formations and bringing them to the border areas in June, but there was a method to their seeming madness.[10] In the meantime, in June, July, and August the greatest possible benefit would have to be derived from the use of the older tanks in the tactical and operational echelons to slow down the German panzer groups and harass their infantry.

The question of exactly where to deploy the operational echelon was a problem that caused some concern for Stalin and his general staff. Zhukov notes that in 1940, Soviet strategic planning was based on the assumption that the southwesterly direction, Ukraine, would be the most likely avenue for a German invasion. The 1940 plan for operations was revised under the supervision of Zhukov and Timoshenko in the spring of 1941, and they, no doubt, were well aware of what the Germans' intentions were, insofar as they had been set down in the Barbarossa Directive of December 1940. As the intelligence documents presented earlier show, highly accurate data was available about the Germans' intentions. Zhukov's May 15 call for a preemptive strike can be taken as positive proof that the general staff and the higher leadership knew exactly what the true situation was.

Taking the Barbarossa Directive itself at face value, the Soviet supreme command logically concluded that the Germans were interested in reaching Leningrad and seizing Ukraine before taking Moscow, and Stalin himself was convinced that this would be the most rational course for the Germans to follow. In the spring of 1941, during a discussion of the operational plan for that year, Stalin told Zhukov, "Nazi Germany will not be able to wage a major lengthy war without those vital resources"—that is, in Ukraine, the Donets Basin, and the Caucasus. Before the war, then, Stalin believed that Hitler would elect to turn his powerful Central Army Group southward and fight a large-scale battle for Ukraine before allowing the advance on Moscow to continue. This belief was based on his personal estimation of Hitler as a shrewd man who took no unnecessary chances, and was confirmed further by the language of the Barbarossa Directive itself.

On the basis of the information at their disposal, Stalin and Zhukov decided to make the operational echelon strong in the areas that would threaten the northern and southern flanks of Army Group Center as it pushed through White Russia north of the Pripyat. It was hoped that the operational echelon could exert enough pressure on the flanks of the Army Group, from around Gomel east of the Pripyat and from Velikie Luki north of the Dvina River, to force the Germans to halt their advance along the Dnepr-Dvina line. In this respect the battle for the Bobruisk-Mogilev-Rogachev triangle northwest of Gomel between the Berezina and Dnepr Rivers was considered to be particularly important. In any case, the Soviet supreme command was well aware that the Germans considered it necessary to allow time for an operational pause in their offensive after reaching Smolensk, a short one at least, in order to regroup their forces and remedy the supply situation.

It was Stalin's conviction that the Soviet forces on the Baltic and in Ukraine would have to bear the brunt of the German offensive from this point on and that the Red Army units in the tactical and intermediate zones escaping from the German advance in White Russia would be enough to arrest the Germans on the approaches to Moscow. It was for this reason that the decision was made to deploy the most important components of the operational echelon deep within western Ukraine, west of Kiev, and also due east of the Pripyat Marshes, where they could be expected to perform three functions:

1. To intensify the direct assaults on the southern flank of Army Group Center if it were indeed checked in its forward movement at the Dnepr-Dvina line, or even if the Germans decided to continue the advance straight on to Moscow

2. To cut off an expected turn from north to south of part of Army Group Center toward the important industrial areas of the eastern Ukraine and the oil-rich Caucasus region

3. To meet head-on a German push into Ukraine from the west if the forces in the Lvov salient proved unable to withstand the pressure from Army Group South

Much of the careful planning carried out by Zhukov in the spring of 1941 had to be undone by early June for reasons that will be explained later, yet the fact remains that the operational echelon was positioned properly in the interior of the Soviet Union in order best to confront all possible contingencies. Zhukov can be criticized, but he cannot be faulted for his lack of prescience. The German army high command's ability to act independently of Hitler's wishes later caught him by surprise, in just the same way it managed to deceive its own commander in chief.

On May 13, 1941, a general staff directive was issued that ordered the movement westward from the interior of units destined for the operational echelon. The Twenty-second Army was moved from the Urals to Velikie Luki north of the Dvina, the Twenty-first Army from the Volga District to Gomel, the Nineteenth Army from the northern Caucasus to Belaia Tserkov south of Kiev, the Sixteenth Army from the Transbaikal District to Shepetovka in the central-western Ukraine, and the XXV Rifle Corps from Kharkov District to the Dvina River. When these forces were joined with the Twentieth, Twenty-fourth, and Twenty-eighth Armies already in the four Western Districts' reserves, they would swell the size of the operational echelon to about ninety-six divisions, though not all of these would be fully deployed before June 22. In addition, eleven more divisions were held back as a reserve directly under the supreme command.

The hefty size of the operational echelon belies the assumption that the general staff was caught napping by the German attack. Quite the contrary; the careful positioning of the operational echelon on what would become the flanks of Army Group Center would cause the Wehrmacht no end of difficulty in the summer of 1941. Army Group Center would have a great deal to contend with, especially from the southerly direction, by the time it reached the Dnepr-Dvina line with its long and exposed flank. The Soviet supreme command could hope for good results from the strong forces located around Gomel, which were shielded from the west by the protective cover of the Pripyat Marshes. They also hoped that the German push from the west into Ukraine could be contained entirely by the tactical echelon there, a force that included only one fully equipped mechanized corps. Had this happened, the operational echelon in the south would have had full freedom to maneuver and face the right wing of Army Group Center if, as expected by Zhukov, Hitler attempted to push down into Ukraine from the north, east of the Pripyat. These plans would be shattered during the first days of war, but no one, no matter how farsighted, could have been any wiser in predicting the course of action the Germans would follow after June 22.

The rather primitive state of telecommunications in the USSR in 1941 will not be discussed in detail here. Most of the communication cable and landlines were operated by the Peoples' Commissariat for Communications, so to a large degree the Red Army depended on the civilian network to handle its message traffic. The post office system managed long-distance telephone and telegraph communications. There was a high-frequency net (VCh) that used landlines with a carrier frequency of 6.3 and 25.5 MHz for voice and telegraph. This system, manned by the NKVD, had the advantage of being non-interceptable aurally at transmission rates over 15 MHz without special equipment. Shortly after the war started, the management of the high-frequency net was handed over to the military, but access to it was limited to higher command structures. By and large, the Luftwaffe attacks on Soviet communication centers on June 22 threw the overland civilian system into confusion and disorder. A large part of the problem that the general staff and Stalin faced in the first few days of the war was trying to make an intelligible whole from the fragmentary reports being transmitted. As an example of how bad conditions were, on the day of the invasion only one signal was wired from F. I. Kuznetsov, the commander of the Third Army in the Bialystok salient. Such prolonged silence from the frontier areas was hardly conducive to planning either at Western Front headquarters in Minsk or in Moscow. Fortunately, the Leningrad radio net command headquarters remained intact and was invaluable in collecting reports from cut-off Red Army units.

The overall effectiveness of the Luftwaffe may be judged from damage reports given in Russian sources. Raids were carried out against sixty-six airfields in the western border areas, and by midday on June 22 fully 1,200 Soviet aircraft were destroyed, 900 on the ground. From June 22 to June 30 the Western Front alone lost 1,163 aircraft, or 74 percent of its total. By 1000 on June 22 all telephone and telegraph communications with the three air divisions based in western White Russia had been completely broken. This contributed to the general disorganization and the high loss rate. But as bad as the situation seemed at first, there was some hope for the future, as only 30 percent of the planes based in the Western Front were newer models such as MiG-3s, Il-2s, and Yak-1s. Even though many older planes were lost, the number of pilots killed was not great. Soviet records show that, although the aircraft were neatly parked on the fields at the time of the German attack, many pilots were elsewhere undergoing training. This charade was worth its high cost, in part because it deluded the Germans about Soviet preparedness. Stalin was willing to take some early losses while not ruining chances for a future rapid buildup of the air force.

The last element in the Soviet supreme command's plan for defense was the strategic reserve. Had the tactical echelon been able to cripple or seriously retard the progress of the German panzer groups, and had the German infantry been delayed for a protracted period in the battles close to the frontier, the operational echelon could have successfully fulfilled the role prescribed for the strategic reserve by launching a counteroffensive in the area of the Dnepr and Dvina Rivers that might have rolled the enemy backward. This did not happen, however, particularly because of the savage effect of the Luftwaffe raids on Pavlov's tank columns and on communications. The only maneuvers the operational echelon could undertake were those that had a purely defensive character.

The shock of the Luftwaffe assault, especially the effect on communications, was much greater than the supreme command had anticipated, and as a result, Zhukov's plans were placed in jeopardy. The true strategic reserve had been only partly mobilized prior to the outbreak of the war, and now the Red Army would have to pay the penalty for this seemingly costly blunder. These delays in mobilization have been attributed to Stalin and his fear of provoking Hitler into attacking the Soviet Union. There is, no doubt, some truth to this argument. Stalin had intended to wait another two to three years before committing the Red Army to war with Germany, but from December 1940, he had no choice left in the matter. War would come to Russia in 1941 despite all that Stalin had done to avoid facing the conflict so soon.

On June 14, Zhukov and Timoshenko appealed to Stalin to order a full mobilization of the Red Army and asked that the country's military forces be brought to a state of war readiness. Stalin's reply was stern: "That means war! Do you two understand that or not?"[11] He still had not relinquished his cherished hope that Hitler would ultimately decide to avoid a further expansion of the European conflict in 1941. One might say that to rely on such prospects, with all the evidence to the contrary, was to clutch at the slenderest of reeds. Yet Stalin must have known that his country could have been placed in a most serious predicament by a German invasion even if the reserves had been fully mobilized before June 22. The strategic reserve could not have saved the situation along the border for the Red Army anyway, and Stalin believed that the fighting power of the tactical and operational echelons, already in the final stage of deployment by June, would be enough to allow the full mobilization of the strategic reserve in time to deal the Germans a crushing blow before they penetrated into the major population centers and industrial heart of the country.

The risk that Stalin took by not mobilizing in May or June 1941 must be weighed against the disadvantages of such an early mobilization. In the first place, Soviet mobilization might have provoked Hitler into military action if his mind had not already been made up in favor of war. Second, if war came, Stalin could reasonably suppose that the Red Army's well-echeloned, in-depth defenses in the tactical and operational zones would act as an effective brake in slowing and perhaps halting the German offensive before substantial damage had been done to the country or the army. Third, the military districts in the west were already bulging with forces, and there was a lack of space to quarter newly created formations. Also, as noted earlier, there was a considerable strain on the carrying capacity of the railroads in the Western Districts after Zhukov's first call-up of 800,000 reservists in March and the movement forward to the west of four armies and one rifle corps in May–June.

The burden on the railroads was further increased by the evacuation of certain key factories and economic facilities from the west to the east before the war began. During a three-month period in 1941 some 1,360 large enterprises, mainly war factories, were evacuated from the western regions. Finally, a full mobilization of all reserves in the Soviet Union would have meant forfeiture of the important elements of deception and surprise that the supreme command believed would catch the Germans off guard. Everything possible had been done in 1941 to convince the German high command that the Red Army was unprepared for war. A larger mobilization of reserves would have been easily detected by the Germans and would have made them more cautious in their plans for aggression. The greater the chances the German high command were willing to take to win a blitzkrieg victory, the better opportunity there would be for the strategic reserve to catch the Wehrmacht unaware in a difficult situation.

Before the war the overall strength of the Soviet armed forces numbered 5,373,000 personnel. Of these, 2.9 million men making up fifty-six divisions were stationed in the border military districts; they would first suffer the shock of the German onslaught. Fully 10,000 out of the 14,200 tanks in the Western Military Districts were obsolete, and many of them required repairs. The qualitative and quantitative advantages enjoyed by the Germans in the early days of the war further increased their commander's beliefs that the Soviet Union was a "colossus with feet of clay" that would "crumble from within" after the initial defeats along the borders. The Russian plans for strategic defense, added to the well-thought-out mechanism for mobilization, redressed the setbacks by the time the Germans reached the upper Dnepr. Nevertheless, the sacrifices of the first and second echelons were both real and severe.

Soviet-German Cooperation Before the War

It is generally believed that the Soviet Union took part in World War II only after the German invasion of June 22, 1941, but this is not true.

The nonaggression pact between the USSR and Germany was signed on August 23, 1939. A secret protocol to this pact, recently made public, envisioned a partition of Eastern Europe into spheres of influence. Later on, the German minister of foreign affairs, Ribbentrop, who had signed the pact and secret protocol in collaboration with Soviet foreign minister Molotov, spoke to reporters about a conversation with Stalin in which he had declined any offer of help against the West from Russia. Germany, he said, "is strong enough to defeat Poland and the western allies."[12]

Stalin reacted to Ribbentrop's rebuff of help in the following way: "Germany's declining our offer of help is worthy of respect. A strong Germany is a necessary condition for peace in Europe; therefore, the Soviet Union is interested in a strong Germany." Stalin also stated that it was "impossible to allow the western allies to put Germany into a difficult position—this is a matter of common interest of Germany and the USSR." The Party newspaper *Pravda* called the Soviet-German treaty a "pact of peace."

At daybreak on September 1, 1939, German forces attacked Poland, unleashing the war. At first, Stalin requested the annexation of the Lublin District. According to the American historian Adam B. Ulam, Stalin's act was extremely cautious: if Great Britain and France succeeded in defeating Germany, he would say that his action was an attempt to preserve the core of Polish statehood. When it became evident that neither Britain nor France was able to give immediate help to Poland, Stalin declared his intention to fully liquidate the Polish state.[13]

Soviet foreign policy in the 1930s after Hitler's rise to power proceeded from Stalin's theory formulated in 1925, concerning the contradictions (frictions or tensions) among western countries and how they could be used. The main thesis of this conception was to manipulate the western countries into fighting each other in the interests of socialism and the Soviet Union. In November 1940, Zhdanov said at one closed meeting, "Comrade Stalin recommends that we carry out our policy against the western powers in secret and not appear as obvious enemies. The role of the bear [Russia] is to walk in the forest, and when the woodcutter wants to fell trees [a western country wants to attack a neighbor] the bear requires him to pay for it [exacts a price for remaining neutral]. Such should be our position . . ."

The common interests between Stalin and Hitler were demonstrated within hours after the German invasion of Poland. The chief of staff of the Luftwaffe, Hans Jeschonnek, sent a telegram to Moscow at 0730 on September 1. He requested that a radio station in Minsk begin transmission of continuous signals around the clock. This was done even though it was obvious that German pilots were using the signal as an aid to navigation during their bombing runs over Poland.

That was only the beginning of military cooperation between Germany and the USSR. On Sunday, September 3, 1939, two days after Germany invaded Poland, Britain declared war on Germany, contrary to Hitler's hopes and Ribbentrop's predictions. Shortly thereafter the German government reversed its pre-war policy in wanting to act in Poland alone and now pressured the USSR in every possible way to send troops into eastern Poland. Ribbentrop's argument was that only an invasion of Poland by the Red Army could fulfill commitments made by the Soviet side in the secret protocols.

Stalin searched long hours for the proper wording of an official communique that would justify an incursion of the Red Army into Poland. He wanted to put the blame of invading Poland solely on Germany. The initial formulation of the communique was as follows: "the Soviet Union brings troops into Poland in connection with the threat to the Bielorussian and Ukrainian peoples by Germany." After receiving this from Molotov, Ribbentrop became furious and protested strongly, stating that it was "incompatible with the principles of the Moscow agreement." After some haggling, another communique was agreed upon. It stated: "the Soviet Union finds it necessary to send troops into Poland due to concern for the fate of Bielorussian and Ukrainian peoples living in Poland and by the overall situation in Poland."

After the fall of Warsaw, Molotov agreed with German representatives that the initial motivation for the military intervention of the USSR in Poland was a sensitive issue for Germany, but he explained that the USSR government could see no other substantial grounds for justifying its intervention. This argument was exceptionally weak, however, in that on no prior occasion had the Soviet Union protested against the treatment of minority peoples in Poland.

On September 17 the Red Army struck at Poland from the east. It was on this day, not on June 22, 1941, that the Soviet Union became a participant in World War II.

Military cooperation between the USSR and Nazi Germany now accelerated in earnest. Aims of the partners were formulated in a joint communique published on September 19. In this document the pledge was made to respect each other's interests and not to act against each other. One day later Stalin said that he was resolutely against the preservation of Polish statehood. One of the most tragic consequences of this decision was the massacre by the NKVD of 10,000 Polish officers in the Katyn forest near Smolensk in April 1940.

On September 20, 1939, representatives of the armed forces of Germany and the Soviet Union signed an agreement in Moscow concerning joint military operations in Poland. From the Soviet side it was signed by the people's commissar of defense, Marshal Voroshilov, and chief of the general staff, Marshal Shaposhnikov.

On September 28, 1939, Ribbentrop again arrived in Moscow to join Molotov in signing a new treaty of peace and cooperation. There were also secret protocols that deepened further the Soviet-German relationship.

After this meeting, Molotov and Stalin forced the Estonian foreign minister to agree to sign a mutual assistance treaty, an act that proved to be the beginning of the annexation of the Baltic states, completed in June 1940.

In the relations between Germany and the Soviet Union during this period, tensions were never far below the surface. In order to settle additional Soviet claims for part of Lithuanian territory, large sums in gold were paid to Germany by the USSR.

The most important consequence for the Soviet Union in the various agreements with Germany was diminished security in spite of substantial territorial gains. Earlier, Poland and the Baltic states had been a cordon sanitaire buffering the USSR against surprise attack from the west because the Soviet Union had no common boundary with the most dangerous potential aggressor, Nazi Germany. Now Germany and the Soviet Union had such a boundary extending for about 5,000 km. and open for invasion along almost its entire length.

Another important consequence of the new cooperation was a profound change in the geopolitical situation of the Soviet Union. The USSR became a major supplier of strategic materials and foodstuffs to help fuel the German economy and its war machine.

The following is an example of how military cooperation between the two countries worked. Soviet and German troops were advancing on Lvov from two directions, making for a dangerous situation ripe for conflict when they met. The German high command found a way out: capture the city alone and subsequently transfer it to the Soviet side. Agreement was reached, and the German military and air attaché in Moscow, Köstring, reported the following on September 24 to the defense commissariat: "Commander of the German XIII Army Corps, General Geyer, met personally with Infantry Corps Commander Ivanov. Close cooperation between the two corps commanders and other unit commanders of the German and the Red Armies was ensured. They agreed about details in a friendly spirit." After the fall of Lvov, a joint parade of Soviet and German troops took place.

After the defeat of Poland, military cooperation between Germany and the Soviet Union continued in various forms. For example, the Luftwaffe was regularly provided with Soviet weather forecasts, which made it easier to bomb England. At Ribbentrop's request Mikoyan and Molotov found a suitable site for a German naval base on Soviet territory. It was situated 35 km. east of Murmansk and was used for repairing various German war vessels, including submarines supporting German operations in Norway. The commander of the German navy, Admiral Raeder, in a message to the Soviet naval commissar, Kuznetsov, expressed his gratitude for all the help Germany had received. At the end of September 1939 a Soviet naval attaché was assigned to Berlin for purposes of "strengthening cooperation between the two navies." Later a Soviet icebreaker piloted a German raider through the Arctic seas to the Pacific Ocean, where it eventually sank several ships carrying weapons and other materials destined for Britain.

In the middle of October, Stalin advanced new slogans for the Comintern (Communist Internationale), which revealed the course of his new policy of cooperation and possible alliance with Nazi Germany. Among the slogans was "Down with governments advocating war!" In order to make his point clear, Stalin made the following comment in a conversation with Zhdanov and Georgii Dmitrov, the general secretary of the Bulgarian Communist Party, on October 25, 1939: "We shall not oppose governments standing for peace!" In other words, the Soviet Union will not oppose the

Nazi government because it, according to Stalin's view, "comes out with peace proposals."

In its support of Germany, the USSR missed no opportunity to expand its sphere of influence and control. In order to realize these plans, the USSR began the war against Finland, suffering serious losses and, in its moral aspect, a crushing defeat. It revealed the weaknesses of the USSR and encouraged Hitler in his belief that Stalin's system was a paper tiger. Weakened by the war against Finland, the Soviet Union demonstrated its faithful loyalty to the Third Reich even more strongly. When German troops invaded Denmark, Molotov wished Germany full success. After the occupation by Germany of Denmark and Norway, the Soviet government closed the embassies of these two countries in Moscow.

On August 1, 1940, after the French capitulation, Molotov, speaking at a meeting of the Supreme Soviet of the USSR, said that Germany could not realize its military plans without Soviet support ("our government ensured quiet confidence for Germany in the East"). He also chastised the attempts of the British press to intimidate the USSR by playing up the German threat. On June 18, 1940, Molotov sent a telegram of congratulations to the German government for its "great success" in the defeat of France.

Four days before the nonaggression pact between Germany and the Soviet Union was concluded, a trade and credit agreement between the two countries was signed. This agreement was a mere prelude to the economic treaty signed on February 11, 1940. In one Soviet document this economic agreement was characterized as unprecedented in the history of world trade.[14] A special department for trade with the USSR was established in the German economic ministry. German business circles welcomed the prospect of expanded commerce with the USSR, which had been quite profitable in the past. During the ten years from 1926 to 1936 Germany sold industrial equipment to the Soviet Union valued at 4 billion marks. The USSR paid for the orders with gold, raw materials, and agricultural goods.

Envoy Karl Schnurre, who was the head of the German economic delegation in Moscow, speaking at the opening of the German Eastern Fair in Königsberg in August 1940, said that the two countries had concluded an unprecedented agreement for delivery to Germany of 600,000 bales of cotton, 1 million tons of food grains, and 1 million tons of crude oil. German industrial and financial interests were quite satisfied with the intense and broad-based Soviet-German economic ties.

Stalin's attention to the Nazi Party as the possible future rulers of Germany became apparent at the beginning of the 1930s. For Stalin, the Nazis were the party of nationalists, struggling against the unjust Versailles peace treaty and the limitations imposed by it on Germany. Stalin himself called for abolishing the Versailles system. During the 1920s, close military cooperation developed between the Red Army and the Reichswehr, including joint maneuvers and use of the armored proving ground at Kazan. This cooperation came to an end after Hitler's accession to power in early 1933.

Hitler's program as outlined in *Mein Kampf* (*My Struggle*), besides being based on the principle of inimicable hatred of Jews as the "back stabbers" of 1918 and the perpetuators of Versailles, called for the return of the German people's rightful "living space" (*Lebensraum*) in the east. Annihilation of the Versailles system and the return of territories lost by Germany after World War I, such as Alsace-Lorraine and Danzig, were only Hitler's intermediate aims as a necessary first step on the way to establishing German hegemony over all of Europe. The next step must be the liquidation of the British Empire. The final goal was the expansion of the power of the master race (*Herrenvolk*) over a vast territory stretching from the Pyrenees in the west to the Urals and the Black Sea in the east. In order to achieve this aim, it was necessary to defeat the USSR.

Being the pragmatist that he was, Stalin believed, falsely, that Hitler was ultimately rational. He underplayed the importance of Hitler's announced final goals as the expedience of politics. He refused to admit that the pact between Germany and the USSR was a skillful political and military maneuver by Hitler aimed, first, at securing Germany against a war on two fronts and, second, at using Soviet-supplied raw materials to fuel the German war machine.

By the fall of 1939 Stalin had almost completely convinced himself that the Nazis were changing their position and that German-Soviet political and economic cooperation had a long-term future.

The Nazi leaders not only tried to increase the deliveries of Soviet raw materials and foodstuffs to an even larger scale but also attempted to use Soviet sources for purchasing strategic materials, especially rubber, tungsten, and tin, in third countries and transshipping these materials, critical for German war industries, through Soviet territory. For its part, the Soviet Union was interested in receiving modern weapons and machine tools in exchange. Gromadko, the director of the Skoda works in Pilzen, one of the world's largest armaments manufacturing concerns, visited Moscow in September–October 1939 and met with people's commissars Vannikov and Tevoshyan. He offered howitzers, antiaircraft guns, naval guns, artillery, armor plates, and various industrial equipment, including tools, molds, and presses for manufacturing small arms. He also offered diesel engines and compressors for submarines and many other goods in exchange for Soviet iron and manganese ore, steel, ferro-alloys, nickel, tungsten, copper, tin, lead, ball bearings, and foodstuffs. Skoda also requested the Soviet side to allow the transit of some goods through Soviet territory to and from Far Eastern countries, particularly Manchukuo (Japanese-occupied Manchuria).

During the seventeen months after the signing of the Soviet-German nonaggression pact, Germany received from the Soviet Union 865,000 tons of crude oil, 140,000 tons of manganese ore, 14,000 tons of copper, 3,000 tons of nickel, 101,000 tons of raw cotton, more than 1 million tons of lumber, almost 1.5 million tons of grains, and 11,000 tons of flax, phosphates, and platinum.

Soviet-German military relations also resumed their former level. For instance, Soviet specialists visited the Messerschmitt, Junkers, and Heinkel German aircraft factories. Among the Soviet visitors were Soviet aircraft designer A. S. Yakovlev; a director of a Soviet aircraft factory, P. V. Dementiev; and the first deputy of the People's Commissariat of Aircraft Industry, V. P. Balandin. Soviet guests were shown everything, including factory floors, design offices, and the newest aircraft on the ground and in flight demonstrations. Soviet test pilots were allowed to fly aboard German aircraft. Additionally, the Soviets were allowed to buy some of the newest Luftwaffe combat aircraft, including the fighters Me-109, Me-110, and He-100, as well as the Ju-88, and Do-217 bombers. Soviet engineers and aircraft designers thoroughly examined these planes and made appropriate changes to their next generation of aircraft.

German specialists also studied the Soviet aircraft industry and, according to the commissar of the People's Commissariat of Aircraft Industry, A. I. Shahurin, they were impressed by its level of output and quality, much higher than they had anticipated. But Soviet specialists drew an unpleasant conclusion; Germany's aircraft industry was much broader and stronger than theirs. As a result of these contacts and observations, the Soviet government set out to modernize equipment and build new aircraft factories on a large scale.

In October 1940 Ribbentrop invited Molotov to make a return visit to Berlin. During these negotiations the Soviet side received a proposal to join the Triple Alliance of Germany, Italy, and Japan, which would become a quad-partite pact. Two weeks later the Soviet government sent a positive reply to Berlin. The USSR, however, expressed some wishes of its own. The Soviet leaders suggested that the sphere of interest of the USSR should include Eastern Turkey, Iran, and Iraq. The USSR must establish a naval base in the straits, meaning that Turkey should join "the pact of four"—it would be a condition of the continued territorial integrity of this country. Otherwise, Germany, Italy, and the USSR must take corresponding diplomatic and military measures to ensure their own interests.

The USSR also insisted on withdrawal of German troops from Finland, but the USSR was obliged to respect Germany's economic interests there. Bulgaria should become a part of the Soviet security zone, and Bulgaria must conclude a mutual assistance pact. Japan should cease demands for oil and coal concessions in the northern Sakhalin islands.

Such was the program of the USSR in the fall of 1940. It should be remembered that in July of that same year Hitler had commissioned his military commanders to begin planning an invasion of the Soviet Union, tentatively scheduled for the second quarter of 1941. It would be hard to decide on the basis of the facts that are now known which side was the more cynical, especially since Stalin had many details of what the Germans' real intentions were.

On Molotov's return from Berlin, the Soviet government decided to increase shipments of goods to Germany, up to 1.6 billion marks' worth, through May 11, 1942. On January 10, 1941, an additional economic agreement was signed with Germany for the period through August 1942. The importance of Soviet shipments to Germany may be measured by the fact that Hitler for a time even ordered the slowing down of some Wehrmacht orders while industrial production was diverted to satisfy Soviet requirements.

After the end of the war with Finland, a critical analysis of the efficiency of the Red Army began in the Soviet Union. Nevertheless, the fundamental basis of Soviet military doctrine—that the main form of combat would be offensive operations by the Red Army into enemy territory—remained unchanged.

The facts presented here show that Stalin hoped to delay the beginning of war with Germany by political maneuvering. But, despite his desperate acts, he knew by the spring of 1941 that war was inevitable. The evidence could not be disputed, and it was increasing daily.

Examining the character of military actions from the beginning of the war, it would be remiss not to mention the widely held opinion among the Soviet leadership that the oncoming war should be used for territorial expansion. Evidence of this is contained in some of A. A. Zhdanov's speeches as well as those of M. I. Kalinin. Zhdanov was the head of the Leningrad Party organization, a member of the elite Politburo, and one of Stalin's trusted henchmen. His mysterious death in 1948 led to a minipurge justified by Stalin as a "doctor's plot." Kalinin was one of the few old Bolsheviks who survived the Great Purge and managed to prosper. He was, in title at least, the head of the Soviet state through his position as chairman of the Supreme Soviet. Despite the rather inflated posturing of his underlings, Stalin could not rid himself of the fear that the very system of terror he had unleashed during the purges might rebound to his disadvantage when war started. An oppressed and fearful people did not make for dedicated fighters in defense of a system they regarded with hatred, especially as territory passed over to the control of occupiers. He could not predict in advance that Hitler and the misguided Nazi ideologists would make his work so easy for him. The brutal nature of the German invasion and the treatment of POWs and the civilian population were all that Stalin could have asked for to ensure his own power and rally the people to defend Mother Russia selflessly with their lives, as they had done in ages past against invaders from east and west.

The danger of war on two fronts in the event of war with Germany also pressed heavily on Stalin's mind. This concern led him to conclude a neutrality pact with Japan on April 13, 1941. The Japanese, of course, had designs of their own and wanted to protect their backs while they undertook the attack at Pearl Harbor in December. On December 5, 1941, Stalin became chairman of the Soviet of People's Commissars and took direct responsibility as head of state. On the same day at a meeting of officers graduated from military academies, he talked about the necessity of readiness for offensive war.

On May 10, 1941, Hitler's deputy, Rudolf Hess, made his spectacular flight to England. Stalin was sure at that time and later said that Hess was sent on his mission by the Nazi leaders in order to secure Britain as an ally in the coming war against the Soviet Union. It seemed to Stalin that his worst nightmare might come true. This was the reason why he authorized even greater materials' shipments to Germany—anything to buy more precious time.

There can be no doubt that Stalin was going to enter the war in Europe at an appropriate time, but, in his conception, 1941 was too soon. Realizing that the major programs of armament production and completion of reorganization of the armed forces were planned for 1942, Stalin tried to delay the beginning of war, but this was not to be.

Deliveries of armaments and other German goods to the Soviet Union began to stretch out further and further in their delays. In the archives of the People's Commissariat of External Trade, there are long lists of German firms late in their shipments to the USSR. This uncharacteristic lateness of German firms was in sharp contrast to the punctual fulfillment of German orders by the Soviet side. It can truly be said that the cynicism of both sides reached to the skies.

It seems that Stalin at that time still harbored the faint hope that Hitler, as a rational human being, would think that he had more to gain from cooperation with the USSR than invasion. Otherwise, it is difficult to understand his words after the war: "Together with the Germans we would have been unbeatable!"

Soviet Intelligence on the Eve of the War

A master spy in Tokyo, Richard Sorge, was one of the first to report Germany's intentions and preparations to invade the Soviet Union. His information was first reported on November 18, 1940. The chief of the general staff intelligence department, Lt. Gen. F. I. Golikov, reported several times to Stalin about the concentration of the Nazi troops close to the borders. On March 20, 1941, he reported that about seventy German divisions were in the vicinity of the borders in a report titled "The Likely Variants of Combat Actions against the USSR."

The document spelled out three possible ways that Nazi troops might attack the Soviet Union. Interestingly, it consistently reflected the German command's Barbarossa plan. The report read in part:

> The following actions intended against the USSR are noteworthy . . .
>
> Option 3 according to information received by us in February 1941 is as follows: Three army groups are being formed to attack the USSR: the first group under the command of Field Marshal Bock will strike toward Leningrad; the second group, under the command of Field Marshal Rundstedt—toward Moscow and the third, under the command of Field Marshal Leeb—toward Kiev. The attacks will start approximately May 20.

Except for the rearrangement of the commanders' names, which is of little importance, this document spelled out the essence of the Barbarossa plan. The report further on read, "According to the information of our military attaché dated March 14, there are widespread rumors in Rumania that Germany has changed its strategic plan of the war . . . A German major said, 'We are changing our plans altogether. We are heading East, against the USSR. We'll capture the Soviet grain, coal, oil. We'll turn invincible then and will be able to continue the war against Great Britain and the United States. . . .' The Rumanian army general staff together with the Germans is engaged in working out a plan of war against the USSR . . ." And finally, Sorge's document cited the Japanese military attaché in

Berlin, indicating that "combat actions against the USSR would most probably start between May 15 and June 15, 1941."

However, the conclusions drawn by General Golikov at the end of this document are not consistent with the magnitude of the threat. This is what he wrote:

1. On the basis of the above mentioned statements and the outlined variants of possible actions in spring this year, I believe that Hitler's first priority is to defeat Great Britain and sign a peace treaty with the western allies. Only after that will it be the most likely time to start a war against the USSR.

2. The rumors and documents speaking of an imminent start of war against the USSR in the spring of this year should be regarded as disinformation coming from the British or, maybe, even German intelligence.

In 1965 Golikov explained these conclusions by the fact that Stalin's personality cult forced him to conform his own views with those of Stalin and "not to provoke a war with the Germans."[15]

During the spring of 1941 Richard Sorge kept informing Moscow of Nazi Germany's preparations to attack the USSR. On May 2, he quoted the German ambassador in Japan, Herr Ott, as saying, "1. Hitler is quite resolved to start a war and invade the USSR, to use the European part of the Soviet Union as its source of raw materials and grain. 2. The critical timing of the beginning of the war depends upon (a) a complete defeat of Yugoslavia; (b) the end of the planting season in Ukraine; (c) the end of the German-Turkish talks. 3. The decision as to the beginning of the war will be finally made by Hitler in May."

Other reliable sources reported the same intelligence.

Admiral N. G. Kuznetsov, the commissar of the navy, reported to Stalin, V. M. Molotov, and A. A. Zhdanov on May 6: "The naval attaché in Berlin, Captain 1st-Class Vorontsov, informs us that a German officer from Hitler's general headquarters said the Germans were planning to attack the Soviet Union by May 14 through Finland, the Baltic region, and Rumania. At the same time heavy air raids against Moscow and Leningrad and airborne landings in the border areas will be carried out . . ."

These facts were as important as those given in Golikov's report. Yet Admiral Kuznetsov as late as May 6 kept supporting Stalin's official point of view. He concluded his report with the comment that "this information is misleading and was deliberately channeled our way to be sure it will reach our government to see its reaction." Sorge informed Moscow on May 19 that nine armies with 150 divisions would be advanced against the USSR. In support of this information the chief of the general staff intelligence department reported to Stalin on June 1 that the German command had concentrated 122 divisions on the western Soviet border and that Finland and Rumania had advanced 16 divisions each to their borders with the USSR.

Admiral Kuznetsov presented a new document to Stalin on June 11. This time there were no conclusions. Here is its full text.

I am reporting a dispatch from our agent in Bucharest: 1. It is known from the official sources that there has been an order in the Rumanian Army and air force to be ready for offensive operations by June 15. Judging by the situation in Bucharest an intensive preparation for combat actions is under way. However, the Rumanians will not be ready by the timetable. As far as the Germans go, it is hard to make any conclusions. 2. Even the Rumanian military is unwilling to fight against the Soviet Union; the people are against any war. 3. The march of the Rumanian-German troops, particularly artillery units, to the north of Rumania continues.

A week before the war, the exact day of Nazi Germany's aggression against the USSR was known. "The war will begin June 22," informed Sorge on June 15. The next day General Golikov excitedly reported to Stalin the same timing for the beginning of Barbarossa that he had learned from still other sources.

These are only a few of the reports informing Stalin of Hitler's preparation for aggression against the Soviet Union. There were dozens of reports of crossings into the Soviet territory by German reconnaissance aircraft, even of forced landings at Soviet airfields, of frequent violations of the Soviet borders by special forces, and much more. All that Stalin could do was continue to buy time and hope that Zhukov and Timoshenko would be able to pull him out of the mess he had made.

On June 14, 1941, the Soviet press published a TASS news agency statement. It read that the rumors being spread by the foreign, particularly the British, press about "an imminent war between Germany and the Soviet Union were quite groundless." With the rumors becoming more and more persistent, Stalin ordered TASS to make the statement that "the rumors were nothing but a clumsy propaganda frame-up by forces hostile both to the USSR and Germany, the forces interested in further escalation of the war . . . The movement of German troops released from the Balkans towards the eastern and northeastern parts of German-held territory was most likely prompted by other motives having nothing to do with Soviet-German relations . . ."

We have shown that the Soviet military-political leadership had at its disposal voluminous and concrete information about the coming Nazi aggression. Until recently Soviet as well as western publications have maintained that the aggression started with a surprise attack, and the Red Army, taken unawares, suffered great losses, especially in the early stages of the war. This explanation has been offered to account for the failures. Archive documents testify, however, that Soviet military intelligence on the eve of the war sent adequate warnings to the Soviet defense commissariat, the foreign affairs commissariat, the NKVD, and other government bodies. These in turn were reported to Stalin and the Politburo members. Since these archives have not been opened yet to public viewers, the authors of this book have an agreement with the *Voenno-istorichesky Zhurnal* (*Military-Historical Journal*) to publish the documents without any references except to the *Voenno-istorichesky Zhurnal* (No. 2, 1992, pp. 36–41). Refer to Appendix A.

TELEGRAPH REPORT
Sent from Berlin 1252, December 29, 1940. Received by Department 9, 1900 December 29, 1940. To the Chief of the In-

telligence Department of the general staff of the Red Army, Berlin, December 29, 1940

From the source . . . informed from knowledgeable military circles, I learned that Hitler had given an order to prepare for a war with the USSR. The war will be declared March, 1941.

The task to check and clarify the information has been given.

Military Attaché

TOP SECRET

A Report from Berlin (March 1941) (from the "Corsican") [According to Pavel Sudoplatov, the agent identified as "the Corsican" was Arvid Harnack] A German aviation ministry employee, when talking to our source, informed:

The German aviation general headquarters is engaged in intensive work in case of military action against the USSR.

Plans of bombing raids of the Soviet most important targets are being designed.

It is believed bombing by the Luftwaffe will start with important bridges to cut off any reserves. A plan for bombing Leningrad, Viborg, Kiev (and Yassy) has been worked out. The aviation staff continues to receive photographs of Soviet cities, Kiev in particular, as well as other targets. The staff has at its disposal the information that the German aviation attaché in Moscow is very interested in the location of Soviet electric power stations. He himself drives around where they are located.

Reports and coded cables from German military attachés, which used to go through the Foreign Ministry, are now directly sent to the headquarters.

The aviation headquarters officers presume that a military attack against the Soviet Union is likely to start either later in April or in early May. The Germans intend to save the crops for themselves, assuming that the retreating Soviet troops would be unable to set the grain on fire, as it will be still green.

Presented to: Stalin, Molotov, Voroshilov, Beria.

Correct: the Chief of Department 1 of the USSR SSPC2 Fitin

TELEGRAPH REPORT

Sent from Tokyo 1140, June 1, 1941. Received by Department 9 at 1745, June 1, 1941. By telegraph to the Chief of the Intelligence Department of the Red Army general staff, Tokyo, May 30, 1941

Berlin has informed Ott that the German attack against the USSR will start in the second half of June. Ott is 95 percent sure the war will start. I see the following indirect proofs to it:

The technical department of the German air force in my city has been instructed to return. Ott has ordered the military attaché not to send any important information through the USSR. The transportation of rubber via the USSR has been reduced to minimum.

The reasons for a German aggression are: the might of the Red Army does not allow the Germans to broaden their war in Africa as they have to keep a strong army in East Europe. To eliminate any threat coming from the USSR, the Red Army must be driven off as soon as possible. This is what Ott has said.

Sorge

Secret Copy 1, INTELLIGENCE SUMMARY No. 16: The situation by June 5, 1941

According to intelligence and other sources, the group of the German troops deployed in the zone against the western Special Military District has increased by two–three infantry divisions since May 25 and by June 5 it amounts to 29–30 infantry divisions, two–four motorized divisions, a tank division, one tank brigade, and seven tank regiments, one cavalry division and two cavalry brigades, three–four antiaircraft artillery regiments, two–three heavy artillery regiments, three aircraft regiments, up to four combat engineer regiments, and presumably two armored "SS" divisions.

More troops, mainly artillery, tanks, and vehicles, were moved from the West to our borders in the second half of May.

According to the information obtained from a deserter, a soldier from a cavalry squadron of the 478th division stationed in

Vlotzlavek, the movement of German troops to our borders is going on.

Infantry, artillery, and tanks are moving nightly from Warsaw along the highway to Vishkov, Ostrov, and Brock.

Radio intelligence traced more than 200 aircraft at the Warsaw airdrome over the period of May 9–May 14.

At the Kalish, Lodz, and Warsaw routes, 86 arrivals of aircraft have been ascertained. A big air formation is being deployed in Warsaw. In the Königsberg area there are 118 aircraft, some of them are STUKAs.

The movement of civil population in the border area has been reduced to a minimum. The entire border zone has been fortified by artillery and machine gun positions, with the telephone communication among the batteries, command, and observation posts well organized.

The urban and rural population has been formally warned that the panic-stricken will be shot on the spot during the war.

All civil medical institutions in large and small residential areas have been taken over as military hospitals all over the general governorship. The hospitals have been provided with the appropriate number of hospital beds and German medical staff (Warsaw). In Warsaw, Malkinya, Ostrolenka, there are several thousand German railway workers, who have come from France, Belgium, and Germany. They are expected to work in various towns and railway stations when the German troops cross into the Soviet territory.

For the Intelligence Department Chief of the western Separate Military Districts Headquarters Lieutenant-Colonel Mashkov, Chief of Unit 3 of the Intelligence Department

The sheer quantity of these kinds of intelligence reports, plus their similar story, led to a comprehensive picture of what the Germans were preparing to do and when they were prepared to do it.

The traditional image of Stalin—passively sitting in his office in the Kremlin quietly smoking his pipe and reading piles of intelligence reports while steadfastly denying his military commanders the slightest latitude in taking measures to defend the nation—should be abandoned forever. The historians' idea of Zhukov and Timoshenko—hoping against hope that the frontier forces would be strong enough to hold back the German onslaught while doing nothing to prepare the rear echelons for an in-depth defense—should be dismissed as ludicrous. Looking at the overall picture, it is suprising that these ideas have persisted as long as they have.

Was the Soviet Union Ready for War?
When all factors are considered, it must be concluded that the decision not to mobilize the strategic reserve completely before June 22 was the correct one. The war mobilization plan worked out in March and April 1941 by the general staff was thorough and provided for a rapid increase in the size of the army immediately after the start of hostilities. For various reasons, however, the strategic reserve would not be used properly, and much of it had to be thrown into battle in an uncoordinated fashion. In all, between June 22 and December 1, 1941, the Soviet supreme command was able to send 194 newly created divisions and 94 newly created brigades to the various fronts. In addition, 97 other divisions, including 27 divisions from the Far East, central Asia, and the Transcaucasus, were sent to the western regions from the interior of the Soviet Union. The well-prepared Soviet plan for mobilization enabled the country's military forces to increase in size from 5 million men in June 1941 to 10.9 million in 1942, despite the large number of casualties sustained in the summer and fall of 1941. The German high command never dreamed that such feats would be possible. Had the German advance been held at the Dnepr and Dvina Rivers, and had the Russians been able to concentrate their strategic reserves properly on the flanks of Army Group Center, in all probability the war would have been over for Germany as far as any offensive efforts were concerned. The worsening weather—first rain, then ice—in October and November could have been the curtain raiser for the counteroffensive by the strategic reserve against the exposed flanks of the Central Army Group. This counteroffensive, as fate would have it, came neither in October nor in November, nor did it come in the area of the Dnepr

and Dvina Rivers. Rather, it came in early December at the very gates of Moscow. By early July 1941, Stalin and Zhukov were forced to make several important changes in the original strategic concept for defense, but the essence of the concept, the idea that Army Group Center must be assailed by attacks on its prolonged flanks as it pushed deeper inside Soviet territory, remained unchanged.

Viewed from any standpoint, the USSR was as well prepared for war in June 1941 as it possibly could have been, considering the late start the general staff under Zhukov's direction had in implementing the strategic defense plan. The tactical echelon on the frontier, some sixty-three divisions in all, although not well equipped with artillery and modern tanks, was theoretically strong enough to cause the Germans some trouble. The operational echelon was also well positioned to fulfill its mission of weakening the main body of the German offensive north of the Pripyat Marshes, mainly by flank attacks, and of arresting the eastward progress of the Wehrmacht at Smolensk in the central area. The operational echelon would also serve to prevent the southern wing of Army Group Center from pushing down into Ukraine east of the Pripyat.

The capstone of Soviet defense planning was the strategic reserve, which by some force of logic ought to have been made ready before the war. For reasons put forward earlier in the chapter, however, Stalin delayed full mobilization until after Hitler made the first move. This decision nearly lost the war for Russia in the early stages, but later in the summer it paid big dividends as fresh forces were continuously being sent to, or directly behind, the battlefronts. Even as early as July 10, the Soviet supreme command could count on reserves of thirty-one divisions. S. I. Bogdanov's Reserve Front alone in mid-July included parts of six armies. The Twenty-first Army's counterattacks against the southern flank of Army Group Center were undertaken on July 13 with a force of twenty divisions, well supported with artillery and armor, the effects of which will be described in detail later in this book. The deception of the German high command was greatly enhanced by Russia's delayed mobilization, and it led Col. Gen. Franz Halder's General Staff to draw many erroneous conclusions about the strength of the Red Army, conclusions that cost the Wehrmacht entire divisions and mountains of material in December at the gates of Moscow. As it was with the fateful turn of Moltke's right wing in 1914, so it was with the collapse of Operation Typhoon. After the curtain rose on Zhukov's Moscow counteroffensive, Germany had no hope of winning the war despite whatever might happen in four more years of desperate struggle.

· 3 ·
THE BATTLE BEGINS:
THE RACE TO THE DNEPR

In the modern era of real-time satellite imagery, AWACS aircraft, the J-STARS command and control system, stealth aircraft, laser-guided weapons, and many other high-tech innovations featured in the Gulf War in 1991, it is easy to forget how blind armies were fifty years ago. Although aerial photoreconnaissance was a sophisticated art in 1941 compared to technology available in earlier wars, today it would be regarded as woefully inadequate for reconnaissance and battlefield command and control. Contact with the enemy on the ground was the only sure method for knowing exactly where he was and at what strength.

Time and again German war diaries express amazement about how much better armed and disciplined the Russian troops were the farther east the battlefronts progressed. This was regarded as an ill omen by many officers who feared that the worst had indeed come true, namely, that Russian reserves in the east were overwhelmingly larger and better equipped than anyone knew and that they were positioned appropriately to inflict heavy damage on the German forces as they advanced into the depths of the country. This impression became pronounced even in the first days of the war as the Bialystok salient succumbed to the German assault.

The Bialystok Salient
When the big guns opened fire in the early dawn hours of June 22 and the first German units crossed into Soviet territory, reports began to flow into army headquarters that did not conform to the preconceived opinions about the enemy's defense plans. Not only was Russian resistance along the border in most cases surprisingly light,

but Soviet artillery activity was scarcely visible. These factors, coupled with the inability of the Luftwaffe to detect any major Russian movement on the roads leading out of the Bialystok salient during the first few days of the war, led some German commanders, particularly those of the larger formations, to wonder if the Russians were hiding out in forests around Bialystok or were much weaker in strength than German intelligence had estimated. Another possibility also existed, one that some generals feared had come true: "Were their masses lying farther east, and did we have a false idea about their deployment?"

The reports about the absence of a Russian retreat from the Bialystok salient were rationalized by Franz Halder as being due to the "clumsiness" of the Russian command, which he considered to be incapable of taking countermeasures on an operational level. He thought that the Russians would have to defend themselves in their current positions, being unable to react properly, because "the Red Army lacked the ability to discern the broad sweep of the Wehrmacht's movements." The absence of any Russian move to retreat from the Bialystok salient also made a strong impression on Guderian, who noted in his Panzer Group 2's War Diary, "It is possible that the Russian High Command knew about the coming attack but did not pass the information down to the forces actually doing the fighting." The fact, however, that the number of Russian prisoners brought in during the first day's action was considerably smaller than had been anticipated, along with the noticeable lack of artillery in the Soviet units, did cause Halder some concern. These unpleasant developments forced the chief of the General Staff to conclude that large portions of the Russian forces were located farther east than had at first been thought, but he believed that the bulk of these forces were no more distant than Minsk and that after Panzer Groups 2 and 3 linked up around that city, the breadth of the gap in the Russian front, plus their heavy losses in the Bialystok pocket, would allow Army Group Center to achieve full freedom of action.

The feeling of uneasiness in the German army high command (OKH) about what the Russians were preparing to do to defend themselves was increased by information sent back to headquarters from Army Groups North and South during the second day of the war. In the Army Group North area along the Baltic it became obvious that the Red Army was making no attempt to defend Lithuania and, in fact, had already begun a withdrawal to behind the Dvina line well in advance of the German attack. Despite this sign that the Soviet command had forewarning about Barbarossa and was implementing a sophisticated and broad-scale plan for defense, Halder refused to believe that the "inefficient and sluggish nature of their command structure" allowed for any kind of planning at all.

Meanwhile, although the northern and central army groups appeared to be making fast enough progress, the situation for Army Group South was developing quite differently. There, in Ukraine, the Wehrmacht had bitten granite because the Red Army was better equipped with the latest-model weapons, including T-34 tanks and MiG-3 aircraft, which the Germans had scarcely encountered on the other fronts and had not expected to encounter at all. In a review of the situation on June 24, Hitler told Jodl, the armed forces chief of operations, that the strong Soviet resistance in Ukraine was confirmation of his belief that Stalin had intended to invade Rumania and the Balkans sooner or later and showed further that Moscow had assigned the protection of Ukraine the highest priority. Hitler and Jodl were still convinced that it had been Stalin's intention for some time to start a war with Germany on his own initiative, and they were not able to see how the powerful presence of the Red Army in Ukraine contributed to the overall strategy for the defense of the Soviet Union. Nevertheless, they were on the right track in determining where the strength of the Red Army actually was.

While Hitler, OKH, and the armed forces high command (OKW) were busily trying to discover where the Russians were, Army Group Center was hard at work trying to erect a solid wall around the Bialystok-Minsk pocket. The first day of fighting went exceptionally well for Hoth's Panzer Group 3. The Nieman River had four crossing points in Panzer Group 3's operational area, the most important of which were three bridges located between 45 and 70 km. from the demarcation line, and all of them were taken undestroyed. In the case of the bridges at Olita, the Russian 126th Rifle Division and the 5th Tank Division tried desperately to defend the Nieman crossings, but the Luftwaffe proved to be effective in keeping the tank division off balance. The bridges could have been demolished in plenty of time, and Maj. N. P. Belov of the Fourth Pontoon-Bridge Regiment of the Eleventh Army had been ordered to accomplish this task as early as 200 on June 23, but this order was not obeyed immediately because adequate studies of the bridge's concrete structure had not been made in advance. Later, as the German tanks drew closer, the commander of the units on the west bank refused to let the engineers do their job, which has led at least one Soviet historian to imply that it was an act of treason that opened the way across the Nieman to the Germans. The swift crossing of this potentially trouble some river barrier ensured Hoth's rapid progress toward the Molodechno–Lake Naroch line, and from there an approach could be made on Minsk from the northwest. The failure of the Russian command to hold the Nieman line also led to the rapid fall of Vilnius, which was taken by the XXXIX Panzer Corps in the early-morning hours of June 24.

The way seemed to be opened also to Vitebsk and the "land bridge" between the Dvina and the Dnepr Rivers to the north, a goal that appeared to Hoth, and von Bock, the commander of Army Group Center, to be particularly worthwhile because this area pre-sented itself as the natural pathway to Moscow from the west. In or-der to further the purpose of securing the Vitebsk-Orsha region, an enterprise that would have left only two motorized divisions available to prevent the Russians from breaking out of the Minsk pocket to-ward the north, Hoth ordered the LVII and XXXIX Panzer Corps to stand by to take Molodechno and push toward Glubokoe north of Lake Naroch.

On June 24, however, Army Group Center informed Hoth that the decision had been made by Brauchitsch to turn his panzer group from Vilnius to the south and east, toward Minsk, not to the north and east as he and von Bock had wished. Panzer Group 3 was now directed to seize the heights north of Minsk and cooperate with Panzer Group 2 in sealing off the Minsk pocket. This order dismayed Hoth, who viewed the Bialystok-Minsk pocket as relatively unimpor-tant compared to the urgent necessity of securing the "land bridge" between the Dvina and Dnepr Rivers before the Russians could group enough forces together along these two rivers to construct a

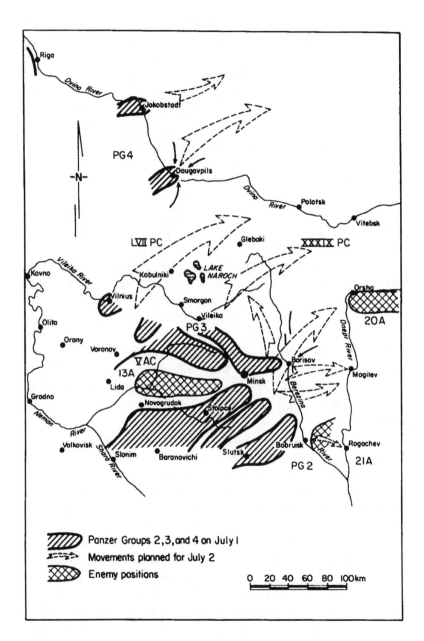

Panzer Groups 2 and 3 in Early July

proper defense. Hoth had made an agreement with von Bock before the invasion about the Vitebsk-Orsha approach to Moscow as the first priority of his Panzer Group 3, and now the entire strategy appeared to be jeopardized by what Hoth believed to be an unconscionable delay. Hoth went so far as to dispatch Lieutenant Colonel von Hünersdorff, who was the OKH liaison officer attached to Panzer Group 3, back to East Prussia to plead directly with Halder to try to get this decision changed, but it was to no avail. The OKH remained steadfast in implementing what Hoth acidly referred to as a "safe but time-wasting tactic." Hoth, like Guderian, in the first few days of the war had already begun to lose faith in OKH.

Actually, Halder's attitude with respect to the Vitebsk-Orsha approach to Moscow was not fundamentally different from that of the panzer generals or von Bock. Nevertheless, Halder saw the need for exercising some restraint in the handling of the vast encirclement now taking place. The biggest problem lay in the area of the Ninth Army after its XX Army Corps was hard hit by Russian tanks on the eastern side of the Lososna River at Kuznica and Sidra. By the evening of June 24, the XX Army Corps was being subjected to attacks from three sides by up to a hundred tanks, including some of the newer, heavier T-34s. The German infantry was hard pressed to repulse the massed Russian armor with no tanks of their own and only a few of the highly prized *Sturmgeschütz* self-propelled artillery vehicles.

To their horror, German infantry commanders discovered that the 3.7cm antitank guns (PAK) used by the Panzerjäger tank destroyer regiments were virtually useless against the latest types of Russian tanks. The XX Army Corps now began to appeal frantically for more antitank weapons and for more armor-piercing ammunition, some of which was flown in by the Luftwaffe. It was von Richthofen's VIII Air Corps that saved the right wing of the Ninth Army from serious damage on June 24 and 25 by responding quickly to the XX Corps' pleas for help. The Ju-87 Stukas, in some cases equipped with phosphorus bombs, proved to be particularly effective in disrupting the large Soviet tank columns in the Lunna-Indura-Sokolka area and also in the area south of Grodno. The problems confronting the Ninth Army were caused by the counterattack by two mechanized corps planned by the commander of the Western Front, D. G. Pavlov, against what he believed would be the southern flank of Panzer Group 3 advancing from the direction of Suvalki toward Minsk. Hoth, however, had crossed the Nieman much sooner than Pavlov could have anticipated for the reasons outlined already, so the bulk of the Russian tanks ploughed into the right flank of the Ninth Army, merely brushing Hoth's southern flank.

The First Days: The Russian Response

In keeping with the fiction that the supreme command really was trying to stop the Germans from overwhelming the Western Front's positions in the Bialystok salient, at 2200 on June 22 Timoshenko issued the following order: "After stopping the enemy advance, the Armies of the Western Front should launch a mighty counterattack with the forces of no less than two Mechanized Corps and the Front's aviation to the flank and rear of Suvalki enemy grouping, destroy it in coordination with the Northwestern Front and by night of June 24 retake the Suvalki area. . . ." There can be no doubt what Timoshenko must have thought about the chances of success of this maneuver, yet a script had been written and parts had to be played. The tragedy was that no one dared to inform the players how their roles would end.

According to a report by the Russian Fourth Army headquarters, the counterattack had begun by 0600 on June 23. The XIV Mechanized Corps advanced in the direction of Vidomlya and the XXVIII Rifle Corps in the direction of Brest. But by 0830 on June 23 this counteroffensive was reported to have failed and the units were said to have retreated to the line of Kuklin-Slobodka-Chahets-Kobrin. The report attributed the success of the enemy to "constant air support with complete absence of aviation on our side" as well as the effectiveness of a meeting engagement undertaken by the Germans with no less than two tank divisions in the direction of Pruzhany and with three infantry divisions with tanks in the direction of Kobrin.

In order to prevent a full-scale retreat from becoming a chaotic rout, Fourth Army reported that: "At night at different places to the east and to the west of Kartus-Beresa checkpoints for stopping the retreating personnel, combat vehicles, artillery and transport have been set up. Some straggler detachments are being re-formed and sent back to the front line." But the big worry of the Fourth Army commander was that he did not have enough aviation or artillery support. This is his sharply worded message to the Western Front.

> I request! I insistently request that: (a) our aviation should be more active in winning air supremacy over the Front. Frontal aviation must stop the advance of enemy tanks in the direction of Pruzhany and Kartus-Beresa; (b) do something about the ammunition situation. The artillery ammunition depot in Bochna Gura has been blown up by the enemy, the units have very little ammunition remaining and there isn't enough transportation to deliver ammunition from the depots in Pinsk.

The notable lack of aviation and artillery support within the Bialystok salient should by now be no surprise. Needless to say, these requests and many others like them from Russian units went unanswered. In a report oozing with frustration, a Northwestern Front headquarters document on June 22 stated:

> Our agents and enemy deserters have pointed out the fact that the German attack against us should have been expected. Almost the exact date of the beginning of the offensive was disclosed—June 20–22, 1941.
> Thus, as the war was becoming a fact, the events demanded that urgent measures should have been undertaken concerning operational deployment of units of all combat arms and their concentration under the existing mobilization plan.
> In the last days before the war the Northwestern Front command had the chance to immediately relocate some units closer to the border. But the momentum of concentration and deployment . . . was extremely slow. The low capacity of the Baltic railroad was to be taken into account as well as the troops being scattered over a large territory and most of them being a long distance from the state border.
> Along with that there was an opportunity under the pretext of field maneuvers to secretly concentrate our main forces near

the state border. It would also have been possible to reinforce and improve the fortifications. At the time of the attack only the 90th, 188th, and 5th Rifle Divisions were fully deployed, but they also were busy with construction work in the field camps and also with training exercises.[1]

After reading many documents of this type, one can say that some of the staff officers in the frontier zone had begun to realize the fate that was in store for them: that the promised reserves and aviation support would never arrive, and that the enemy would not be checked and thrown back across the border. It must be remembered that the men who wrote these reports were intelligent and experienced soldiers who knew their jobs. This was not the sort of treatment they expected. Did they deserve to be so callously used in this way?

The fact is they were put into this position by a misguided offensive-minded strategy. Once those lines had been drawn, there was no other way for Timoshenko and Zhukov to deal with the problem posed by the German invasion. What better strategy could have been devised?

The German air bombardment of Grodno itself wreaked havoc on Russian communications in this area, and despite all efforts, well-coordinated counterattacks were made impossible. Pavlov's virtually clean miss of Panzer Group 3 meant that Minsk was left without armored protection, and Hoth's penetration to that city from around Molodechno on June 26 was thus left largely unimpeded. Pavlov was under the erroneous impression that Hoth would veer his tanks to the south after reaching Lida, not Molodechno. As a result, he did not prepare an adequate defense of Minsk but instead sent the XXI Rifle Corps from the intermediate echelon reserve off toward Lida from west of Minsk. Pavlov's maneuver in this respect can be called a mistake, but Hoth's rapid capture of Minsk was not the only important result of the two mechanized corps' clash with the Ninth Army.

The gap that was steadily opening up between the motorized units of Panzer Group 3 and the infantry units of the Ninth Army was widened further by Pavlov's counterattack, and the Russians were able to use this delay in the progress of the German infantry to effect the escape to the north and east of important units that would otherwise have been securely trapped. The holding up of the Ninth Army's right wing near Grodno also meant that Grodno would have to be the turning point for the German infantry to press down to the south to link up with the Fourth Army around Bialystok in order to contain the Russian forces around this city. For the Ninth Army, the ring around Bialystok would initially have to be formed with five infantry divisions, each having a front of approximately 25 km. A 25-km. front would be difficult enough for an infantry division to defend under favorable circumstances, but very troublesome indeed in the thick forests around Bialystok. To try to extend the front of the Ninth Army closer to the main part of Panzer Group 3 farther to the east was, by June 25, an impossibility, yet von Bock was not deterred from ordering one entire army corps from the Ninth Army to turn to the northeast toward Vilnius. This turn was planned to aid Hoth's projected drive toward Vitebsk-Orsha but would have seriously impaired the Ninth Army's ability to hold a continuous front around Bialystok.

From the point of view of the Russians on the front lines, the first day of Barbarossa caught them totally by surprise. In an operational review at the I Rifle Corps of Tenth Army, held at 1900 on June 22, the comments made were:

> Approximately up to two infantry divisions of the enemy supported by artillery and aviation at 0500 of June 22, 1941 violated the state border, overcame the resistance of the border guard units, and continued their advance to the east and southeast. The units of the 8th Rifle Division were not able to occupy the forward positions before the enemy got there and they are now on the defensive line Schuchyn-Grabovo-Vorkovo-Konty. During the day there was no communication with the HQ of the Tenth Army either by radio or telegraph. Phone communication with the divisions is frequently disrupted. Heavy losses in the units are being reported.

This commentary is typical of the confusion and disorientation that prevailed in the units in position to bear the full fury of the German invasion. These are reports by men who would almost surely die in the defense of their homeland, victims of a bizarre twist of fate that compelled the leadership of the country to sacrifice them without any hope of salvation. This is how in real life mistakes in strategy are "fixed." Soldiers pay for such mistakes with their blood.

The Battles for the Upper Dnepr

The dimensions of the battles that developed around the upper Dnepr in mid-July 1941 were large by any standard. Overall, the battle for the Dnepr in the area of Army Group Center encompassed 600–650 km. of front, stretched from Sebezh and Velikie Luki in the north to the Loev and Novgorod-Severskii in the south; from Polotsk, Vitebsk, and Zhlobin in the west to Toropets, Yartsevo, and Trubchevsk in the east. Not only was the physical setting of the struggle immense, but the duration of it was protracted, from July 10, when Guderian succeeded in crossing the Dnepr, to the last days of September, when the advance toward Moscow was resumed under the code name Operation Typhoon.

After Pavlov's sudden dismissal as commander of the Western Front (and his subsequent execution), Marshal S. K. Timoshenko, the commissar for defense, was picked by Stalin on July 1 to serve as Pavlov's successor. It has been said that Timoshenko's assignment was due to Stalin's desire to take direct control over military affairs, yet the evidence now in hand shows that in early July Stalin was relying heavily on the men who had devised the February defense plan to actually implement it. The Soviet dictator went into seclusion after June 22 and made no public appearances of any kind until his radio address to the nation on July 3 (see Appendix A). Timoshenko was now the man of the hour who had to answer for the success or failure of the Western Front, and he must have been aware that he, too, could share Pavlov's fate.

The situation that confronted Timoshenko when he and his staff arrived at Smolensk on July 2 was anything but enviable. Pavlov's counterattacks with three mechanized corps had not worked the desired effect on the two German panzer groups coming into the Bialystok salient from the north and south; nor had the enemy failed to take advantage of its overwhelming air superiority close to the frontier. Communications in the forward areas of the Western Front were in shambles; it was difficult for a commander to make intelligent decisions under such conditions.

By June 26 it had become obvious to Zhukov, still the chief of the general staff, and Timoshenko that emergency measures had to be taken by the operational echelon if German armor was to be checked before a breach was torn in the Dnepr line of defense. Zhukov could not have foreseen how rapid the advance of the German tanks was to be after the bridges over the Nieman were captured intact and after the Luftwaffe had made short work of the large Russian mechanized corps. In his memoirs Zhukov acknowledged one other mistake: "We did not envisage the nature of the blow [on June 22] in its entirety. Neither the People's Commissar [Timoshenko], nor myself . . . expected the enemy to concentrate such huge numbers of armored and motorized troops, and, on the first day, to commit them to action in powerful compact groupings in all strategic directions."[2] Zhukov evidently believed beforehand that the Germans would be more cautious in crossing the border, putting infantry and artillery ahead of the tanks, as Halder had proposed. A decision had to be made at once to strengthen the Dvina-Dnepr line in the area of the operational echelon of the Western Front. A delay or postponement of this decision was not possible, because no one could predict how long the forces within the encirclements could resist the strong German pressure. One bright spot in the picture, however, was that the Russian forces, parts of three armies cut off by the Germans west of Minsk, were continuing to put up a stiff fight. The tactical reserve was, in actuality, fulfilling its function by holding its ground while the German armor passed on to the east, and many German units were tied down by the Bialystok-Minsk encirclement operation until after July 8.

But Zhukov could not count on the German infantry being held west of the Dnepr for long. Positive action was required to ensure the position of the forces on the upper Dnepr.

In the afternoon of June 22, Zhukov was dispatched to the Southwestern Front by Stalin to ensure that the grave situation there would not turn into a rout, thus endangering their strategy on the southern flank of Army Group Center. On the evening of June 26, Stalin summoned Zhukov back to Moscow to discuss the situation with Timoshenko and Vatutin, who was then chief of the operations section of the general staff. Since Vatutin had issued the order inviting key naval and air force personnel to participate in the clandestine February war game, he was well aware of the overall strategy. It was decided at this conference that the forces of the operational echelon already on the Dvina-Dnepr line in the area of the Western Front—the Twentieth, Twenty-first, and Twenty-second Armies, plus other units—would now have to be augmented by other armies taken from the main part of the operational echelon in Ukraine and from reserves directly controlled by the supreme command. The final recommendation made to Stalin on June 27 called for the Thirteenth, Nineteenth, Twentieth, Twenty-first, and Twenty-second Armies to defend the line Dvina-Polotsk-Vitebsk-Orsha-Mogilev-Mozyr. In addition, the Twenty-fourth and Twenty-eighth Armies from the supreme command reserve were to be held in readiness near and to the south of Smolensk. The recommendation also called for the immediate formation of two or three more armies from the Moscow militia. Stalin approved of this proposal without objection.

The German move across the Dnepr could not be made immediately, because Army Group Center would need several days, approximately until July 5, in order to resupply and regroup its Panzer Groups 2 (Guderian) and 3 (Hoth). More time would also be needed to complete the transfer of the command of Panzer Groups 2 and 3 from Army Group Center's direct control to von Kluge's Fourth Army command, a task that was finally accomplished on July 3. It was von Kluge's intention to postpone Guderian's crossing of the Dnepr until the two infantry corps of his new command, the so-called Fourth Panzer Army, could be brought up to lend assistance. Guderian too was worried about the feasibility of cracking the Dnepr line without the help of infantry units being brought forward by train, but the army group could reply only that the entire rail-carrying capacity was strained to the limit in bringing enough supplies up to the front. Another problem that caused Guderian some difficulty was that his units had already suffered 3,382 casualties up to July 3, and on July 7 he had to report to OKH that 10 percent of his tanks had been lost and only 35 percent of the tanks in the 3d and 18th Panzer Divisions were battle worthy. The 10th Panzer Division was in the best condition, with 80 percent of its tanks in service, but the overall repair and breakdown situation in the panzer group's armored vehicles did not auger well for a blitzkrieg victory over the Red Army.

The creation of the Fourth Panzer Army was actually a subterfuge by Halder to allow Guderian the maximum amount of freedom to continue his plunge eastward toward Moscow. The problem was that Hitler believed that Army Group Center's two panzer groups should turn back to the west and help forge a tight ring around the Bialystok encirclement. By removing Guderian from the direct control of von Bock, Halder hoped that this would give Guderian an excuse to "misunderstand" and disobey orders. Guderian, however, needed no stimulation to disobey orders from the higher command authorities, as Halder would discover to his everlasting sorrow.

By July 4 the XXIV Panzer Corps, led by the 3d and 4th Panzer Divisions and followed by the 10th Motorized Division, had secured several crossings over the Berezina and had come up to the Dnepr near Rogachev and at Stary Bykhov. The Soviet strength west of the Dnepr was, however, far from depleted, as their operational echelon had transformed Rogachev, Mogilev, and Orsha into formidable strongholds. On July 5 a Russian probing attack composed of units of F. I. Kuznetsov's Twenty-first Army crossed the Dnepr near Zhlobin south of Rogachev and moved toward Bobruisk. Although this attack was shoved back by the 10th Motorized Division with some help from the 3d Panzer Division, nevertheless, the area between the Dnepr and the Berezina remained hazardous, as many Russian units continued to operate here, destroying bridges and causing supply difficulties.

On July 12 Guderian pleaded with Army Group Center to do something about putting the Minsk-Bobruisk railroad into service, but the army group had to reply that "this area was still too dangerous to work in." Guderian, however, could not wait for these problems to be cleared up; he was determined to leave the securing of the area west of the Dnepr to the infantry of von Weichs's Second Army, which, for the most part, was still near Minsk.

In order to cross the Dnepr as easily as possible and open the way into Smolensk from the south and west, Guderian made a fateful decision. He decided to bypass the main crossings of the river at

Zhlobin, Rogachev, Mogilev, and Orsha, where the largest concentrations of Russian forces were located, and transfer his units over to the eastern bank at Stary Bykhov, to the north of Rogachev, and at Shklov and Kopys between Mogilev and Orsha. This area was covered by the Russian tactical reserve. These Soviet units were banded together with other fragmented forces and given the designation "Thirteenth Army." Guderian's decision to cross the river here looked good on paper because it allowed Panzer Group 2 to push through the Russian line at its weakest points, thereby leading to the capture of Smolensk in a rapid stroke by July 16, the earliest date that the Fourth Panzer Army commander had set for the arrival of the mass of the infantry of the Second Army on the Dnepr. Maneuvers of this kind were dear to Guderian's heart—to hit the enemy at its weakest link with armor and let the infantry deal with the strongpoints later. Guderian drummed this philosophy into the heads of his subordinate commanders; on July 7 he addressed them all in a briefing session prior to the crossing of the Dnepr: "All commanders of the panzer group and their troops must disregard threats to the flanks and the rear. My divisions know only to press forward."

The idea, however, of pushing across the Dnepr, thus exposing the right flank of the panzer group to the danger of a counterattack by Timoshenko's forces east of the river, while leaving the powerful Russian concentrations around Rogachev-Zhlobin, Mogilev, and Orsha unmolested in the rear, was too much for some of Guderian's own commanders to accept. On July 8 Gen. Geyr von Schweppenburg's XXIV Panzer Corps had captured a Russian map showing the strength of the Red Army at Rogachev-Zhlobin and showing a connection between these forces and the large Russian grouping around Gomel. This map also indicated that a planned Russian counterattack from the southeast would take place as soon as the panzer group crossed the river. As a result of this information, von Schweppenburg earnestly recommended that the attack be postponed either until the infantry had been brought up to Bobruisk or until his panzer corps could be strengthened. It is likely that this map, plus another similar one captured by the LIII Army Corps on July 15, was based on the defensive strategy worked out at the time of the February war game.

The same concern was voiced by von Kluge, who appeared at Guderian's headquarters early on the morning of July 9. He, too, was opposed to Panzer Group 2's crossing the Dnepr without waiting for the infantry and more artillery support, but Guderian would hear nothing of such arguments. He told von Kluge, half truthfully, that the XXIV and XLVI Panzer Corps had already been concentrated in their takeoff positions and that to hold them there for too long would be to expose them to the danger of attack by the Russian air force. Guderian went on to say that if this attack succeeded, then the campaign would probably be decided within the year. After listening to Guderian's barrage of excuses, and knowing full well that he was speaking with the authority of Army Group Center and OKH, the field marshal reluctantly backed down, though he warned Guderian prophetically, "Your operations always hang by a thread!" For the next few days Guderian seemed to be proud of this, repeating von Kluge's warnings to his staff, which elicited the hoped-for gales of laughter.

As an illustration of what kind of improvisation was necessary by early July, a battalion of the 255th Infantry Division, without the approval of Army Group Center or the Second Army, was loaded onto trucks provided by the 3d Panzer Division and moved from southeast of Minsk to Bobruisk during the night of July 9. The main part of the LIII Army Corps, however, could not reach Bobruisk before July 12. The hurried progress of Panzer Group 2 and its consequent lack of infantry support led to another sticky situation on July 4, after the 3d Panzer Division managed to establish a bridgehead on the Dnepr's eastern bank near Rogachev. Continuous attacks by the LXIII Rifle Corps of the Russian Twenty-first Army forced Lieutenant General Model to order his units back over to the western bank on July 6. Also, on July 8, Guderian's headquarters asked the Fourth Panzer Army to speed up the transfer of ammunition supplies through the Second Army supply area, as both the XXIV and XLVI Panzer Corps were reporting shortages, especially of heavy artillery shells. Army Group Center's "Order of the Day" on July 8 announced the end of the Bialystok-Minsk battle and the capture of 287,704 Russian prisoners. Of this number only about 100,000 were taken in the smaller pocket around Bialystok.

By July 10, the Soviet Western Front had sixty-five divisions. Despite the rough equality with Army Group Center in the numbers of large units, the Red Army was way behind in overall firepower, especially in tanks. Although the reserves were not fully in place, they would arrive in time.

The immediate task of the Western Front was to block the enemy's breakthrough to Moscow and to ensure the prerequisites for the planned counteroffensive. For this reason, it was necessary to complete as quickly as possible the concentration and deployment of the troops that were rapidly being brought up to the newly organized defenses along the line Disna-Polotsk-Vitebsk-Orsha-Dnepr River-Loev.

Of the seven armies at his disposal on the Western Front, Timoshenko assigned the Twenty-second, Nineteenth, Twentieth, Thirteenth, and Twenty-first to the forward part of the operational echelon. Behind them was a newly constituted Fourth Army, while the Sixteenth Army was moved into the Smolensk area immediately after its arrival from Ukraine.

The main concern of the front command was to defend the "Smolensk gates," also referred to by the Germans as the "land bridge" between the Western (*Zapadnaia*) Dvina and the Dnepr. Here the Twentieth Army was positioned, reinforced by units of the Nineteenth and Sixteenth Armies. Much in the way that NATO for forty years expected the Red Army to pour through the Fulda gap in an invasion of Germany, terrain funneled the Wehrmacht along certain prescribed routes. As stated earlier, this is why the defense and the counterattack plans by Timoshenko and Zhukov focused on the Dvina–upper Dnepr area.

A German blow was also expected at Mogilev in the operational area of the Thirteenth Army. This army, like the Fourth, was given the same unit designation as the one cut off and destroyed in the Bialystok-Minsk encirclements. It was planned to deploy the Fourth Army and the IV Airborne Corps there also, but the concentration of troops was slowed by German air superiority. The commanding general of the Nineteenth Army, Ivan Konev, ordered his units to conduct a defense near Vitebsk, but by July 10 the army managed to have only one division near the town and by then it was too late—the enemy had already occupied Vitebsk. The same thing happened to the Sixteenth Army. Only one of its divisions entered Smolensk before the Germans got there.

The arriving troops took up defensive positions that had been under construction since the beginning of July. In spite of the fact that more than 2 million service members and civilians were taking part in the construction, they had succeeded only in throwing up barricades and digging trenches and communications lines. There was simply not enough time to properly prepare defensive positions with such bare necessities as wire entanglements and mines. The German timetable had so far been much faster than anyone had expected. The question was, could they be slowed down and then arrested in their progress?

But things were not all so bleak as they might have appeared on the surface. Already, 100 km. to the east of Smolensk, a third echelon was being formed composed of six reserve armies. The Germans, of course, had no idea what was soon to be in store for them. In fact, in the Smolensk-Yelnia region the presence of large numbers of artillery and mortar tubes, which began pounding them as soon as they arrived, was quite a shock. Halder and the German General Staff were still comfortable with the illusion that the main defensive barriers of the Red Army had been crushed along the frontier and that the hinterland of the vast country was open to free-ranging operations.

Von Bock, the commander of Army Group Center, concluded on the basis of the reconnaissance data he had at his disposal that the Western Front had only eleven divisions remaining, thus underestimating the real number several times. The Soviet general staff for its part reported in early July that the Germans had thirty-five divisions facing the Western Direction, underestimating them by about a factor of two. Such was the state-of-the-art in reconnaissance in 1941. This explains why Timoshenko and Zhukov were so bullish about destroying the German bridgeheads over the Dvina and the Dnepr. They thought they were solidly in the superior position in terms of overall resources.

Now, we must say a few words about unit names that may help avoid confusion. By the second week in July the Russian supreme command had come to believe that a greater level of coordination was needed between the various army fronts that were facing three large German army groups. As a result, the STAVKA adopted a cumbersome command structure that added direction staffs in between the supreme command in Moscow and the fronts actually doing the fighting. On July 10 the supreme command ordered the creation of three special "front groups": (1) the Northwestern Direction under Marshal K. E. Voroshilov and commissar A. A. Zhdanov, which had control over the Northern and Northwestern Fronts plus the Northern and Baltic Fleets; (2) the Western Direction under Marshal Timoshenko and N. A. Bulganin, which controlled the Western and later the Reserve Fronts (Timoshenko still retained direct command over the Western Front); and (3) the Southwestern Direction under Marshal Budenny and N. S. Khrushchev, which controlled the Southwestern, Southern, and later the Central Fronts plus the Black Sea Fleet. When reference is made to the Southwestern Direction, it means this staff; the Southwestern Front was subordinate to the Southwestern Direction. This command structure would prove to be troublesome in the near future, as friction grew between Moscow and the directional and front staffs; opportunities for misunderstandings multiplied now that another level of organization had been created.

If the possibilities for confusion here were not enough, one must bear in mind that at this time the Red Army had a dual command structure. The political officers referred to, such as Khrushchev, were outside the ordinary command structure of the Red Army and reported to the higher command structure of the Communist Party. It may help to visualize the organizations of the army and Party as being separate but intertwined, as most senior officers were Communists. It should also be noted that Stalin was head both of the military and of the Communist Party.

By July 10, only thirty-seven divisions of the Western Front had managed to arrive in defensive positions, and only twenty-four of them were deployed in the second (the new first) echelon. Many arriving units had to engage in combat immediately after disembarking from troop trains. Part of the Twenty-second Army was fighting in the Polotsk fortified region; the Twentieth Army was fighting around Lepel, and the Twenty-first at the Dnepr crossings near Stary Bykhov and Rogachev. With a front defense zone of 800 km., every division was responsible for defending at least 33 km.; in some sectors the main line of resistance (MLR) was 70 km. The creation of stable front lines was impossible under such dynamic and fluid conditions.

The Luftwaffe was devastatingly effective in the early months of the war, particularly because at that time the Western Front had only 400 antiaircraft guns and extremely weak fighter protection. This made the Soviet troops defenseless against German air operations.

On July 10 Guderian's panzer group split the seam of the Twentieth and Thirteenth Armies in the Shklov area with a force of 460 tanks. At Shklov were three Soviet rifle divisions covering an MLR of 37 km., and they had no tanks at all. Guderian's forces broke through the Thirteenth Army's defenses and started to cross the Dnepr. By the night of July 11 they managed to secure bridgeheads to the north and south of Mogilev. The most vulnerable part of the Western Front's defenses turned out to be the seam between the Twentieth and the Twenty-second Armies, where only one division of the Nineteenth Army was engaged in combat. It was at this very point that Hoth's Panzer Group 3 delivered its blow. With 500 tanks Hoth broke through the defense lines and captured Vitebsk.

Timoshenko immediately saw how serious the situation near Vitebsk was and that Hoth's breakthrough represented a threat to the rear of the main body of the Western Front. It was possible to counter the strong German armored penetration with the powerful second echelon, but, thanks to Stalin's delays, it was not yet fully in place.

Despite the agreement to form a second echelon after the February war game and not pin all hopes solely on fortifying the Bialystok salient, Stalin, in his lack of wisdom, failed to see how rapid the eastward plunge of the German panzers would be. In this respect, Guderian's rash disregard for the problems of the infantry in grappling with Russian forces in the salient had brought grief for the Russian high command. Stalin had ordered the troop trains not to roll before the invasion started, afraid that this movement would be detected and that the Germans would be alerted to the new strategy. He had reckoned that Bialystok would cost the Germans at least three weeks to reduce, thus the recklessness of the German panzer leaders in effectively bypassing the salient caught him off guard. Zhukov's memoirs reflect the frustration he felt when Stalin would not allow the second echelon to be properly positioned in time to meet the German tanks when they reached the Dnepr. But, as it turned out, the panzer leaders had problems of their own. They had outrun their logistics train, as Major General Paulus, the head quartermaster (OQI) of the German army, pointed out would happen in the summary of his own war game held in mid-December 1940. This war game showed convincingly that the army would overreach its logistics pipeline by the time it reached the Dnepr. The panzer leaders were forced into an operational pause by a law as inflexible as the law of gravity; without supply no army can move. This gave Zhukov and Timoshenko the time they needed to bring the second echelon into play. As shall be seen, Guderian's forces had to pay dearly for their lack of infantry and adequate artillery support when the pressure of the second echelon began to make itself felt. This pressure was manifested most severely around the Yelnia salient and around Propoisk (now Slavgorod) along the Sozh River. The Sozh River events will be examined much more closely in the next chapter.

The fall of Smolensk was now but a short time away, but such haste in the end gained nothing for Guderian. The problems confronting his panzer group from the southeast, and from the rear as well, would absorb ever more of his attention, and the chimera of Moscow would slowly recede into the background as the Russian pressure gradually intensified against his units and against the Second Army coming up from the west.

The Fall of Smolensk
Guderian's main drive across the Dnepr toward Smolensk, Yelnia, Dorogobuzh, and Roslavl came on July 10–11 and was carried out with only light casualties, as no attempt was made to eliminate the Russian bridgeheads on the western bank beforehand. The Russian bridgehead at Orsha was screened by two battle groups while the XXIV Panzer Corps was to protect its own flank against attacks from the area Zhlobin-Rogachev and its northern flank against the enemy at Mogilev.

As Smolensk was now in jeopardy, by July 14 Timoshenko subordinated all troops in and around the city to the commander of the Sixteenth Army, M. F. Lukin. By that time he had only two rifle divisions at his disposal, which were not enough to create a solid defense along the approaches to the city with time running out. On July 15 Guderian's 29th Motorized Division captured the southern suburbs of the city. The units of General Lukin's Sixteenth Army fought together with the Twentieth Army. The commander of the Sixteenth Army's 152d Rifle Division, Colonel Chernyshev, was wounded twice in one day but kept on fighting. General Lukin reported to Marshal Timoshenko: "The 129th Rifle Division, composed of detachments which have retreated from the front and separate units of other divisions, has become one of the most stable and stubborn divisions." It was commanded by General Gorodnyanski, a veteran of the First World War, who became the commanding general of the Thirteenth Army a month later.

It seemed that nothing could prevent the German command from developing their success. Hitler was satisfied with the course of the offensive. On July 14, in his talk with Japan's ambassador to Berlin, Hiroshi Oshima, he said that Napoleon's fate was awaiting not him but Stalin. He was delighted with his generals at that time, calling them "personalities of historic scale," and characterized his officers as "extraordinary." By the middle of August, however, his confidence in this respect had waned.

The XLVII Panzer Corps was given the direct assignment of capturing Smolensk, and this was done in remarkably short order by Lieutenant General von Boltenstern's 29th Motorized Division. The push across the Dnepr by the 29th Division of the XLVII Panzer Corps began at 0515 on July 11 in the area of Kopys and at Shklov. Although Russian artillery fire was lively, it was soon suppressed with the aid of a nearby self-propelled artillery (*Sturmgeschütz*) unit. Even while the Russian artillery was still active, and the Red Air Force as well, the pioneers of the 29th Division went to work building a bridge, completing it by 0400 that day. After a diversion to the northwest to help the 17th Panzer Division in its crossover near Orsha, the 29th Division made its way straight for Smolensk. It met no determined resistance until the lead elements of the 15th Infantry Regiment reached Khokhlovo, and here Russian artillery and air strikes caused heavy casualties. Again, the self-propelled artillery proved its worth in combination with the infantry, and the Russian machine-gun nests and strongpoints were soon overcome. The last resistance near Smolensk was broken in this way, and by the evening of July 15 the battle-hardened 15th Infantry Regiment drove into the southwestern edge of the city. Then, by order of the XLVII Panzer Corps, the 71st Infantry Regiment (from Khokhlovo) and the 29th Artillery Regiment were turned directly into the city's south side. This action was fought on foot and across fields, mostly against militia units hastily formed by the Russian Sixteenth Army command. By nightfall this second German group had also entered Smolensk.

Colonel Thomas's 71st Infantry Regiment had taken the Russian heavy artillery positions on the Koniukovo hills southwest of the city and learned from prisoners that Smolensk was strongly defended from this direction. After learning this, the regiment pressed on farther east to the Chislavichi-Nikitina-Smolensk road, escaping observation by the Russians. By 0400 they were in the city's outskirts, but within an hour a heavy barrage of Russian artillery fire began to rain down on them. Not until nightfall were the troops of the 71st Regiment able to reach the southern bank of the Dnepr. During the night the 29th Artillery Regiment brought up some support guns placed at its disposal, including 100mm cannon, Nebelwerfer rocket launchers, 88mm flak antitank guns, and regular antitank guns. The 15th Infantry Regiment was to the west of the 71st Regiment, also on the city's south side.

The final assault on Smolensk began at 0400 on July 16. Due to the narrowness of the streets, the German artillery could offer the infantry only a little direct help. The main part of the Russian force in the city seemed to be on the northern bank of the river, and other Red Army motorized columns were observed coming in from the north and east. German artillery opened fire on the Russian reinforcements; the Russians replied in kind and also with an aerial bombardment. Already in the morning of July 16 Smolensk began to take on a shattered appearance, as only a few undamaged buildings protruded from the rubble. By late morning, with the aid of some self-propelled artillery and the flame-throwing tanks of the 100th Panzer Regiment, a secure foothold was carved out on the southern bank. Around noon Russian artillery fire of all calibers picked up considerably, and in this way many fires broke out among the city's predominantly wooden houses, creating dense clouds of smoke; the cathedral tower with its golden cupolas provided a colorful contrast.

Around 1600 the 15th and 71st Infantry Regiments began crossing the Dnepr in rubber boats, while the 29th Artillery Regiment on the southern bank poured fire into the Russian-controlled northern bank. This assault was ordered by von Boltenstern, who had his headquarters in the Hotel Molokhov. After arriving safely on the opposite side, the men of the 15th Infantry Regiment soon reached the main railroad station and by 0530 had fought all the way into Peter's Church, smoking the Red Army men out of their hiding places as they moved along. Particularly rough fighting occurred at the cemetery on the northern bank, where parts of the Russian 129th Rifle Division under Gen. A. M. Gorodnyanski managed to use the tombstones as effective cover. By 1800 the fighting had moved out to the northern city limits, with the struggle growing ever more bitter; the streets had to be cleared systematically block by block, in many cases with grenades, flamethrowers, and machine pistols. Right at the city's northern limits some military barracks with well-dug-in field fortifications proved to be a tough nut to crack. Nevertheless, by 2300 the whole city had been subdued. The struggle, however, was far from over. Russian artillery fire continued to rain down on Smolensk from the hills close in on the north side. The stricken city glowed red in the night as Russian attacks, backed up by tanks, persisted until the morning. The next day's mission for the 29th Division would be to hold positions south of Smolensk along the Dnepr line, mainly along the Roslavl road, in order to prevent the Russians from breaking out of the large semipocket that had been formed by the two panzer groups around Smolensk from the north and south. The Russian Sixteenth, Nineteenth, and Twentieth Armies were now cut off. Only one crossing over the Dnepr was available for retreat farther to the east in the vicinity of the village of Solovev. On July 16 Marshal Timoshenko reported to the STAVKA: "We have not enough regular forces to cover the direction of Yartsevo-Viazma- Moscow. It is most significant that we have no tanks."

Although the actual taking of Smolensk went well enough, the broad encirclement of the city had been carried out neither smoothly nor with great effectiveness. After Guderian's conversation with von

Kluge on July 9 and the panzer general's emphatic statement that his assault over the Dnepr would decide the campaign within the year, von Kluge, the commander of the Fourth Panzer Army, ordered the 12th Panzer Division, since July 8 relieved from duty on the Minsk encirclement front, not to join Panzer Group 3's 7th Panzer Division at Vitebsk, but rather to drive through Senno to cover Guderian's northern flank. Panzer Group 3's assault north of Smolensk was thereby weakened in order to aid Guderian's push toward Smolensk-Yelnia-Dorogobuzh from the southwest, much against the protests of Hoth and von Bock.

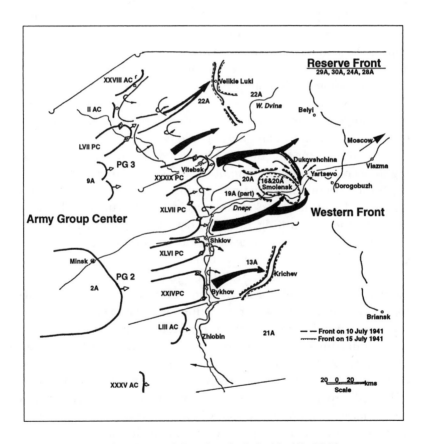

Battles Around Smolensk, July 10–15, 1941

Guderian's only thought was to reach the high ground to the east and south of Smolensk between the upper Dnepr and the headwaters of the Desna, thus securing an opening to Moscow from the west, whereas Hoth was more immediately concerned with the integrity of the planned encirclement around Smolensk. On July 10 Hoth ordered the XXXIX Panzer Corps to swing around Smolensk from the north through the line Lesno-Surazh-Usiavits toward the northeast, hoping that the heaviest enemy resistance would thus be skirted; but destroyed bridges and mines in the roads reduced the speed of the motorized units to that of the infantry. On July 13 the lead elements of Panzer Group 3's XXXIX Panzer Corps reached Demidov and Velizh, and on July 14 the 12th Panzer Division reached Lesno and then turned in a more easterly direction toward Smolensk. The 12th Panzer Division was checked near Rudnia after being hit by Russian attacks from three sides, but the 7th Panzer Division managed to hold fast to the Demidov highway northwest of Smolensk while Guderian's northerly XLVII Panzer Corps crowded up toward Orsha, leaving a great conglomeration of Russians more or less boxed in from three directions to the north and west of Smolensk.

It was at this time that the STAVKA decided to unleash a new and highly secret weapon in the fight for the upper Dnepr. On July 14 the Soviet Twentieth Army fired the first "reactive artillery"—later known as "Katiusha"—rocket salvos against the German 5th Infantry Division, then occupying Rudnia northeast of Smolensk on the Vitebsk highway. The famous Katiushas (also known as the "Stalin Orgel," or "Stalin's organ pipes," by the Germans) were quite unexpected by the Wehrmacht. At 0015 on July 14, Capt. Ivan Flyorov's battery launched 16,132 rockets from seven Katiushas within a period of fifteen seconds. This rate of fire was equal to one volley fired simultaneously by three artillery regiments. The Katiusha truckborne, rail-launched rockets created havoc in the area of the 5th Infantry Division, largely because the Germans had never encountered them before. If used against a relatively flat or open area, a large salvo of Katiusha rockets would create a veritable blizzard of shrapnel. A memorial now stands at the spot where this weapon was first fired. The Germans failed to capture even one of the Katiushas despite strenuous efforts. Eventually, some of these weapons were taken to

Germany for analysis, but no production copies of it were ever made for the German army. By contrast, the Geman Nebelwerfer 41 could fire six 150mm rockets in about ten seconds.

For his part, Stalin was furious with the commanders whom he considered responsible for allowing the ancient garrison town of Smolensk to fall. In his rage he accused the Western Front commanders of "having a defeatist and lighthearted attitude towards the loss of Smolensk." In reading the documents of the State Defense Committee, one sees clearly that Stalin considered his generals to have almost betrayed the Motherland. Stalin thus laid down the law: either recapture Smolensk or die trying. Anything less was treason. The example of Pavlov must have hung over their heads like an ax beginning to descend.

The cause of the panic and confusion was that although many units of the Red Army were standing fast and giving superb accounts of themselves, such as the 172d Rifle Division at Mogilev, others were not. Many officers were confused about what their assignments were and what was expected of them. Most of all there was much rumormongering about where the enemy was and what his plans were. This is what happens when senior officers are not given any idea as to what the overall strategy is and where they fit into a plan of coordinated, echeloned defenses. Individual initiative had a different meaning in the Red Army under Stalin than it did in the West. Only later, when the Red Army was bolstered by the delayed reinforcements and the defenses began to hold, did confidence in the upper leadership begin to reassert itself. Meanwhile, all Stalin had to rely on to keep control over his forces was fear, and this he knew how to use. Looking back at the records, we can conclude that if the Soviet Union ever came close to collapse, it was during the time just after the fall of Smolensk. Clearly, something had to be done, and done quickly. There could be no further thought of holding back the strategic reserve.

It should come as no surprise that shortly after Stalin's violent tirade, the Western Front command reported to Stalin and Molotov that its most important objective was to retake Smolensk. Several sporadic attacks went on in and around the city until about the end of July, when the effort had to be abandoned. Other tasks were taking priority. As an example of this, the counterattacks of the Nineteenth and Twentieth Armies, commanded by Generals Konev and Kurochkin, missed their aim. Their units tried to attack the Germans in the center of the Western Front's defense line, but the attacks were not synchronized properly and did not enjoy adequate artillery support. During the desperate fighting, the Nineteenth Army lost its command and control means, and after breaking up into scattered units its forces retreated eastward trying to avoid encirclement by the fast-racing panzers. Some of them made their way into Smolensk.

The success of the Twentieth Army under Kurochkin was more promising. A particularly bright spot was the 73d Rifle Division's defense of Orsha led by Col. Alexander Akimov. The 1st Motorized Rifle Division of Gen. Yakov Kreiser eventually fought its way out after being cut off for four days. Reports from Panzer Group 3's war diaries show that the Germans were continuously surprised by such staunch defenders obviously well equipped and positioned in areas where they were not supposed to be. After all, had not the bulk of the Red Army already been destroyed along the frontier? The truth began to manifest itself in the growing numbers of casualties being inflicted on Army Group Center. As an example of this, by the end of July Panzer Group 2 was reporting a casualty rate of more than 18 percent total losses. As will be seen, the casualty rates rose significantly for the units engaged around Yelnia as well as in the Second Army on the southern flank of Army Group Center.

The Smolensk Counteroffensive

On the whole, in the period July 10–20 the Germans advanced about 200 km., encircling large groups of the Western Front near Smolensk and Mogilev. These encirclements created a serious threat to Moscow. Emboldened by this success, Hitler, in his Directive 33 of July 19, ordered that Army Group Center should undertake an offensive toward Moscow after destroying the encircled troops in the Smolensk pocket.

In order to relieve the threat to Moscow, the STAVKA accelerated the accumulation of its reserves in this direction. Along the line Staraia Russa-Ostashkov-Bely-Yelnia-Briansk in the rear of the Western Front, a new Reserve Front was created commanded by Gen. S.I.

Bogdanov, former head of the Bielorussian Border District. The new front was composed of divisions recruited by the People's Commissariat for Internal Affairs (the infamous NKVD) as well as from the border guards and other internal troops. All in all the front comprised four armies: the Twenty-ninth, which was commanded by the commissar of internal affairs, General Maslennikov; the Thirtieth, by the head of the Ukrainian Border District, General Homenko; the Thirty-first, by the head of the Karelo-Finnish Border District, General Dolmatov; and the Twenty-fourth, by the former head of the Baltic Border District, General Rakutin.

On July 18 the STAVKA deployed the third strategic echelon behind the Western Direction forces now in direct contact with the enemy. On the far approaches to Moscow along a line to the west of Volokolamsk-Mozhaisk-Maloyaroslavets, what became known as the Mozhaisk line of defense was organized. This force, which would grow rapidly in strength, included the Thirty-second and Thirty-third Armies and was under the command of the chief of the Moscow Military District, General Artemev.

The strategic defense of Moscow was constructed in three defensive lines with a depth of deployment of 300 km. At the same time the idea of a counteroffensive was never far removed from the thoughts of everyone on the STAVKA. Stalin made reference to this in his direct wire discussion with the commander in chief of the Western Direction, Timoshenko, on July 20. He criticized the marshal for dispersing his troops and said, "I think that it is time for us to give up pitching pebbles, let's get ready to throw some big rocks."

On that same day, the chief of the general staff issued a directive concerning the encirclement and destruction of the German forces around Smolensk. For this operation sizeable resources had to be allocated. Eventually, twenty divisions were formed out of the reserves and organized into five operational groups led by Generals Homenko, Kalinin, Rokossovsky, Kachalov, and Maslennikov. Their task was to "destroy the enemy with synchronized blows from the northeast, east, and south in the general direction of Smolensk and to link up with the encircled troops of the Sixteenth and Twentieth Armies." At the same time, a raid deep into the enemy rear was undertaken in the operational zone of the Twenty-first Army by a cavalry group of three divisions led by Gen. O. I. Gorodovikov. Overall command of the Smolensk counteroffensive was entrusted to A. I. Eremenko, who was appointed new commander of the Western Front on July 19.

The engagement in combat of twenty fresh divisions immediately changed the balance of forces in the west. The German forces around Smolensk had already suffered heavy losses there and were not expecting reserves to appear this soon. But because of the direct pressure by Stalin to relieve the approaches to Moscow, too little time was allowed for preparing the counteroffensive. Two short days were not enough for ensuring supplies and support of command and control, especially coordination with the Twentieth and Sixteenth Armies. As a result, not all units managed to arrive in their staging areas on time. Many of them suffered heavy losses from enemy air action before the jump-off.

The forces of the Western Front began offensive operations at different times during the period July 20–25. As the offensive picked up steam, the hottest fighting developed around Dukovshchina, Yartsevo, Smolensk, and, most violently of all, around Yelnia. Intensive fighting also continued around Velikie Luki on the northern flank of Army Group Center.

On July 26–27 the troops of the five Russian operational groups kept on the offensive. The Germans were now forced to send to Smolensk troops from quieter sectors. Some of these suffered from attacks by cavalry units operating with some vigor on the flanks and in the rear of Army Group Center, disrupting communication lines and supplies of ammunition and fuel, thus contributing to the success of the counterattacking operational groups. As an example of this success, General Rokossovsky's group was able to retake Yartsevo. These were hardly the actions of a defeated and disorganized enemy. By this time it should have become clear to the Germans that they had big problems on their hands, much larger problems in fact than even Paulus's worst-case scenario had envisioned.

Remembering these crucial combat operations after the war, Marshal Konstantin Rokossovsky paid tribute to the mass heroism of officers and men. At the same time the marshal wrote, "Adding to the difficulty of the situation, which we don't have the right to keep silent about, there were some acts of cowardice, panic, desertion and self-inflicted wounds with the aim of avoiding combat. First, there were the so-called 'left-handers' who shot themselves in the left palm or shot off fingers from their left hands. When some attention was paid to that, the 'right-handers' appeared who did the mirror image of the same thing. Mutual self-wounding also happened."[3] Soon rules were adopted that set forth the death penalty for desertion, shirking combat, self-inflicted or mutual wounding, and insubordination. As harsh as these penalties might be, in a fight to the death the individual soldier had to be shown that self-interest could not be placed above the good of all.

Lt. Gen. Vasilii Kachalov's group had to pass the hardest tests. It was encircled in the region north of Roslavl in one of the rare sectors of the front where the Germans still managed to move forward. Breaking the encirclement at the end of July, the troops of the group suffered heavy losses, and on August 4 the commander of the group, General Kachalov, was killed. After his death the STAVKA issued the following order on August 16: "The Twenty-eighth Army Commander Lt. Gen. Kachalov, together with his group's headquarters, were encircled, displayed cowardice and surrendered to German fascists." This statement, signed by all members of the STAVKA, was announced to all companies, squadrons, batteries, teams, and headquarters. These false accusations of betrayal of the Motherland against the general who fulfilled his duty to the ultimate were dropped only many years after the war.

Still, despite immense efforts, the troops of the Western Front were unable to destroy the enemy in the vicinity of Smolensk. The attempted counteroffensive had failed for a second time. Although the effectiveness of uncoordinated attacks by weak groupings along a broad front seemed to be small, these blows threatened the flanks of Army Group Center and restricted the Germans' freedom of maneuver. The offensive also relieved some of the pressure on the Soviet forces encircled near Mogilev and Smolensk, allowing important elements of the trapped Sixteenth and Twentieth Armies to break out. On August 1, Rokossovsky was able to effect this breakout by coordinating his forces with those trapped inside the encirclement, surely one of the most difficult and risky of maneuvers.

In the course of the battles near Smolensk, the Western Front suffered heavy losses. By the beginning of August no more than 2,000 men remained in any of its divisions; 184,000 Soviet soldiers were taken prisoner in July.

As a result of the steady resistance of the Soviet troops near Smolensk, Army Group Center lost its offensive momentum and found itself restricted on all sectors. Field Marshal von Bock wrote at the time: "I am compelled to engage all my combat-ready divisions from the army group reserves . . . I am in need of every single man at the front line . . . Despite their great losses, every day the Russians attack at several sectors which until now made regrouping our forces and mustering fresh reserves impossible. If no strong blow is delivered against the Russians on some sector in the near future, then it will be hard to accomplish the task of their complete destruction before winter."

At the beginning of August the STAVKA continued to think that the enemy forces would be used in the direction of Moscow. Since their frontal assault along the most direct route had failed, the expectation was that the Germans would try to envelop the flanks of the Western Front. The STAVKA ordered the troops of the Western Direction to keep the bridgeheads open near Gomel and Velikie Luki, preserving the strong positions on the flanks of Army Group Center and to continue inflicting blows in the Smolensk region at Dukovshchina and Yelnia. In order to strengthen the defense lines protecting Moscow from the west, on July 30 the STAVKA created the Reserve Front along the line Rzhev-Viazma and named Zhukov as its head. By this time Zhukov had fallen out of Stalin's favor due to a sharp disagreement over strategy regarding the Kiev situation, which will be examined later in some detail. Zhukov was replaced as chief of the general staff by Marshal B. M. Shaposhnikov.

We must explain how the Germans managed to cross the Dnepr River as quickly as they did and what they encountered afterward. The point to remember is that Timoshenko and Zhukov were almost, but not quite, ready for Guderian when he approached the upper Dnepr. The Timoshenko-Zhukov timetable was upset by the impetuous Guderian's rapid plunge to the east with no thought given to the difficulties of containing and then mopping up some 300,000

Russians left in his rear; that was for the infantry to deal with. The gap, however, between the fast-racing panzers and the slower foot-bound infantry created no end of problems for the Germans and contributed greatly to later Russian success. Already in the early days of the war it is possible to see some of the differences between blitzkrieg versus combined-arms tactics. The failures of the blitzkrieg will be apparent after a close examination in Chapter 4 of what happened to the Germans when they attempted to hold on to the Yelnia salient with no armored support against resolute combined-arms attacks personally directed by Zhukov.

In Chapter 5, we will discuss the effect of Russian pressure on the southern flank of Army Group Center. The reader can avoid confusion by remembering that many of the events in Chapters 4 and 5 occur at the same time. We describe the events around Yelnia and the action on the southern flank of Army Group Center in separate chapters because the vast scale of the front made it seem like separate wars to the participants. Also, in this way, we believe, it is easier to see the overall effect Russian strategy had in forcing the Germans to make several bad decisions that ultimately determined the course of the rest of the war.

·4·
YELNIA: THE END OF THE BLITZKRIEG

The Yelnia Salient: A Crucible of Fire and Steel
In mid-July, Guderian made a critical choice. He elected not to turn the XLVI Panzer Corps toward the area west of Yartsevo to link up with Hoth northwest of Smolensk. Instead, he aimed for the heights of Yelnia and Dorogobuzh, thinking ahead about Moscow, and in the process forfeited the chance of forging a strong wall around the Smolensk pocket. The availability of an opening leading out of Smolensk to the east saved the Russian Sixteenth and Twentieth Armies from complete disaster and led directly to the precarious situation that would soon develop around Yelnia (the name means "spruce grove" in Russian), a small town 82 km. to the southeast of Smolensk, near the headwaters of the Desna River. The responsibility for the creation of the conditions that led to the battles around Yelnia, battles that raged with such fury that some of the older German officers compared them to their experiences at Verdun in 1916, must be shared equally by Fedor von Bock and Heinz Guderian, although Halder perhaps could be given a portion of the blame. Yelnia is a name that was burned into the collective consciousness of the German army, and the memory of it faded only after the larger disasters outside Moscow and at Stalingrad.

Lieutenant General Schaal's 10th Panzer Division of the XLVI Panzer Corps received orders to take Yelnia at 0900 on July 16, before the battle inside Smolensk had been brought to a conclusion. At this time Yelnia was defended by the 19th Rifle Division of the Russian Twenty-fourth Army. It was not until the early morning hours of July 18, however, that the bulk of 10th Panzer Division could pull up to Pochinok and to Prudki, at the intersection of the Smolensk-

Roslavl and Mstislavl-Yelnia roads. Forward units of the division were held up at Strigino where the bridge over the Khmara had been damaged by a Russian attempt to burn it down. The worries about that particular bridge at least were ended when one of the tanks of the 7th Panzer Regiment crashed through it attempting to cross over at 0545. Because of this and other delays, Schaal decided to hold the division at Petrova-Berniki and attack Yelnia the following day at 1000. The attack had to be further postponed until 1315 on July 19, however, because of the bad roads and the collapse of another bridge. During the night of the eighteenth and the morning of the nineteenth, the Russians had used the delay to fortify an antitank ditch that had been dug across the Pochinok-Yelnia road. Two Russian heavy artillery pieces began to shell the road from a long distance in midafternoon, making the situation very uncomfortable. Later, by 1430, a way was found around the antitank ditch, and the 7th Panzer Regiment resumed the advance on Yelnia along the railroad tracks from the northwest, from the direction of Smolensk. Soon the panzer troops drove into the western and the southern edge of the town.

Hardly had the 10th Panzer Division penetrated into Yelnia when the XLVI Panzer Corps command flashed an urgent message for reinforcements to be sent to help the SS "Das Reich" Division pushing from Baltutino to Dorogobuzh. Schaal replied that he could not take Yelnia and Dorogobuzh at the same time, but the corps commander, von Vietinghoff, was insistent. As a result, parts of a motorized rifle regiment and an artillery regiment, along with one tank destroyer (Panzerjäger) unit, were ordered to take and hold the Dnepr bridge at Dorogobuzh, but it would be an ill-fated attempt, as the Russian defense around Yelnia and along the Dorogobuzh road was too strong.

By 1800 on the nineteenth, the 10th Motorcycle Battalion had cleared the eastern side of Yelnia all the way to the cemetery, 800 meters north of the town limits. By 1830 the church in the center of the town was taken, but a sharp fight was still being waged on the railroad embankment west of the main station. Russian artillery fire now was beginning to pour in at a steady rate from the south and the southeast. Around 2000, the whole south side of the town was under

heavy shell fire from big guns, and the German division commander had to comment, "It is questionable whether we can take and
hold Yelnia." It was not until nearly 2200 that the costly battle around
the railway station was ended and the combing out of the rest of Yelnia could be completed. This final operation was finished within the
next half hour. The Germans owned a crucial piece of real estate,
but how long they could hold it was in question.

It was almost at this moment, however, that the 4th Panzer Brigade
ran entirely out of engine oil. This shortage came about because by
mid-July German tanks were using twice the amount of oil they con-
sumed during normal operations. The dust clouds encountered
on the Russian roads ruined the tanks' air filters and increased wear
on the engines. By July 22 the 10th Panzer Division had only nine
battle-ready tanks remaining (five Panzer IIs and four Panzer IIIs).
All the rest had been put out of commission by breakdowns or enemy action. Now, despite orders to the contrary, Schaal decided to
postpone the push toward Dorogobuzh by parts of the three regiments mentioned. To continue with so many tanks immobilized
would mean his division would have a difficult time hanging onto
Yelnia, much less expanding its area of control. On July 21 von Vietinghoff reported from the XLVI Panzer Corps headquarters that
despite the most strenuous efforts the 10th Panzer Division could not
be supplied with oil or, for that matter, with ammunition, which also
was in great demand. Because of the supply problem and strong Russian presence, with well-emplaced artillery positions, south of Yelnia,
behind the Desna, it was decided by von Vietinghoff and Schaal to
pull the stalled SS "Das Reich" Division back from the road to Dorogobuzh and use it to guard the 10th Panzer's northeastern flank,
while the armor pushed farther out to the east and south. On July
20 a tank battalion of the 10th Panzer Division, along with some infantry, overran a few Russian artillery positions to the east and south
of Yelnia. These emplacements were reported to have been especially
well constructed, with accommodations for both men and horses,
and had obviously been completed for some time.

The infamous "Yelnia salient" had now been created, and it would
soon become a cauldron of fire and steel that would consume the
lives of tens of thousands of German and Russian soldiers. The bat-

tles around Yelnia would be more costly than any the German army had fought since 1918 and reminiscent of that earlier war in many ways. For the first time the Wehrmacht would have to face the Red Army across a static front lined with trenches and foxholes, enduring almost continuous artillery barrages and having to beat back savage infantry attacks, sometimes supported by armor. In the summer of 1941 at Yelnia, it was the Red Army that came out the victor, with the last stage of the battles coming under the personal direction of Georgii Zhukov, an ominous foreshadowing of the fate of the German army.

On July 19 Guderian issued Panzer Group Order No. 3, which stated that "after reaching the area southeast of Smolensk [that is, around Yelnia] Panzer Group 2 will come to a halt for refitting and replenishing supplies." However, on July 20 this order was canceled due to the "changed situation." Guderian was now ready to give his battle-worn panzer group a much-needed rest after reaching Smolensk-Yelnia, but the Wehrmacht had set only one foot inside Great Russia, and the Red Army had just begun to bring the main part of its force into action. Halder and the generals in the field had wondered about the absence of large quantities of Russian artillery in the Bialystok-Minsk pockets, but by the third week in July they wondered no longer. The Russian thunder was on the Dnepr River.

After the formation of the salient there was little else the German armored and motorized units of the XLVI Panzer Corps of Panzer Group 2 could do but hold on grimly to the territory they had won and hope for relief. The marching infantry of von Kluge's Fourth Panzer Army was, however, far to the west, and this army's IX Army Corps would not arrive in the salient in force until July 28, nine full days after the fall of Yelnia.

On July 24, 1941, the XLVI Panzer Corps ordered its SS "Das Reich" Division and its 10th Panzer Division to rectify the defense line around Yelnia and prepare to hold the area as economically as possible, making the best use of the irregular terrain. By 1300 the SS was already fighting off Russian assaults with heavy tanks near hill 125.6. The SS had to defend a long front of more than 30 km. on the northern side of the salient from this hill to Koloshchina, Vydrina, Lavrova, Uzhakovo, and the Glinka railroad station. In order to shorten "Das

Reich's" front, von Vietinghoff, the commander of the XLVI Panzer Corps, decided to pull the motorized infantry regiment "Gross Deutschland" into the salient, also to the northern side, to the immediate left of the SS.

The "Gross Deutschland" unit was particularly interesting. In the German army, at least at this time during the war, divisions were raised in communities and, for the most part, were allowed to keep their local identity. This traditional method of organization was not only intended to keep morale high, but also to ensure bravery: men were less likely to show cowardice under fire if they knew that the stories of their actions would be carried back home to their friends and families. "Gross Deutschland" was, however, composed of men from all over the Reich representing the supposed best of Adolf Hitler's new army. No less interesting was the Waffen SS unit "Das Reich." The Waffen SS was the field army component of Heinrich Himmler's "Schutzstaffel," or "Protection Squad," and, as a rule, its men did not take orders directly from regular army commanders. The beastly activities of this division in France in 1944 have been amply chronicled in Max Hasting's book *Das Reich.*

The northern front of the salient was particularly dangerous to the Germans at this time, for the Russian divisions, both inside and outside the semipocket around Smolensk, were doing all they could to keep open an escape route to the east. Early in the afternoon of July 25, several Russian tanks broke through the seam of the SS and the 10th Panzer Division, three of them penetrating nearly to Yelnia itself. In about an hour this attack was beaten back, with the Russians leaving sixteen broken tanks on the battlefield. Only one German gun position had been overrun, but the damage would have been considerably worse had the Russians sent in infantry behind the tanks. The Russian commanders, especially on the tactical level, still had much to learn, but the Germans would not be able much longer to consider themselves so fortunate. Von Vietinghoff, realizing that the 3.7cm antitank guns his troops were using were worthless against the big Russian tanks, managed to get one 88mm antiaircraft weapon brought in from a Luftwaffe unit. This gun had an extremely flat trajectory of fire, and it could accurately track and score a *Volltreffer* (direct hit) on a Russian tank at 3,000 meters. It and others like it proved to be indispensable for the prolonged defense of the Yelnia salient.

The Luftwaffe also provided welcome support in other ways. Ju-87 Stuka dive-bombers were constantly in action over and around the salient, disrupting Russian tank columns. Later the Stukas would be gone, for they would follow Guderian during his march to Ukraine, and Guderian would not allow any of his units to remain at Yelnia. When the panzer general left, he would not only take the air cover and some artillery away from the salient, he would also remove virtually all the motorized units, critically important behind a static defense to provide a mobile reserve in case of Russian breakthroughs. This was a factor readily appreciated while the XLVI Panzer Corps was within the salient but ignored when the unit was ordered to pull out and head to the south. On the morning of July 26, the Russians hit SS "Das Reich" along its entire front with aircraft and tanks, so the division pleaded for a mobile reserve to be sent by the 10th Panzer Division, which was done in short order.

During the afternoon of July 25, von Geyer's IX Army Corps received orders from von Kluge's Fourth Army to proceed as rapidly as possible to Yelnia and relieve the forces of Panzer Group 2. On the way into the salient, near and to the east of Voroshilovo, the 485th Infantry Regiment of the 263d Infantry Division was hit hard by the Russian 149th Rifle Division. Two German battalions were cut off and had to beat back attacks from all sides by Russian tanks fighting in close coordination with their infantry. The German division had no reserves, and so the battalions were ordered to fight their way out of the encirclement as best they could; they succeeded in doing so on July 27 "after suffering considerable losses in personnel and materiel." The rest of the IX Army Corps began the relief of the 18th Panzer Division and the infantry regiment "Gross Deutschland" to the west and northwest of Yelnia, an operation that was completed by July 28. "Gross Deutschland" was moved out of line to a position in and generally to the west of Yelnia. "Das Reich's" western flank was now covered by units of the XLVII Panzer Corps, including the 17th Panzer Division; these were then linking up east of Smolensk with Panzer Group 3's 20th Motorized and 7th Panzer Divisions. Meanwhile, the V and VIII Army Corps of Strauss's Ninth Army were employing four divisions in rounding up the trapped Russians to the north and west of Smolensk. By the end of July the divisions of the Russian Sixteenth and Twentieth Armies caught in the Smolensk pocket were down to about 1,000 to 2,000 men each. The Twentieth Army had only 65 tanks and 177 guns remaining, yet the battles went on with neither side yielding or expecting quarter. The Smolensk pocket would not finally be eliminated until August 5, when Army Group Center's "Order of the Day" proclaimed that the Russians had lost 309,110 prisoners, 3,205 tanks, 3,000 guns, and 341 aircraft.

After coming into the salient, the IX Army Corps took up positions on the southern side of the front, with the 292d Infantry Division being farthest east, next to the 10th Panzer Division, and the 263d Infantry Division being farthest to the west. The final move by the infantry divisions into the salient was aided by the charitable willingness of General Schaal, the commander of the 10th Panzer Division, to allow his empty trucks to be used for this purpose.

During the next two days, the units of the IX Army Corps discovered for themselves what others in the Yelnia salient had already come to know: that the Russian attacks with heavy tanks could not be stopped with ordinary antitank weapons. Fortunately, the IX Corps had a few self-propelled artillery pieces, allowing it to bolster its front with a kind of mobile reserve. Without these and some antiaircraft guns brought into action at the end of July, IX Corps would have been in serious trouble. Other problems for the corps were caused by the swampy ground around the upper Desna, on the southern side of the salient, and by the thick scrub that grew everywhere and allowed the enemy to creep up to the front lines without being observed. The worst problem that the German troops had to face at Yelnia, however, was a difficulty that became more troublesome every day: the growing power of Russian artillery being moved into the range of the salient. On July 30, the 10th Panzer Division was attacked heavily while trying to disengage itself from the front. The artillery support that the Russians had brought up for these attacks caused some surprise. The 10th Panzer received word from the Luftwaffe that "outside the range of our own artillery large numbers of Russian guns are firing from open country; closer in to our front their guns are well hidden under the low trees." It was taken as an ominous sign by many at Yelnia in late July that the Russians appeared

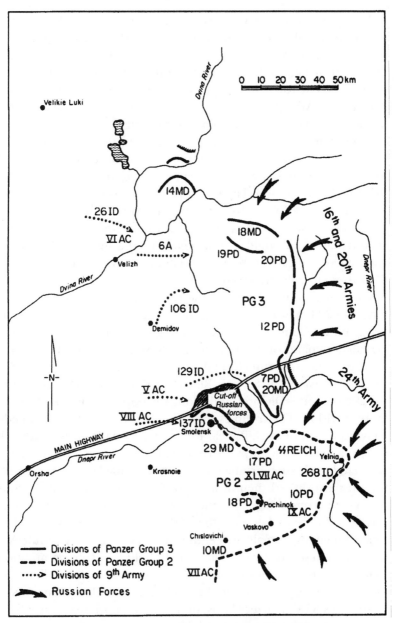

Panzer Groups 2 and 3 on July 27, 1941

to be so well provided with artillery and ammunition behind the Dnepr. It was also regarded as an ill omen that Russian prisoners taken during the attacks on the salient were fresh and clean cut with military bearing, unlike the rather motley soldiers captured in earlier battles. The Russian strategic reserve was already making its presence felt on Army Group Center: so far only the advance elements had arrived; the rest would come soon enough.

When Guderian began to make plans on July 28 for the march southward with Roslavl as the first objective, as ordered by OKH and Army Group Center, he also made provision for two army corps, the VII and IX, to join him. The IX Corps was to push south and east toward Kovali and Kosaki along the western bank of the upper Desna. This would mean that, for a time, the corps, augmented by the 137th Infantry Division, would be removed from the Yelnia salient. It was compelled to return to Yelnia at a later date, however, after conditions there had deteriorated.

On August 8 the defense of the Yelnia salient, now some 30 km. long and 20 km. wide, was temporarily transferred to the XX Army Corps under General Materna, although Panzer Group 2 retained overall command of the area until August 26. Around the perimeter of the salient, starting from the southwestern end, were the 268th Infantry Division, the SS "Das Reich" Division plus one regiment of the 292d Infantry Division, and, along the northern rim, the 15th Infantry Division. The troubles for these units began almost immediately, especially in the hills near Klematina, a small village northwest of Yelnia near the swampy Ustrom rivulet. This area was repeatedly subjected to Russian artillery, tank, and air attacks. On August 10, the Russians shifted their assaults to the Uzha stream, which flows due north from Yelnia into the Dnepr. Here the Russians broke through the seam between the 15th Infantry Division and "Das Reich," retaking a small village. In order to contain this assault, XX Corps had to send 3,000 rounds of light field howitzer ammunition to its 15th Division. Despite this heavy dependence on artillery, the next day the corps was ordered to give up two artillery regiments to Guderian's XLVI Panzer Corps, preparing to move the "Das Reich" Division out of the salient toward the south, along with the regiment "Gross Deutschland" and the 10th Panzer Division, which had already moved out. Materna protested violently against this decision, which he described as "a significant weakening of our defense strength," but to no avail. The Russians now attacked the 15th Division in dense waves, losing heavily in the process but bloodying the Germans as well. On August 10–11 alone, the 15th Division lost twenty officers. By August 11, the German shortage of artillery ammunition was critical, and units of the 292d Division had been pushed off the hills around Klematina. As a matter of urgent necessity, "Das Reich" was temporarily forced to move back into line along the Uzha. The position at Klematina was soon restored without major difficulty, although the corps command had been seriously worried about the integrity of the front lines. On August 13, the rest of the 292d Infantry Division began to filter back into line (having returned from the mission northeast of Roslavl) in order to bolster the beleaguered 15th Division and the SS, whose front had been pushed back 3 km.

When he was informed about the situation along the Uzha and about another breakthrough in the front of the Ninth Army north of Yelnia, von Bock remarked that Army Group Center had no reserves left except the Spanish "Blue Division" (Division Azul) and the 183d Infantry Division, scheduled to arrive in Grodno sometime in mid-August; "From Grodno to the front is 600 kms! . . . I need every man at the front." Von Bock was known to have a low opinion of his country's allies—he had observed that the Spanish were wont to pound their MG-34 machine guns into the ground with shovels instead of using the tripods. There were also stories of their carrying pigs and chickens in their trucks, as well as taking women for rides. As diverting as these tales must have been, von Bock would have done better to worry about the behavior of his own countrymen. In a report by "Einsatzgruppe B" of the SS operating in the rear areas of Army Group Center, it was claimed that 45,467 Jews had already been shot by mid-November 1941.[1]

In a report dated August 13, Materna outlined the situation of the XX Army Corps to Army Group Center, describing the heavy losses along the salient, especially the northern perimeter, and stated that it was impossible to respond adequately to the Russian "drum fire" artillery barrages because of the ammunition shortage. The three divisions then under his command, the 268th, the 292d, and the 15th, had fronts of 25, 14, and 22 km., respectively, in very difficult terrain. At the end of the report, in the gravest possible language, he prophesied that if the Russian attacks were better coordinated and came in larger-than-battalion strength, then his divisions might not be able to hold. On August 14, Materna flew to Guderian's headquarters to plead for help: he asked either to be allowed to reduce the size of the salient or for Panzer Group 2 to send forces to the Desna and the Ugra, south and east of Smolensk. Guderian did not give a definite reply to this request, saying only that the decision would be made within the next two days. The first time the panzer general had been asked to make a decision about maintaining the position at Yelnia had been on July 20 when, in response to a query from von Kluge, he had refused to consider the possibility of abandoning the salient. The next occasion on which Guderian's opinion was solicited came on August 4, when Hitler visited Army Group Center. In order to ensure the smooth running of this conference, Halder had telephoned Greiffenberg, Army Group Center's chief of staff, on August 3 and warned him "to use caution in outlining the Yelnia situation" to Hitler so as to avoid any possibility of interference from the führer. Halder did not need to worry about what Guderian would say about Yelnia, however. The panzer general told Hitler that Yelnia was indispensable for a future operation against Moscow, and even if an offensive against Moscow were not envisioned, "the maintenance of the salient still remains a question of prestige." This was the second time that Guderian had referred to the Yelnia salient as being important for certain metaphysical reasons, such as troop morale or prestige, but Hitler would not listen to any such talk from one of his generals; in his words, "Prestige cannot be permitted to influence the decision at all." In his memoirs Guderian mentioned only the first part of his argument—that Yelnia had importance for future operations against Moscow. Hitler, however, was unable to decide the question about Yelnia immediately, and so a final decision was postponed. On August 14, however, after his confrontation with Materna, Gu-derian realized that something had to be done.

In a telephone conversation with von Bock on this same day, Guderian said that Yelnia could be held only if (1) the Russians were pushed back to the edge of the great forest east of the Desna, (2) much more ammunition was made available for the salient, and (3) the Luftwaffe concentrated strong forces for use against the Russians around Yelnia. Von Bock decided to pass this thorny problem on to OKH, telling Brauchitsch essentially what he had heard from Guderian but adding that he doubted that a short push over the Desna would help Yelnia at all. Von Bock also said that he could do nothing more about either the ammunition supply or the Luftwaffe, the latter being in Hermann Göring's province. Brauchitsch promised an early answer.

Late in the afternoon Halder telephoned Greiffenberg at Army Group Center and notified him that OKH would leave the final decision about Yelnia to von Bock, although Halder was of the personal opinion that the salient should be held "because it is harder on the enemy than it is on us." The OKH also left open the possibility of Army Group Center pushing farther east, a possibility that von Bock was "overjoyed" to hear. When von Bock contacted Guderian the next day to ask his advice, the panzer general said the salient should continue to be held, although two infantry divisions of the IX Army Corps would have to relieve two of his motorized divisions there. Another infantry division could be held behind the salient in reserve. In his memoirs Guderian noted that his plan to push his panzer group to the northeast toward Viazma was rejected by OKH on August 11 and that soon after that he advocated giving up the Yelnia salient, thus attempting to rid himself of any responsibility for this bloody affair. Notations after August 11 in von Bock's diary and in the diary of Guderian's own panzer group, however, contain no such record that the panzer general wanted to abandon Yelnia. On the contrary, Guderian's advice to von Bock was key to the question of holding the salient. The decision to hold on to Yelnia had thus firmly been made by mid-August, but no one from OKH or Panzer Group 2 had any reason for doing so other than that the Russians were wasting more lives there than the Germans—a true reversion to Falkenhayn's strategy at Verdun in 1916—or that the location was valuable to hold in case another immediate offensive operation were to be carried out against Moscow, a decision that had been repeatedly put off by Hitler. It is also a sad commentary on the state of German military planning in 1941 that some generals advocated maintaining a position for reasons of prestige. To say that Yelnia was a costly blunder would be to minimize its true horror; it would also ignore the skill and perseverance of Georgii Zhukov.

On August 15 at 1030 the IX Army Corps received orders from Panzer Group 2 to move both of its divisions, now the 137th and 263d Infantry Divisions, back into the Yelnia salient to relieve the elements of SS "Das Reich" Division and infantry regiment "Gross Deutschland," both belonging to Guderian's XLVI Panzer Corps. The panzer corps provided trucks to hurry the infantry into place on the northern side of the salient west of the Uzha. In the area of the XX Army Corps, IX Corps' neighbor to the east, the 78th Infantry Division was brought in on August 16 to replace the badly mauled 15th Infantry Division. By August 17, after the XX Army Corps had been in the salient only one week, its three divisions had lost 2,254 men, including 97 officers.

Taking notice that his IX Army Corps had a 40 km. front and that the infantry units lacked the mobility to react to crises along it (the XLVI Panzer Corps was mobile), General von Geyer on August 18 urgently requested Panzer Group 2 to send some self-propelled artillery and heavy artillery units back into the salient. This request was prompted by the fact that on the previous day Panzer Group 2 had ordered nearly all of the heavy artillery and the engineers taken away from the XX Army Corps. It was the opinion of the chief of staff of the XX Corps that this loss of artillery and engineers, plus the casualties the corps had suffered, had weakened the front. On August 20 General Materna drove to see Guderian near Roslavl to tell him personally about the "extremely difficult and threatening situation" faced by the XX Army Corps. The only concession Guderian was willing to make was that the 268th Infantry Division on the southeastern side of the salient would not have to undertake the immediate relief of 10th Panzer Division to the south of the XX Corps. Guderian would not relent on the question of artillery—it had to be moved elsewhere. At noon on August 22, von Kluge's Fourth Panzer Army officially took command over the three army corps within the salient, the IX on the northern and western sides, the XX on the eastern and southern sides, and the VII along the Desna front leading to the

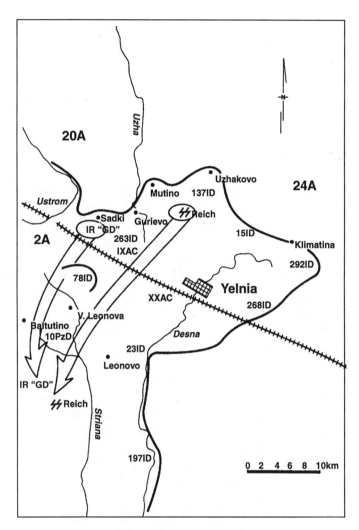

The Yelnia Salient, August 17, 1941

south. Since von Kluge was ill, however, Guderian retained command over the salient until August 26.

On August 23 the 263d Infantry Division of the IX Army Corps lost 150 men repulsing a penetration at a hill, Chimborasso, accompanied by a heavy Russian artillery barrage. This division was in a bad position because it was located on the extreme northwestern corner of the salient, at the "neck of the bottle" the Russians were trying to break off. The division lost a hundred men a day for the five days it was in the salient. By August 24 the line strength of the division's infantry companies had dropped to thirty to forty men. Geyer pleaded for the 15th Infantry Division to be sent back into the salient to help the 263d, but this request was shelved until von Kluge could return and make a decision.

On August 25 the 263d Division suffered another penetration south of Chuvashi, which it could not rectify. Russian artillery continued to rain shells at a steady rate, the division losing more than 200 men that day. Meanwhile, von Bock refused to allow the self-propelled artillery of "Das Reich" to return to the salient, although other heavy artillery batteries were sent. The self-propelled artillery units were supposed to remain with "Das Reich" and "Gross Deutschland" because they were supposed to move south to join the rest of Panzer Group 2, and Guderian did not want to split up his mobile units. Von Bock did agree to allow the 263d Division to have the artillery from the 15th Division, but this was only a small help. During the next day, the 263d Division lost another 150 men trying to repair the ruptured front line at Chuvashi. This carnage had to stop, and so both Materna and Geyer flew to see von Kluge at Minsk, the field marshal having just returned to duty, and convinced him that he should visit the salient and gain a firsthand impression.

The first result of von Kluge's visit to the front on August 27 was that the 15th Infantry Division was sent immediately to the relief of the 263d Division, which by then was down to 25 to 50 men in each of its companies. Before leaving its sector of the front for refitting, the 263d Division finally managed to restore the old front line south of Chuvashi, the Russians leaving 300 dead behind. The second result of von Kluge's visit to the IX and XX Army Corps was that the next day he drafted a report to von Bock with the forecast that if the Russians ceased attacking only in battalion strength and instead mounted assaults with whole divisions, concentrating on a small area, then, with their bountiful artillery support, they would succeed in permanently cracking the German front. Von Kluge went on to say that Yelnia was originally taken by Panzer Group 2 as an offensive measure and that the position was very difficult for defense. Each division in the salient was losing 50 to 150 men a day, and only one road led out of the salient to the west, through a zone only 18 km. wide under German control. Von Kluge recommended either rapidly resuming the offensive toward Moscow or giving up the salient.

The conditions von Kluge surveyed on the front lines of his army were indeed depressing. There were no trenches as there had been in the First World War; instead the defense at Yelnia was conducted using "a string of pearls" kind of dugout system, with each small dugout holding one or two men and being spaced 10 to 20 meters apart. In most areas there was no depth to the line, such as in the area of the XX Army Corps' 78th Infantry Division, which was compelled to hold an 18-km. front. No company or division had any reserves, and the enemy was able to creep up to within 25 meters of the German lines. As a result of the close contact with the enemy, movement by daylight was impossible, and all but the most essential movement was prohibited at night, for it was then that the Russians were most likely to attack. Barricade and construction work of any kind was also hindered, and food could be supplied to the dugouts only at night with attending risk. The men in the dugouts had little contact with their comrades to the rear and to either side, a condition that made for shaky morale. During four days' fighting up to August 26, the 78th Infantry Division had lost 400 men, and the overall casualty rate since the beginning of the war was 30 percent for the division. Most of the losses were caused by twenty-five to thirty Russian guns firing with an "unlimited" ammunition supply. A daily average of 2,000 shells fell on the 78th Division, and 5,000 shells rained down on the night of August 24–25, mostly of 120–170mm caliber. Two 210mm guns were also used, along with many heavy mortars, with telling effect. The Russians were using excellent sighting and ranging techniques and frequently changing the positions of their batteries. On August 26 the commander of the 78th Division, General Gallenkamp, predicted that the division would be "used up" very soon. Similar reports flowed in to Fourth Army headquarters virtually every day. The older officers in the field considered the unsteady static front (*unruhige Stellungsfront*) situation at Yelnia to be worse than conditions during the First World War and wanted either to resume the offensive or to give up the position. Merely to hold it for reasons of prestige was asking too much.

Zhukov Closes the Trap

In late July 1941, after a disagreement with Stalin over strategy (to be explained later), G. K. Zhukov was removed from his post as chief of the general staff and replaced by B. M. Shaposhnikov, who had been the supreme command's representative at the Western Front opposite Army Group Center. Zhukov was demoted and given command of Bogdanov's Reserve Front, receiving from Stalin the mission of rubbing out the Yelnia salient. He arrived to take up his new assignment in early August. After taking the measure of the job and his resources, Zhukov decided to postpone any major action until later when reinforcements could be brought up to support K. I. Rakutin's Twenty-fourth Army. The main assault on the salient by three Russian divisions was not to begin finally until August 30. All other attacks up to this time were only probing efforts to pinpoint the enemy's artillery positions and find the weak spots in the German defenses. Although these small attacks were not calculated to produce big results, they nevertheless caused the Germans many difficulties, especially the XX Army Corps. When Zhukov's main effort began, he departed from the tactic of using only battalions in the assault. The Russians would now attack with entire divisions, with armor and artillery support on small fronts. It was this kind of pressure that finally forced the German lines to give way. These tactics were again used with great effectiveness during the later war years.

The breakthrough of the German defenses was to be undertaken by nine of the Twenty-fourth Army's thirteen rifle divisions, while four other divisions maintained defensive positions on the eastern side of the Uzha. The decisive offensive operation was to be carried out by the troops west of the Uzha on the northern rim of the salient, where the 102d Tank Division and the 107th and 100th Rifle Divisions were located. These units had the greatest strength and were deployed on a narrow 4.5-km. front. The southern group was composed of the 303d Rifle and the 106th Motorized Divisions, but these units had to move against a front of 8 km. around Leonova. Two rifle divisions, the 19th and the 309th, were positioned due east of the

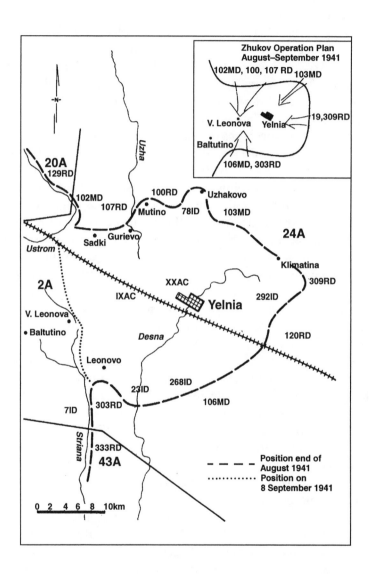

Russian Victory at Yelnia

salient and assigned the task of pushing straight in toward Yelnia from its leading edge.

The main assault was launched early on August 30 with infantry attacks in certain key areas; then at 0730 all of the Twenty-fourth Army's 800 guns plus many mortars and some Katiusha rocket launchers opened fire on the salient. The artillery density achieved by Zhukov at Yelnia was 60 guns and heavy mortars per kilometer of front, or two to three times more than during the earlier counteroffensives around Smolensk in August. After the artillery preparation, close support tanks with infantry following behind them began to move out against the enemy's positions. Some 60,000 Russian soldiers were flung against 70,000 Germans, who were well dug in although spread very thinly along a 70-km. front. Under withering fire from the Germans, the advance was lucky to progress only 1.5 km. in some sectors. Due to insufficient reconnaissance of the enemy's position, the attacks continued to make slow progress. Other problems for the Russians now emerged; the artillery ammunition was virtually used up and the troops were totally exhausted after four days of the bitterest kind of fighting at close quarters.

After the German 263d Infantry Division, with the help of the 15th Infantry Division, had repaired the crack in the front at Chuvashi, no one seriously expected the Russians to resume the offensive immediately. During the early-morning hours of August 30, however, the eastern flank of the 137th Infantry Division on the northern rim of the salient was hit by a surprise attack carried out without any advance artillery preparation. The Russians first made a small break in the German front along the Uzha. Later, the 137th Infantry Division was pounded by a three-hour artillery barrage, and six Russian battalions succeeded in opening a bigger gap in the German front at Sadki, northwest of Yelnia and east of the Ustrom. In this attack some Russian tanks penetrated 1 km. behind the German front, overrunning several machine-gun emplacements in the process. The Germans temporarily lost Sadki but regained it by early dawn of August 31. Still early in the morning of August 31, Zhukov renewed the pressure on Sadki, this time with forty tanks, which were well handled in close cooperation with infantry. Instead of bursting into the German rear areas alone, where they could be picked off singly by direct artillery fire, the Russian tanks this time remained in the frontline area and systematically rolled over the German weapons positions. This was where the German infantry dearly paid for its lack of self-propelled artillery, which could have played a vital role in the defense of Yelnia. In the words of the commander of the IX Army Corps, von Geyer: "The IXth Army Corps could have been spared the loss of hundreds of lives and our achievements would have been much greater . . . had our indispensable self-propelled unit not been taken away from us."

The new penetration at Sadki and farther east widened the gap in the German front to 3 km. and pushed the salient front inward by 2 km. The German commanders now believed that the Russians were trying to pinch in the sides of the salient, from the north along the Uzha and in the south against the 268th Infantry Division of the XX Army Corps at Leonova. Actually, the attacks against the 268th Division in the south were only designed to draw German reserves, if any, in the wrong direction while the major blow fell along the Uzha. The Germans believed that the Russians were using poor tactics, failing to coordinate their assaults on both sides of the salient, but Zhukov had not made this mistake. The German army would have a lot to learn from Zhukov during the coming months.

While the IX Army Corps had its hands full on the eastern bank of the Uzha, the XX Army Corps was also experiencing extreme difficulties along the other side of the stream. On August 31 the 78th Infantry Division was hit hard north of Gurev and had to pull back 2 km. On September 1 the Russians reached Voloskovo and cut the railroad to its south. Some Russian units in this area, with infantry and tanks, crossed behind the 78th Division's front and penetrated into the rear area of the 292d Infantry Division farther to the east, destroying some supplies. The 292d was already hard pressed trying to control another Russian penetration south of Vydrina, on the northeastern side of the salient at its juncture with the 78th. On September 2, the operations chief of the 292d reported to the XX Army Corps that the division "was close to the limit of endurance." Not only could the gap at Vydrina not be closed, but the Russian group at Voloskovo in the 78th Division area immediately to the west of the 292d Division could not be dislodged. Thus, the entire northwestern flank of the XX Army Corps was in danger of crumbling inward, and the eastern flank of the IX Army Corps was under the same threat.

In his memoirs Zhukov singled out the Voloskovo action for special attention. A rifle regiment of the 107th Rifle Division led by I. M. Nekrassov particularly distinguished itself by continuing to hold out for three days while completely surrounded. In order to close the gap at Vydrina and recapture hill 240.3, General Materna of the German XX Corps ordered every artillery battery in the salient to direct fire at the target for twenty minutes. By committing its last reserves, the 292d Division retook hill 240.3 during the evening of September 2, but it was obvious to all that the XX Corps had been strained to the limit. The IX Corps, too, had suffered heavily. The 137th Infantry Division on August 30–31 lost 500 men and another 700 on September 1. In all, since coming into the salient the division had suffered at least 3,000 casualties. On September 2 the commander of the 78th Infantry Division, Gallenkamp, reported that he believed the 137th Infantry Division was "fully used up" and could no longer repulse a Russian attack. These sympathies were echoed on the same day by von Geyer, who stated that during the past ten weeks each infantry regiment of the XX Army Corps had lost 1,000 men, including 40 officers. He urgently requested that infantry no longer be used in critical areas without armored support.

On September 2 Halder and Brauchitsch flew to Army Group Center headquarters at Borisov to review the situation with von Bock. No one at this conference had any idea when the advance on Moscow could be resumed; that project would depend on several factors beyond the control of OKH. Halder was inclined to leave the question of whether Guderian's Panzer Group 2 could cooperate with Army Group Center in the advance on Moscow up in the air for the moment. At this time, Halder viewed either a closer-in solution in which Guderian would cooperate directly with Army Group Center or a wider-ranging solution in which he would drive directly from the south toward Moscow on his own if possible. In any event, everyone agreed that no offensive eastward could take place before the end of September, and so a final withdrawal was ordered from the Yelnia salient.

The actual task of pulling out of the salient devolved on von Kluge, and he immediately set to work to confer with the commanders and the staffs of the IX and XX Corps. The withdrawal would take place in three stages: (1) during the night of September 4 the rearward services and supply units would retreat; (2) during the night of September 5 the troops farthest east would pull back to the west of Yelnia; and (3) during the night of September 6 all forces would complete the move westward and take up new positions along the Striana-Ustrom front.

Early on the morning of September 5, the last elements of the 78th Infantry Division east of the Uzha, including fragments of the 137th Division that had been separated from their unit, began to move around the Sadki bulge ("the Russian dumpling") toward the west. The Russians in Sadki probed lightly here and there, but the 137th Division fended off the attacks. Around 0600 the Russians laid down a strong artillery barrage against the 137th Division, but this ceased by nightfall. Mercifully, as if sent from heaven, the showers that had fallen the day before turned into a downpour, making the ground treacherous for movement but masking the German withdrawal. A thick fog also blanketed the area, making it impossible for Russian observers to detect the opportunity to attack the weak German lines. On September 6, the Russian Twenty-fourth Army reentered Yelnia with the 100th, 103d, and 19th Rifle Divisions commanded by Gens. I. N. Russianov and I. I. Birichev and Col. A. I. Utvenko.

Zhukov reported to Stalin that Russian forces, particularly the tank forces, were not strong enough to cut off the salient completely from the west, but this probably was not true. If the Germans had not evacuated Yelnia when they did, they most assuredly would have suffered an encirclement of their IX and XX Army Corps. Also, had it not been for the bad weather during the last two days of the withdrawal, a stroke of luck for the Germans, the Russians would have been able to inflict much heavier losses on the two corps. The overall cost to the Wehrmacht in terms of lives during the battles around Yelnia in late July and August and early September is difficult to assess from the German records. Zhukov gives the figure of 45,000 to 47,000 casualties, and this figure may be accurate. The six divisions in the salient from July 29 to August 29 probably lost an average of 50 to

100 men dead or wounded per day, which would make for around 9,000 to 18,000 losses for this period. From August 30 through September 3, however, the casualty rate was much higher, and the figures could easily approach those given by Zhukov. This would certainly be true if the losses suffered by the VII Army Corps along the Desna front to the south are taken into account. The total loss to the German army from the battles around Yelnia should not be considered less than three full divisions, a dreadful price to pay for prestige. For that matter, it was a terrible price to pay for a springboard to Moscow, especially since no one knew when such an operation could be undertaken. Some historians have commented on the passivity and slowness of von Kluge's Fourth Army to advance after it reached the Nara River in late November during the Operation Typhoon offensive against Moscow. The fact is that the divisions of the Fourth Army never recovered from the wounds suffered at Yelnia during the summer. Zhukov may not have completed the destruction of the enemy at Yelnia, but he had done his job well enough so that the results of his efforts would be seen in November and December when German armies neared Moscow.

During the Yelnia operations the Red Army learned many things about German tactics, and new ways were devised to take advantage of the enemy's weaknesses. In the first phase of the battles they learned that German mobile units by themselves, without strong infantry or extra artillery support, were not able to overcome a stout defense supplied with ample artillery in rugged terrain. This was the situation that prevailed in late July when the SS "Das Reich" Division and the 10th Panzer Division were unable either to advance along the Dorogobuzh road or to close the gap around Smolensk. These units also could not advance into the high country much beyond Yelnia to destroy Russian artillery emplacements that were already well dug in along the upper Desna. The Red Army at Yelnia learned how vulnerable German static defenses were if they relied solely on infantry and artillery and lacked a mobile reserve. Once the tanks and self-propelled artillery units were removed from the salient, it could only be a matter of time before breakthroughs were achieved that the Germans would not be able to close. It was important also that the power of artillery in modern war was demonstrated clearly to those who might have believed that in a mechanized age cumbersome, heavy artillery pieces had no place on the battlefield. After Yelnia was taken, Zhukov toured the battlefield and was greatly impressed by the destruction that artillery and rocket artillery had produced. Zhukov remarked that the main German defense bastion on the Uzha at Uzhakovo was completely smashed, including underground shelters. This was information that he would file away for future reference, especially for the time in 1944–45 when the battle lines would cease to be flexible and the Germans would rely increasingly on static defenses.

Finally, Zhukov demonstrated beyond a doubt how close cooperation between infantry, armor, and artillery in a combined-arms operation could achieve excellent results against a strongly fortified enemy. His combined-arms tactics on a narrow sector of the front proved that they were superior to those being employed by the Germans. If Guderian had allowed the XLVI Panzer Corps to remain at Yelnia, the battles might have turned out differently, but he did not and so the end was predestined. In 1944 the German army would not have mobile reserves capable of defending hundreds of kilometers of static front, and the end then would be the same.

In several ways, the battles around Smolensk and Yelnia in the summer of 1941 can be said to have been strikingly representative of the entire war on the eastern front from 1941 to 1945. The first phase consisted of wide, sweeping German armored movements covering tremendous distances in a short time yet failing effectively to cut off or surround the Russian armies between the encircling arms of two panzer groups. The second phase developed around stationary German front lines increasingly subjected to stronger Russian artillery barrages. The Russians also used the pause in the German forward movement to accumulate more reserves, armor, and artillery, all the while probing for weak spots in the enemy's defenses. During the third and final phase, Zhukov directed a powerful combined-arms offensive against a vulnerable German position, and the Red Army carried the day. The battles, then, foreshadowed the war of movement leading up to Stalingrad in 1942–43 and Kursk in July 1943, the war of stationary fronts from mid-1943 to mid-1944, and the war of massive Russian manpower, armor, and artillery superiority from mid-1944 to 1945 that crushed all German attempts to create defensive barriers in the east.

It is necessary now to say a word about the Russian high command's defense strategy of positioning the operational echelon behind the upper Dnepr and the Pripyat Marshes immediately after the beginning of the war. At Smolensk and Yelnia the fruitfulness of this strategy was manifest as the pressure on Guderian's southern flank kept Panzer Group 2 from closing the Smolensk pocket. The wise decisions by Zhukov regarding the operational echelon, coupled with the mistakes of Guderian, Halder, and others, all contributed to the German setback on the upper Dnepr in July, August, and September. The advantages secured by the Russians were not permanent, however, and the tides of war would fluctuate before Zhukov could win a decisive victory over the enemy. Also, Stalin's decisions about not allowing the operational echelon to be prepositioned proved to be unwise. The failure of Pavlov's mechanized corps to retard the advance of the two German panzer groups on both sides of the Bialystok salient led to the rapid fall of Smolensk, an omission that, temporarily at least, caused Stalin to react with dire threats against his commanders. Stalin's overreaction led these commanders to waste lives and materiel in uncoordinated counterattacks around Smolensk. These wasteful exercises should be compared with the much more successful and coordinated attacks by the Red Army on the southern flank of Army Group Center and around Yelnia. Planning in advance had made all the difference.

In regard to the strategic reserves, Zhukov was able to call on them for extra divisions during the last phase of the battles around Yelnia. Russian losses at Smolensk-Yelnia were high, perhaps three times higher than German losses, but no permanent damage had been done to the Red Army's strategic posture. The German position in July and August, by contrast, was awkward and out of balance. German flanks in the north and south were easily subjected to strong pressure from the operational echelon, which in mid-July was joined by the first elements of the strategic reserve. These forces did the job of slowing and then stopping the enemy advance. Stalin had been right: full mobilization had not been necessary before June 22; but in late August and early September he would take his biggest risk of the war, and he nearly lost everything for Russia in the process.

At Yelnia, the Soviet Guards were born, with the four rifle divisions that had carried the day along the salient being granted that distinction. For the rest of the war, and in other Russian wars since, the "Guards" designation is strived for, and the men who serve in Guards units do so with special pride.

On September 10, the two-month-long battle of Smolensk ended. Hitler's offensive toward Moscow had been halted. Some historians attribute the fact that the Germans were forced to go on the defensive in this important sector to indecisiveness in the German high command, but the compelling force that stopped them was not Hitler or the German high command. It was the Red Army.

But the Red Army had paid a price. Losses in the ranks were about 300,000 men, with another 200,000 missing or taken prisoner. The tank and motorized divisions of the Western Direction suf-fered disproportionately greater losses: almost half of their personnel and equipment. No matter what the cost, however, Red Army officers and men gained vital experience in coming to grips with the enemy.

The Northern Flank: Velikie Luki

The attempt to block and destroy the northern flank of Panzer Group 3 with attacks led by Gen. Fedor Yershakov, commander of the Twenty-second Army, had already come to grief by July 12. The Twenty-second Army defended a zone of 280 km. with only six divisions. Until July 16 units of the 174th Rifle Division under Col. Andrei Zygin defended the Polotsk fortified region, hampering the progress of Hoth's 18th Motorized Division. But the main body of the German panzer group still managed to break through. Having analyzed the situation, Timoshenko ordered Yershakov "to draw his Army to the rear step by step, calmly, exhausting the enemy. To destroy enemy tanks every division should have special detachments which should be under Twenty-second Army unified command. Their task is to encircle and destroy the enemy." To retard the tanks' progress, the marshal ordered that tank traps be erected with the help of the local populace. Aviation was also to be used. An order was given to destroy tanks with "special incendiary means," that is, Molotov cocktails. But none of these measures was effective in slowing the push of Panzer Group 3 against the right flank of the Western Front.

What ensued now was a contest of wills that took place between Brauchitsch at OKH and von Bock at Army Group Center. The crux of this argument was whether Panzer Group 3 should be sent farther north to aid in the assault against Leningrad, as Hitler wished, or whether some excuse could be found to keep it in Army Group Center, where it could be used against Moscow. The form this argument took is illustrative of how a consistent strategy became impossible on the German side.

During the evening of July 13, OKH ordered part of Panzer Group 3—it was unclear to von Bock what part was meant—to turn north and cooperate with the southern flank of Army Group North to encircle the Russians in the Kholm–Lovat River area south of Lake Ilmen. In order to clarify the somewhat confused directives coming from East Prussia, von Bock telephoned Brauchitsch on the afternoon of July 14 and told him that any such wide-ranging operation by Panzer Group 3 would have to wait until after the fall of Smolensk. Brauchitsch agreed but added that a farther eastward plunge of the tank units was now out of the question and that the mass of the German infantry could not then move far beyond the Dnepr, due to problems of supply. Brauchitsch believed, however, that some sort of armor-infantry combined "expedition corps" could be used to reach further goals, such as Moscow. But the commander in chief did not relent on the question of sending Panzer Group 3 northward.

On July 16, the day Smolensk fell, the 19th Panzer Division was ordered to take Velikie Luki on the Lovat, with von Bock continuing to protest despite his earlier agreement with Brauchitsch that after Smolensk the operation would take place. Also on that day, the 19th Panzer Division captured the city of Nevel and surrounded the LI Rifle Corps, operating to the west of the city. The LXII Rifle Corps was now threatened with deep envelopment from its flanks, so it began a retreat to the northeast, opening the door for the Germans to take Velikie Luki.

The assault on Velikie Luki by the 19th Panzer Division began on July 17. After the Germans took the central railroad station, a Russian train rolled in loaded with tanks, a wholly unexpected gift! On July 18 the Russian Twenty-second Army fought stubbornly to retake Velikie Luki without success, suffering considerable losses in the process.

The rest of the LVII Panzer Corps—that is, the 12th Panzer Division and the 18th Motorized Division, screening the 19th Panzer Division's southeastern flank at Nevel—was not as lucky as the 19th Panzer Division. During the night of July 19, the screening front at Nevel was put under strong pressure by a well-organized attack from the west by Russian units being pushed back from the front of Army Group North's Sixteenth Army. In the early morning of July 20 two Russian regiments broke through the LVII Panzer Corps' front from west to east at Borok. Also on July 19 two Russian divisions set upon Hoth's XXXIX Panzer Corps and with powerful artillery support broke through the front of its 14th Motorized Division south of the Nevel-Gorodok road. The German attempt to surround the Russians northwest of Nevel by coordinating movements between Army Group North and Panzer Group 3 apparently would not work.

After some discussion, it was agreed by everyone except Hoth that Velikie Luki would have to be given up. Hoth later blamed the loss of Velikie Luki on von Kluge and von Bock, both of whom were against the operation from the start because it jeopardized the attempt farther south to close the armored ring around Smolensk. In fairness it must be said that von Kluge and von Bock cannot be blamed for the failure of an operation that they had done all they could to prevent. The real blame, in our opinion, belongs to Halder, for it was he who convinced Hitler that such a maneuver was necessary before the Smolensk pocket was closed. Halder was willing to admit now that Velikie Luki would have to be given up, in spite of the fact that the Russians would turn the city into a strongly fortified position. As Hoth noted, a month later in August, seven infantry and two panzer divisions would be needed to retake Velikie Luki. The order for the 19th Panzer Division to abandon Velikie Luki and pull back to Nevel was given at 0700 on July 20.

On August 14 the southern flank of Army Group North south of Lake Ilmen was hit hard by about seven Russian divisions crossing over the Polist River and driving westward into a gap between the II and X Army Corps. In order to counteract this strong Russian push south of Staraia Russa, Army Group North hurriedly pulled in units of the LVI Panzer Corps to assembly points east of Dno. Although Halder referred to this Russian breakthrough near Staraia Russa as a "pinprick," on August 15 the commander of Army Group North, von Leeb, reported to Brauchitsch that the X Army Corps was no longer able to maintain a front to the east and would now have to pull back the 290th Infantry Division to the west and north. The corps' new front would face southward and would have its rear abutting on Lake Ilmen. The situation around Staraia Russa seemed so serious that on August 14 Jodl of OKW asked for and received permission from Hitler to send Hoth's XXXIX Panzer Corps from the northern flank of Army Group Center toward Staraia Russa. The crisis for the X Army Corps was alleviated, however, by a counterattack on August 19 by Manstein's LVI Panzer Corps of Army Group North, which succeeded in restoring the front along the Polist River on August 21.

Now that the XXXIX Panzer Corps was no longer needed in the Staraia Russa sector, Hitler decided not to return it to Army Group Center but to send it on to the northern wing of Army Group North to aid in the assault on Leningrad. This decision to give up part of Panzer Group 3 to Army Group North was deeply resented by von Bock and Hoth, and it must be said that from their point of view, the splitting up of Panzer Group 3 was largely unnecessary. The sending of this corps from Army Group Center to the Leningrad front would have an important effect on German strategic planning, as we will see later. Again, the baleful effects of the failure to close the Smolensk pocket rapidly enough and the inability of Panzer Group 3 to retain control of Velikie Luki in the third week of July made themselves felt. The gap existing between Army Groups North and Center in mid-August afforded the Red Army an excellent opportunity to drive a sharp wedge westward in the area of Staraia Russa. After the transfer of the XXXIX Panzer Corps to Army Group North, the problem of Velikie Luki again advanced into the foreground, and a solution was undertaken on August 22.

The task of retaking Velikie Luki was given to the Ninth Army and the LVII Panzer Corps of Panzer Group 3. Since August 3 Ninth Army had been occupying defensive positions after having retreated from

Velikie Luki and Toropets. Despite several attempts to organize a renewed assault on Velikie Luki by the 251st and 253d Infantry Divisions of the XXIII Army Corps, the forces of Ninth Army were simply too weak to move against the determined enemy. Halder and von Bock decided on August 9 that no large encirclement around Velikie Luki should be attempted. Instead, a close-in solution with a movement of the Ninth Army from south to north, west of Lake Ilmen, would be undertaken. Panzer Group 3's tanks would not be used directly against the city, because the refitting of these units would require eleven more days. Halder and von Bock hoped that the tanks could be held back from a major battle at Velikie Luki and reserved for a push toward Moscow.

The problems faced by Ninth Army in preparing for an attack by its northern wing were exacerbated by repeated Russian assaults along its long defense front, especially in the area of the Vop River. On August 12 the 5th Infantry Division of the V Army Corps suffered a Russian breakthrough of its front that reached all the way into the division's rearward battery positions. The following week, the Russian Thirtieth, Nineteenth, and Twenty-fourth Armies intensified their attacks upon the German Ninth Army along a front stretching from the source of the Western Dvina to Yartsevo. K. K. Rokossovsky's re-formed Sixteenth Army kept up such continuous pressure on the Ninth Army from around Yartsevo that by mid-August the Russians had succeeded in digging in on the eastern bank of the Vop. On August 18 the German 161st Infantry Division on the northern flank of the VIII Army Corps, which held a front along the Dnepr, Vop, and Loiania Rivers, was flailed by strong Russian attacks, and the division was forced to withdraw from its frontline positions to previously prepared defenses farther west. The V and VI Army Corps were also subjected to some pressure. By August 20, the situation on the front of the 161st was so serious that Hoth, who temporarily commanded Ninth Army because Strauss was ill, committed his last reserves, the 7th Panzer and 14th Motorized Divisions, to holding the line. The 7th Panzer Division from the VIII Army Corps reserves drove into the northern flank of the Russian breakthrough southwest of Frol and penetrated to southwest of Makovia, thus saving the situation along the Loiania and preventing any further delays in the attack on Velikie Luki, although the Russian counterattacks had cost Ninth Army heavy losses.

On August 22 General Stumme's XL Army Corps launched the long-awaited attack on Velikie Luki, with help from the LVII Panzer Corps. The XXIII Army Corps joined in the attack on August 23, and a pocket was soon formed east of the city. The battle for Velikie Luki ended on August 26 with the capture of 34,000 prisoners and more than 300 guns. Immediately after the fall of Velikie Luki, Hoth ordered the XL Army Corps and one panzer division on to Toropets, which was taken on August 29.

The conquest of Gomel in the south and of Velikie Luki in the north relieved the pressure on the flanks of Army Group Center at the end of August. For a month and a half Army Group Center had been stalled in the Dvina-Dnepr area while the difficulties on its flanks were being resolved. By early September the Russian operational echelon in the Dvina-Dnepr area had largely been exhausted, but new formations were already in place along defense lines farther east. Although Army Group Center was now in a more favorable position with regard to its own flanks, its neighbor to the south, Army Group South, had still not broken the Dnepr barrier in force, and the Kiev stronghold remained a formidable obstacle. The path to Moscow was not yet open, and there would be harsh and complex clashes of personalities among Hitler and his generals before an advance eastward could be resumed. The German military high command structure was chronically incapable of formulating clear and consistent plans for success in the Soviet Union. No important strategic decisions could be made without a contest of wills ensuing among Hitler, Halder, Jodl, von Bock, Guderian, and others. One can only wonder how the German army did so well despite such burdens. No army, however, could withstand the ravages of such jealous, egotistical, contradictory, and ill-informed leadership for long. The foundation of the army had already begun to crack at Yelnia under the weight of the leadership superstructure. A virtual collapse would be barely avoided before Moscow.

But the mistakes made on the German side should not obscure the right things that were being done by the Russians. Documentary evidence of the heroic resistance of Soviet troops is preserved in the archives of the Soviet general staff. During the period August 12–30, 1941, according to a dispatch from the Thirty-fourth Army of the Northwestern Front, 2,375 out of 4,434 officers and 4,565 out of 7,764 noncommissioned officers were lost. In the lower ranks, 25,929 out of 42,714 were casualties. This army also suffered great losses in materiel: 24 out of 26 armored vehicles, 349 out of 369 mortars, 600 out of 6,299 heavy machine guns, 782 out of 900 light machine guns, and 36 out of 40 motorcycles were destroyed or damaged beyond repair. These statistics, when they are extrapolated across the total numbers of Russian units in combat, would have spelled disaster had it not been for Zhukov's and Timoshenko's third echelon of defense. Had the strategic defense plan not been implemented, the sword would have been struck from Stalin's hands and the war would have been indeed lost in the first few days.

· 5 ·
PRESSURE ON THE SOUTHERN FLANK OF ARMY GROUP CENTER

The Soviet High Command's Defense Strategy in Action

Using the forces put on near-full mobilization status after the February war game, the STAVKA managed to restore the Western front despite the speed of Pavlov's collapse along the border. The troops of the Front were now under the command of Marshal Timoshenko, commander in chief of the newly designated Western Direction. Timoshenko's main concern was to stabilize a defense line along the Dvina and the Dnepr Rivers, for, as noted earlier, the troops assigned to the Western Front for the operational echelon were not yet completely concentrated due to Stalin's hesitation. The full mobilization of the strategic reserve had also been delayed by Stalin.

Zhukov knew that manpower alone would not be enough to halt the German advance, so by July 14, the supreme command began to deploy the armies of the strategic reserve as soon as they became mobilized along lines east of the Dvina-Dnepr behind the Western Front.

This action, and the movement northward of important units of the operational echelon from Ukraine, represented a partial breakdown of the careful strategy that Zhukov and Stalin had plotted before the war. By July 8 the former tactical reserve of the Western Front had ceased to exist, and what the supreme command had intended to be the operational echelon along the Dnepr-Dvina line was now transformed into the new tactical echelon, with fronts that were becoming rapidly less flexible and maneuverable as German pressure toward the east continued. As a result of the supreme command's decision to deploy the strategic reserve on and immediately behind the Western Front, the strategic reserve would be unable to fulfill the

200

function for which it had originally been intended, that is, launching a counteroffensive as soon as the German army had been halted, presumably along the Dvina-Dnepr line. Now, instead of holding back the strategic reserve and using it all at once against the Wehrmacht in a massive counteroffensive, the supreme command decided by mid-July to use it piecemeal, to deploy it as soon as the mobilization schedule would allow, in order to supplement the armies already on the Dvina-Dnepr line and to establish other lines of defense farther east between the battlefronts and Moscow.

The situation with regard to the large armored formations, the mechanized corps, also had to be brought sharply into focus. The Luftwaffe's work had been so effective against them in White Russia that Zhukov's intended plan to hold the new models back for a counteroffensive by the strategic reserve also had to be given up. Pavlov's failure in White Russia also meant that many factories, including tank factories, had to be dismantled and moved eastward as quickly as possible. For example, the Kirov factory in Leningrad, the Kharkov Diesel Works, and the "Red Proletariat" Factory in Moscow were all moved to Cheliabinsk in the Urals. Eventually, part of the Stalingrad Tractor Factory was moved there, causing the vast complex at Cheliabinsk to be nicknamed "Tankograd."

The combination of higher-than-expected initial losses coupled with production interruptions in key tank factories forced the STAVKA on July 15 to order the breakup of the mechanized corps. A few tank divisions were kept, but most were split up into their component regiments. The motorized divisions were at the same time made into rifle divisions. The goal was to concentrate on building smaller armored units that could be used more easily to support the rifle divisions in a combined-arms role. The point is that Zhukov was forced to fritter away the new tank production piecemeal in order to shore up the tattered operational echelon. Despite this seemingly desperate situation, however, Soviet industry managed to rise to the occasion and produced 4,800 newer model tanks in the second half of 1941. Some western commentators have remarked about the severity of the economic dislocations resulting from evacuations of factories to the east, but it should be remembered that the Russians produced more tanks in the last six months of 1941 than the Germans did during the whole year—3,796, including self-propelled guns.[1] This impressive feat not only allowed the Red Army to keep pace with the numbers of German tanks on the front despite continuous heavy losses, but it also permitted Zhukov the luxury of being able to concentrate 774 tanks, including 222 T-34s and KVs, along the key axis of the Moscow counteroffensive against the flanks of Army Group Center in December. Paradoxically, the enforced reliance on combined-arms tactics and the forsaking of large armored formations proved to be an advantage for the Red Army in the end. In fact, the Germans would have done well to have taken a leaf from Zhukov's book at Yelnia and themselves learned more about combined-arms tactics, especially in defensive situations. Later in March 1942, after an increase in the numbers of tanks, the Red Army was able to re-create the tank corps, which added significantly to its ability to exploit breakthroughs. The basic reliance on combined-arms operations and the close mutual support of tanks, artillery, and infantry was, however, not discarded.

The important strategic decisions made by the supreme command in late June and the first half of July, to strengthen the approaches to Moscow as rapidly as possible with armies from the interior and from Ukraine, should be understood within the context of the prewar strategy. A large, uncommitted part of the original operational echelon was still located in Ukraine, and although Panzer Group 1 of Army Group South had broken through the "Stalin line" of fortifications south of Novograd-Volynskii on July 7, another month was to pass before Army Group South could bring the Uman battle of encirclement to a close. Even though the Southwestern Front suffered a serious blow, its units had performed well, and the major prize, Kiev, seemed to be out of the Germans' immediate reach. The supreme command still retained operational freedom by early August and still possessed the ability to maneuver on a large scale since there were still large forces, particularly in the south, that had not yet come into direct contact with the enemy. In a sense, this relative freedom fostered a false overconfidence in the supreme command. The powerful Russian Fifth Army, operating just south of the Pripyat Marshes and west of the Dnepr around Korosten, did not begin its withdrawal to the eastern bank of that river until after August 21. As the huge mass of prisoners gathered in by the Germans during the Kiev encirclement would show, the supreme command had not yet completely abandoned its hopes of using the operational group in Ukraine to good advantage against the flanks of Army Group Center. It is true that the pre-war strategy had been placed in jeopardy by mid-July, but it was not changed entirely. By mid-July the war was less than a month old and the mobilization of the strategic reserve was still in its first phase. Bigger things could be planned for the coming weeks once mobilization got into full swing. Despite the altering of their strategy, Zhukov and Stalin were not yet faced with a crisis; there was another trump card to be played.

Action on the Flanks of Army Group Center

Simultaneously with the defense of Smolensk, the Western Front launched its much-hoped-for counteroffensive by Gen. Fyodor Kuznetsov's powerful Twenty-first Army with a force of about twenty divisions against the southern flank of Army Group Center on July 13. General Kuznetsov had been handpicked by Timoshenko and Zhukov to lead the counterattack, and he had been one of the select few to attend the clandestine February war game. A major role in this counteroffensive was played by the VI Rifle Corps under Gen. Leonid Petrovsky. On the first day, the corps crossed the Dnepr using boats and temporary bridges and recaptured Rogachev and Zhlobin. These were the first cities retaken from the Germans in the course of the war. In these battles the 154th Rifle Division commanded by Col. Yakov Fokanov particularly distinguished itself in suppressing resistance near Zhlobin.

Advancing along with Petrovsky's corps was the LXVI Rifle Corps of General Rubtsev. Its 232d Rifle Division commanded by Gen. Sergei Nedvigin exploited the cover of the dense forest, advanced almost 80 km., and captured a crossing of the Berezina. These attacks did not immediately concern Guderian, who was determined to continue his plunge eastward with few or no interruptions. The "big picture" in his mind was to capture Moscow; the Russian pressure on the southern flank of Army Group Center and Panzer Group 2 could be considered meddlesome but not overly threatening. This fundamental belief among the German high command that the Russians were still suffering from surprise and shock and had no coherent strategy or ability to coordinate on a broad scale was eventually fatal to their cause.

The events on the southern flank of Army Group Center were critical, for it was here and at Yelnia where the Zhukov-Timoshenko strategy first began to manifest itself and succeed. An important aspect of the Twenty-first Army's counterattack was the effect it had on overall German strategy. What follows is an account taken from German sources showing how serious the Russian pressure was on the southern flank of Army Group Center and how, even though Guderian tried to ignore the threat for as long as possible, his subordinate commanders, such as Geyr von Schweppenburg of the XXIV Panzer Corps, were not able to deal effectively with the crisis. The situation on the southern flank grew so desperate that Guderian's superiors at OKH, Halder in particular, were forced to respond in ways that Guderian did not want to admit were necessary and that he considered prejudicial to the whole eastern campaign and the Moscow operation in particular.

Guderian's XXIV Panzer Corps reported early in the morning of July 16 that the 1st Cavalry Division had to repulse repeated assaults by one or two Russian divisions on both sides of the Dnepr 8 km. south of Stary Bykhov. The panzer corps also reported that the 10th Motorized Division on the eastern side of the Gomel-Mogilev road was being pressed hard from a northerly direction. The commander of the corps, Geyr von Schweppenburg, urgently requested that the infantry of the XII Army Corps from von Weichs's Second Army be brought up immediately or else the corps was in danger of losing its rearward communications. The next day Guderian telephoned von Kluge and asked him if part of the XII Army Corps could not be used to attack Mogilev and thus relieve the XXIV Panzer Corps. The commander of the Fourth Panzer Army had to decline this proposal because the XII Army Corps was already being turned southward to deal with problems on its own flank.

The difficulty confronting von Weichs and his Second Army staff was that too many demands were being made on his infantry by too many people and all at the same time. Von Weichs needed the XII Army Corps badly at Stary Bykhov in order to close a gap that had

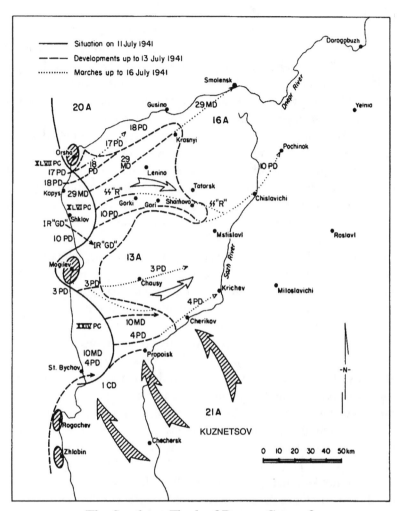

The Southern Flank of Panzer Group 2

opened up between it and the LIII Army Corps, the latter unit having its own hands full contending with Russian units crossing to the western bank of the Dnepr in the region of Novy Bykhov. In the early afternoon of July 16, the LIII Army Corps estimated that it was being assailed by seven Russian divisions and could not hold out much longer. Although the XII Army Corps reached Stary Bykhov just in the nick of time after a strenuous forced march, the Russians still managed to push west of Rogachev on July 18 and retake Strenki from the 167th Infantry Division with rolling artillery fire and tanks.

By July 18, Second Army had to deal with four groups of Russians: (1) a weak group that penetrated through the Pinsk swamps; (2) two divisions, including one motorized, that attacked to the south of Bobruisk; (3) the Zhlobin-Rogachev group, which pinned down the LIII Army Corps; and (4) the Russian units bypassed by Panzer Group 2 at Novy Bykhov and Mogilev, also west of the Dnepr. The third (Zhlobin-Rogachev) group had powerful artillery support and was being strengthened by additional units brought up from Gomel; its strength was estimated at eight or nine divisions, with more on the way. There were also more Russians around Shklov, Kopys, and Orsha. This situation seemed so serious to von Weichs that he urgently recommended that Gomel be taken at once, or else the flank of the Second Army would continue to be imperiled. Meanwhile, as he said, the Russians would be able to bring up more reinforcements against the XXIV Panzer Corps at Propoisk.

When von Bock learned of von Weichs's request, he turned a deaf ear to it and said that the task of the army was to cross the Dnepr and push to the northeast, toward Smolensk and Moscow, leaving "only the bare minimum protection for the southern flank." Von Bock then issued von Weichs a written order for the Second Army to move its main force to the northeast and to turn the XII Army Corps to the south only insofar as it was "absolutely necessary." Von Bock concluded by referring to the Russian units on Guderian's southern flank as being only "makeshift units" and expressed his belief that the threat to the southern flank of the Second Army was overestimated. Now the Second Army would be permitted only to screen itself from the direction of Gomel, and the bulk of the IX, XIII, and VII Army Corps would have to move toward the northeast.

While the infantry corps of the Second Army were still preparing to cross the Dnepr, Guderian's XXIV Panzer Corps continued in a state of unrelieved crisis. The corps command fully expected the Russians to cross the Sozh between Propoisk and Krichev and cut off all German units east of the Sozh. Already by July 19, the 1st Cavalry Division had sustained a Russian breakthrough 10 km. southeast of Stary Bykhov. On this day the Russians made a continuous attack with tanks and artillery all along the front of the 10th Motorized Division of the XXIV Panzer Corps at Propoisk, and the division was now very close to the end of its ammunition supply. Guderian put in another request to von Kluge for the help of the XII Army Corps, but the commander of the Fourth Panzer Army was powerless; von Bock had already made his decision. This request for infantry was renewed again on July 21, this time directly from the 10th Motorized Division, but von Weichs replied that he would not turn another division to the south without an express order from Army Group Center. Guderian noted in his panzer group's war diary that the battered German troops at Propoisk "regarded with bitterness" the fact that the XII Army Corps was not sent to their aid but turned to the northeast instead. Guderian now realized rather bitterly himself that in order to relieve their comrades at Smolensk, the Russians had taken advantage of Panzer Group 2's long, open southern flank.

The predicament of the 10th Motorized Division had become so severe by July 21 that von Bock had to relent and allow the Second Army to send the XIII Army Corps to Propoisk: in his words, ". . . an impressive result for an enemy already so badly beaten!" This relief operation was carried out by the 17th Infantry Division of the XIII Corps on July 23, but the battle still raged on northwest of Propoisk. By July 25, other infantry units from the IX Army Corps had begun to relieve the 18th Panzer Division in the area of Vaskovo, the 29th Motorized Division near Strigino, and the 10th Panzer Division within the Yelnia salient. Guderian's chestnuts had been pulled out of the fire by several redoubtable infantry divisions. For the first time, Guderian was forced to admit that his tanks could not get too far ahead of the slower infantry. On July 22 Guderian addressed a personal letter to von Kluge in which he made a most revealing statement:

> The panzer group is locked in a battle in an area over 100 km. deep and we are forced to operate over huge distances with very poor roads. The securing of the flanks . . . of the widely separated panzer corps has become very difficult and takes away the strength from our spearheads.

He concluded the letter by requesting an infantry corps of two or three divisions to be attached directly to the panzer group that would be used to secure the rearward areas and the flanks. Von Kluge's reaction to this letter has not been recorded, but he must have reflected grimly on the words that he had said to Guderian on the eve of his rash crossing of the Dnepr on July 10.

While Guderian and von Bock were clumsily trying to solve their problems along the Sozh, the battles still raged furiously on the western bank of the Dnepr. The VII Army Corps was given the task of assaulting Mogilev, an undertaking that promised to be difficult since the Russians there showed no signs of giving in. Even though the ground forces had been cut off from the east, Russian planes were still flying in at night and parachuting munitions to the besieged garrison.

The situation at Mogilev, where the Thirteenth Army, headed by Gen. Fyodr Remisov, was operating, proved to be difficult for attackers and defenders alike. After Guderian's panzer group crossed the Dnepr on July 11, the flanks of Thirteenth Army were seriously threatened. The tempo of combat now picked up with sharp firefights continuing day and night. Four Soviet rifle divisions as well as separate units from the 61st Rifle Division and the XX Mechanized Corps were encircled near Mogilev. On July 17 the 3d Panzer Division captured Krichev and appeared in the rear of the Thirteenth Army, encircling part of its forces in the region of Chausa. The Thirteenth and Fourth Armies had to wage heavy combat particularly around Mogilev, Chausa, and Krichev. The total depth of the zones of resistance from west to east reached 100 km. In a fierce battle the troops of Thirteenth and Fourth Armies inflicted serious losses on the Germans. In the period from July 11–17 in the battles between the Dnepr and the Sozh, they destroyed 186 tanks, 25 armored vehicles, 227 trucks, 27 guns, 11 aircraft, 109 other motor vehicles, and many German soldiers. These two Russian armies stopped the German advance at the Sozh River and stabilized the defenses in the sector from Mstislavl to Krichev until August 1 and farther south along the line Krichev-Propoisk until August 8.

The local population also took part in support of the troops encircled near Mogilev. Some 45,000 civilians aided in constructing fortifications after being mobilized by the Communist Party. Within a week they had dug trenches and tank traps in an arc stretching some 25 km. around the city in addition to constructing barricades within the city itself. A "people's guard" of some 12,000 men was formed and given training with weapons for fighting as well as sabotage. On July 1 General Bakunin, who headed the defenses around Mogilev, reported to the Thirteenth Army commander, General Gerasimenko: "For the second day in a row we are waging fierce struggle with an enemy who is much stronger. For now we are holding firm, but we are running short of ammunition. When will more be supplied?"

The encircled troops managed to repel the enemy's attacks until July 26, fulfilling Timoshenko's order to defend Mogilev at any cost. The 172d Rifle Division of Gen. Michael Romanov was extremely active. Together with the divisions on the right flank of the Twenty-first Army, who counterattacked the enemy in the direction of Mogilev from the south, the encircled troops restricted the maneuvering ability of Guderian's XLVI and XXIV Panzer Corps. On July 11–12 the Germans tried to break through the positions of the 338th Rifle Regiment of the 172d Rifle Division, which defended the approaches to the city. In one day of combat the regiment commanded by Col. Sergei Kutepov destroyed thirty-nine German tanks as well as three aircraft, not bad for an army that supposedly had been routed and in full retreat after the battles on the frontier. Guderian had been telling Hitler that the gates to Moscow were open and all they had to do was continue the reckless plunge to the east.

Bloody fighting also took place along other sectors of the defense zone of the 172d Rifle Division. From six to eight attacks daily were repulsed by units of the 747th Rifle Regiment, commanded by Lt. Col. Andrei Scheglov. They kept fighting until their last cartridge was spent.

Having exhausted all opportunities for further defense, the commander of the 172d Rifle Division ordered a breakout from Mogilev on the night of July 26. After heroic efforts, part of the division escaped the encirclement and succeeded in joining the main forces. Many perished under enemy fire. Survivors melted into the woods to continue their struggle as partisans.

The troops remaining in the city kept on fighting to the last as there was no hope for a breakout. To deny the enemy the opportunity to advance to the east, they blew up the last remaining bridge. Doomed to death they fought for still another day. On July 27, the enemy entered the city. German historian Paul Carell states that in the fighting for Mogilev 12,000 defenders of the city were taken prisoner. There were small numbers of officers among them, as they, the author thinks, preferred to perish in combat or to shoot themselves rather than be captured. It impressed the Germans that the majority of the city's defenders fought bravely, fulfilling their duty to the end.

A participant of those battles, Marshal Ivan Yakubovski, remembers that near Mogilev he saw for the first time how cruel and savage the enemy could be. In the village of Stary Chemodany they burned three houses filled with wounded Soviet soldiers.[2] Such acts only infuriated the Russians and stimulated greatly their desire to fight to the death to drive the Germans from their soil. The hero of Mogilev's defense, General Romanov, was badly wounded during the breakout attempt, was captured, and then died in a *Dulag* camp, as did countless other prisoners.

Although after Mogilev another Russian stronghold on the Dnepr had been eliminated and the Germans had a secure foothold on the Sozh to the east (thanks to the timely arrival of the XIII Army Corps), the Red Army showed no evidence of letting up its active defense along either of the two rivers. It still maintained a strong presence on the Dnepr at Rogachev-Zhlobin and on the Sozh at Krichev. In addition, Russian cavalry units were still active far behind German lines, threatening the Minsk-Bobruisk railroad. On July 23 the Western Front troops launched a strike in the region of Roslavl and during the following two days from south of Bely and Yartsevo. Overcoming sturdy German resistance, they made some headway, forcing the enemy to use all of Panzer Group 3 to stop them. The operations carried out by Homenko, Kalinin, and Rokossovsky managed to advance 5–12 km. Gorodovikov's cavalry group enjoyed particular success. On July 24 it broke to the region to the west of Bobruisk and penetrated deep in the rear of Panzer Group 2 and Second Army, effectively cutting their communications. Having no forces to counter the breakthrough, von Bock asked OKH for help. At a loss to do otherwise, Brauchitsch assigned three infantry divisions from the reserves that managed to stop Gorodovikov.

On July 28, the German LIII Army Corps west of Rogachev was raked by a fourteen-hour artillery barrage and a full-scale assault by a Russian division. The XIII Army Corps was subjected to similar treatment after it took over the Krichev bridgehead from the XXIV Panzer Corps. On July 30 the Second Army had to cancel plans for the continuation of the offensive across the Dnepr and the Sozh during the next four to five days because the divisions of the army were 20–65 percent short of their normal ammunition supply.

Halder's concern about the activities on the flanks of Army Group Center was reflected in the conference he held with Hitler on July 13. He recommended that the problem of the flanks be solved before resuming the offensive toward Moscow. Halder's views on this subject were transmitted on the same day to von Bock through Greiffenberg, the chief of staff of Army Group Center. According to Greiffenberg, Halder favored turning Panzer Group 2 to the south, behind the main group of Russian armies in Ukraine, after first giving it a chance to rest and refit in the Smolensk area. Greiffenberg added that Hoth should perform a similar maneuver in the north by turning part of his Panzer Group 3 toward Army Group North. The rest of Hoth's panzer group could be used to aid the main drive of the Fourth and Ninth Armies to Moscow. Von Bock reacted swiftly (as could be expected) to this shift in the wind from OKH. After first conferring with von Kluge, who was still prepared to see Moscow left as the first priority, von Bock dispatched Colonel Schmundt, Hitler's adjutant, who happened to be present at army group headquarters, back to East Prussia with a message to Halder protesting this impending decision. Halder, however, was not deterred from putting his plan into effect, and he dispatched two of his emissaries to Army Group Center. OKH had decided that it was time to make major adjustments in strategy in order to deal with the worsening flank situation. The problem was, however, that some of the generals in the field, notably Guderian and von Bock, still naively believed that Moscow could be taken before the onset of winter.

Vacillation by OKH: Trouble Brewing with Guderian
On the morning of July 21 Brauchitsch and Heusinger arrived at

Army Group Center's headquarters in Borisov in order to clarify the latest views on strategy entertained by OKH. During a preliminary discussion Brauchitsch set forth the first goal as the sealing off of Smolensk and the elimination of the pocket of trapped Russians. Then he said preparations could be made for sending Second Army and Panzer Group 2 toward the south and Ukraine by the beginning of August, a judgment that was unpleasant music to von Bock's ears. During this conversation, when von Bock was temporarily absent from the room, von Kluge took the opportunity to make some disparaging remarks to Brauchitsch about von Bock's methods of command. When the commander of Army Group Center returned, he overheard part of the conversation and flew into a rage, saying that von Kluge had been his enemy for a long time and that his vanity was well known. The origin of the two field marshals' dislike for each other can be traced back to the planning phase of Barbarossa when they argued over the best method for employing tanks.

When Brauchitsch returned from his trip to Borisov that same day, Halder was ready to reveal to the army commander in chief in greater detail his plans for the future conduct of operations by Army Group Center: (1) von Kluge, then the commander of the Fourth Panzer Army, should take command of the southern flank of Army Group Center, that is, over Panzer Group 2 and the southern part of the Second Army; (2) von Kluge's force was then to split off from Army Group Center and push to the southeast and come under the overall direction of von Rundstedt's Army Group South; (3) von Kluge's force would then push eastward with Stalingrad as its ultimate objective; (4) Strauss's Ninth Army would be divided, with its southern wing joining von Weichs's Second Army and its northern wing uniting with Army Group North, which in turn would shift some of its forces to the south, including the Sixteenth Army and Panzer Group 4; (5) Army Group Center, now to be composed of the Second Army and Panzer Group 3, would proceed through Kholm and Bologoe toward the east, approaching Moscow from both the north and south, envelop the city, and reduce it with some help from Army Group North; and (6) Army Group Center would then move its front to Kazan on the middle Volga before the end of 1941. After the war Halder stated that "the ultimate goal of Hitler was to eliminate Russia as a European power in a brief period of time. This OKH knew to be a military impossibility, but Hitler was never able to realize this." As the Halder plan outlined above shows, however, the chief of the General Staff was at least as much to blame for overestimating the Wehrmacht's capabilities in 1941 as was Hitler.

In his memoirs Guderian quotes Halder's words in an OKH memorandum of July 23, 1941, in which the chief of the General Staff set forth his plans as outlined above. The panzer general attempted to show that Halder favored putting Ukraine ahead of Moscow in terms of importance, but this certainly was not the case. Von Bock also reacted strongly to this OKH communique and dispatched an immediate objection to East Prussia, saying that his army group command would become "superfluous" if the proposed order went into effect and that his post should be abolished if his army group were to be split up into three separate groups. In fact, the chief of the General Staff had been forced to take cognizance of reality and change his original plan so as to alleviate the problems faced by Army Group Center on its southern flank and to remedy the difficulties confronting Army Group South in Ukraine. The essence of Halder's new strategy was that by early August a general shift of German forces to the south should take place. Important parts of Army Group Center, including Panzer Group 2 and units of the Second Army, should be sent to Army Group South, while portions of Army Group North should also be moved south to supplement the main drive on Moscow by the rest of the Second Army and Panzer Group 3—some parts of the Ninth Army would remain with the Second Army, and some of its units would come under the direction of Army Group North. Presumably, Army Group North would have to forgo the assault on Leningrad until after Moscow had been taken.

By arriving at this solution at such a late date, however, Halder would have serious problems persuading Hitler to go along with it, for he had already convinced the führer once, prior to July 17, of the necessity of sending Panzer Group 3 to cooperate with Army Group North. This idea had been Hitler's ever since Jodl convinced him of it on the basis of the so-called "Lossberg Study" undertaken by OKW back in December 1940. The setback that Hoth had suffered by July 20 at Velikie Luki would further strengthen Hitler's conviction that the Russians in front of Army Group North would have to be dealt with before any rapid plunge eastward was made in the direction of Moscow. Halder's blunder at Velikie Luki would thus have a double-damning effect, not only on the situation along the northern flank of Army Group Center, but on Hitler as well. The führer had furthermore been unimpressed by Army Group Center's failure to form a tight pocket around Smolensk, a factor due more, however, to Guderian's unwillingness at any cost to give up Yelnia than to any direct fault of Halder's. The course of events had begun to catch up with Halder by the third week in July, for he had already set forces in motion that would shortly prove to be beyond his power to control. Fate would soon play a cruel trick on the chief of the General Staff, but it was of his own making.

On July 27, Guderian and his chief of staff, Freiherr von Liebenstein, flew to Army Group Center headquarters at Borisov expecting to hear that the new assignment for Panzer Group 2 would be to advance either on Moscow or Briansk, but to Guderian's surprise he was told by von Bock that his next order of business, as ordered by Hitler, would be to cooperate with the Second Army and encircle the eight to ten Russian divisions in the direction of Gomel. In Guderian's words this would mean "sending tanks toward Germany." Guderian's reaction to this order was predictable, and it was also a portent of things to come. The panzer general first replied to von Bock that his units would not be ready to undertake any new operations before August 5 and only then if supplies arrived soon enough to allow the repair and refitting of his tanks. In truth, some of what Guderian said did have a basis in fact. On July 29 Panzer Group 2 reported that as of July 25 only 263 Panzer IIs, IIIs, and IVs remained in battle-worthy condition. Up to this same date the panzer group had lost 20,271 men and had received approximately 10,000 men as replacements. Panzer Group 2 had begun the war with 113,500 men and 953 tanks. The overall tenor of his speech, though, was designed to pressure von Bock. Guderian also described the terrain toward the south and southwest as being "impossible" and pleaded with von Bock to allow his tanks to continue east.

After von Bock managed to calm Guderian down, he told him that he would not have to send his tanks all the way back to Gomel on

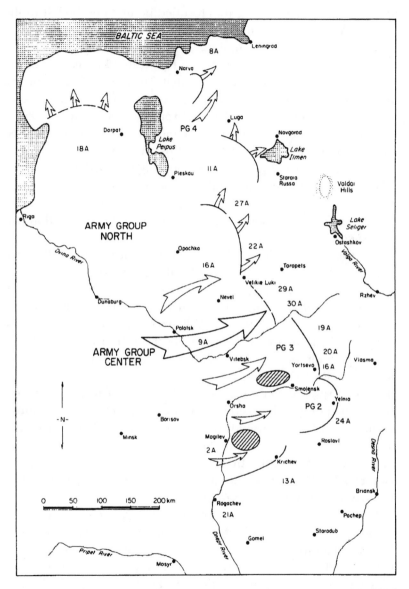

The Situation of Army Groups Center and North on July 21, 1941

the Sozh; the job of taking that fortified point could be left to the Second Army, which, it might be added, was already having a rough time with Rogachev and Zhlobin. Von Bock then broke the news to the panzer general that Brauchitsch had visited him earlier in the morning and that both had agreed that Panzer Group 2 should be used against Roslavl and not Gomel. In order to sweeten the task for Guderian, the commander of Army Group Center further informed him that two infantry corps, the VII and the IX, were to be placed directly under his command for the Roslavl operation.

The pressure was now, at least temporarily, lessened for Guderian. The Roslavl operation was similar to the one that he had been advocating ever since July 20 as the best way to secure the southern flank of Panzer Group 2 in a drive toward Moscow. The attacks that had punished the XXIV Panzer Corps along the Sozh since July 18 had come from the direction of Roslavl, as well as those launched against the XLVII Panzer Corps since July 24 along the Stomat River east of the Sozh. Guderian had already made plans before July 27 to finish with Roslavl before going on to Moscow. It was for this reason that on July 23 he ordered the XXIV Panzer Corps to remain in the Propoisk-Cherikov area after its relief by the XIII Army Corps. There the corps could be supplied with the fuel and ammunition needed to push on Roslavl. Guderian was further pleased by the fact that two infantry corps would be added to his panzer group instead of the one that he had originally asked for on July 22. With this extra complement, Panzer Group 2 would also be able to take Krichev on the Sozh, another troublesome thorn in the group's southern flank. Guderian had at first told von Bock that he would not be able to move against Gomel before August 5 at the earliest. The operation against Roslavl-Krichev, however, began on August 1.

For Guderian, the major confrontation with Hitler and OKH could be postponed until after the Roslavl-Krichev operations had been brought to a close. The panzer general knew well enough that OKH would do what it could to convince Hitler that a rapid drive on Moscow was necessary, but he did not care for the way Halder had outlined his view of things in an OKH communique of July 23. Guderian believed that a wide sweep by his panzer group south of Moscow, perhaps through Briansk and across the Oka, might be necessary, but he strongly disagreed with Halder's plan to take Moscow with only two infantry armies and Panzer Group 3, and to detach his panzer group from Army Group Center entirely and dispatch it to Ukraine and the lower Volga. The panzer general's vanity was much too great for him to endure the slight offered to him by OKH. If Moscow could be taken, Guderian was sure that it could only be done with his panzer group in the vanguard. His self-esteem was well known to his colleagues, and it was a factor that von Bock had already taken into account.

On July 9, before the crossing of the Dnepr, von Bock seriously considered the possibility of moving the armored and motorized units in the rearward areas toward Panzer Group 3, which had already crossed the Dvina and was thus in a good position to drive down from the north toward Smolensk and eastward. Von Kluge's chief of staff, Blumentritt, however, argued von Bock out of this idea, saying that he was afraid of Guderian's reaction at being slighted in such a manner. Earlier, at the time of the operations around Minsk, Guderian had shown himself to be ferociously protective of his units whenever it seemed that some of them, even temporarily, might be taken from his command. The personality of the man was such that before the campaign in France he ordered every vehicle in his panzer group to be painted with a large white letter "G," a practice he continued in Poland and Russia. It would have been better for Halder if he had remembered this important feature of Guderian's forceful character. After the communique of July 23, the panzer general firmly considered Halder to be hostile to his cause, and he would not hesitate to betray the chief of the General Staff in the future if given a chance. Although Halder had not yet fathomed the depths of Guderian's psyche, Hitler knew his man, so he sent his adjutant, Schmundt, to Guderian on July 29 to present him the Oak Leaves to the Knight's Cross. The award earned the gratitude of the panzer general, who was now more convinced than ever that he could manipulate the führer toward his own ends. Guderian used the occasion of Schmundt's visit to ask him to carry a personal message to Hitler stressing the importance of Moscow over Ukraine. Hitler, in the end, was not one to brush off Guderian casually, as he was prone to do with Halder, and this quirk in his personality would have a telling effect later on Halder's schemes and on the course of the war.

The time was near for a momentous resolution of forces to take place between Hitler, OKH, and Guderian. The losers in these struggles were, as they have always been, the men who had to die for their leaders' mistakes.

Guderian and Roslavl-Krichev

The battles around Smolensk in July and August that have already been examined in detail did not concern Guderian as much as did the operations at Roslavl-Krichev, which, in his mind, were absolutely necessary if an advance toward Moscow were to be undertaken. By the end of July, after the fall of Mogilev on July 27, units of the Second Army began crossing the Dnepr in increasing numbers to the north and somewhat to the south of Stary Bykhov. The approach to the Sozh River by the Second Army had actually occurred on July 25 when the XIII Army Corps reached the Propoisk-Cherikov area. More reinforcements arrived when the XII Army Corps relieved the XXIV Panzer Corps in the Krichev bridgehead east of the Sozh on July 28. Meanwhile, well back to the west, the LIII Army Corps still had not been able to cross the Dnepr due to the strong Russian presence at Rogachev-Zhlobin.

In preparation for the assault on Roslavl, Guderian decided to introduce the commanders of the two army corps recently added to his panzer group, the VII and the IX, to his plans for winning a victory. This introduction had an inauspicious beginning when Guderian told General Geyer, the commander of the IX Army Corps, that the "newly subordinated infantry corps, which up to then had scarcely been in action against the Russians, had to be taught my methods of attacking." Guderian noted that Geyer, his old superior officer at the Truppenamt of the Reichswehr ministry and while he was stationed at Würzburg in the V Military District, disagreed with him at first, but after the Roslavl operation began, according to the panzer general, he saw the light. Actually, Geyer took Guderian's comment about his troops being untested in battle as a personal insult. Geyer could not refrain from pointing out that the 137th Infantry Division of his IX Corps alone had suffered 2,050 combat losses since June 22. The panzer general's words with Geyer are illustrative of the attitude that Guderian had toward infantry units. It seemed to be Guderian's position that, since his armored units were always in the forefront of the advance, only they were actively engaged in overcoming the enemy's resistance.

Guderian was not alone in his way of thinking. Infantry units typically were expected to strain themselves to the limits of human endurance in making long forced marches over rough terrain and then defend difficult positions with inadequate weapons. The infantry was no longer considered to be the backbone of the army, and infantry units were more poorly armed, clothed, and equipped and more parsimoniously provided with replacements than any other branch of the military. The OKH constantly overtaxed the infantry and made generally bad use of it during the entire war.

The plan for the encirclement at Roslavl was simple enough to execute. One arm of the trap would be provided by the XXIV Panzer Corps, in cooperation with the VII Army Corps in a push across the Sozh. The armored units were to cut off Roslavl from the south and east while the VII Army Corps approached the city from a westerly and somewhat northerly direction. The other arm of the encirclement was to be provided by the IX Army Corps, in a push due south from the Yelnia salient along the Desna toward Kovali and Kosaki. The infantry of the IX Army Corps and the armor of the XXIV Panzer Corps would later link up northeast of Roslavl, west of the Desna, creating a relatively small pocket; it eventually netted 38,561 prisoners.

The attack on Roslavl began on August 1 with the advance of the XXIV Panzer Corps. The movement of the VII and IX Army Corps did not begin until August 2. Guderian was afraid that the infantry of the IX Corps would be delayed by possible procrastination on the part of General Geyer, so the panzer general went to the corps headquarters in person and stressed to his former superior the importance of cutting and holding the Roslavl-Moscow road. Leaving nothing to chance, Guderian marched along with the troops of the IX Corps to impress upon them the urgency of their mission and the necessity for haste. The panzer general was a strong believer in the power of his presence to inspire his troops to great achievements. Despite, however, the initial success of the XXIV Panzer Corps, particularly "Group Eberbach" of the 4th Panzer Division, which approached Roslavl from the south side on August 3, the IX Army Corps was unable to make fast progress. The 137th and 292d Infantry Divisions tried and failed to reach the Roslavl-Moscow road on August 2, for even though resistance was light, the roads were bad and the 292d Division became bogged down in the swamps around Kostyri. Both infantry divisions, however, succeeded in marching 30 km. on this warm, sunny day. The next day, August 3, the 4th Panzer Division completed the conquest of Roslavl and sent units down the Moscow highway to make contact with the 292d Division, closing the Roslavl pocket.

The sealing of the Roslavl pocket had proceeded smoothly, with few delays or changes in the plan of operations. The maneuver was a textbook case of the results armor and infantry can achieve through close cooperation. The goals were not set impossibly high for the infantry to reach in a short time and, in contrast to the encirclements at Velikie Luki and Smolensk, Roslavl represented a definite improvement of the tactical situation. This is not to say that the elimination of the Roslavl pocket was accomplished altogether without difficulties. On August 5 forward elements of the 137th Infantry Division reached the Desna near Bogdanovo, under harsh urging from Guderian, while the right flank of the division was still trying to maintain the northeastern side of the Roslavl pocket along the Oster against strong Russian breakout attempts supported by artillery and armor. Finally, the Russians did manage to break through on the Oster front near Kosaki in the afternoon of August 5 after the 137th Division nearly ran out of ammunition, faced as it was with Russian pressure from the Roslavl pocket from the west and along the Desna front from the east. Elements of the 4th Panzer Division were ordered to help the 137th Division, but they arrived too late to prevent the temporary loss of Kosaki on August 6. It was not until units arrived on the scene from the 292d Division and from the 137th Division's Desna front that Kosaki was retaken and the pocket finally sealed late in the day on August 6. Closer coordination between infantry and armor could have made for a perfect outcome; nevertheless, the results were good enough, due to the small geographical area in which the encirclement took place.

Guderian was so encouraged by the success of the Roslavl operation that, after an inconclusive conference with Hitler at Borisov on

August 4, he ordered his staff to prepare for an advance on Moscow. During the evening of August 9, the panzer general proposed to von Bock that the XXIV Panzer Corps, then pushing southwest of Roslavl to a position east of Krichev, should reverse its front and advance toward Viazma, to the northeast. Guderian wanted his tanks to press eastward on his southern flank along the Roslavl-Moscow highway while the infantry of his two army corps advanced in the center and on the northern flank. The general direction of the offensive would be through Spas-Demensk toward Viazma. Such a maneuver, according to him, would also aid an advance by Hoth's Panzer Group 3 toward Moscow from the north. Guderian believed that the enemy front was very thin in front of his panzer group and that the Russians here were exhausted and would no longer be able to offer firm resistance. This plan would succeed, he was convinced, because reconnaissance had shown that for a wide area around Roslavl no enemy was seen.

Von Bock, too, was aware that there was a gap in the Russian armies around Roslavl and that the 3d and 4th Panzer Divisions of the XXIV Panzer Corps had pushed into this vacuum, seemingly having found a way open for a further thrust to the east. There were, however, other problems that Guderian either could not see or could not fully appreciate that militated against a decision to allow Panzer Group 2 to drive eastward. To the contention that the enemy in front of his units could now offer only a weak resistance, von Bock replied, "The enemy at Yelnia is not exhausted—quite the opposite." The commander of Army Group Center said that a push from south to north by Panzer Group 2 would be endangered by the strong Russian reserves around Yelnia. Von Bock did not reject the idea totally, but he did say that the forces opposing the Second Army on the Dnepr would have to be defeated first. The Russian pullback on the southern flank of Army Group Center south of Roslavl also made an impression on Halder. He believed it possible that the Russians were drawing all available strength eastward to the line Lake Ilmen-Rzhev-Viazma-Briansk in preparation for constructing a new line of defense. Already, some six weeks into the war, at least some in the German high command were thinking about what to do if the Russians really did have a strategy. Halder's thoughts along these lines would lead him to fundamentally question the tactics being employed by

Guderian. Eventually, these questions would lead to a head-on collision between Halder and OKW on one side and Guderian on the other, profoundly affecting the outcome of the war.

The situation along the Dnepr front of Second Army at Rogachev and Zhlobin and also the still open question of what to do about the Russian forces around Gomel compelled Halder to fly to Army Group Center and confer with von Bock and the commander of Second Army, von Weichs, on August 6. A solution to the problem along the Dnepr would have to be postponed, everyone agreed, until Second Army could build up stronger forces, since at that moment each of its divisions had a 12-km. front to maintain, and only one regiment and a cavalry division remained in army reserve. Halder's opinion, supported by the others, was that Panzer Group 2 should transfer one panzer division to the northern flank of the Second Army to enable the XII and XIII Corps of that army to push southward along the Dnepr and the Sozh toward Gomel.

Guderian, as might have been expected, reacted violently to this proposal by OKH and Army Group Center, maintaining that his units badly needed rest. He went so far as to threaten to refuse to obey orders to give up even one panzer division to Second Army. In his memoirs Guderian defended his objections by saying that the distance from Roslavl to Rogachev was 200 km.—that is, a 400-km. round-trip—and that his panzer units could not have undertaken such a mission, given the need for refitting the vehicles. Sending tanks to Propoisk on the Sozh, insisted Guderian, would have been difficult and would have resulted in an unconscionable loss of time. Guderian's memoirs do not, however, give a true picture of the nature of his resistance to the plans of Halder and von Bock on this issue. Guderian fully realized that something had to be done to hasten the long-delayed advance of the southern flank of the Second Army over the Dnepr, as well as to remedy the situation at Krichev and Gomel, which acted as thorns in the side of his panzer group.

On August 7, Guderian had asked Army Group Center's permission to send the 3d and 4th Panzer Divisions to Krasnopole, east of the Sozh, and thereby eliminate Russian strength on the northern flank of Second Army. The following day, he was ready to send the XXIV Panzer Corps even farther south, past Krasnopole all the way to Chechersk and Gomel. This idea was postponed at the time only because the XLIII Army Corps on the extreme southern flank of the Second Army was still so far back to the west that the second arm of an encirclement would have been missing. The key to Guderian's adamant refusal to give up one panzer division to the Second Army was not a fear that the distance was too great for his battle-worn tanks, for two days later on August 9, as mentioned above, he felt confident enough about the capabilities of the XXIV Panzer Corps to advocate sending it all the way to Viazma, a distance of no less than 100 km. from its grouping points east of Roslavl. His refusal can be traced to the fact that he was resistant to any attempt by any authority to remove armor units from his command, even temporarily. This consistent behavior by Guderian should have been taken more into account by Halder, for it would cause him much grief in the future.

While smarting from von Bock's and Halder's refusal to allow him to proceed to Viazma, Guderian turned his full attention to the encirclement operation around Krichev on the Sozh being carried out by the XXIV Panzer Corps and the 7th Infantry Division of the XIII Army Corps. This operation was begun on August 9 but made slow progress because of bad roads. By August 12, the Russians at Krichev had been fully cut off, but the fighting there lasted two more days, resulting in the capture of 16,033 Russian prisoners and seventy-six artillery pieces. An attempt by the XXIV Panzer Corps to utilize this success and push rapidly on to Gomel came to grief when the 4th Panzer Division ran into a strong group of the enemy at Kostiukovichi. Guderian had lost one round of his continual battle with Halder and von Bock, but after Krichev the victory was his—the situation on the northern flank of the Second Army had been saved without Panzer Group 2 having to surrender any of its units to another command.

The Beleaguered Southern Flank of Army Group Center

The problem for the Second Army along its southern flank at Rogachev-Zhlobin was, however, far from being solved, although hope was in sight. After the fall of Krichev the Russian Twenty-first Army had begun a deliberate pullback toward the east. Now, nearly two months after the beginning of the war, the front of the operational

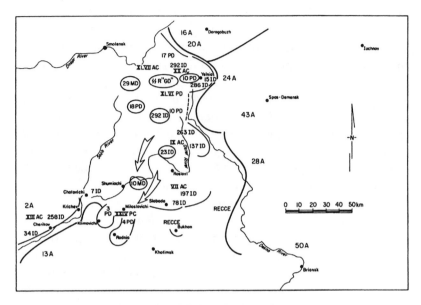

The Krichev Operation

echelon along the Dnepr north of the Pripyat Marshes had begun
to give way entirely, but the echelon had fulfilled its function. New
Russian armies were already manning lines of defense farther east,
and, meanwhile, German Army Group South had not yet cracked the
Dnepr front south of the marshes. The Russian operational echelon
in eastern Ukraine was still largely intact, although some of its units
had been transferred to Timoshenko's Western Front. To Stalin, Kiev
seemed to be an unconquerable bastion that would anchor the Red
Army's flank in the south while the newly mobilized armies of the
strategic reserve could be sent direct to the Western Front. By the
third week in August, Stalin could afford to be satisfied with the general situation, for even though the operational echelon north of the
Pripyat was in its final stage of disintegration, adequate forces were
on hand to counter almost any foreseeable German strategy. Overconfidence in war, however, breeds disaster, and the Red Army had
not yet suffered its greatest calamity of 1941.

By August 13, the staff of Army Group Center had formulated a plan for encircling Rogachev-Zhlobin and solving the thorny problem of Gomel as well. Von Bock now wanted the Second Army to hold the Russians in check at Rogachev-Zhlobin and press on toward Gomel along the Zhlobin-Gomel railroad, although the three army corps that were supposed to participate in the Gomel operation, the XII, XIII, and XLIII, were forced to halt their movements to the south and east because of Russian pressure from the direction of Gomel and because parts of these corps had to be used to prevent the Russians at Rogachev and Zhlobin from escaping eastward. Early on the morning of August 14, the LIII Army Corps moved directly against Zhlobin with its southern wing of two divisions. To aid the initial breakthrough of the Russian front here, the Luftwaffe supplied a squadron of Ju-87 Stukas. By the evening of this same day, these two divisions took Zhlobin after a hard fight and managed to capture both the highway and railway bridges over the Dnepr intact, although the rail bridge was damaged. Meanwhile, on the eastern side of the encirclement, the XII Army Corps turned its entire front westward to face the Russian breakout attempts coming from the direction of Rogachev. The XIII Corps also was unable to proceed southward toward Gomel because the Russians now began stepping up their pressure against its 17th Infantry Division. The Russians used tanks in these attacks, and one assault from the direction of Gomel pushed deeply into the flank of the 17th Division before it was stopped. By August 15 the XLIII Army Corps also had been thwarted in its advance on Gomel even though F. I. Kuznetsov, the commander of the Russian Central Front, had now decided to abandon Rogachev and Gomel. As a result of this withdrawal, Rogachev was taken by the German 52d Infantry Division of the LIII Army Corps in the late morning of August 15, although the Russian rear guard left behind to protect the retreat of the main force eastward toward Novozybkov was strong enough to cause some trouble at Gomel.

By August 16 the German Second Army had been divided into four separate parts: (1) the XXXV Army Corps in the area southwest of the Berezina poised to strike at Mozyr to the south on the Pripyat River (if ordered to do so by OKH); (2) the Rogachev-Zhlobin encirclement front formed by parts of the XLIII, LIII, XII, and XIII

Army Corps; (3) parts of the XIII and XLIII Army Corps moving toward Gomel; and (4) a group formed by the 167th Infantry Division at the Chechersk bridgehead on the Sozh and "Group Behlendorff," made up of most of the 258th and part of the 34th Infantry Divisions, which was moving eastward from the Sozh due north of Gomel. On August 16 both the XLIII and XIII Army Corps were stalled on the way to Gomel, but no forces could be taken from the Rogachev-Zhlobin encirclement front where the Russians were trying to make their escape. During this day, the 267th Infantry Division of the XLIII Army Corps was hit hard by an entire Russian division that succeeded in pushing through German lines between Rudenka and Zavod. Only in a very few cases did the Russians in this area surrender. One company of the 267th Division had only sixty-eight men remaining after trying to fend off the frantic Russian assaults.

In order to help contain the Russians fleeing from Gomel, Guderian decided to send the XXIV Panzer Corps farther south to Starodub, to the east of Gomel. This movement was begun on August 16, also the day on which the 3d Panzer Division succeeded in capturing the Mglin crossroads. On August 17 the western flank of the XXIV Panzer Corps came under strong pressure from the enemy, but the 10th Motorized and 3d Panzer Divisions still managed to cut the Gomel-Briansk railroad. Early in the morning of August 19, however, some units of the 3d Panzer Division at Unecha were hit hard from the west and were soon surrounded by Russians. In one instance a T-34 tank penetrated the German lines and made its way to the Unecha railroad station, overrunning everything in its path. It was finally stopped when a brave lieutenant jumped up on the tank, pulled off the motor grid, and tossed in a grenade. The situation there grew so desperate that some forward elements of the 3d Panzer Division had to reverse their course and head back northward from Starodub to Unecha. Although the crisis around Unecha soon abated somewhat, the road from Mglin to Unecha was still blocked by Russians, and the units of the 3d Panzer Division that were to strike at Novozybkov were held back, prepared to move toward Unecha or Starodub if necessary. Moreover, the XXIV Panzer Corps was dangerously near the end of its gasoline supply, and only the timely arrival of Luftwaffe transport planes loaded with oil and fuel for the corps on August 21

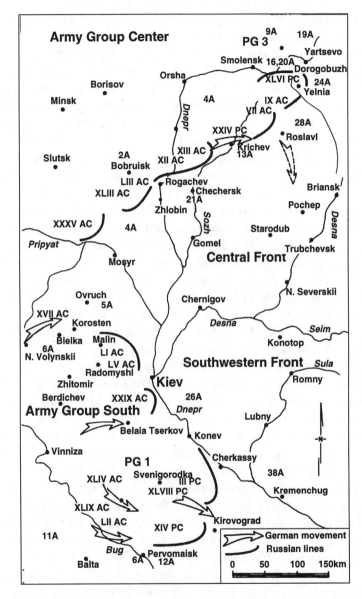

Russian Defenses on the Southern Flank of Army Group Center

averted yet another crisis. Guderian at this point might have welcomed close infantry support for his tanks, as he had enjoyed around Roslavl, but at Unecha such help was far away.

Guderian recalled in his memoirs that on August 17 Second Army still had not launched its attack on Gomel and that the reason for this delay was that Army Group Center had ordered strong units of Second Army toward the northeast, far behind the front of the XXIV Panzer Corps. The commander of the XXIV, Geyr von Schweppenburg, said his troops regarded the tardy progress of the Second Army with bitterness, believing their relief at Unecha should have come sooner. This complaint was identical to the one he had voiced earlier, in the third week of July, when he desperately required relief at Propoisk. The Germans had to pay a high price for operating their tanks over long distances without close cooperation from the infantry, but this was a lesson that Guderian had not yet taken to heart.

As a matter of fact, on August 16 von Bock had ordered von Weichs's Second Army to leave only the forces barely essential to hold the Zhlobin-Gorodets pocket and to press on to Gomel with all deliberate speed. Yet parts of four army corps were needed to secure this encirclement, which by August 18 had yielded 50,000 Russian prisoners. The force that had been sent eastward by the Second Army "Group Behlendorff," left the Chechersk bridgehead on the Sozh on August 16 to provide cover for the northern flank of the XXIV Panzer Corps when that corps was ordered by OKH to turn westward from Starodub and advance on Gomel from the east. For the reasons outlined above, however, the XXIV Panzer Corps was unable to advance beyond Starodub, a failure that cannot be blamed on the tardiness of the infantry divisions of the Second Army, for they were too far behind to offer any assistance. The crisis at Starodub was due to Russian pressure at Unecha against the XXIV Panzer Corps and the difficulties with supplies, as well as the magnitude of the Russian force doing battle in the Zhlobin pocket sufficient to tie down several large German units. Unlike the operation at Roslavl, but similar to those at Bialystok-Minsk and Smolensk, the Gomel operation had turned sour because of lack of coordination between the various arms of the Wehrmacht.

The final assault on Gomel, situated on the Sozh above its confluence with the Dnepr, was begun at 0700 on August 19 by units of the XIII Army Corps that pushed in toward the center of the town from the northwest and the northeast. The 17th Infantry Division was the first to break into Gomel from the west and north that same day, and there the Germans were forced to engage in the bitterest kind of house-to-house fighting. By the early evening, the Russians had been pressed all the way back to the downtown area and into the southern side; they now used their last opportunity to demolish all the bridges over the Sozh. The struggle around Gomel continued for one more day until the Russians gave up entirely. The 17th Infantry Division continued its advance through the town and began to carve out a bridgehead east of the Sozh while the final clearing of Gomel itself was carried out by parts of the 131st Infantry Division.

The results of the operations at Krichev and Gomel on the southern flank of Army Group Center were satisfactory, at least in the numerical sense, to the Germans. The two battles cost the Red Army 78,000 prisoners, 700 artillery pieces, and 144 tanks. The successful conclusion of these battles allowed Second Army to complete the elimination of Russian forces between the Dnepr and the Sozh and thus exert strong pressure on the northeastern flank of the Russian Fifth Army facing the German XXXV Army Corps north of Mozyr. After the fall of Gomel, Fifth Army began to pull back from Mozyr and from the front on the northern flank of German Army Group South, southwest of the Pripyat Marshes. Not only was "the specter of Mozyr dead," according to von Bock, but the victories at Krichev and Gomel, coupled with the anticipated success of the resumed advance toward Velikie Luki on the opposite or northern flank of Army Group Center, meant that "the entire army group can begin again the advance to the east." The Velikie Luki operation this time would bring good results, but whether or not Army Group Center would be able to advance east depended on factors beyond von Bock's control.

The Hinge of Fate: The Halder-Jodl Compromise
In order to accomplish what he now had in mind, the splitting up of Panzer Group 2, the chief of the General Staff had to undertake yet another visit to Army Group Center headquarters, a visit that he saw fit to give only the briefest mention of in his diary. After his arrival

in Borisov during the afternoon of August 23, Halder presented to von Bock a copy of Hitler's memorandum of the previous day and told the field marshal that at least part of Panzer Group 2 would now have to be sent to fight against the Russian Fifth Army and thereby aid Army Group South in its push across the Dnepr. Halder sought to disguise his true intentions and said that the only recourse was to obey Hitler's orders. This was a trick that OKH had already tried to use on von Bock, and he was no less wise to Halder on August 23 than he had been to Brauchitsch on July 27. Previously, the chief of the General Staff had done nothing to encourage anyone at Army Group Center to knuckle under to Hitler's will, and so such sympathies must have sounded strange emanating from Halder. Von Bock was horrified at the thought of trying to advance on Moscow without all of Panzer Group 2 under his command. The battles then in progress around Yelnia were clear proof to him that the enemy was far from beaten along this front. The commander of Army Group Center decided to muster all the resources at his disposal to force Halder to come to his senses, and so he hurriedly summoned Guderian from the front to participate in this makeshift conference.

The panzer general, still in a dusty uniform, and von Bock discussed with Halder at some length how Hitler's attitude toward Moscow could perhaps be changed. The chief of the General Staff gave the appearance of agreeing that the diversion of Panzer Group 2 to the south would be a great mistake and that to use it in an operation east of Kiev would be folly. Guderian told Halder that his tanks, especially those of the XXIV Panzer Corps, which had not had a day's rest since June 22, were incapable of carrying out a broad mission to the south. Also, he said, the road and supply situation would make such a maneuver virtually impossible. Guderian's real purpose on this occasion could be seen in the following comment:

> These facts provided leverage which the chief of the general staff could bring to bear on Hitler in still another attempt to make him change his mind. Field Marshal von Bock was in agreement with me; after a great deal of arguing back and forth he finally suggested that I accompany . . . Halder to the führer's headquarters; as a general from the front I could . . . support

a last attempt on the part of the [OKH] to make him agree to their plan.[3]

When Guderian finished his explanation of how he would deal with Hitler and persuade him to see the light about Moscow, Halder must have believed that he had the panzer general in the palm of his hand. Once it was decided to use Guderian in this fashion, von Bock telephoned Schmundt, Hitler's adjutant, and arranged an interview for Guderian at Hitler's Wolfschanze (wolf's lair) bunker in East Prussia that same evening. The chief of the General Staff had prepared a surprise for Guderian at the Wolfschanze, but it was Halder, in the end, who would find that tables could be turned in more than one direction.

It can, at present, be only a matter of conjecture, but several bits of circumstantial evidence, especially the behavior of the other participants at Guderian's meeting with Hitler on August 23, point to the fact that Halder and Jodl finally succeeded in ironing out a compromise on strategy sometime during the period August 22–23, probably on August 22. The Halder-Jodl agreement called for the pursuit of both objectives, Moscow and Ukraine, at the same time, an idea that both generals had agreed upon earlier. This time, however, since Panzer Group 3 had been weakened by one panzer corps, the XXXIX, it was decided to make up this deficiency by removing one panzer corps from Guderian's Panzer Group 2—the XLVI, then still in the area around Yelnia—and withdraw it behind the front for rest and refitting for use later in von Kluge's Fourth Army command as a spearhead in a renewed thrust against Moscow. The remainder of Guderian's force, the XXIV and the XLVII Panzer Corps, would then be sent to aid Army Group South in the destruction of the Russian Fifth Army, an undertaking that had been termed essential by Hitler on August 22. The formation of this new *Kraftgruppe* (task force) under von Kluge, a force that included some other infantry units as well as the XLVI Panzer Corps, would have meant the splitting up of Guderian's panzer group, with two of his panzer corps being sent to Ukraine.

This compromise had several features that appealed to Halder and Jodl and, it could be hoped, would appeal to Hitler as well. Aside from answering all of Hitler's objections against renewing the thrust on Moscow and ensuring substantial help for Army Group South, the new strategy would allow the southern flank of Army Group Center's advance on Moscow to enjoy the support of an entire panzer corps. Under the Halder-Jodl compromise, von Kluge's Fourth Army could have formed an integrated combined-arms task force, with both armor and infantry cooperating toward joint objectives. The same would have been true for the operation against Korosten; there, Guderian's armor would be able to concentrate upon a limited goal with

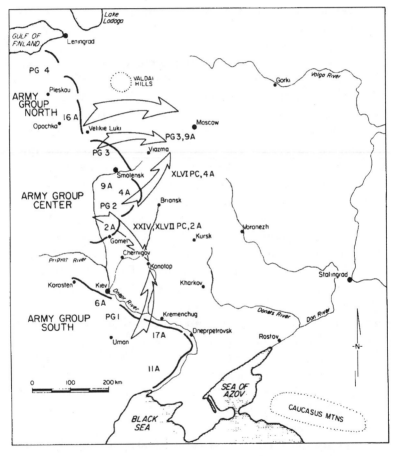

The Halder-Jodl Compromise of August 22, 1941

the infantry of von Weichs's Second Army. Halder had called for this kind of cooperation in his proposal of August 18, at that time perhaps cynically, but by August 23 he, too, like Hitler, may have had enough of Guderian's wide-ranging thrusts by large masses of armor. Another feature of the compromise would have been that parts of the XLVI Panzer Corps could have been used to brace up the Yelnia salient where, as has been seen, by the end of August severe Soviet pressure was being exerted and where the infantry units were in sore need of armored help. The Halder-Jodl compromise was the closest thing to good planning that the Wehrmacht was to enjoy in 1941. It is open to speculation how successful it might have been, since the Russians had plans of their own. Nevertheless, the new plan represented careful thought and was a real effort to deal with tangible facts, not just wishful thinking. The trouble was that Halder's past and continued reliance on intrigue would now ensnare him, and he would be unable to put the new plan into action.

The order for the breaking up of Panzer Group 2 was issued on August 23 before Guderian went to the Wolfschanze, but Halder did not inform Guderian of this in the meeting during the same afternoon at Borisov. It was for this reason that Brauchitsch instructed Guderian not to mention Moscow in Hitler's presence; he told the panzer general that the decision about Ukraine had already been made, and that it would be useless for him to object. It was true— the decision had already been made by OKH and OKW to sacrifice Guderian's command. It had probably also been agreed that Jodl would assume the responsibility for persuading Hitler of the need for the compromise, and probably for this reason no one from OKH bothered to appear at the last conference on August 23. Guderian's assigned role in all this was simply to go before Hitler and state his case about the condition of his armored units. This would confirm the impression that Jodl presumably had already planted in the führer's mind, that Panzer Group 2 could pursue only limited objectives south of the Pripyat and that at least part of the panzer group should be retained by Army Group Center and refitted for use later as a spearhead against Moscow.

The possibility exists that von Bock may have received advance warning about the Halder-Jodl agreement and that he may have briefed Guderian about this danger before the panzer general's flight to East Prussia. At 10:30 on the morning of August 23, before the Borisov conference, Greiffenberg, the chief of operations of Army Group Center, telephoned Guderian and told him that some of his units might have to go south toward Nezhin and Konotop. Greiffenberg: "What if this is required of you?" Guderian: "Then I will ask to be relieved." Greiffenberg: "What if your supplies can be sent through Roslavl-Gomel, then could you do it?" Guderian: "That is still too far. . . . By going only half that distance I could be in Moscow. I could take the whole panzer group there. . . . I hope this thing has not been ordered already." Greiffenberg: "It has not been ordered yet."

Actually, by August 23, Guderian's visit to Hitler was superfluous so far as Halder was concerned, and he agreed to this idea only because of von Bock's adamant insistence. Halder may have been afraid to push von Bock too far on this issue, and he may have yielded to the commander of Army Group Center and allowed Guderian to make his fateful journey, hoping that Guderian would be caught unawares by the turn of events. Or he may have believed that the panzer general would merely speak his piece and leave. Yet, knowing that Hitler was highly sympathetic to the views of "front soldiers," he should have been aware of the risk. Brauchitsch's warning to Guderian before his conference with Hitler was another sign that Halder was worried about what the panzer general might do. It is open to conjecture what compelled Halder to go along with von Bock on this matter; it was a decision that Halder would regret for the rest of his life.

Guderian's Coup in East Prussia

When Guderian arrived at the Wolfschanze, he was ushered into a room where he met Hitler in the presence of a large number of officers, including Keitel, Jodl, and Schmundt. It struck him as peculiar that no one from OKH was in attendance, not Brauchitsch, Halder, or anyone else. It would not have taken an overly clever man to figure out that something strange was in the wind, and Guderian must have known from the moment he stepped into the conference room that Halder was trying to use him as a tool. The chief of the General Staff had, however, met his match in Guderian.

The panzer general began the evening with a report to Hitler about the condition and the situation of his panzer group. When he finished, Hitler asked him if he still thought his units could undertake yet another important task, and Guderian replied that "if the troops are given a major objective, the importance of which is apparent to every soldier, yes." Then Hitler asked whether Guderian meant Moscow when he used the phrase "major objective," and Guderian launched into a long explanation of why he thought Moscow should be the primary target. The panzer general told Hitler that he knew the troops in the field and that it was important for their morale that they be given Moscow as their goal. He also used some other military and economic arguments to support his position as to the importance of the Soviet capital. But it was probably Guderian's insistence on the necessity of taking Moscow in order to bolster the morale of the ordinary soldiers that really affected Hitler. He, too, had been in the trenches and he knew how important morale was, and thus he was inclined to accept Guderian's comments.

After listening patiently to the panzer general, not interrupting him a single time, Hitler then repeated some phrases that he must have gotten from Göring, the commander in chief of the Luftwaffe, about the danger of the "Crimean aircraft carrier" to the Rumanian oil fields. He also charged that his generals knew nothing about the economics of war. Finally, the führer stated that Kiev must fall, and that the capture of this city would be the next primary goal. According to Guderian, "All those present nodded in agreement with every sentence Hitler uttered, while I was left alone with my point of view." The panzer general then recorded that he asked Hitler for permission to keep his panzer group intact so that he could carry out his task in Ukraine quickly before the beginning of the fall rainy season. Hitler gladly acceded to Guderian's request.

The following day Guderian reported to Halder on the results of the previous evening's conference, whereupon the chief of the General Staff, according to the panzer general, "suffered a complete nervous collapse" and began to heap all sorts of abuse on his head. Then

Halder telephoned von Bock and cursed Guderian for his unwillingness to split up his panzer group. It was very hard for Halder to believe that Guderian had not pleaded the weakness of his units and insisted to Hitler that Panzer Group 2 was not strong enough to carry out a wide-ranging maneuver around Kiev, as written in his diary:

> Guderian's report of yesterday [at the meeting at Borisov on the afternoon of August 23] was designed to give OKH leverage to restrict the operation to the south. After he saw that Hitler was convinced about the necessity of the operation, he believed that it was his duty to perform the impossible and carry out Hitler's wishes.
>
> This conversation showed with shattering clarity how irresponsibly official reports have been used.
>
> The army commander in chief has issued a sharply worded order regarding truthfulness in reports, but this will do no good. A person's character cannot be altered by orders.

On June 29 Halder boldly stated that he hoped officers such as Guderian would disobey orders, if need be, in order to do "the right thing," that is, push ahead to Moscow as rapidly as possible. The command structure that Halder had created in Army Group Center in early July had been intended to give Guderian and Hoth the maximum amount of freedom to forge ahead eastward without interference from above. Halder may have been right about Guderian's character, but the chief of the General Staff was himself largely responsible for encouraging him to act in the way that he did. British historian Alan Clark is correct in writing that Guderian's refusal to allow even a part of his armored strength to stay in Army Group Center while he carried out the Kiev encirclement may have been crucially important during the final push on Moscow, which began only at the end of September. Clark pointed out that Guderian's conference with Hitler on August 23 finished off his relationship with Halder, for the chief of the General Staff believed that Hitler's promise to the panzer general not to divide his command amounted to nothing more than a bribe on the part of the führer that Guderian accepted.[4]

Göring and Jodl would still be able to convince Hitler to resume the thrust on Moscow after Kiev, but then it would be too late in the year for the attempt to have any real chance of success. It seems safe to say also that Hitler's final decision about Moscow in September would not have been made had Guderian not given voice to his emotions regarding the intangible importance of the Soviet capital. The damage that had been done to the formulation of strategy and the conduct of the war simply could not be repaired. The mistakes that had already been made up to August 23 would only be compounded later. A major catastrophe, vaster by far than what was in progress at Yelnia, could not be postponed for long.

·6·
KIEV

Stalin's Mistake

After the fall of Smolensk, the operations of the Red Army at the center and on the left flank of the Western Front were divided into two relatively independent foci of combat—one in the vicinity of Smolensk, and the other farther south near Gomel. To facilitate command and control, on July 23 the STAVKA established the Central Front, including the Thirteenth and Twenty-first Armies and some time later the newly formed Third Army. The front commander was F. I. Kuznetsov, who had acquitted himself well as commander of the Twenty-first Army. The task of the new front was to protect the seam of the Western and the Southwestern Fronts and, with active probes in the direction of Gomel and Bobruisk, contribute to the overall success of the Western Front. The Central Front was integrated into the Briansk Front, however, about a month later after the fall of Gomel, an event that did not please Stalin. Instead of being punished, however, Kuznetsov was restored to his command of the Twenty-first Army, and eventually he and his staff managed to fight their way out of the Kiev encirclement.

By the end of July, Zhukov considered the situation along the western approaches to Moscow to be well in hand. Not only had additional forces been sent to the Western Front from the supreme command reserves, but units had also been transferred to the Smolensk area from Ukraine and the Orel Military District. Beyond this, the Germans had been temporarily checked at Velikie Luki, Yelnia, and Gomel, and, after July 14, the supreme command had ordered the construction of another line of defense for Moscow with three new armies: the Thirty-second, Thirty-third, and Thirty-fourth. These armies would occupy the line Volokolamsk-Mozhaisk-Malo-yaroslavets, and later Kaluga. This barrier would become known as the Mozhaisk line of defense. The units deployed here, for the time being, were directly subordinated to the command staff of the Moscow Military District headed by Lt. Gen. P. A. Artemev. The Mozhaisk line of defense was thinly manned in August and September, but as the Red Army began to fall back eastward in October, the density of the forces along the line began to increase significantly.

On July 29, Zhukov reported to Stalin in the presence of L. Z. Mekhlis, the chief of the main political administration of the Red Army (PUR), and informed him that a continued German advance from the Smolensk area toward Moscow was not likely. The chief of the general staff knew that German losses around Smolensk had been heavy, and he believed that Army Group Center had no remaining reserves to strengthen its northern and southern flanks. Zhukov correctly saw that the weakest and most dangerous Russian sector was in the area of Kuznetsov's Central Front, then covering the approaches to Unecha and Gomel with the Thirteenth and Twenty-first Armies. He told Stalin that the Central Front should be given three additional armies, one each from the neighboring Western and Southwestern Fronts and one more from the supreme command reserve. These units would also have to be given extra artillery, presumably from the reserves. Stalin, however, was opposed to any weakening of the direct route to Moscow, even though Zhukov pointed out that within twelve to fifteen days another eight full divisions, including one tank division, could be brought from the Far East, which would result in an overall strengthening of the Western Front in a short time. Furthermore, Zhukov said that the entire Central Front should be pulled back behind the Dnepr and no less than five reinforced divisions deployed in a second echelon behind the junction of the Central and Southwestern Fronts. In conclusion, Zhukov said, "Kiev will have to be surrendered." He also expressed his opinion that the Yelnia salient ought to be eliminated right away in order to prevent any possibility of a renewed German thrust against Moscow in the near future.

Stalin took Zhukov's words as a sign of loss of nerve, and the suggestion to surrender Kiev cost him his position as chief of the general staff. Zhukov was demoted and reassigned as commander of the Reserve Front. His replacement as chief of the general staff was Marshal B. M. Shaposhnikov. It is important to remember, however, that he remained a member of the STAVKA despite Stalin's temporary lack of confidence in him, and he used this position later with telling effect. The overall result of this move was that although Zhukov was unable to affect the looming disaster at Kiev directly, he was, as commander of the Reserve Front, able to wreck havoc against the Germans at Yelnia, as has been seen. If the most important part of the overall defense strategy was to protect Moscow and stop the Germans along the main route to the capital, then Stalin's choice of Zhukov to head the Reserve Front was not a bad idea. Certainly, Zhukov well understood the importance of what he was doing, and the STAVKA begrudged him little in terms of support for his operations against the Yelnia salient.

Despite the increasingly dangerous situation, Stalin was not about to surrender Kiev, the third most populous city in the Soviet Union, without a fight. The chief political officer of the Southwestern Direction, Khrushchev, and the commander of the Southwestern Front, Kirponos, are to a great extent to blame for this decision, which resulted in the heaviest losses Russia suffered throughout the war. Nikita Khrushchev, as he himself recalls in his memoirs, met with Stalin prior to the disaster and assured him that it was possible to save Kiev.

Despite his unswerving resolve about Kiev, however, Stalin was still convinced that the Wehrmacht was not yet through with Moscow. In this way, the Red Army was whipsawed by the same kinds of contradictions in strategy that so badly crippled the Wehrmacht. The fundamental contradiction on both sides was that Stalin and Hitler were incapable of objective analysis of real conditions. Both were too easily influenced by their own preconceived opinions of strategy and superiority and by the devious self-aggrandizing agendas of advisors that they admitted into their councils and listened to: Eremenko and Khrushchev on the Russian side, and Göring and Guderian on the German. The corrective intrusions of reality early in the war made more of an impact on Stalin than they did on Hitler; thus, Zhukov was given the necessary leeway to win the war.

Stalin's preoccupation with the defense of Moscow, despite the push of Panzer Group 2 and the Second Army southward, appeared in a conversation that he had on August 12 with A. I. Eremenko, then deputy commander of the Western Front. Summoned to the supreme command headquarters in Moscow late at night, Eremenko was first given a briefing by the new chief of the general staff. Shaposhnikov explained that the supreme command expected a Crimean offensive in the immediate future and also a push by Panzer Group 2 from Mogilev and Gomel toward Briansk, Orel, and Moscow. Stalin then asked Eremenko which assignment he preferred, Briansk or the Crimea. Eremenko replied that he wanted to be sent where the enemy was most likely to use armor, for he himself had commanded mechanized forces and understood mobile tactics. Eremenko was thus dispatched to command the Briansk Front, which was created on August 16. He was given specific orders to prepare to stop the resumption of the German offensive against Moscow, expected momentarily. The Briansk Front was formed from the Fiftieth and Thirteenth Armies and had about twenty divisions, although the Thirteenth Army was far understrength. To the north of the Briansk Front was Zhukov's Reserve Front, with the Twenty-fourth, Thirty-first, Thirty-second, Thirty-third, Thirty-fourth, and Forty-third Armies, and to the south of it was Kuznetsov's Central Front, now composed of the Third and Twenty-first Armies. The original Third Army had been virtually wiped out in the Bialystok salient in June, but it was reconstituted from supreme command reserves in August and assigned to the Central Front. The Fiftieth Army also was a new unit making its appearance for the first time in August, as was the Forty-third Army of Zhukov's command. Altogether, the Briansk Front was assigned a stretch of 230 km., roughly from south of Smolensk to Novgorod-Severskii.

Zhukov's anxiety about German intentions grew after Guderian sent the XXIV Panzer Corps south toward Starodub and Unecha on August 16, after the encirclement at Krichev. On August 17, Guderian broke through the front of the weak Thirteenth Army of Maj. Gen. K. D. Golubev and cut the Briansk-Gomel rail line, placing the entire Briansk Front in a difficult position. Panzer Group 2 had exploited the success at Krichev after August 12 to drive a wedge between the Reserve and the Central Fronts, and this gap in the Russian line widened as a result of the pullback of the Twenty-first Army from Gomel. The supreme command had created the Briansk Front on August 16 in order to prevent Guderian from passing between the Reserve and Central Fronts and pushing straight to Moscow from the south through Briansk, as indeed the German panzer general wanted to do; but contrary to Stalin's expectations, Panzer Group 2 continued its drive to the south against the hapless Thirteenth Army.

Eremenko's armies had been supposed to hit the southern flank of Guderian's panzer group as it moved north and east toward Moscow, but now the Briansk Front itself and the weakest army in that front had become the direct target of Guderian's assault. Zhukov sent a warning telegram to Stalin on August 19, spurred by the threat of disaster to the entire Southwestern Front in Ukraine with its Fifth, Sixth, Twelfth, and Twenty-sixth Armies—in all some forty-four divisions.

As an official member of the STAVKA, Zhukov continued to receive high-level reports, and through his analysis of the strategic situation he grew more convinced that his assessment of the possibility of a German strike at the flank and rear of the Central and later of the Southwestern Fronts was correct. He was especially disturbed by the information from POWs and Soviet intelligence about the fact that Army Group Center had been ordered to assume a defensive posture on the approaches to Moscow. This aggravated Zhukov's concerns more than he could stand. It was impossible for him to keep his hands off the situation and not try to convince Stalin again that his assessment of the situation on July 29 was correct: that Kiev and the Southwestern Front were in imminent danger of encirclement.

On August 19 he telegraphed Stalin with the message:

The enemy, seeing the major concentration of our forces on the direct approach to Moscow, having at his flanks the Central Front and Velikie Luki grouping of our forces, has temporarily given up the plans of striking at Moscow and, beginning active defense opposite the Western and Reserve Fronts, has sent all of his assault and mobile tank units against the Central, Southwestern, and Southern Fronts.

Probable plan of the enemy: to destroy the Central Front and advance to the area of Chernigov-Konotop-Priluki to destroy the armies of the Southwestern Front from the rear. After that, the main strike at Moscow by-passing the Briansk forest will follow and then will come a strike at the Donbas (Donets Basin industrial area). To frustrate these threats by the German command I consider it useful to create as quickly as possible a major grouping of our forces in the area of Glukhov-Chernigov-Konotop such that it could strike the enemy's flanks as soon as he starts to implement his plan.

In his message, Zhukov contended that the Germans knew that the main force of the Red Army was now being deployed on the approaches to Moscow and that they considered it to be too dangerous to proceed toward the capital while a threat existed to the flanks of Army Group Center from the direction of Velikie Luki in the north and from the Central Front in the south. Zhukov predicted that after the fall of Kiev, German mobile units would be able to bypass the Briansk forests and push on to Moscow from the south and also, at the same time, strike toward the Donets Basin. In order to foil the enemy's plans, Zhukov proposed that a powerful group be concentrated in the area Glukhov-Chernigov-Konotop in the northern Ukraine along the Desna and Seim Rivers, which would thus be in a position to land a hard blow on Guderian's eastern flank as his panzer group moved south. This additional force was to be supplied by the Far Eastern Front and Moscow Zone of Defense (MZO) and other internal military districts and should have eleven or twelve rifle divisions, two or three cavalry divisions, no less than a thousand tanks, and 400 to 500 aircraft. The size of the reinforcements requested by Zhukov shows clearly how far the mobilization of the strategic reserve had progressed by mid-August. There can be little doubt that the thousand tanks and the divisions he asked for were not all that the supreme command had at its disposal. The German high command, of course, had no idea of the magnitude of the Russian reserves they would be facing soon; needless to say, the Wehrmacht could not match the quantities of personnel and materiel replacements that had begun to appear on the eastern side of the front.

In his prompt reply Stalin agreed with Zhukov and informed him that resolute measures were being undertaken. Among these measures was the creation of the Briansk Front under Col. Gen. A. I. Eremenko. The return wire ended with the comment that other measures would be taken. Zhukov's uncomfortable feelings did not desert him, however, and within two days he telephoned Shaposhnikov to find out exactly what the "other measures" were. The reply from Moscow was that the northern wing of the Southwestern Front, a force including the Fifth Army and XXVII Rifle Corps, would be pulled back over the Dnepr, but Kiev would be held for as long as possible. Zhukov said that he doubted that the Briansk Front would be able to accomplish all that was expected of it, and Shaposhnikov tended to agree, but according to the new chief of the general staff, Eremenko had promised Stalin that the Briansk Front would be able to prevent Guderian from hitting the flank and the rear of the Southwestern Front, and this promise had apparently made a good impression on Stalin. Zhukov was troubled by what he had heard from Shaposhnikov, so he contacted Stalin directly over the high-frequency telephone line. Stalin affirmed his conviction that Kiev must be held, and he said that the military and political commanders of the Southwestern Front, Kirponos and Khrushchev, were in agreement with this point of view. It is interesting to note that in Eremenko's record of his conversation with Stalin on August 12, no mention was made of Panzer Group 2's threat to the Southwestern Front and Ukraine. According to Eremenko, the Briansk Front was established solely to prevent a drive by Guderian toward Moscow from the south. This version is repeated in the account given by the Khrushchev-period official history of the war. It is also a matter of interest that Zhukov recorded a conversation held on August 8 between Stalin and Kirponos in which the commander of the Southwestern Front gave his assurances that Kiev could be defended.[1]

Stalin had made an ironclad decision about Kiev, and he would not yield an inch on the question. Like Hitler, Stalin would take advice from those he trusted, but the Soviet dictator, once his mind was made up, would not waver on important issues. In this way, Stalin's leadership was much stronger than Hitler's; the führer was unable to adhere for long to one plan. It is interesting to observe that the greatest mistakes of the war were made because Hitler was too weak and flexible, whereas Stalin was not flexible enough.

It was Budenny who convinced Stalin to pull back all of the Southwestern Front to the eastern bank of the Dnepr. The supreme command order issued on August 19 directed the Southwestern Front to defend the Dnepr line from Loev to Perevolochna and prevent the enemy from advancing toward Chernigov, Konotop, and Kharkov. Stalin's assent to Budenny's request demonstrated that he realized the potential threat to the rear of the Southwestern Front posed by Guderian. But in his telephone conversation with Zhukov a few days later, the dictator reaffirmed his decision not to yield Kiev. Neither Zhukov nor Budenny believed that Kiev could be held if Panzer Group 2 continued its march to the south, but for better or worse, Stalin insisted that the Southwestern Front do everything it could to defend Ukraine. In the meantime, Stalin and Shaposhnikov were mainly concerned about the danger to Moscow, and the supreme command continued to do everything it could to protect the capital from the west and southwest.

For his part, Eremenko continued to promise Stalin that he would successfully accomplish the destruction of Guderian's panzer group. The Briansk Front was reinforced by infantry, tanks, and aviation, including the reserve aviation group of the STAVKA, which consisted of four air regiments under the command of Col. D. M. Trifonov. The front's mobile group was headed by deputy commander Maj. Gen. A. N. Yermakov. As Eremenko himself points out in his book *At the Beginning of the War*, near Trubchevsk alone on August 31 some 250 to 300 tanks were engaged. In addition, the front possessed one other tank brigade and two independent tank battalions.

STAVKA's plan was to try to stop Guderian by interdiction from the air. The aviation forces of the Reserve and Briansk Fronts, in all some 460 aircraft, were deployed for action against Panzer Group 2. This was the first time in which an all-out air campaign was waged with the specific intent of destroying massed enemy armor, so the plan was personally reviewed and approved by Stalin. During the period August 29 to September 4, more than 4,000 sorties were flown destroying more than a hundred tanks, twenty armored vehicles, and a fuel dump. In addition, fifty-five Luftwaffe planes were shot down in dogfights. Another fifty-seven enemy aircraft were destroyed on the ground in raids on eight airfields on August 30.

Still, Guderian's panzers were not deflected from their goal, the encirclement of Kiev and the Southwestern Front. It was clear that airpower alone was not enough. The Briansk Front also failed in its mission and could not exploit the successes of the air raids. The most combat-capable army of the Briansk Front, the Fiftieth, was not assigned objectives in accordance with the goal of stopping Guderian. Rather, it was set off to the northwest against the southern flank of the Fourth Army of Army Group Center. As a result of this frittering away of opportunities, by September 10 Guderian had advanced to the line Konotop-Chernigov, seriously threatening the deep rear of the Southwestern Front.

Instead of concentrating and massing his tank forces to confront Guderian, Eremenko since early September had dispersed his mobile units, which he himself describes:

> For the strike in the direction of Roslavl by the Fiftieth Army, a grouping of four Rifle Divisions was created in addition to one tank brigade and a separate tank battalion. The Third Army, also engaging in the strike, had four divisions. Of these, only one tank and one cavalry division had so far seen combat. The Third Army was to thrust in the direction of Pochep. The Twelfth Army created an assault group of four Divisions that had been exhausted in course of previous fighting, and one tank brigade. They were to advance in the direction Pogar- Starodub.[2]

Dividing his combat forces in such a way meant that Eremenko's forces would be unable effectively to oppose Guderian.

Zhukov quite skeptically observed all of Eremenko's actions and did not conceal his attitude about them in front of the STAVKA and Stalin, which aroused Eremenko's annoyance; he complained about it in his memoirs.

Again and again Zhukov turned to Stalin with insistent recommendations about the quickest possible withdrawal of the troops of the right wing of the Southwestern Front to the eastern bank of the Dnepr. According to Zhukov:

I knew what the combat value of the troops of the hastily formed Briansk Front was and that is why I considered it necessary to report to the commander in chief once again that it was necessary to withdraw all the troops from the right wing of the Southwestern Front to the eastern bank of the Dnepr as quickly as possible. . . . My recommendation again was ignored. I. V. Stalin said that he had just talked with N. S. Khrushchev and M. P. Kirponos and they had persuaded him that under no conditions should Kiev be abandoned. He himself is also convinced that even if the enemy were not destroyed by the Briansk Front, it would be stopped.

In order to allow the Briansk Front more latitude for maneuver, Stalin telephoned Eremenko on August 24 and asked him if he agreed that the Central Front be abolished and its forces added to those of his command. Eremenko concurred, and so the Central Front's Third and Twenty-first Armies were combined into one army, the Twenty-first, and subordinated to the Briansk Front. In addition, the Briansk Front received two new rifle divisions, made up of about 27, 000 men, which had just been brought up to the Desna River. On August 24, Shaposhnikov informed the commander of the Briansk Front that Guderian's main blow would fall upon the northern flank of the front, against the 217th and 279th Rifle Divisions of Fiftieth Army, probably the next day—first toward Briansk, then Moscow. Guderian's continued movement southward, however, struck at Pochep and the southern flank of Fiftieth Army, not at the northern flank, as Eremenko had expected. These developments forced him to conclude that the supreme command had been taken by surprise by the switch of Panzer Group 2's thrust to the south. This impression was strengthened by the fact that on August 30, the supreme command ordered an attack by the Briansk and Reserve Fronts to begin with an advance of Fiftieth Army on Roslavl. An attack against Starodub and Guderian's main force was also ordered, but this was to be carried out by the weak Thirteenth Army; no good result could have been expected from it. Eremenko was ordered to prepare a defense of the approaches to Moscow from the southwest, not to stop a German push toward Chernigov-Konotop-Priluki and against the northern flank of the Southwestern Front. It was for this reason that the Briansk Front "permitted" Guderian to push southward largely unmolested. Eremenko was told by the supreme command to expect Panzer Group 2 to turn to the north and east, to hit Briansk and then move toward Moscow, and this was what he was trying to prevent.

When Fifth Army of the Southwestern Front began its withdrawal over the Dnepr, its commander, Maj. Gen. M. I. Potapov, elected not to turn his northern flank toward the north to defend Chernigov—a serious mistake, as von Weichs's Second Army began a push toward that city after August 25. This advance by the German Second Army endangered the rear of the entire Fifth Army, which was trying to establish defenses along the eastern bank of the river from Loev to Okuninov. At the end of August, the Southwestern Front ordered Potapov to protect Chernigov, but by August 31 the Fifth Army was able to send only weak units of the XV Rifle Corps there. Maj. Gen. K. S. Moskalenko was named commander of the XV Rifle Corps on September 3.

The order that the supreme command issued on August 19 for the withdrawal of the Fifth Army behind the Dnepr was not the only action taken to save the Southwestern Front and Kiev from disaster. Soon thereafter the supreme command directed the Southwestern Front to create a new army, the Fortieth, in part made up from units first brought to the Kiev area around August 10. The commander of this new army was Maj. Gen. K. P. Podlas, and he was given the task of blocking Guderian along a defense line running from north of Bakhmach and Konotop to Shostka and along the Desna River to Stepanovki. The problems faced by the Fortieth Army were, however, severe.

On August 26 Panzer Group 2 succeeded in establishing a bridgehead over the Desna near Novgorod-Severskii, and the eastern flank of the Twenty-first Army was thus imperiled. Its commander, Kuznetsov, ordered his units to continue the retreat begun on August 15 from around Gomel. The first stage of the retreat carried the Twenty-first Army over the Dnepr, and now it would cross the Desna, seeking to avoid encirclement. Kuznetsov, however, did not inform his neighbor to the east and south, Fortieth Army, about his decision. As a result, Fortieth Army was unable to advance against Guderian's

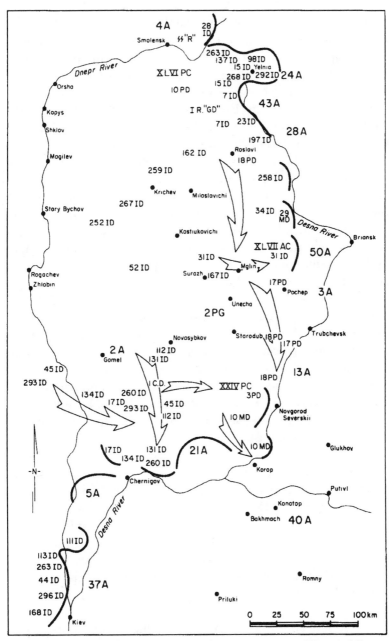

Panzer Group 2 Crosses the Desna at Novgorod-Severskii

bridgehead near Novgorod-Severskii from Konotop, and Podlas was forced to withdraw toward the southeast. The Twenty-first Army was now completely cut off from the Briansk Front, and on September 6 it was transferred to the command of the Southwestern Front, opening a large gap between the two fronts.

Kirponos ordered the Twenty-first Army on September 6 to stop its retreat and attack the rearward areas of the 3d and 4th Panzer Divisions, but the Briansk Front was unable to support this attack. Since August 28 the Thirteenth Army on the southern flank of the Briansk Front had been trying to form a line from Pochep to south of Starodub and along the River Sudost, but it had been badly mauled by the XLVII Panzer Corps and was forced to pull back behind the Desna. On September 2 the Briansk Front launched a series of counterattacks against Guderian's eastern flank as they had been ordered by the supreme command. These counterattacks lasted until September 12 and were supposed to have been carried out in two main directions: toward Starodub in cooperation with the Twenty-first Army to the south and toward Roslavl with the help of four rifle divisions from Zhukov's Reserve Front to the north. Eremenko criticized this decision, which he claimed was made by Zhukov, because it frittered away the Briansk Front's strength by sending the Fiftieth Army toward Roslavl instead of concentrating the counterattacks against Guderian's main force around Starodub. Eremenko still believed that Panzer Group 2 was striving to bypass the Briansk Front from the south and then push toward Moscow:

> Here it must be said that we regarded the German attack south of Trubchevsk as an attempt to envelop Moscow during the summer of 1941 . . .
>
> During this period we did not have complete information about the enemy's plans. Therefore, the push southwards by Guderian's tank units in August and September was regarded by us strictly as a maneuver to strip the [southern] flank of the Briansk Front.

The root of all this trouble was that Stalin and the supreme command had been caught off guard by the movement of Panzer Group

2 to Ukraine. The Soviet dictator knew in his heart that Moscow was Army Group Center's prime target for the fall of 1941; after all, had not OKW and OKH, with its General Staff, agreed on this priority? The ability, however, of a general in the field, Guderian, to manipulate Hitler and essentially carry out his own strategy independent of OKW and OKH had thrown Stalin and the Soviet intelligence apparatus into confusion.

Even if the underhanded dealings in the German high command had been explained to him, it is doubtful that Stalin would have understood or believed what was going on. His political police apparatus inspired a wholly different kind of "loyalty" in the Red Army. He could not imagine that Hitler and the Nazis did not have the same kind of control over the German armed forces.

That Stalin was certain about the plans of the German high command there can be little doubt. The Soviet spy network was functioning in high gear, transmitting streams of high-level intelligence to Moscow. According to Sudoplatov, an agent in Switzerland by the name of Rudolf Rossler, code named "Lucy," was responsible for transmitting the orders of the German high command, troop movements, and many operational details to Moscow. The information being provided by "Lucy" was actually supplied by the British secret service. The British were able to decode top-secret German messages because they had full knowledge of the German Enigma cipher machines, a fact they tried to conceal from the Russians. What the British did not know was that the infamous Cambridge ring in London was sending the same information in an unedited version directly to Moscow, thus giving Soviet intelligence the ability to compare the information from both sources.

Other intelligence information was provided by Hans Schulze-Boysen in the air ministry, code named "Senior." The penetration of the Luftwaffe staff by Soviet agents was particularly valuable since Göring and his subordinates, such as Kesselring, were not only aware of strategy but were in fact active in making it. The Abwehr counterintelligence agency under Admiral Canaris was not aware of the Soviet spy network nicknamed "Rote Kapelle," or "Red Choir," until late 1941 and did not effectively begin to break it up until early to mid-1942, but by then much of the real damage had been done. One

Soviet spy station was caught transmitting details of the Stalingrad operation a month before it was to be carried out. After the war, Abwehr officers admitted that only the surface of the Soviet spy net had been neutralized.

Stalin's mistaken belief in the course of German strategy for 1941 would, however, be set right before the end of the year. The German attempt on Moscow would not come in September and October, but rather in November and December, the Wehrmacht playing into Stalin's hands. But first the Red Army would have to suffer for Stalin's error.

The Fall of Kiev

In September 1941 the Southwestern Front was encircled and suffered heavy losses on the left bank of the Dnepr east of Kiev. (In traditional Russian geographical and mapping terms, "the left bank Ukraine" is actually the eastern bank of the Dnepr. This makes sense if one looks at Ukraine from the northern perspective of Moscow.) There are differing views and opinions concerning the mistakes and miscalculations of the supreme command and Stalin personally, as well as the general staff and its chief, Marshal B. M. Shaposhnikov. Also participating in the tragedy that was to come was the commander in chief of the Southwestern Direction, Marshal S. M. Budenny. Budenny was one of the true heroes of the Russian Civil War and remained above the purges that had decimated the rest of the senior officer corps. The chief political officer of the Southwestern Direction was N. S. Khrushchev, who in the 1950s became Party chairman and denounced Stalin as incompetent for ignoring the threat of invasion in 1941. At the level of the Southwestern Front the commander was Col. Gen. M. P. Kirponos, and his chief of staff was V. I. Tupikov. Kirponos had been decorated with the Hero of the Soviet Union medal for his generalship in the war with Finland—and there had not been many medals handed out in that war. Zhukov had his eye on the man and picked him as one of his army commanders in the January war games. In February 1941, Kirponos succeeded to Zhukov's old command as head of the Kiev Special Military District after Zhukov became chief of the general staff in January, so it is clear that he was one of his handpicked protégés. Tupikov was an interesting character, having served as military attaché in Berlin for a few months in late 1940 and early 1941.

The criticism of the direction and front commands is generally concerned with the collapse of the plans to defend Kiev and the failure to withdraw the troops of the Southwestern Front behind the Psel River in time to avoid encirclement. There are controversies also in the assessment of the operations of the Briansk Front and the actions of its commander, Col. Gen. A. I. Eremenko. The primary mission of the Briansk Front was to prevent Army Group Center from enveloping Moscow by destroying Guderian's Panzer Group 2, a mission that it was woefully incapable of fulfilling.

How did this monumental disaster happen, the biggest Soviet defeat of the war, dwarfing by far the disaster at Bialystok? Was it possible that the Southwestern Front could have been saved and the war shortened?

Guderian's continued drive southward in the first part of September produced an ever-growing level of uneasiness in the Soviet supreme command, but Stalin still could not accept the fact that all of Panzer Group 2 was being used in the Kiev operation and that, temporarily at least, Moscow was in no danger. On September 7 the Southwestern Front flashed another warning to the supreme command asking for permission to pull back the Fifth Army behind the Desna. Shaposhnikov then contacted Budenny and found that he concurred. The next day Zhukov was summoned to Stalin's office, where he was told that he would be sent to Leningrad; upon Zhukov's recommendation, Stalin selected Timoshenko as Budenny's replacement as commander of the Southwestern Direction. Lt. Gen. I. S. Konev was to occupy Timoshenko's position at the Western Front. Just as Zhukov was preparing to leave, Stalin queried him about German intentions. The former chief of the general staff replied that since Guderian and von Weichs had already advanced as far as Chernigov and Novgorod-Severskii, it would not be long before Twenty-first Army was shoved back even farther, and the Germans would be able to penetrate to the rear of the Southwestern Front. He also prophesied that the bridgehead established by the Seventeenth Army of German Army Group South on the eastern bank of the Dnepr near Kremenchug, below Kiev, could be used as the starting place for a mobile strike force that would move to the north and east to link up with Panzer Group 2. Zhukov advised Stalin to transfer all Russian forces to the eastern bank of the Dnepr and deploy all available reserves in the Konotop area for use against Guderian. Stalin then asked, "What about Kiev?" and Zhukov answered, "Sad as it may be, Kiev will have to be given up. We have no other way out." Stalin then telephoned Shaposhnikov and told him what he had just heard. Zhukov did not listen to the entire conversation, but Stalin said that the problem would be discussed later with the Southwestern Front staff.

Zhukov's words affected Stalin, for the next day, September 9, Shaposhnikov informed the Southwestern Front that the supreme command had decided that the Fifth Army and the right wing of the Thirty-seventh Army, defending Kiev, must withdraw to the eastern bank of the Dnepr and turn their fronts to face Panzer Group 2 coming down from the north. This maneuver, however, was difficult, because on September 7 Guderian crossed the Seim River and drove southward toward Bosna and Romny. Kirponos now called Budenny on September 10 (at a time when the whole northern wing of the Southwestern Front appeared to be caving in), after Chernigov had fallen to the Second Army on September 8, and asked for immediate reinforcements, especially for Podlas's Fortieth Army, which was now in a desperate situation along the Seim River in the Konotop sector. On September 10, the 3d Panzer Division already had taken Romny on the Sula River, well to the south of the Seim and almost due east of Kiev. Budenny had to reply, however, that the supreme command had placed no more reserves at the disposal of either the Southwestern Direction or the Southwestern Front. As a stopgap, Shaposhnikov authorized movement of two rifle divisions from the Twenty-sixth Army, immediately to the south of Kiev, toward the Fortieth Army to help stop Guderian's breakthrough in the region of Bakhmach and Konotop. Budenny, whom Stalin had already decided to replace, and Kirponos, however, considered this tactic to be wholly unsatisfactory, as this would leave Twenty-sixth Army with only three rifle divisions to hold a 150-km. front. The situation below Kiev was now also worsening rapidly because the Twenty-sixth Army's neighbor to the south, the Twenty-eighth Army, had been unable to eliminate the German bridgehead near Kremenchug between the Psel and Vorskla Rivers on the eastern bank of the Dnepr. It was expected that at any moment Panzer Group 1 would burst out of this bridgehead and plunge north and east to meet Guderian.

The conversation between Shaposhnikov and Budenny in the morning of September 10 testifies to the fact that Stalin still believed in Eremenko.

SHAPOSHNIKOV: The commander in chief ordered me to give the following order to you: the I Cavalry Corps should be urgently relocated to the area of Putivl where it will be subordinated to Eremenko. The corps is necessary to cover the breakthrough between the Southwestern and Briansk Fronts at the sector of Konotop–Novgorod-Severskii. You should report when the mission is accomplished.

BUDENNY: The enemy is enveloping the right flank of the Southwestern Front from the north. If the corps is sent there then why should it be given to Eremenko? I think that the story with the corps will be like that with the Twenty-first Army. I request that you should pay attention to Eremenko's actions in general. He was to destroy the enemy group [Guderian] and failed. If you are well aware of what is going on at the Southwestern and Southern Fronts and, despite the fact that neither of them has reserves, you still want to move the corps and give it to the Briansk Front, then I will be compelled to order the move . . .

SHAPOSHNIKOV: I understand all that, Semyon Mikhailovich. To allow the Southwestern Front to fight it is necessary to cover the breach at the sector of Novgorod-Severskii–Konotop. This is why the move of the cavalry corps is ordered. And the responsibility for the operation rests with Eremenko. . . .

BUDENNY: All right . . . I request that my opinion be reported to the commander in chief and in particular about the operations of Briansk Front . . .

SHAPOSHNIKOV: I'll do that by all means. Good-bye!

Meanwhile the situation at the front was developing as Zhukov had foreseen. Guderian's forward units broke into Romny, and the tanks of Colonel General Kleist in Army Group South started to attack from the Kremenchug bridgehead. The encirclement of the main body of the Southwestern Front had begun.

Shortly after midnight on the morning of September 11 the Southwestern Front's military council sent the following telegram to the supreme command:

> A tank group of the enemy has penetrated to Romny and Graivoron [not far west of Belgorod]. The Fortieth and Twenty-first armies are not able to check this group. We request that forces be sent immediately from the Kiev area to halt the enemy's movement and that a general withdrawal of the front [to behind the Psel River line] be undertaken. Please send approval by radio.

In response, around 0200 Marshal Shaposhnikov summoned Kirponos to the telephone and gave him Stalin's directions:

> The STAVKA considers it necessary to keep fighting at the positions of the Southwestern Front as our orders demand. Already yesterday, September 10, I told you that three days later Eremenko would start the operation aimed at covering the breach to the north of Konotop . . . Hence, you should destroy the forward units of the enemy near Romny . . .

Some hours later Budenny again appealed to the STAVKA:

> Being late with the retreat of the Southwestern Front might entail huge losses in personnel and materiel. Anyhow, if the decision can't be revised I ask for permission to withdraw at least the troops and good combat equipment from the Kiev fortified area.
>
> They will undoubtedly help the Southwestern Front to counter the encirclement. . . .

The requests of Budenny and Kirponos annoyed Stalin, as they contradicted his forecasts and calculations. He accused the commanders

of the front of incompetence and loss of nerve and decided to replace
Budenny with Marshal Timoshenko. But even Timoshenko could do
nothing about the catastrophe that was approaching.

Somewhat later in the morning, Stalin, Shaposhnikov, and Timoshenko telephoned the staff of the Southwestern Front—Kirponos,
Tupikov, and M. A. Burmistenko, the chief political officer of the
front. Stalin said that if the front withdrew from the Dnepr, the Germans would rapidly secure strong footholds on the eastern bank.
Consequently, the Southwestern Front, during its withdrawal, would
have to face enemy pressure from three directions instead of two—
from the west as well as from the north around Konotop and from
the south around Kremenchug. Then, he said, the encirclement of
the front would follow if the Germans coordinated the thrusts of
their panzer groups east of Kiev. Stalin recalled that the earlier withdrawal of the Southwestern Front from Berdichev and Novgorod-
Volynskii to behind the Dnepr had resulted in the loss of two armies
at Uman, the Sixth and the Twelfth; the retreat had turned into a
rout, allowing the Germans to cross the Dnepr on the heels of the
fleeing Red Army. A debacle of this sort must not be repeated. Stalin
explained that, in his opinion, the proposed retreat of the Southwestern Front would be dangerous for two reasons. In the first place,
the Psel River line had not been prepared for defense, and in the
second place, any withdrawal would be risky unless something were
done first about Guderian's panzer group around Konotop. Instead
of ordering an immediate retreat, Stalin made three proposals: (1)
that the Southwestern Front use all available forces to regroup and
cooperate with Eremenko to hit toward Konotop; (2) that a defense
be prepared on the eastern bank of the Psel with five or six rifle divisions and that the front artillery be brought behind this line and
positioned to face the northern and southern approaches; and (3)
that after the first two conditions had been fulfilled, preparations
be made to abandon Kiev and to destroy the bridges over the
Dnepr. While the withdrawal was actually under way, a screening
force would have to remain on the Dnepr to protect the front from
the west.

In his answer to Stalin, Kirponos said that no withdrawal would
take place without first discussing the situation with the supreme

command. However, he did hope that since the defense line now exceeded 800 km. the supreme command would send him some reserve forces. Kirponos referred to what Shaposhnikov had said on September 10, that two rifle divisions from the Twenty-sixth Army should be sent northward to help Podlas and Kuznetsov fight Guderian's panzers pushing toward Romny. He stated further that the Southwestern Front had no more units to spare for this task, as another two and a half rifle divisions had been sent in the direction of Chernigov to help the Fifth Army. In regard to reinforcements, Kirponos asked only that promises already made by the supreme command be fulfilled. Stalin's final statement was that though Budenny favored a pullback to the Psel, Shaposhnikov opposed it, and that for the present Kiev was not to be evacuated or the bridges destroyed without the approval of the supreme command. He announced his decision to replace Budenny with Timoshenko as commander of the Southwestern Direction. Budenny's career, however, was far from finished. He was assigned command over the Reserve Front defending the approach to Moscow in the Yelnia-Roslavl region. In 1942 he took charge of operations in the Caucasus.

Timoshenko was present when Stalin ordered Kirponos by telephone not to withdraw from Kiev, and the new commander approved of this decision. His optimism on September 11 was based partly on the fact that he knew of reinforcements that were on the way. These reserves were, however, inadequate to stem the German tide: only one rifle division and two tank brigades with 100 tanks. Timoshenko may also have believed that the counteroffensive by the Briansk Front ordered by Stalin against Panzer Group 2 might bring good results, but it is hard to imagine how he could have put much faith in such an operation. The counterattacks by the Briansk Front on August 30 had brought scanty returns because the front had been expected to push in two different directions, toward Starodub and Roslavl, simultaneously. A new counteroffensive ordered by Stalin to begin on September 14 was to be directed solely toward Roslavl and the southern flank of Army Group Center, not toward Konotop at all, as he had promised Kirponos over the telephone on September 11. On September 10 the gap between the Briansk and the Southwestern Fronts had widened to 60 km., and Eremenko was correct in saying that the supreme command knew there were no forces at hand strong enough to close this breach. All of Eremenko's armored brigades together had only twenty tanks in running condition. The questions must be asked: Why did Stalin, Shaposhnikov, and Timoshenko order the Southwestern Front to hold Kiev at all costs? What purpose could this act of mass sacrifice possibly have served?

Stalin now was forced to use Kiev in the same way that he had used the Bialystok salient in June, only this time the gamble was far more risky. The large hole that would soon be torn in the Red Army's defenses in Ukraine simply could not be patched. Too much of the strategic reserve had already been used to bolster the front along the Dnepr and the Dvina ahead of Army Group Center to allow the supreme command to save Kiev and Moscow at the same time. The sacrifice of Kiev would, however, exact from the Germans a high price, greatly exceeding that of the Bialystok encirclement in lives, materiel, and, most importantly, time. Stalin was right when he pointed out to Kirponos on September 11 the impossibility of withdrawing the entire Southwestern Front with its 677,000 troops behind the Psel River line in time to prevent its encirclement by Guderian and by von Kleist's Panzer Group 1. The Southwestern Front would have to stand and fight in the same way that the Third, Tenth, and Fourth Armies had fought in the Bialystok salient.

Pavlov, prior to the earlier catastrophe, had not been told what the true task of his forces was to be. Stalin was always a man who played his cards very close to his chest, and likewise he would not tell Kirponos, or for that matter Eremenko, what he really expected of them. Zhukov, Budenny, and Timoshenko, however, knew Stalin's true intentions; thus, Zhukov lost his position as chief of the general staff in late July, and Budenny was sacked on September 11. Timoshenko, who had agreed with Stalin in early September, would lose his nerve by September 13 and place Stalin under intense strain. He could have Pavlov shot, but Zhukov, Budenny, and Timoshenko were men of a different sort. Stalin could put them in their place, but he could not liquidate them. Timoshenko and Zhukov had saved the nation with their in-depth strategy for dealing with the German invasion, and Budenny, the dashing cavalry officer of the Civil War, was a national hero.

What if the Germans continued their offensive in the south, through eastern Ukraine, to the Donets Basin and the Caucasus? What if the entire southern flank of the Red Army were to be rolled up and the offensive against Moscow by Army Group Center postponed until the following spring? What if all the careful defensive preparations to the north, west, and south of Moscow, the massing of the strategic reserves around the capital, had all been for naught? How could the Soviet Union survive without its industrial base in the south while Army Group Center remained intact east of the Dnepr, poised for a spring offensive against Moscow with the aid of three panzer groups? These were questions that Zhukov and the other generals put to Stalin, and for them he had no effective answer. His only hope must have been that the Germans would somehow choose to rupture themselves in a final assault on Moscow before the end of 1941—a vain hope, it would seem, after nearly all of Guderian's panzer group had been committed to Ukraine in early September. If the XLVI Panzer Corps had remained in Army Group Center, as Halder and Jodl wished, Stalin's strategy would have seemed unquestionably correct to his generals. But as has been seen, Guderian had his way with Hitler on August 23, and all of his tanks were sent to the south except the 18th Panzer Division of the XLVII Panzer Corps, which Halder managed to retain in the rear near Roslavl as an army group reserve. In this way, by mid-September, Stalin's plans were placed in extreme jeopardy, for it could not be certain that a German assault on Moscow would be carried out during the remainder of the year. As it turned out, the Soviet dictator's fondest dreams were realized.

On September 12 von Kleist sent his tanks across the Dnepr near Kremenchug, at a point a considerable distance downstream from Kiev. Panzer Group 1 then unleashed its fury against the 297th Rifle Division of the Russian Twenty-eighth Army and pushed north and east toward Khorol. As Guderian's units were already south of Romny, there could be no doubt about German intentions. Altogether on September 12, Army Group South had twenty divisions concentrated against the five rifle and four cavalry divisions of the Twenty-eighth Army on the southern flank of the Southwestern Front. There was no way now for that front to stop von Kleist; all available forces had been sent to the north in a futile effort to block Guderian. North of Kiev, also, the situation had deteriorated badly during the previous two days. Under heavy pressure Potapov's Fifth Army had begun pulling back across the Desna, but when several divisions reached the river, it was discovered that the Germans already held the eastern bank. Some units, such as Moskalenko's XV Rifle Corps, managed to cross the Desna south of Chernigov relatively unscathed, but for the most part, the Fifth Army suffered heavy losses. The steadfastness of the Thirty-seventh Army around Kiev saved Fifth Army from being cut off from the south.

Now that the encirclement of Kiev and the entire Southwestern Front had become all but an accomplished fact, the front staff dispatched telegrams on the evening of September 13 presenting the situation in the gravest possible terms. Somewhat later, in the early-morning hours of September 14, the chief of staff of the front, Maj. Gen. V. I. Tupikov, on his own initiative sent a personal wire to Shaposhnikov that ended, "The catastrophe has begun and it should be obvious to you within a couple of days." The chief of the general staff's reply, sent to both the front and directional commands, was immediate and harsh:

> Major General Tupikov has sent a panicky report to the general staff. The present situation demands calmness and self-control at all levels of command. It is necessary not to yield to panic. It is important that all vital positions be defended, especially the flank areas. It is necessary to stop the retreat of Kuznetsov [Twenty-first Army] and Potapov [Fifth Army]. It is vital to impress upon the entire staff of the front the need for continuing the battle. You must not look backward, you must fulfill Comrade Stalin's order of September 11.

Shaposhnikov's answer was nothing less than a death sentence for the Southwestern Front. Now that two German panzer groups were actually linking up east of Kiev, there could be no question about the fate that was close at hand for the forces defending the middle Dnepr. Faced with the indisputable fact that a disaster of enormous proportions was about to take place, however, Stalin and Shaposhnikov stood fast. The Southwestern Front would have to stand and fight, to die, in order to drain the Germans of men and materiel and deprive them of time—all in order to permit the deployment of the strategic reserve around Moscow to proceed unimpeded. But what if Hitler chose not to attack Moscow in 1941? Would all of Stalin's plans then collapse in ruins? Now that all of Panzer Group 2 had been sent to Ukraine, it seemed that Hitler had found the perfect antidote to the strategy that had proven so fruitful at Velikie Luki, Yelnia, Roslavl, and Gomel.

Since July, Stalin and Zhukov had been painstakingly preparing a strong defense of Moscow, a strategy that now appeared to be useless. Zhukov and Budenny believed that Army Group South, strengthened by an additional panzer group, would have no trouble in overrunning all of the Soviet Union in the south up to the Volga, including the Caucasus. It was for this reason that they broke with Stalin and refused to agree with his adamant insistence not to allow a retreat of the Southwestern Front. Zhukov and Budenny could not accept a strategy that required that the 677,000 troops of the Southwestern Front be used in the same fashion as the three armies that had been sacrificed in the Bialystok salient. The first disaster had cost the Red Army losses of about 300,000 men—a heavy price, yet not unbearable—but the prospective losses at Kiev might be intolerable. Unless the Germans chose to put their own necks in the noose that had been so carefully prepared for them around Moscow, there could be little hope of winning the war.

At the beginning of the Kiev catastrophe Stalin had relied on Shaposhnikov, Zhukov's replacement, and Timoshenko, Budenny's replacement, to do his bidding, but by September 15 Timoshenko also had begun to break under the strain. On that date he told Shaposhnikov in Moscow that he favored an immediate withdrawal for the front, an attitude that represented a complete reversal of the position he had taken on September 11 when he, Stalin, and the chief of the general staff had telephoned Kirponos and ordered his units to remain in place. The extent of Timoshenko's influence over Shaposhnikov at this point is uncertain, but the next day he returned to the Southwestern Direction headquarters near Poltava and called in I. Kh. Bagramian, chief of the operations staff of the Southwestern

Front, for a conference. At this conference, with Khrushchev also present, Timoshenko announced that a decision to allow the Southwestern Front to withdraw behind the Psel River would have to be made without delay while the enemy's ring of encirclement was not yet tight. After pacing the floor for a time, Timoshenko asserted that he was certain the supreme command would go along with such a decision, but there was simply no time to waste in securing confirmation from Moscow. Bagramian noted in his memoirs that Timoshenko appeared deeply troubled when he made this statement and obviously doubted the truth of what he had just said—as well he might, considering the language of Shaposhnikov's abovementioned telegram.

When he finally managed to get hold of himself, Timoshenko ordered Bagramian to fly to Piriatin and give Kirponos an oral command to "abandon the Kiev fortified region and, leaving covering forces along the Dnepr, to begin immediately the pullback of the main force to behind the rearward line of defense [along the Psel River]." Kirponos was also to be instructed not to attempt the withdrawal without first carrying out counterattacks in the Lubny and Romny areas in order to slow down Panzer Groups 1 and 2 as much as possible. There can be no question that Timoshenko lacked the authority to issue such an order, for it clearly violated Stalin's wishes. Hence he refused to give Bagramian any sort of written document, explaining to him that the flight would be very dangerous and no important written orders should be allowed to fall into enemy hands. Timoshenko was right on one point—the flight would be risky—and the mission nearly came to grief when German patrol planes gave pursuit, but Bagramian was not fooled by the marshal's artificial excuses. As far as he knew, Timoshenko could have been executed for contravening Stalin's orders, and he could have shared his fate for relaying an unauthorized command. It was better not to incriminate oneself any more than necessary, so Timoshenko decided not to commit his order to paper. In the end, Timoshenko was not punished for his disobedience. The Southwestern Direction was abolished at the end of September, and he was made commander of the new Southwestern Front, with the Fortieth and the re-created Twenty-first and Twenty-eighth Armies.

When the front chief of operations finally met with his commander on September 17 in a forest grove north of Piriatin, Bagramian duly delivered Timoshenko's orders, but Kirponos decided not to act hastily. He asked Bagramian to produce a written command from headquarters. None existed, of course. Then, brushing aside Bagramian's objections, he chose to send a wire to Moscow requesting confirmation of the order instead of accepting his subordinate's word at face value. In those grave hours Marshal Timoshenko took all the responsibility for the order to retreat. Then Timoshenko got in touch with Shaposhnikov and requested confirmation of the order, as it was the only chance to save part of the troops. Having learned from Shaposhnikov that Timoshenko had issued the order of retreat, Stalin allowed it to be confirmed. The STAVKA informed Kirponos of Stalin's decision, but it was too late. The reversal of strategy took three days, September 15–17, and by the time the final decision was reached, the encirclement was already complete. The troops of the Southwestern Front were compelled to fight their way to the east, with great losses. All the members of the front staff together with the commander Colonel General Kirponos, were killed. The majority of those who survived—more than 600,000 officers and men—were taken prisoner.

Stalin had purposely delayed the withdrawal of the Southwestern Front until the German trap had been sprung. What appeared to Eremenko and Kirponos as uncertainty and procrastination and to the Germans as sheer stupidity actually was a desperate gamble on Stalin's part to win the war. The elimination of the Southwestern Front would cost the Germans much in terms of personnel, materiel, and time. Stalin was now certain that the strategic reserve could be mobilized and deployed in strength around Moscow, but all would depend on the enemy's next move. Stalin's willingness to sacrifice the Southwestern Front may have been foolhardy, as Zhukov believed, but if so, the Soviet dictator was easily surpassed in this respect by the German high command. Guderian notes that Potapov, the commander of the Russian Fifth Army, was captured and that he himself had the opportunity to question him. When asked why his army had made no attempt to abandon Kiev until it was too late, the Russian general answered that such an order had been issued but was

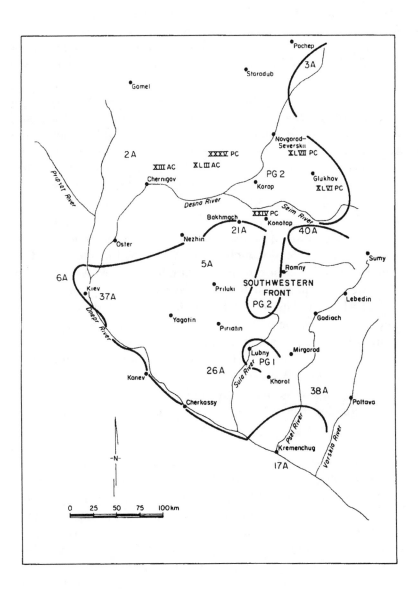

The Closing of the Kiev Encirclement

rescinded on September 11, and his forces were ordered to defend Kiev at all cost. Guderian and the other generals were startled at this seeming ineptness on the Soviet side. Although wounded, Potapov survived the war, was freed by the Americans in 1945, and returned to Moscow.

Despite the fact that by September 26 the Southwestern Front would largely cease to exist, some elements of the beleaguered armies did manage to escape eastward. A group of fifty men under Bagramian escaped to Godiach on September 24. Several thousand soldiers of the Fifth and Twenty-first Armies also made their way to safety, including 500 men of the Twenty-first Army staff headed by Kuznetsov. The commander of the Twenty-sixth Army, Lt. Gen. F. Ia. Kostenko, also escaped with a large group, as did a cavalry unit with 4,000 men led by A. B. Borisov. Several corps commanders, including Maj. Gens. K. S. Moskalenko and A. I. Lopatin, evaded the German trap as well. Kirponos and his staff, however, were not so lucky. They were all killed near Shumeikovo on September 20. The Red Army had suffered its worst defeat of the war, but Guderian was right when he said that Kiev was only a tactical, not a strategic, victory even though Russian losses had been enormous. German losses before and during the battle of Kiev were also heavy. From June 22 to September 28 the Wehrmacht suffered 522,833 casualties, or 14.38 percent of its total strength of 3.4 million. On September 26, the organization department of the General Staff reported to Halder that the forces in the east lacked 200,000 replacements.

The cumulative impact of all that happened in the summer of 1941 could not be felt at the time by either side; it would be a while before the damage inflicted on the Germans along the upper Dnepr took its toll. But all of this would soon dramatically change, and it would become glaringly apparent who was going to win the war. In early September the German high command undertook the planning of an operation that they believed would end the war in the east before the end of the year but actually was guaranteed to save Russia—an assault on a strongly fortified Moscow in the fall of 1941.

J. V. Stalin in his Kremlin study.

Colonel General
D. G. Pavlov.

Marshals S. K. Timoshenko and G. Kulik in the Kremlin during the January 1941 war games.

Stalin and his generals at the January 1941 war games.

Foreign Commissar V. M. Molotov and Stalin.

Marshal G. K. Zhukov.

General A. M. Valilevskii.

General K. K. Rokossovsky.

General I. S. Konev.

Marshal S. M. Budenny.

Fording the Dnepr River, 1941.

Yelnia in August 1941 shortly after being abandoned by the Germans.

Aircraft overflying Smolensk during the July 1941 battle.

Gun crew defending Kiev, September 1941.

Burned out Smolensk in mid-July 1941, shortly after its capture by the Germans.

Soviet tank crewmen receiving their orders, autumn 1941.

Barriers in Moscow, 1941.

Soviet aircraft overfly Moscow, autumn 1941.

Stalin in the Kremlin, autumn 1941.

Field Marshal Fedor von Bock.

Colonel General Heinz
Guderian.

Generals Franz Halder
and Walter von
Brauchitsch.

Colonel General
Hermann Hoth.

Colonel General Alfred Jodl.

General Walter Warlimont.

Field Marshal Gunther
von Kluge.

General Leo Geyr von Schweppenburg.

Colonel General Friedrich Paulus.

Field Marshal Albert
Kesselring.

German Infantry on
the march July 1941.

Germans crossing the Dnepr River, July 1941.

German attack on hills
of Lukty, near Vitebsk,
July 1941

·7·
MOSCOW

Operation Typhoon: The Gathering Storm

Once Guderian had made his pact with Hitler regarding the inviolability of his panzer group, von Bock and Halder were powerless to control the situation. The operation east of Kiev would take place on Guderian's terms, with the use of nearly his entire panzer group, and there was nothing his superiors could do now that the panzer general had Hitler's backing.

Jodl and Göring were, however, in a different position; they could influence Hitler to change his mind about Moscow, and the evidence shows that they were prepared to do so. A major alteration in Hitler's mood became apparent during a conversation he had with Brauchitsch on August 30, a week after Guderian's coup at the conference in East Prussia. The army commander in chief's talk with the führer went so well that Halder could say that "all was again love and friendship. Now everything is fine." On August 22 Halder had been on the verge of handing in his resignation, and on August 24 Guderian had practically provoked him into a nervous breakdown, but within a few days a thaw had become perceptible in Hitler's attitude. Brauchitsch was informed by the führer on August 30 that the strength of Army Group Center then operating in the Desna area should not be employed for the operation in Ukraine but rather should be readied for action against Timoshenko in the direction of Moscow. It should be noted here that although Lt. Gen. I. S. Konev took over Marshal Timoshenko's command of the Western Front on September 11, subsequent German documents still referred to the Western Front as "Army Group Timoshenko." The forces on the Desna that Hitler and Brauchitsch discussed were the units of XLVI Panzer Corps promised to Guderian on August 23. Hitler had begun to have second thoughts about releasing the XLVI Panzer Corps to Guderian, for as Halder correctly pointed out, once these divisions were committed to such an operation, they would be tied down for some length of time and it would be the enemy who would determine how and when they could be used again for other missions. Guderian, however, would not relent so easily. No matter how much Hitler might vacillate or how hard Halder and von Bock might struggle against him, the panzer general was determined to have his way.

The role of Jodl in bringing about the gradual shift in Hitler's opinion regarding Moscow is not easy to trace. The chief of the Wehrmacht operations staff had been convinced of the importance of taking Moscow ever since August 7, and although he had not always agreed with Halder on exactly how this task should be accomplished, he had remained dedicated to the project, as shown by his conversations with Halder and the studies produced by his department. Jodl's compromise with Halder over strategy had been brought to ruin by Guderian at the Wolfschanze on August 23, but he had not ceased trying to change Hitler's viewpoint. On August 31, Halder conferred with his chief of operations, Heusinger, and they discussed a telephone conversation that Halder had just held with Jodl, who referred to the Kiev operation as an "Intermezzo" and said that after the task in the south was fulfilled, the Second Army and Panzer Group 2 should be used against Timoshenko, perhaps in the second half of September. This possibility was also discussed with the view that the northern wing of Army Group Center could be strengthened by some units from Army Group North. It is obvious that Halder was not wholly surprised at Jodl's breakthrough with the führer. On the previous day OKH dispatched an order to Army Group Center that all units from Panzer Group 2 and the Second Army that crossed the Desna would come under the command of Army Group South, but it is clear from the way Halder phrased this order that he believed that not all of Panzer Group 2 would have to cross to the southern bank of the Desna. Brauchitsch's talk with Hitler on August 30 seemed to give some substance to this idea. The information Halder received from Jodl the following day appeared to be even more encouraging, although the situation was still indefinite and the chief of the General Staff had to tell Heusinger "these things are so unclear that we cannot give Army Group Center any concrete plans."

Von Bock, however, had other sources of information, and he was not left in the dark about the shifts in position of the high command. During the afternoon of August 31, the same day that Halder conferred with Jodl, Field Marshal Albert Kesselring of the Luftwaffe appeared at Army Group Center headquarters with news that probably emanated from Göring. Von Bock was informed that Hitler was considering halting the push southward of the Second Army and of Panzer Group 2 at the Nezhin-Konotop railroad and then allowing all of Army Group Center and part of Army Group North to move eastward toward Moscow. Kesselring advised the commander of Army Group Center that the OKH order of August 30 would now not be put into effect. Considering the problems that von Bock had been having with Guderian over the disposition of the XLVI Panzer Corps, it is no wonder that he saw the change in orders as a chance to bring Guderian "back under rein."

After listening to Kesselring, von Bock immediately telegraphed Guderian and ordered his units to move no farther to the south or east than the line Borana-Bakhmach-Konotop. But the forceful panzer general had ideas of his own. Guderian had given Hitler a promise that Panzer Group 2 would link up east of Kiev with Panzer Group 1 to destroy the Russian Southwestern Front, and he held to his promise. By fulfilling his end of the bargain, Guderian hoped that Hitler would keep his word and not allow his panzer group to be split apart. The panzer general had astonished von Bock on August 24 when he told him, rather flippantly, how he had consented to Hitler's wishes and informed the führer that his panzer group could take part in the Kiev operation; in fact, he had insisted that all of his units be sent to Ukraine. Now Guderian would continue to torment both von Bock and OKH with constant requests for the release of "his" XLVI Panzer Corps from Army Group Center. Halder was prepared for big trouble from the panzer general, and on August 28 he cautioned von Bock to try to keep Guderian strictly under control.

Guderian had first asked for the release of the XLVI Panzer Corps from OKH on August 26 and had received a flat refusal, even though he claimed that the spearheads of his panzer group were running into heavy resistance in their push southward. Failing in this approach, he then turned to Army Group Center on August 27, after the XLVII Panzer Corps crossed the Desna near Obolonie and Novgorod-Severskii. During the evening he repeatedly telephoned Greiffenberg, the army group chief of staff, and cursed the Second Army, which, he said, was marching in the wrong direction, that is, due east, perpendicular to his own axis of movement. Guderian again demanded that the XLVI Panzer Corps, then being held in reserve southeast of Smolensk along with the 18th Panzer Division of the XLVII Panzer Corps, be sent immediately to rejoin the main part of his panzer group. Von Bock finally telephoned Halder for instructions, and they agreed, temporarily at least, to do nothing. The commander of Army Group Center referred to Guderian's request as "light-headed" (*leichtsinnig*) because the 18th Panzer Division was located south of Roslavl, so far behind Guderian's front that he could not help but wonder what use the panzer general could make of it. Matters were complicated even more when Paulus appeared at army group headquarters on the evening of August 28. He had been on a short visit to Panzer Group 2 and during this time had been won over to Guderian's cause. Halder's deputy now went so far as to telephone his chief in East Prussia and plead that not only should the XLVI Panzer Corps be returned to Panzer Group 2 but all of the Second Army should be turned to the south and be subordinated to Guderian's command. Halder's decision was emphatic:

> I see the difficulties of the situation but this whole war is made up of difficulties. Guderian wants no army commander over him and demands that everyone in the high command should yield to his limited point of view. Unfortunately, Paulus has been taken in by him, but I won't give in. Guderian agreed to this mission, now let him carry it out.

The next day, August 29, Guderian again repeated his demands, this time maintaining that the western flank of his XXIV Panzer Corps was seriously threatened, but von Bock found this difficult to believe, because the panzer corps had already "incautiously" reported to the Second Army that its flank was not in danger. Von Bock again contacted Halder for advice, but the chief of the General Staff seemed to relish Guderian's predicament. Halder believed that Panzer Group 2 would soon be subjected to attacks from three sides and that Guderian would find himself in a great deal of trouble. In order to ease the situation as much as possible for von Bock, and also to facilitate the splitting up of Panzer Group 2, OKH issued the directive of August 30 (already mentioned) that would have subordinated the main part of Guderian's force to Army Group South. It was an order, however, that von Bock was happy not to have to put into effect. Kesselring's visit on August 31 had given him new hope that Moscow might once again become the main goal of the German advance. Halder, too, seemed to think things would again be brought onto what he considered the right track. When von Bock queried him about what he had heard from Kesselring about Moscow, the chief of the General Staff replied, "I can't confirm it, but it has been talked about."

Despite the fact that the attacks on the Yelnia salient were growing in intensity and that on August 30 the 23d Infantry Division of the VII Army Corps along the Desna front south of the salient suffered a rupture in its lines up to 10 km. in depth, Guderian continued his demands for all of the XLVI Panzer Corps to be sent to the south. Von Bock was of the opinion that the penetration in the area of the 23d Infantry Division had to be taken seriously and ordered the 10th Panzer Division of the XLVI Panzer Corps to stand by for an immediate counterattack, which was indeed successfully launched the next day. Although it is hard to imagine what the fate of the 23d Infantry Division would have been without the timely aid of the 10th Panzer, on August 31 Guderian told the commander of Army Group Center that he would appeal directly to Hitler unless this panzer division and all other units of the XLVI Panzer Corps were dispatched southward immediately. Halder was further infuriated by Guderian's cheek, which he labeled "unheard-of impudence."

When Halder and Brauchitsch called on von Bock on September 2, the visit that led to the abandonment of the Yelnia salient, there was still a great deal of uncertainty about when the offensive against Moscow could be resumed. Von Bock did not think that his army group could renew the offensive unless both Panzer Group 2 and the

Second Army were turned toward the east and unless some help was also received from Army Group North. The situation was still unclear, since Guderian had succeeded so thoroughly in wrecking everyone's plans. Halder, Brauchitsch, and von Bock could all agree that Moscow should be taken before the winter of 1941, but as the commander of Army Group Center pointed out, "The Intermezzo, as General Jodl of OKW referred to the turning of my right flank to the south, can cost us the victory." Until it was decided what to do about Guderian, and about Hitler, no definite plans could be made regarding Moscow. The consensus was that in any event another push toward the Soviet capital could not take place before the end of September.

When Halder returned to headquarters on September 4, he found, to his delight, that the prospects for the Moscow project looked a good deal brighter. Hitler had become irritated with the way Guderian had carried out his drive to the south, especially his allowing the XLVII Panzer Corps to move far to the east of the Desna, causing a big gap to develop between his armored units and the infantry of Second Army. Keitel finally telephoned von Bock to say that Hitler would personally intervene to bring Guderian back farther west if neither Army Group Center nor OKH would do so. By this time von Bock had become so fed up with Guderian that he asked Brauchitsch to replace him, but the panzer general still retained too much popularity with the führer for this to be done. Since Guderian's progress had been so rapid, Hitler decided to allow him to continue his movement southward to link up with Panzer Group 1, which would erupt from the Kremenchug pocket south of Kiev on September 12.

Nevertheless, Jodl and Göring had done their work well. Von Bock found out once more what Hitler's future strategy would be from Kesselring, who appeared at Army Group Center headquarters on September 6. In the words of von Bock: "How curious it is that I get all my news first from the Luftwaffe." Hitler was about to make what may well have been the most momentous decision of his life, a decision leading directly to the sharpest setback the German army had suffered since 1918 and a defeat of such magnitude that it crippled Germany's chances for victory over the Soviet Union. By September

5 Hitler had become convinced that Russia could not be beaten unless Moscow was taken in 1941.

Shortly before 0600 on September 5, Hitler summoned Halder for a conference and revealed to him his plans for the future:

1. The goal of encircling Leningrad had already been achieved; that sector would now become of "secondary importance."

2. The attack against Timoshenko (that is, the Russian Western Front guarding the shortest path to Moscow) could begin within eight to ten days. Army Group North would aid this attack by sending one panzer and two motorized divisions to Army Group Center. Some help could also be provided by Army Group North's Sixteenth Army.

3. After the conclusion of the battles in Ukraine ("history's greatest battle"), Panzer Group 2 was to be turned north toward Moscow.[1]

This new plan, of course, suited Halder, for he still believed that Moscow was of primary importance if the war were to be won in blitzkrieg fashion, although he thought that the advance eastward could not possibly be resumed for at least three more weeks. That evening Halder conferred with Heusinger and Paulus about the plans for the coming operation. The order for the renewed Moscow offensive, which took the name Operation Typhoon, was issued by Hitler on September 6:

1. On the Central Front, the operation against the Timoshenko Army Group will be planned so that the attack can begin at the earliest possible moment [end of September] with the aim of destroying the enemy forces located to the east of Smolensk by a pincer movement in the direction of Viazma with strong concentrations of armor on the flanks.

2. On the Northeastern Front . . . we must . . . so surround the enemy forces fighting in the Leningrad area that by 15 September at the latest substantial units of the motorized forces and of the 1st Air Fleet . . . will be available for service on the

Central Front. Before this, efforts will be made to encircle Leningrad more closely, in particular in the east, and should weather permit, a large-scale air attack on Leningrad will be carried out.

Göring had promised Hitler that the Luftwaffe could undertake the destruction of Leningrad, a promise that he felt was necessary after the air arm had failed to force England to its knees in 1940. The genesis of the idea that large metropolitan areas in the Soviet Union could be subdued with airpower alone goes back to Hitler's conference with Halder on July 8; the idea was further developed in Directive 34 of July 30, which stated that the VIII Air Corps was to be transferred from Army Group Center to support Army Group North's advance on Leningrad. Clearly, this was done with Göring's approval. On August 8, Hitler's press secretary, Otto Dietrich, released a statement for publication that said in part, "It is the first time in world history that a city of two million [Leningrad] will literally be leveled to the ground." This statement was made three days after the elimination of the Smolensk pocket and the capture of 309,000 Russian prisoners, which no doubt contributed to the atmosphere of euphoria in the Reich's chancellery.

Later, on October 7, shortly after the commencement of Typhoon, an OKW directive signed by Jodl stipulated that large Soviet cities such as Leningrad and Moscow were not to be assaulted by infantry or tanks but rather were to be "pulverized" by air raids and artillery. The population of the large cities was to be impelled to flee into the interior of the country: "The chaos in Russia will become all the more pronounced and our administration and utilization of the occupied eastern lands will thus become easier. This desire of the führer must be communicated to all commanders."

This was not the last time that Göring would overestimate the capabilities of the Luftwaffe; the next occasion would come in late 1942 and early 1943 during the battle of Stalingrad. In the summer of 1941 Hitler believed that the air force could neutralize Leningrad, and it was for this reason that he was willing to order the resumption of the Moscow offensive before the metropolis on the Gulf of Finland had actually fallen. That Hitler should have

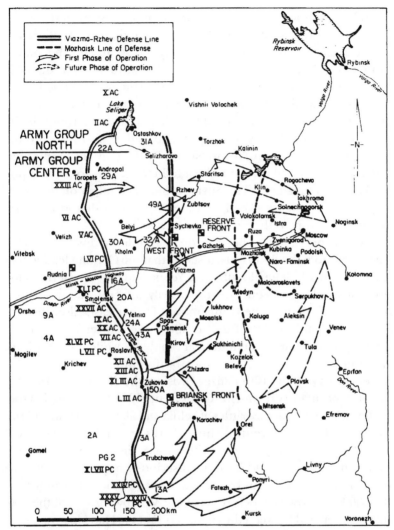

The Operations Plan for Army Group Center During Operation Typhoon

known better, that he should have realized the gravity of the situation should the Luftwaffe be unable to carry out its mission, seems all too clear in retrospect. But Hitler was too dependent on his closest advisors and he was under too much pressure from the army generals to be able to resist the temptation of Moscow in the early fall of the first year's campaign. Göring, like Jodl, had initially been against beginning the Moscow operation so soon, and this had a telling effect on the führer, but after Jodl's conversion on August 7 and Göring's reconsideration of strategy somewhat later, Hitler could not deny his generals any longer. On September 10 Kesselring visited von Bock and assured him that Hitler was strongly in favor of all available forces being concentrated against Moscow, including units from Army Group North. By the end of the summer of 1941, Moscow had ceased to be a military target—or even a political or economic goal. The Soviet capital had taken on an air of magical enchantment; it had become the Lorelei that would lure unwary navigators to their deaths on the rocks.

Once the decision had been made to assault fortress Moscow, all else flowed from the disastrous mistakes that the German leadership had already made. The bloodbath at Yelnia had cost the German infantry of von Kluge's Fourth Army heavily, a factor that would become more evident as the fronts moved farther east. Also, the significance of Guderian's refusal to allow one panzer corps of his panzer group to remain behind near Smolensk while the rest of his units were sent to Ukraine cannot be forgotten. Had the XLVI Panzer Corps with the 10th Panzer Division, the SS division "Das Reich," and the infantry regiment "Gross Deutschland" remained in the Smolensk-Yelnia area, the battles at Yelnia and along the Desna might have turned out differently. Zhukov's reserves might have been mauled badly in trying to reduce the Yelnia salient, so badly that the defense of Moscow could have been seriously impaired. As it was, Guderian had his way, but by the end of September his armor had 500–600 km. to traverse before reaching Moscow instead of the 300 km. that stretched between the capital and Yelnia. Had Moscow fallen in late 1941, the war would have been far from ended. It would have been better for the Wehrmacht to first conquer the south of Russia, then Moscow in the spring of 1942. By the early fall of 1941, however, German strategy had fallen between two stools. The German army may have been able to take all of Ukraine or Moscow in 1941, but not both. After Hitler's change of mind about Ukraine in September, however, and after Guderian's refusal to allow the splitting up of his panzer group, neither goal was attainable. The Red Army was too strong to be so casually bent to its opponent's will. Zhukov had done all he could to make Moscow impregnable, a task that could not have succeeded without Guderian's help.

In spite of having made movements of 600 km. and 400 km., respectively, Panzer Groups 2 and 3 on September 11 were assigned objectives for a renewed push in the direction of Moscow. This time Army Group Center was bolstered by the addition of Panzer Group 4 from Army Group North. At the beginning of October the strength of Army Group Center, including these additional forces, amounted to 1,929,406 men and 1,217 tanks. The Luftwaffe, however, was able to operate less than 700 aircraft in the Army Group Center area during Typhoon. By order of Army Group Center on September 26, Panzer Group 4 was subordinated to Fourth Army command, renamed 2d Panzer Army, and was given the mission of wheeling around Viazma from the south, from the direction of Roslavl. The beginning phase of Operation Typhoon went well enough, with Gu derian's force launching its attack on September 30 and rapidly taking Orel and closing the Briansk pocket with the help of Second Army. The rest of Army Group Center began its assault on October 2 with Panzer Group 3 from the north and Panzer Group 4 from the south closing an armored ring around Viazma. The Viazma operation was a particular success because there the encirclement took place only 100 km. east of Yartsevo and 170 km. from Roslavl—in other words, close enough to the starting point of the offensive for the infantry to move in rapidly and help the armored units seal off the pocket.

In such a manner the battles along the Dnepr, which lasted from mid-July to late September, were brought to a close. But even after the great victories of Briansk and Viazma, the panzer generals charged with opening a way to Moscow found little to be happy about. Guderian went so far as to say that after the initial success of Typhoon, his superiors at OKH and at the headquarters of Army Group Center "were drunk with the scent of victory." Even before the end of the Briansk-Viazma operations, Brauchitsch was confident enough to comment: "Now the enemy has no noteworthy reserves remaining around Moscow. We can, however, expect him to try to build defense lines in and to the west of the city." The army commander in chief went on to describe the advance of the central part of Army Group Center toward Moscow as a "pursuit."

An aura of mystery still hangs over Guderian's thoughts about the resumption of the Moscow offensive in the fall of 1941. In his memoirs, he gives the impression that he had some doubts about whether such an operation would succeed, yet materials contained in his panzer group's war records show that he was in favor of it. It is generally believed that Hitler alone was responsible for the decision to turn again to Moscow after the battle of Kiev, a decision that probably crippled for all time any chance the Germans might have had for winning the war in the east, but as the previous chapters have shown, this was not the case. Hitler was not strong-minded enough to chart a course and hold to it.

Soon after Guderian reached Orel on October 3, the first snow began to fall and the panzer general himself knew that his troops would never mount a guard on the Kremlin parapets. After Orel, Guderian had only one thought—shift the blame to someone else, accuse the high command of being drunk with the scent of victory. Guderian told Hitler on August 4 at a meeting at Army Group Center headquarters in Borisov (which we will examine in detail in the next chapter) that the Soviets were scraping up their last proletarian levies and had no remaining reserves. Recall, also, how on August 23 Guderian told Hitler and OKW staff that Kiev could be taken only if his panzer group were not split up or otherwise reduced in strength. At this meeting he also stressed the significance of troop morale and the necessity for making Moscow the near objective of the crusade. It was this intangible foundation so cleverly laid by Guderian that provided the support for Jodl and Göring to press their cause, the Moscow project, with Hitler in September. Guderian was right about the intoxication of the high command after Briansk-Viazma, but it was he who had uncorked this bottle of heady wine and served it to his superiors.

The twin battles of encirclement at Briansk and Viazma in early to mid-October seemed to open the way to Moscow, but von Bock knew that other Russian reserves were positioned even farther to the east. Hitler and OKH learned enough from the experiences of Bia-

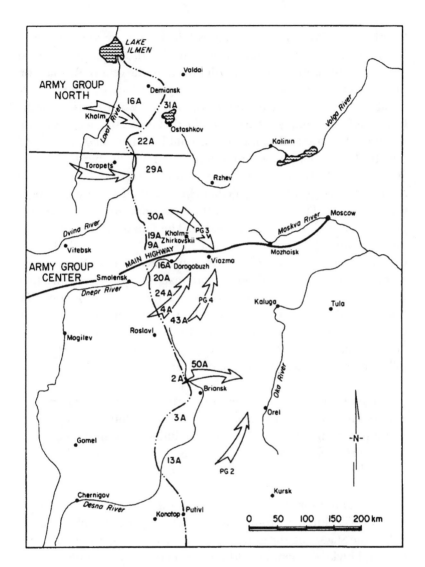

The Briansk-Viazma Twin Battles of Encirclement

lystok-Minsk and Smolensk to know that close encirclements that afforded a good opportunity for cooperation between infantry and armor offered the best chance for success. The Briansk-Viazma operation produced spectacular results; the twin battles ended on

October 19 with 657,948 Russian soldiers taken prisoner. But von Bock could sense the troubles that lay ahead. In his view, deeper panzer thrusts were needed in order to cut to the rear of Russian fortifications and reserves massed to the west of Moscow. In all likelihood, however, such tactics would have led to a worse disaster for the Germans than actually occurred. In the first place, the pockets of surrounded Russians at Briansk-Viazma could not have been contained effectively had German armored units been sent farther to the east. Second, deeper thrusts would have meant longer and more exposed flanks for armor units, dangers that Hitler and OKH were no longer willing to risk. The toughness of the opponent, too, was obviously growing instead of becoming weaker. The fate of some of the prisoners captured at Briansk-Viazma illustrates why the Red Army would not surrender. On the march route back to a POW camp near Smolensk, some 5,000 prisoners were machine-gunned before they reached their destination. At Smolensk Camp 126 it is estimated that some 60,000 Soviet prisoners were killed, mostly under the direction of SS "Special Commander" Eduard Geyss. Why not fight to the death—what was there to lose? Marshal I. S. Konev has written the following words about the battle of Viazma:

> Finally, the battle assumed the form of an encirclement. If one is forced to fight such a battle, it is important not to panic but to continue the combat, even in difficult circumstances. In the fortunes of war such situations are always possible and should not be excluded from contemporary military practice.[2]

In the end, more than anything else, the misguided racial prejudices of Nazi ideology toward the Soviet peoples, the minorities as well as the Slavs, dug the grave for the Wehrmacht. Without mass surrender, blitzkrieg tactics could not succeed in Russia. The German policy toward Russian prisoners did not favor mass surrender for trapped Red Army units. The Prisoner of War Department of OKW (*Abteilung Kriegsgefangenenwesen*) issued a report in May 1944 that put the total number of Soviet prisoners at 5,165,381. Of these, 2 million deaths were placed under the heading "wastage," whereas another 280,000 were recorded as having died or disappeared in transit camps (*Durchganglager*, or *Dulags*). The number 1,030,157 was given for the total of Soviet prisoners who were either shot while trying to escape or handed over to Himmler's SD for liquidation in special camps. If these figures are extrapolated, it is possible that 5.7 million Soviet prisoners had been captured by the Germans by the end of the war in May 1945. The final count of surviving prisoners is usually approximated at 1 million. When this number of survivors is added to the number of Russians estimated to be serving with or aiding the Wehrmacht as volunteers (*Hiwis*) or in the Vlasov all-Russian units, together a total of about 800,000 to 1 million, we can estimate that about 3.7 million Soviet prisoners simply vanished from the face of the earth.

The battle of Kiev required nearly a month to bring to a conclusion; the battles of Briansk-Viazma lasted almost three weeks. These delays in the German advance eastward, coupled with the delays already experienced along the Dnepr and in the Bialystok salient, proved fatal for Germany's campaign in the east.

The Blade Descends: Zhukov's Moscow Counteroffensive

On October 10, Zhukov was named commander of the Western Front, replacing I. S. Konev, who was sent to head the newly formed Kalinin Front. It is evident from Zhukov's post-war statements that after the resumption of the German offensive against Moscow, his faith in Stalin had been somewhat restored. Despite Zhukov's reluctance to submit to Stalin's plan to sacrifice the Southwestern Front, the Soviet dictator had a high respect for his abilities, and he would now call upon him to save Russia in its hour of greatest need.

By the time Zhukov arrived to take charge of his new command, parts of five armies of the Western and Reserve Fronts had already been surrounded at Viazma. The twin battles of encirclement at Briansk-Viazma have been described by German historians as great successes brought about by the passivity of the Russian leadership and by the Russian inability to understand the new principles of armored warfare. Why else would the Red Army attempt to ward off powerful German tank thrusts by relying on the kind of static-front tactics utilized during the First World War?[3] Yet there is another possible interpretation. In the words of Zhukov:

The most important thing for us in the middle of October was to win time in order to prepare our defense. If the operations of parts of the Nineteenth, Sixteenth, Twentieth, and Thirty-Second armies and the Boldin Group [a force made up of three tank brigades and one tank division] encircled west of Viazma are assessed from that point of view, these units must be given credit for their heroic struggle. Although they were cut off in the enemy's rear, they did not surrender. They continued to fight valiantly, attempting to break through to rejoin the main force of the Red Army and thus held down large enemy formations that would otherwise have pursued the drive toward Moscow.

And again:

In the beginning of October the enemy was able to achieve his first objective, taking advantage of his superior manpower and equipment and of errors made by commands of Soviet fronts. But his ultimate strategic objective, the seizure of Moscow, failed because the main forces of the enemy were held down by the Soviet troops surrounded in the Viazma area. The limited forces thrown in by the enemy against the Mozhaisk line with the aim of breaking through to Moscow succeeded in pushing the Soviet troops back to a line running through Volokolamsk, Dorokhovo, the Protva River, the Nara River, Aleksin, and Tula. They were not able to break through.[4]

The "errors" referred to by Zhukov probably are an indirect criticism of Stalin and Budenny. Some Soviet historians have charged that at the beginning of October the supreme command and Budenny had positioned the Reserve Front too close to the rear of the Western Front to allow a true defense in depth or adequate freedom of maneuver for the Western Front.[5] Zhukov's comment about German manpower being superior should be taken to mean superior only on narrow sectors of the front where the German offensive strength was the greatest.

The battles of Briansk and Viazma were fought by the Russians on the same principles used in the battles of Bialystok-Minsk and Kiev.

In 1941, the Red Army lacked the capability of rapid maneuver of its large formations, so it was impossible for Stalin and his generals to entertain seriously the idea of ordering sudden retreats for entire army fronts. Recall that at one point in September, Zhukov was prepared to risk the withdrawal eastward of the whole Southwestern Front in order to save it from being cut off. The real disagreement between Stalin and Zhukov here concerned the likelihood of a future thrust against Moscow in the fall. Had the Germans failed to live up to Stalin's expectations, had they denied themselves the temptation of Moscow, then Zhukov and Timoshenko would have been proven right. For his part, Zhukov had no qualms about exacting enormous sacrifices from the men under his command if the situation so demanded. This point was true not only at Bialystok-Minsk and Briansk-Viazma, but also in battles later in the war against Army Group Center in White Russia and Poland. Other generals in history, such as Grant, Haig, and Neville, also had a reputation for producing long casualty lists. In certain cases such tactics were the height of folly (Haig and Neville), but Grant and Zhukov were winners, however terrible the price.

The time gained by the Red Army in the great battles of encirclement and annihilation that took place during the first four months of the war was used by the Russian command to transform Moscow into a strongly fortified area. Most importantly, time was gained for the mobilization and deployment of the strategic reserve along what would become the northern and southern flanks of Army Group Center as the Germans continued their advance toward Moscow. As has been seen, a considerable portion of the strategic reserve had already been sent to the various fronts, mainly the Western Front, to bolster the forces along the Dnepr, but important elements of the reserves were held back to play a decisive role in December as the Wehrmacht neared the capital.

At the end of November, the Twentieth and First Shock Armies of the strategic reserve were moved into the Moscow region to join the newly formed Twenty-fourth, Twenty-sixth, and Sixtieth Armies. In addition, the Tenth Army was concentrated south of Riazan, and the Sixty-first Army deployed around Riazhsk and Ranenburg. From November 1 to 15, 1941, the Western Front received 100,000 officers and men, 300 tanks, and 2,000 guns from the strategic reserve. From

November 15 to December 15, the Moscow Zone of Defense was able to send 200,000 fully equipped troops to the Western and Kalinin Fronts as well as to the remnants of the Southwestern Front defending the line Belopole-Lebedin-Novomoskovsk. From mid-November on, Artemev's Moscow Zone of Defense was in actual charge of the deployment of the strategic reserve. Some of the units that Artemev had at his disposal for use around Moscow, at least three rifle and two tank divisions, came from the Far East, thanks to the timely advice sent from Tokyo by Richard Sorge, the master spy who correctly notified the Kremlin on September 14 that the Japanese would make no move against the Soviet Union. In the main, the First Shock Army, which was to play a key role in the Moscow counteroffensive, was made up of men from Siberia and the Urals, as well as the Gorki and Moscow regions.

As the battles neared Moscow, fresh units arrived continuously from the northern, eastern, and southern parts of the country. Ski troops came mainly from the Gorki and Kirov regions; rifle divisions and tank formations arrived from the Volga, Urals, Trans-Urals, and the Far East; and several cavalry units were transferred from Central Asia. In large measure the German November offensive was repelled by reserves from the interior of the country. Units from the Fifth, Thirty-third, Forty-third, and Forty-ninth Armies as well as from reserve units were regrouped in the direction of Volokolamsk, where Panzer Group 3 was attempting to envelop the capital from the northwest. Reserves of the Kalinin Front and the STAVKA reserve were used there only sparingly. To repel the attack of Guderian's Second Panzer Army[6] from the south toward Tula and Moscow, the Tenth and Fiftieth Armies and the Western Front's reserves were engaged. Constant reinforcement of the troops along the northwestern and southern approaches to the capital allowed the density of Russian troops to be gradually increased. By the time Army Group Center neared Moscow, the Red Army was prepared to deliver devastating blows to both the northern and southern flanks of von Bock's hapless force.

The size of the strategic reserve forces concentrated around Moscow on the flanks of Army Group Center by early December spelled disaster for the Wehrmacht. Not only had the Red Army been able to send seven new armies to the Western Front for the Moscow counteroffensive, but several other armies received substantial reinforcements. Altogether, the Russian forces gathered around Moscow numbered 1.1 million men, 7,652 guns and mortars, 774 tanks (including 222 T-34s and KVs), and 1,000 aircraft.

The decision about exactly when the counteroffensive should occur was made easier when reports from the front indicated that the German troops were so weakened by the cold and lack of nourishment that they could not withstand an all-out assault. Inspired by their growing successes in defense, Russian troops were able to shift to the counteroffensive with little or no transition time.

On November 29, 1941, Zhukov called Stalin by telephone and, having briefed him on the situation, asked for permission to start the counteroffensive. As Zhukov recalled, Stalin listened to him attentively, and the following coversation ensued:

STALIN: "Are you sure that the enemy is close to a crisis and has no opportunity to engage any fresh troops?"

ZHUKOV: "The enemy is exhausted, but if we don't destroy their spearheads they will be able to reinforce their troops near Moscow with major reserves from their northern and southern army groups and then the situation will become a good deal more complicated."

Stalin ended the conversation saying that he would consult with the general staff.

"Late at night on November 29," recalled Zhukov, "we were informed that the STAVKA decided to begin the counteroffensive and demanded our plan for the operation. In the morning of November 30 we presented to the STAVKA a planning map of the counteroffensive which marked the disposition of forces on November 30 and indicated the assignments for the right and left wings of the Western Front in the attack."

It was Zhukov's goal to use the forces at his disposal to drive the enemy all the way back to Staraia Russa-Velikie Luki-Vitebsk-Smolensk-Briansk and, if possible, to encircle the Germans in the areas of Rzhev, Viazma, and Smolensk. The main weight of the counteroffensive was to fall north of Moscow, where the Russians were able to achieve an overall numerical superiority. In some areas, such as on the southern wing of Konev's Kalinin Front, their edge rose to 50 percent—more than enough to nullify the superiority in tanks and aircraft of Panzer Group 3 and the Ninth Army. South of Moscow, Guderian's Second Panzer Army and von Weichs's Second Army also were to face an enemy stronger than they were in manpower, although here the difference was not so decisive.

On November 30 the STAVKA adopted Zhukov's plan for the counteroffensive against Army Group Center by the Western Front and the right wing of the Southwestern Front.

Preparations for the operation proceeded rapidly, as the situation in early December permitted no delays. The enemy's offensive power was spent, the severe winter having taken its toll. In the process of trying to deeply envelop Moscow, the spearheads of the Wehrmacht were themselves surrounded on three sides by Soviet troops. Zhukov recalled:

> Guderian's troops began to retreat without orders from the high command. The same thing happened also to the northwest of Moscow. The troops of Hoepner's tank army also started to retreat without Hitler's orders and in absence of the order from the commander of Army Group Center. What do these facts demonstrate? They show to us that the enemy's spearheads were already unable to accomplish offensive missions.

Zhukov realized that any delays in kicking off the counteroffensive would mean giving the enemy a chance to pull back to more defensible positions behind the Rzhev-Viazma-Briansk-Orel line, and to draw in forces from other fronts. This would have been an unforgivable mistake and might have prolonged the war, with unpredictable consequences for the Soviet side. Thus, the decision was made to exploit the enemy's weaknesses immediately without waiting to regroup. This also explains why the forces used in the counteroffensive were not able to overwhelm the enemy numerically on all sectors. The Western Front stretched 700 km. from north to south, and most of its armies had fronts extending 20–80 km. and more. An average rifle division had a front extending 5–14 km. The average density of artillery was no more than 1,427 guns and mortars per kilometer, whereas tank and armored vehicle density was 0.5 to 2.0 per kilometer. Although these densities were low, Zhukov reckoned the margin of safety lay in the exhaustion and demoralization among the enemy soldiers, who were so obviously ill equipped to fight a winter war in the Russian taiga.

A rapid shift to the counteroffensive without an operational pause was not originally planned, and the spontaneity of it caught the German high command totally off guard.

Even on December 4, when little more than twenty-four hours remained until the beginning of the counteroffensive, Army Group Center reported that "the combat power of the Red Army cannot be estimated as high enough to be able to begin the counteroffensive." It is interesting that the daily situation maps of the German General Staff, which reflected the situation on the Soviet-German front, by December 6 showed only seven out of ten armies of the Western Front. Comparatively heavy Soviet formations such as the First Assault Army and the Twentieth and Tenth Armies, which later played important roles in the course of Zhukov's counteroffensive, were beyond the horizon of German intelligence. The German General Staff failed to discover significant concentrations of Red Army units ready for the long-awaited counteroffensive. At the beginning of December on the northwestern approaches to Moscow, seven rifle and one cavalry division were redeployed, as well as sixteen rifle brigades, three artillery regiments of the STAVKA reserve, four tank and eleven ski battalions, and five battalions of Katiusha artillery. To destroy the enemy groups in the south, STAVKA covertly concentrated eight rifle and two cavalry divisions, one artillery regiment of the reserves, and four Katiusha artillery battalions. In addition, by mid-December STAVKA reinforced the central sector of Konev's Western Front with four rifle divisions, one rifle brigade, one artillery regiment, and two Katiusha artillery battalions.

The German high command, unaware of these units, stated that the Soviet army had no reserves, and ordered its troops to continue the offensive with the aim of capturing Moscow. The trouble was that the Germans had no strategic vision or any scenario that would have enabled the Soviets to accumulate reinforcements of this magnitude and position them so appropriately for a counteroffensive.

We should note that, according to Zhukov's plan, various units were committed to the counteroffensive at different times. The Germans, having no reserves, were compelled to maneuver their forces to respond to the attacks while they were in close contact with Soviet troops—always a dangerous undertaking. Along the main axes of the counteroffensive, the Germans transferred some units from quieter sectors. But the Kalinin Front began its counteroffensive on December 5—a day earlier than the others. The fact that the Germans shifted some units farther north to bolster the line there resulted in a weakening of the forces opposite the center of the Western Front, making its mission easier to accomplish. Zhukov realized above all else that it was essential to destroy the most serious menace to Moscow—Panzer Groups 3 and 4—from the north.

The shocks that compelled Army Group Center to reel backward after December 6 might have succeeded to an even greater extent than they actually did had Stalin followed Zhukov's advice. It had been Zhukov's original intention to launch two minor counteroffensives in mid-November against Army Groups North and South, one at Tikhvin and the other at Rostov, in order to prevent Army Group Center from calling for help from its neighbors after the main action got under way around Moscow. Although Zhukov had command over only the Western Front, his position on the supreme command staff permitted him to voice opinions about the situation in other areas as well. Stalin, agreeing with this idea in principle, wanted to make the counteroffensives against Army Groups North and South considerably stronger than Zhukov desired. In this way, the counterattack around Moscow was weakened and the maximum results were not achieved.

After the initial success of Zhukov's counteroffensive, the Germans had little time to prepare defensive positions and to construct fortified zones. In his memoirs Gen. Kurt von Tippelskirch said, "Russian troops, which were opposing Army Group Center, obviously were waiting only for the moment when the attacker was completely exhausted to begin a counteroffensive with newly arrived reserves." He was right, of course, but he wrote these words many years after the fact. On November 18, 1941, Halder wrote in his diary: "Field Marshal von Bock, just like ourselves, thinks that at present both the sides are at their extreme limits of endurance . . . The enemy lacks reserves in the depth, or even at its front, and he is sure to be in a much worse position here than we are." Even three days before the beginning of the offensive, Halder was certain that the resistance of the Soviet troops had reached its maximum. This was another great miscalculation by the German high command.

The main axes of the Western Front in the December 6 counteroffensive were directed against German panzer groups on the northern and southern flanks. The troops of the Kalinin Front, the Thirtieth and Tenth Armies of the Western Front, and the forces of the right flank of the Southwestern Front were to hit the poorly protected flanks of Army Group Center with the aim of rolling them back and enveloping as many Germans as possible. There is a direct connection here with the general German conception of operational art. The German General Staff, basing its ideas on the experience of operations against France in 1940, issued a directive on November 20, 1940, that contained recommendations about conducting an offensive. "Decisive breakthrough, without any fear of threats from the flanks, accomplishes the destruction of the enemy's front." In this view, the positive outcome of battle was seen as dependent only on the momentum of advance, regardless of threats to the flanks. Actually, this may have been a hangover from September 1914 when the powerful right-wing thrust of the Schlieffen Plan through Belgium was brought to a halt at the Marne River, prematurely some thought. Only by a reckless disregard of dangers in areas separate from the main offensive thrust could a blitzkrieg war be won. This was certainly the message of Guderian's pre-war book *Achtung Panzer!* and it was a philosophy that he constantly harped on to his subordinates and superiors alike.

If such tactics could be somehow justified in a war with a weak enemy, in the war against the Soviet Union they proved to be an unmitigated disaster. Adhering to this pattern of tactics and operational art put the Germans into a critical situation during the battle of Moscow. Panzer Groups 3 and 4 punched like wedges into Soviet defenses, but then they themselves were exposed. This also happened to Guderian near Kashira, when his exposed and weakened flanks were vulnerable to strikes from Mikhailovo and Serebrianye Prudy (Silver Ponds).

Close coordination was achieved between the armies of the fronts. For example, the destruction of Panzer Group 3 on the northwestern approaches to Moscow both in accordance with the idea of the offensive plan and in actual fact was implemented by coordinated operations of the armies of the right wing of the Western Front. The Thirtieth and First Assault (*Udarnye*) Armies advanced from opposite directions toward Klin to encircle and destroy the Germans there. The Twentieth and part of the forces of the Sixteenth Army overcame the Germans at Solnechnogorsk while the main forces of the Sixteenth Army and part of the forces of the Fifth Army fell upon the Germans around Istra. Coordination among the forces of multiple armies was achieved also along the left flank of the front. Here, thanks to coordinated operations of the Tenth and Fiftieth Armies and Belov's operational group, Guderian's Second Panzer Army was decimated near Tula.

An analysis of the preparation and conduct of the counteroffensive shows that surprise was achieved not only due to the covert concentration of reserves but also due to the increased availability of newer weapons. The ground assault aircraft Il-2, or Sturmovik, was particularly devastating. This plane was well armored and could absorb tremendous punishment from ground fire. The Germans nicknamed the Sturmovik *fliegende Panzer* (flying tanks). Also, the T-34 and KV tanks appeared in ever-larger numbers closer to Moscow, as did Katiusha rocket artillery.

Surprise, however, played a positive role only in the first days of the counteroffensive operation. Later, after December 8, when the German command admitted that taking up defenses along the whole Soviet-German front was necessary and ordered the construction of fortified lines, taking advantage of the terrain, Soviet troops were faced with the problem of breaking through prepared lines. For example, the troops of the Twenty-second and Twenty-ninth Armies of the Kalinin Front that joined the counteroffensive on December 18 failed to advance for three full days in the direction of Staritsa to the southwest of Kalinin. To alleviate this situation the STAVKA had to rush the Thirty-ninth Army into combat to encircle and destroy the main body of the German Ninth Army.

The practice of frontal attacks against enemy strongpoints, as had been the case in the war against Finland in 1940, led to scanty results and significant losses in personnel and materiel. It was not long be-

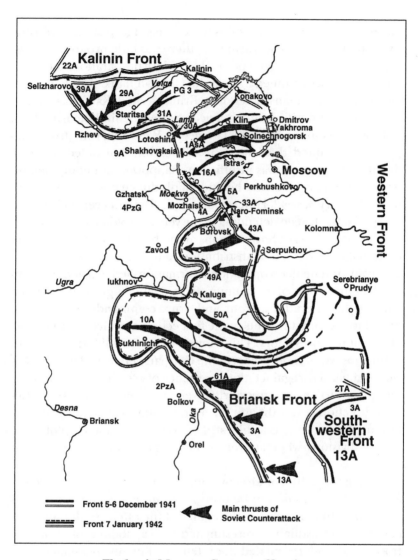

Zhukov's Moscow Counteroffensive

fore these kinds of wasteful assaults were stopped. In the winter of
1941–42, as German defenses consisted mainly of isolated strongpoints, it was possible to use enveloping maneuvers, which generally
forced them to retreat to avoid being cut off. On December 7 the

Sixteenth Army, using part of its forces, began its push toward Istra. Even though surprise was achieved, there was little progress. On December 8, this time after a powerful artillery preparation, the counteroffensive was resumed against the German flank. To avoid encirclement the Germans defending Kriukove and Kamenka had to abandon their positions and hurriedly retreat behind the Istra River.

From December 25 until January 7, Western Front troops repeatedly assaulted the Lama–Rusa River line but failed to break through. Here there was insufficient manpower and equipment to overcome enemy resistance behind solidly dug-in positions. In his order of January 3, 1942, Hitler demanded, "Defend every village, not a step of retreat, keep defending to the very last soldier and bullet . . ."

The operations of Soviet troops along broad fronts with low operational densities, equal distribution of forces and materiel along the front, and no deep operational formations led to a general slowdown in the course of the counteroffensive and its gradual cessation. During the operations, front and army commanders were compelled to regroup the units of the first echelon, concentrating their efforts at narrow sectors. This allowed them to inflict sharp attacks at the most vulnerable points in the German defenses. Thus, the Soviet command first gained the experience of creating powerful striking groups to ensure superiority over the enemy in decisive localized directions even though an overall numerical superiority was lacking. In an army, as a rule, strike groups were made up of three or four divisions, whereas over a frontal region several armies might be involved.

During the battle for Moscow the Red Army made many mistakes as well, which should not be overlooked no matter how successful the results. In particular, in the course of the offensive the supreme command unjustifiably overestimated the capabilities of their own troops and underestimated the intensity of enemy resistance. As a result, the mission of encircling and destroying Army Group Center assigned to the troops of the Western Front in January 1942 as a follow-on to the Moscow counteroffensive was not accomplished. Several STAVKA decisions about deploying the strategic reserve did not help matters either. At the crucial moment of battle the First Assault

Army was sent to the northeast and three reserve armies near Moscow—the Twenty-fourth, Twenty-sixth, and Sixtieth—were not used. Front and army commanders failed to use their reserves effectively in many cases. Their piecemeal deployments resulted in a dispersion of forces and did not produce the desired results. These mistakes apparently were due to the euphoria caused by initial successes in the counteroffensive.

Careful analysis of the Red Army's experience in the battle of Moscow exposes significant shortfalls in the deployment of various service components. For example, the fact that organic aviation divisions were incorporated into the fronts and armies denied STAVKA the opportunity of focusing aviation properly in key directions. Its use, especially deep into enemy defenses, was largely ineffective. Long intervals between air strikes and the jump-off of the ground troops allowed the Germans to restore cohesive defenses, thus endangering operations. When the counteroffensive was already in full swing it became clear that constant air support was necessary. This problem was imperfectly solved after some improvisation. The problem of centralized employment of air support at the front level was lessened when major operational air units were formed as well as mobile reserve units becoming separate corps and divisions of the STAVKA reserve.

Lack of experience in destroying the Germans during offensive actions could also be seen in the use of artillery. The planning of artillery preparations before the counteroffensive received detailed attention. Typically, troops began the counteroffensive after a ten- to fifteen-minute barrage that was supposed to hit every assault direction simultaneously, but in practice this did not happen often. Artillery was equally distributed along the front lines instead of concentrated behind main jump-off points, where it would have done the most good. During the initial stage of the counteroffensive when the enemy had not yet shifted to defense, the improperly dispersed artillery fires were virtually undetectable at the very time when they should have had their greatest effect. Later, after the Germans began to organize resistance in prepared positions, artillery fires should have been concentrated even more, but this was generally not done.

Without constant artillery support, the infantry was frequently unable to accomplish its missions. Finally, in accord with a STAVKA directive in January 1942, artillery preparation was replaced by the "artillery offensive." This concept presupposed massive use of self-propelled artillery, enabling constantly advancing fire support for assaulting troops. The first experience with a prototype artillery offensive was by the Twentieth Army in January 1942 while cracking the German defenses at the Lama River.

Problems also existed in the use of airborne troops. To assist the Kalinin and Western Fronts in encircling Army Group Center in January 1942, the STAVKA decided to conduct an airborne operation. In accord with the planned scenario, units of the IV Airborne Corps landed in an area to the southwest of Viazma. Their actions in the enemy rear during a six-month period played an important role, but the major goal of the operation was not achieved. This was due mainly to the absence of the necessary preliminary work in defining the mission of the troops and the scope of the landing as well as poor timing and coordination between the landing forces and the troops assaulting from the front. Here once again no objective estimate of the relationship of forces took place, as had happened earlier. Such an operation needed a more detailed analysis of all relevant questions. Mistakes were made not only in planning but in the practical training of the troops of the landing force and the support and supply troops, and coordination with the main groupings of the Kalinin and Western Fronts. Because of a lack of airlift capacity, landings took too much time and the element of surprise was forfeited. Apart from that, insufficient training of pilots and their lack of experience in some cases resulted in misdirected landings and the dispersion of paratroopers over areas that were much too large. Several days were frequently necessary for paratroops to assemble at predetermined checkpoints.

Looked at from a broad perspective, the Moscow counteroffensive was not conveniently timed. It was conducted when large Wehrmacht forces were being shifted from Western Europe. German forces near Viazma were significantly strengthened while the offensive potential of Soviet troops was greatly reduced. Coordination between headquarters and troops engaged in the operation was unsatisfactory. In fact, the airborne troops were dropped into combat without any external or nonorganic support. There was no support even when the artillery resources of the fronts could have directed fires to help them. The airborne troops also did not enjoy protection from the air; no air support existed, and air-dropped reinforcements and materiel were nonexistent.

For the counteroffensive to be successful there had to be timely reinforcement in order to sustain a high momentum in the advance. Close to Moscow this was not a problem, as plenty of troops were available; every army had two or three divisions in reserve as a second echelon. But even this was insufficient to sustain a rapid advance over long distances. It became obvious that more armored and mechanized units were needed. These had to have great striking potential, high maneuverability, and independence in order to achieve and sustain high rates of advance. These mobile forces could inflict cutting blows and penetrate defensive systems deeply, encircling large enemy groupings, quickly exploiting breakthroughs on key sectors, and conducting deep raids in the enemy's rear. In formulating these concepts, strategies and tactics were evolved that had potential use later against NATO in the post-war period.

Front and army commanders tried to compensate for the lack of armored and mechanized units by creating improvised mobile combined-arms groups composed of tank, rifle, and armored cavalry units. For instance, the mobile group of the Thirtieth Army of the Western Front consisted of the 8th and 21st Tank Brigades, the 46th Motorized Regiment, and the 145th Tank Battalion. Similar groups were formed in the Sixteenth Army and in others as well. Infiltrating through the enemy rear, they destroyed headquarters and supply units, cut the routes of transportation, and interdicted the evacuation and retreat of the enemy. Their bold and decisive strikes caused fear and panic in the enemy and helped the troops attacking from the front to seize important road junctions and inhibit the enemy's movement.

Taking into account the fact that the Germans were highly active in the daylight hours but preferred to dig in at night for warmth, special night action detachments were formed. In the dark hours of the morning on December 6, forward battalions of the first echelon of the Thirtieth Army, supported by tanks but without artillery preparation, attacked the positions of the 1st Panzer and the 36th and 14th Motorized Divisions along a 60-km. front, achieving great success.

At the concluding stage of the counteroffensive, forward detachments were organized in divisions consisting mainly of rifle and ski battalions. They were able to maneuver ahead of the main body, capturing important objectives and ensuring freedom of action for main forces, striking at the enemy's rear and flanks.

The experience of organizing and conducting defensive operations at both the distant and close approaches to Moscow demonstrated convincingly that, by exploiting the advantages of terrain, defending troops can hold their positions despite enemy superiority in strength. If proper attention is paid to field fortifications, minefields, and laying out fire grids, defending troops can inflict heavy losses on the enemy and break an offensive. Success depended above all else on firm command and control of the troops on the part of supreme command as well as the front and army commanders.

The Wehrmacht suffered serious losses at Moscow. Although the Germans would retain the tactical initiative in the south until the time of the battle of Kursk in July 1943, never again after Kiev and the commencement of Operation Typhoon would they have a strategic advantage. The losses incurred by Army Group Center during Operation Typhoon from October 1, 1941, to January 31, 1942, were 369,500 men. In all, twenty-three divisions were destroyed or severely attrited. German losses in tanks were so significant that industry was unable to replenish them. German artillery suffered even greater losses.The fact that thirty-five Wehrmacht generals were removed from their posts after Moscow also testifies to the graveness of the defeat.

These failures seriously undermined the morale of German troops and forever laid to rest the myth of their invincibility. Operation Typhoon was a monumental catastrophe fraught with further long-range consequences. As Halder put it, "the outcome of the battle of Moscow was the beginning of the tragedy in the East." A strong case can be made, however, for putting the beginning of the tragedy earlier, back in July and August when Army Group Center was forced to pause along the upper Dnepr first to deal with the advance of the Twenty-first Army against its southern flank at Propoisk-Rogachev-Zhlobin, and then to confront the situation at Yelnia. As has been seen, Zhukov's bloodletting of the Germans at Yelnia was the first real sign that Germany was going to lose the war.

The inexorable law uttered by Gen. Erich von Ludendorff at the end of World War I—"A single mistake in strategy cannot be made good in the same war"—could not be repealed. The German high command had thrown away any chance of winning a strategic victory after the battle of Kiev, and the results of the battle of Moscow were a confirmation of this fact: the blitzkrieg died a natural death. The German high command should have recognized this truth after the development of the struggle along the Dnepr—they should have admitted to themselves and to Hitler that the war was bound to be long and grueling—but they would not or could not make the admission.

Although three and a half more years of war were needed to defeat the enemy and bring the war to a successful conclusion, a Soviet victory was confirmed by the results of Zhukov's Moscow counteroffensive that were visible in the snows drenched with German blood around Kalinin and Rzhev. Zhukov's success in saving Russia from an overwhelming disaster in 1941 was due much more, however, to his own genius than it was to the ineptness of the Germans. The strains and mistakes in the German high command occurred because they encountered a prepared enemy, well equipped and in possession of a strategic vision for winning the war. The Germans had not expected that, and they were in no way capable of dealing with this new reality.

Stalin's strategy of massing the reserves around Moscow while ignoring the encirclement of the Southwestern Front until it was too late should have led to the defeat of the Red Army in the spring campaign of 1942. That it did not was the fault of the German command system. Had the Germans not undertaken Operation Typhoon, instead holding their positions on the Rzhev-Viazma-Oka River-Orel line in the central region of the front while continuing to exploit the gains in the south after the fall of Kiev, then the situation would have been considerably worse, probably fatal for the Russians. Zhukov's reserves, so skillfully massed north and south of Moscow, would not have been in position to inflict grievous damage on Army Group Center, certainly not to the extent they did in December. Instead of tearing into the German flanks at the gates of Moscow, Zhukov's reserves would have had to hold where they were anticipating a German assault on the capital, which would never come, or they would have been expended in counterattacks that largely batted the breeze.

It may be wondered how effective the Russian strategy was that allowed entire fronts to be encircled by the German panzers without permitting a retreat. In the case of the encirclements at Smolensk and Roslavl, no timely retreat was possible, but this was not true at Bialystok-Minsk or at Kiev. It was Zhukov's intention at first to allow vast forces to be surrounded by the German panzer groups, thus forcing the enemy to spend time and materiel in the reduction of the large pockets of trapped Red Army units. Zhukov and Timoshenko did not disagree with Stalin about the necessity of sacrificing the three armies in the Bialystok salient, but Kiev was a different matter. Not only were the forces deployed there much larger than at Bialystok, but Stalin went so far as to refuse to order an all-out attack by the Briansk Front on Guderian's eastern flank in late August and early September, preferring instead to conserve the forces of the front in order to blunt a later advance by Army Group Center directly on Moscow. This plan was too much for first Zhukov and then Timoshenko to accept, and so they temporarily parted with their chief over this issue. The German high command, however, set things right for Stalin in Operation Typhoon.

The final choice about the deployment and use of the strategic reserve was made by Stalin in the face of intense pressures placed on him by his most trusted commanders. Whether or not the risk the Soviet dictator took in postponing full mobilization until after the war began was justified is a question that still can be debated, as can Stalin's plan to wait until the enemy approached the gates of Moscow before committing the reserves to an all-out counteroffensive. Had the reserves been sent to the Southwestern Front in the fall, as Zhukov and Budenny had wished, the defense of Moscow in December would have been seriously jeopardized, if not impossible. It appears at first glance that Stalin was right and Zhukov was wrong about the reserves, but the issue is too complex to permit a simple resolution. Zhukov believed that Kiev was to be the stepping-stone for a continued German offensive in the south toward the Donbas and the Caucasus. It did not seem plausible to him that Army Group Center would resume the advance on Moscow in late September and that Guderian would attempt to drive on the capital from the south through Orel and Tula. In retrospect, Zhukov's assessment was the one that was most rational.

By the end of January 1942, Army Group Center had managed to stabilize its front along the line Rzhev—west of the line Staritsa-Lukhnov-Suchinitsi-Belev-Chern—points much farther east than Zhukov had planned. Had Stalin followed his recommendations, the setback of Army Group Center might have turned into something more significant, but the opportunity was lost. Stalin may have been fortunate in sticking by his guns and refusing to accept Zhukov's dire warnings in September, but he should have listened to him more carefully in November—although even if Zhukov's plan had been carried out, the war would still have been far from over.

The battle for Moscow in the winter of 1941–42 did not end the war for Germany in the east, but this colossal defeat went a long way toward sealing the fate of the Wehrmacht. Although the battle served as dramatic proof that Germany's era of rapid victories had come to an end, the actual collapse of the blitzkrieg method of warfare had come during the struggles along the Dnepr River in the summer of 1941. The German high command was not able to make its strategy and tactics conform to reality. The reality of the battles at Smolensk-Yelnia, Gomel, Velikie Luki, and Kiev all pointed to the fact that the war would be a long trial. In the last analysis, however, no one in either of the two military command organizations, OKW or OKH, was willing to take the final step and advise Hitler about the truth of the matter. The ultimate responsibility for Germany's debacle must belong to Hitler, but he should not shoulder this blame alone. Also, to place the blame for Germany's defeat solely on the Germans would be a serious distortion of the truth. The truth is, the Russians—despite egregious errors on the part of some, such as Stalin, Pavlov, and Eremenko—were able to capitalize on German mistakes and win the war.

It can only be said that Stalin was right about Moscow, although the price he paid for the victory—the loss of the Southwestern Front—was fearful. Stalin had the ability to force his generals to bow to his will, a task that Hitler, by contrast, would not attempt, however halfheartedly, until Rundstedt, Brauchitsch, and Guderian were dismissed or resigned in November and December 1941. It would appear that the Soviet leadership at the highest strategical-political level was a long distance ahead of that of its antagonist. But it was not Stalin who was the mastermind—it was Zhukov. Even when the Soviet dictator pulled Zhukov down after his warnings about Kiev, his innate sense of survival compelled him to keep the general close at hand, and when the fateful hour of decision came, he let him work his will against the enemy.

·8·
A WAR WON AND LOST: AN ANALYSIS

Soviet Strategy in Transition

It is now possible to make some judgments about Soviet wartime strategic leadership that could not be made earlier. Rather, opinions could have been held, but only as conjecture. Today, the relevant facts at hand and opinions can be offered based on a level of information that historians in the west at least could never have even dreamed about a few years ago. Since it is strategy that determines the outcome of war, provided that the opponents are relatively equal in the amount of resources they can mobilize and bring into the conflict, it is the most important issue. With resources, the problem of objectively estimating their effectiveness is a severe one. The best question to ask is, "Would you trade forces with the enemy?" or, put another way, "Would you rather be the Russian or the German commander in a Barbarossa war game?" With fifty years of hindsight, the answer to these questions seems fairly obvious, yet why should this be so?

The quote from Geoffrey Blainey's book *The Causes of War,* used as the epigraph of this book, brings the strategy issue sharply into focus. It is true that both sides in a looming war feel that they will be victorious; why else would they fight? Nations that know they will be defeated usually surrender or make some kind of peace accommodation, as was the case when Germany occupied Lithuania in 1940 or when China opened its doors to foreign occupiers in the late nineteenth century. With the information presented here, we can demonstrate that not only did Stalin and the Soviet high command believe that they would win a war against Germany, some of them advocated a preemptive or first strike against the enemy. Thus, the myth that Stalin and his generals were caught off guard by the German onslaught must forever be laid to rest. Quite the contrary, the difficulties they had in countering the German invasion were caused in the main by their reliance too long on a first-strike strategy based on a scenario of using the Bialystok salient as a springboard for an offensive into the heart of Central and Western Europe. The dilemma faced by Stalin and the high command in early 1941 was how to adapt a strategic situation designed for a first-strike offensive war to better answer the changed conditions of an enemy first strike.

In Stalin's mind, the enemy striking first was a scenario that was not supposed to happen. France was supposed to remain in the war with Britain, and the United States was supposed to come to her aid, tying down the German Wehrmacht in a war of attrition on the Western Front, as had happened in 1914–18. But the best-laid plans of Stalin and his armored warfare expert, Pavlov, were dashed with the rapid defeat of the French in May 1940. The crucial turning point in Soviet strategy was the two Kremlin war games in January 1941. These convinced Stalin with crystal clarity that Pavlov's makeshift attempt to adapt Bialystok into a defensive bastion would lead to a colossal disaster. Zhukov and Timoshenko, however, came to the rescue literally at the last minute with plans of their own for a deeply echeloned defense strategy. The super-secret defense plan was tested in February 1941 at a clandestine war game, the existence of which we reveal here for the first time. Although this plan was not fully implemented with all the reserves that Zhukov and Timoshenko had asked for in a timely fashion, the resources allocated to them by Stalin were sufficient to halt the advance of the Wehrmacht in the crucial central sector along the upper Dnepr River. This halt was forced on the Germans by the threat to their southern flank, a fact that has been seriously underplayed by the German generals in their memoirs but that stands out in stark relief in the war diaries of the units undergoing assaults from the south, particularly in the region along the Dnepr River near Rogachev-Zhlobin.

The February 1941 plan had one feature to it that has kept it hidden to this very day. Stalin decided to keep the plan secret from Pavlov and the others charged with the forward defenses to the west. Even though Zhukov and Timoshenko, with Stalin's approval, had no intention of launching a counteroffensive so close to the frontier to provide relief to Pavlov when the war started, Pavlov could not be told the truth. His arrest, trial, and subsequent execution were pre-ordained in a course of events that, once set in motion, could not be stopped. Was Khrushchev right in condemning Stalin for failing to fortify the western borders as Pavlov wanted? Could blood and territory have been spared by the implementation of what Pavlov had advocated?

In light of today's evidence, the judgment must be "no." Pavlov made himself a victim once the strategic situation had changed and Germany was able to bring up the full might of its armed forces to the east. The trap that Pavlov fell into had no exit other than death. In the human sense, what happened to Pavlov was a tragedy of great proportions, and the ramifications of it are still with us, in that the true story of his sacrifice, and the sacrifice of the men in his command, has not been told until now. Yet, the ultimate conclusion is inescapable that although Pavlov's fate could have been softened, the outcome of it could not have been fundamentally altered.

Much has been made in this book of the defeat inflicted upon Army Group Center in the battles around the Yelnia salient in July–August 1941. We can say that these battles signaled the beginning of the end for German victories because here all the elements were present that presaged the end. The mistakes by the German high command, notably by Halder and Guderian, which were exacerbated by Hitler and Göring, were fatal to any hopes that Germany had for winning the war. Had the German high command eschewed the assault on fortress Moscow, too late in the year for the attempt to have any chance of success, then the war could possibly have been won by Germany, or certainly prolonged. As we have already mentioned, if the Wehrmacht had held the Rzhev–Oka River line on the Central Front instead of plunging east to fall within reach of Zhukov's reserves, hundreds of thousands of lives and mountains of equipment could have been spared. The Wehrmacht could have pursued its strategic advantage in the south, through Ukraine and the Donbas. In the spring or early summer of 1942, Moscow could have been enveloped from all sides, the difference being that there would no longer have been a threat to the southern flank of Army Group Center.

Thus, there were two grave errors on the part of the German high command that forfeited their chance of winning the war on the Eastern Front. The first error was that all of Guderian's panzer group was sent to Ukraine instead of the parts of it that were actually needed. This error led to the mauling of the infantry in the Yelnia salient that was stripped of its armored protection. After the abandonment of Yelnia, the German high command should have realized that an assault on Moscow was impossible for the remainder of the year until after the threat to the southern flank of Army Group Center had been fully eliminated. The second error, the truly fatal mistake, as we have explained, was Operation Typhoon.

The damage the Germans did to themselves was compounded by the things the Russians did right. Zhukov brought everything into play in the cauldron of Yelnia that proved to be the recipe for future victories throughout the remainder of the war. The right mix of combined-arms support of tanks and artillery along with redoubtable Russian infantry brought up from a strategic reserve that was superbly handled by Zhukov proved far too much for the Germans to deal with. They could not imagine how such reserves could have existed. Zhukov and Timoshenko saw to it that enough of the reserves were in the right place at the right time to do the job needed—that is, inflict the greatest damage on the enemy at the cheapest cost to themselves given the circumstances.

We hope that this book will succeed in righting the distortions of history that have mainly blamed Hitler's blunders for what happened on the Eastern Front. The truth is that the blame for the blunders on the German side must be spread out among a larger group of key players. But, most of all, history must give the credit where it really belongs. Zhukov and Timoshenko were able to exploit fully the errors of the German high command, and thus saved their nation and its peoples from a fate that can only be imagined. There is no higher criterion for good generalship. A German occupation of a defeated Russia surely would have surpassed what happened in countries such as Poland in its breadth and ferocity.

Of no lesser significance were the important battles along the Dnepr and Sozh Rivers in the region Rogachev-Zhlobin-Gomel in July and August. Here was tested the Zhukov-Timoshenko strategy of stopping the eastward thrust of Army Group Center by well-planned and coordinated counterattacks against its southern flank. Not only did these succeed in stopping Army Group Center, but they forced the crack in the German leadership to widen, making it impossible for the Germans at one time to solve their problems in the south and take Moscow in 1941. The mistakes made by the German high command in August–September 1941 in essence were considerably worsened by the pressures brought to bear on them by the successes of the Red Army along Army Group Center's long and exposed southern flank.

Combined Arms: The Wave of the Future

The experience of the first three months of the war bore out the correctness of Zhukov's decision to rely on combined-arms operations to defeat the wide-ranging encirclements of the German panzers. The physical characteristics of the USSR and the ability of the Russian people to support a large although poorly mechanized army in 1941 imposed natural limitations on defense planning. With the exception of a brief and faltering attempt in late 1940, after the success of the blitzkrieg in the west, the Russians after 1936 never seriously considered utilizing armor alone in deep penetration maneuvers. The experiences of the Red Army in Spain in 1936, at Lake Khasan and Khalkhin-Gol against the Japanese in 1938 and 1939, and in Finland in 1939–40, were convincing proof that tanks could not play a completely independent role apart from infantry and artillery. This was especially true for an army that could put fewer of its infantry units in vehicles than the Germans. In the Red Army's projected Field Regulations for 1941, tanks were considered part of the complement of the rifle divisions and were thought of as vital for the support of the infantry in the breakthrough of an enemy's tactical zone of defense. As the war progressed, the Russians learned from their mistakes how to neutralize German armored tactics. In the evolution of Russian antitank operations, the battles of Bialystok-Minsk and Smolensk-Yelnia played an important role. The failure of Pavlov's counterattack with three mechanized corps in June, coupled with the German failure to close the Smolensk pocket rapidly in July, confirmed Zhukov's belief that combined-arms tactics would eventually carry the day. His success at Yelnia in late August and early September, a success that rested on the lavish use of artillery and infantry to support tanks in a drive against a well-prepared German position, was crucially important in the development of Russian tactics for the remainder of the war. After the summer of 1941, the Western Front command issued instructions forbidding tank attacks without reconnaissance and a careful coordination of the assault with infantry and artillery. In a defensive role, tanks were to be used to support infantry by direct fire from ambush or dug-in positions. Tanks could be used in semi-independent counterattacks, but only to protect the flanks and the seams of rifle divisions. Throughout the remainder of the war, these tactics were not fundamentally changed. After the summer of 1941, when an increased number of tanks were available, some armored vehicles were attached to rifle regiments.

The problems with the use of infantry support tanks (NPP) proved to be so serious that in January 1942 the STAVKA issued a new set of directives, followed by further directives from the defense commissariat in October of that year. These regulations provided that tanks must support the infantry, particularly along "the axis of the main blow." NPP tanks were to carry out their operations never allowing gaps of more than 200 to 400 meters to develop between them and the following infantry. Instead of allowing NPP tanks to be flung into battle without proper support, where they had in practice incurred heavy losses, the directives required that artillery be used to counter German tanks. Tank-to-tank battles were to be avoided unless the terrain conditions and number relationships were highly favorable. The role of the infantry was to scout for, mark, and, if possible, destroy enemy antitank mines and obstacles. After the initial phase of an assault, the infantry would carry out the crucial mop-up operations that often had been neglected. Pockets of resistance would be closed off and neutralized, not left to be troublesome thorns in the rear of an advance. Artillery and support aviation were to coordinate their operations with the armor and infantry as closely as possible.

During the counteroffensive at Stalingrad in late 1942, these tactics were brought to a finely honed point and used with great success. There, tank regiments and brigades were integrated into rifle divisions. Since each tank battalion had at least one artillery battery and an engineer unit, they were able to penetrate and hold positions in the depths of German defenses. These lessons were incorporated in the Field Regulations of 1943.

It was not until mid-1943, however, with the advent of self-propelled guns on the Soviet side—the Su-76, the Su-122, and the superb Su-152 built on the KV tank chassis—that armored close support of infantry came into its own. The renowned German self-propelled guns had proved their usefulness in close cooperation with infantry many times in 1941, but they were always in critically short supply. Late in the war Soviet breakthroughs were usually accomplished with tanks and self-propelled guns distributed to the infantry regiments. Typically, tanks and self-propelled guns would be assembled 10–15 km. behind the front a couple of days before the attack. In the predawn hours before the assault, these units would move up to their jump-off areas 1–3 km. in back of the main line. If the German resistance was expected to be heavy, the attack would take place in two or three echelons. The first wave would be composed of a battalion of T-34s or a company of KVs. The second wave would move out about 200 to 300 meters behind the second line of the first wave. The reserve elements, the motorized rifle battalion, would operate about the same distance in back of the second wave. The goal was to keep about 25 to 50 meters between the tanks and self-propelled guns. In practice, however, a density of approximately thirty to forty armored vehicles was achieved per kilometer of front along the main axis of the assault. Usually, this combined-arms attack was accompanied by a rolling artillery preparation at a depth of 1.5–2.5 km. In 1943, a great deal of emphasis was placed on moving forward and shifting fire after the enemy began to pull back. As stated earlier, the techniques of advancing artillery fire and employing self-propelled guns became refined enough to earn the name "artillery offensive."

The Failure of the German Command and Control System

According to the interpretation usually favored by historians and memoirists of the war on the Eastern Front, the strategy pursued by Hitler in 1941 was erratic and inconsistent, based less on sound military reasoning than on a confused political, social, and economic ideology.[1] By contrast, the policies of the General Staff and OKH are portrayed as having been clear and consistent but continuously frustrated by incompetent interference from Hitler and OKW. However, careful examination of the events leading up to the postponement of the advance on Moscow until after the battle of Kiev in September 1941 does not support the conclusion that Hitler alone was responsible for the confused strategy that led to the German army's shocking reversal of fortunes at the gates of the Soviet capital in December. The General Staff, OKH, OKW, and some generals in the field, specifically von Bock and Guderian, must share the blame for the blunders that produced the Wehrmacht's first major setback at Yelnia and the later one at Moscow. In many ways, errors in strategic planning made by the German high command and the tortured convolutions of policy and underhanded dealings typifying German military leadership were reflections of the contradictions coming from deep inside the fabric of the Nazi system.

In a real sense, one can say that the Wehrmacht had no strategic guidance in 1941. Instead, the assault on Russia was launched without a unified and coordinated plan of action for all levels of command on all sectors of the front. In June 1941, essentially two strategies were followed, one favored by Hitler and OKW, the other by Halder and OKH. In addition, by mid-July other strategic plans began to emerge, further clouding the situation. Halder and Jodl reached a compromise during the fourth week of August that could possibly have produced desirable results for the Wehrmacht. The nature of this compromise was such, however, that it ran afoul of the plans of Heinz Guderian, who, for a variety of complicated reasons, managed to achieve almost total independence from his superiors. Guderian's autonomy was due in part to the machinations of Halder, for the chief of the General Staff wished to see Guderian gain the cherished goal of Moscow as rapidly as possible. In order to ensure the panzer general's chance of success, Halder systematically insulated Guderian from interference from above. The creation of the Fourth Panzer Army under the nominal command of von Kluge was an artificial device to confuse the command structure and keep Guderian closely tied to OKH. Hitler was able to issue orders immediately to Army Group Center, but von Bock was unable to issue orders direct to Guderian. By making use of Halder's awkward command system, it was easy for the panzer general to devise delays and to "misunderstand" directives sent to him by army group headquarters. Von Bock soon recognized what Halder and Guderian were trying to do. He endeavored repeatedly to regain control over Panzer Group 2, but to no avail.

When Halder first analyzed the strategic problem posed by the Soviet Union during the last half of 1940, Moscow seemed to be the only objective in the country worthy of consideration. In remaining faithful to his first plan to achieve victory, he ignored the best advice given to him by members of his own General Staff organization (such as Greiffenberg, Feyerabend, and Paulus) and made bad use of other strategic studies by Marcks and Lossberg. Throughout 1941, Halder did not waver from his opinion that Moscow should be considered the primary goal in Russia; but he did, as the battlefront situation deteriorated, modify his operational plans a great deal, and his outlook changed significantly in regard to how the enemy should be defeated.

Before June 22 and the beginning of the War in the East, Halder made it known in no uncertain terms that a consideration of economic objectives had no place in the formulation of strategy. The campaign in Russia was to be a purely military exercise, army against army, conducted to destroy the enemy's main force by vast armored encirclements, with infantry bringing up the rear of the advance to secure pockets of surrounded enemy formations. These tactics would be effective because he thought that the Russians would be compelled to position the bulk of their defensive forces along the main approaches to their capital from the west and to defend west of the Dnepr-Dvina line in order to protect their vital industrial bases.

By July 13, however, during the third week of the war, Halder's opinion of the Red Army's toughness underwent a fundamental change. It was clear then that the Red Army had not exhausted its reserves, as more units were known to have arrived in the Smolensk, Orsha, and Vitebsk areas from Ukraine. This, plus the strong Russian pressure from the direction of Velikie Luki on the northern flank of Army Group Center, compelled Halder to advise Hitler to postpone the direct advance on Moscow until after the problems on the flanks of the Army Group Center had been rectified. The troubles for Panzer Group 2 and Second Army on the southern flank of Army Group Center that began after July 13, the starting date for Kuznetsov's counteroffensive with the powerful Twenty-first Army, confirmed Halder's change of mind.

Halder had taken great pains before and during the campaign in the east to see that no one interfered with his plans. The OKH's Deployment Directive Barbarossa in January 1941 set the stage for a major push through White Russia directly toward Moscow, and the creation of the Fourth Panzer Army command under von Kluge in early July was designed to give the panzer generals Guderian and Hoth the maximum amount of freedom to attack eastward as rapidly as possible. By July 13 Halder was willing to postpone the assault on Moscow for the time being. His desire to delay the push on the Soviet capital was increased after the failure of Fourth Panzer Army to close the gap around Smolensk.

On the morning of July 21, Brauchitsch and Heusinger visited von Bock at Army Group Center headquarters and agreed with him that the army group should continue to press east until the last enemy reserves were crushed, but instead of insisting that Guderian and Hoth have the free rein they had enjoyed in the past, Brauchitsch established the precondition that, first and above all else, the Smolensk pocket would have to be secured and eliminated. The OKH was not in the mood to order Guderian to abandon the Yelnia salient completely, but Brauchitsch and Halder were prepared by the third week in July to exercise a restraining hand over the panzer groups to prevent any further extension of their already badly exposed flanks. Following this explanation of OKH's policy, the army commander in chief told von Bock and von Kluge essentially what Halder had told Hitler on July 13: after the closing of the Smolensk pocket and after the refitting of Panzer Groups 2 and 3, Guderian should prepare to turn south and east toward Ukraine; Hoth's Panzer Group 3 alone would remain as Army Group Center's armored force, to support the drive on Moscow by pressing ahead toward the east or the northeast. According to the OKH timetable, Panzer Groups 2 and 3 should have been readied for their new tasks by the beginning of August.

This alteration in the OKH strategic plan was reaffirmed by Halder in a conference held after Brauchitsch returned from his visit. This conference, on July 21, was summarized in a communique on July 23, a document that convinced Guderian that OKH was preparing to throw overboard the entire plan of placing Moscow above all other objectives. This was not, however, the truth of the matter. Halder wished to form a special task force composed of Panzer Group 2 along with part of the Second Army, to be commanded by Field Marshal von Kluge, to be sent to Ukraine, with Stalingrad on the lower Volga as its ultimate objective. The main target of Halder's plans was—as it had always been—Moscow. The Soviet capital could be taken, he believed, by the remaining part of Army Group Center along with some help from one army and Panzer Group 4 from Army Group North. On July 23, the day the communique so despised by Guderian was issued, Halder laid his case before Hitler. In his discussion with the führer, Halder noted that the infantry of the Second and Ninth Armies alone would not be enough to take Moscow after von Kluge's group had been diverted to the southeast. That objective could be accomplished only by Panzer Group 3 first clearing its own flank toward the northeast and then aiding the final drive on both sides of Moscow to begin between August 5 and 10. Army Group North could continue its advance to the north and east, but with the Sixteenth Army moving its southern wing along the line Kholm-Bologoe, a maneuver that would cover Army Group Center's approach to Moscow from the north.

The chief of the General Staff justified his revised proposals to Hitler on the basis that it was proving to be impossible to eliminate Russia's military forces without eliminating its economic base. For this reason, he submitted, the Volga line in the south must be reached by von Kluge's group, a force of about ten infantry divisions plus Panzer Group 2. This group would have the mission of moving through Briansk and Gomel toward Kharkov. In terms of territorial objectives, Halder called for reaching the Caucasus-Volga line, an objective that perhaps could be extended to Kazan if the situation warranted. In Army Group North area, the territory between Rybinsk and Lake Onega was considered particularly important. Army Group

North would have to consolidate its hold here and prepare to send an expedition into the Urals.

In presenting his case to Hitler on July 23, Halder appealed to the führer's sense of reason in terms that, for him, were unusual. Halder had finally realized that Russia's inexhaustible reserves of manpower could not be defeated by the methods heretofore used. He now advocated the shattering of Russia's economic capacity to make war instead of concentrating simply on destroying the enemy's armed forces. One might think that Halder was resorting to a subterfuge, engaging Hitler's sympathies by advancing a consideration dear to his heart—that is, the importance of economic strategy in winning a victory over the Soviet Union—but there is other evidence to show that this was not the case. The earnestness of Halder's newfound interest in economic matters was manifested in a conference held at OKH headquarters on July 25. In this conference, Brauchitsch, who never deviated far from Halder's way of thinking, addressed the chiefs of staff of the three eastern army groups:

> Our main task remains to shatter Russia's capacity to resist. A further goal is to bring their population and production centers under our control. The Russians have a wealth of manpower; we must seize their armament centers before the onset of winter. . . .
>
> Although their armament production is high, it is limited, nevertheless. If we succeed in smashing the enemy strength before us, their superiority in manpower alone will not win the war for them.

Halder now genuinely believed, in contrast to his earlier and narrower philosophy of the war, that economic considerations must be taken into account if the enemy were to be defeated within a reasonable length of time. This change of mind on Halder's part was not, however, a complete departure from the past, for he still had not abandoned the strategy that placed Moscow above all other objectives. In other words, although he now recognized the importance of economic factors in the War in the East, he still stopped short of recommending to Hitler that measures be taken to prepare Germany for a protracted war instead of one short and swift campaign.

Although Hitler was willing to listen to Halder's arguments, he was disinclined to change the wording of a new directive, Directive 33-A, that he caused to be issued that same day, July 23. This directive was a supplement to the Directive 33 that had appeared on July 19, an order that called for armored units from Army Group Center to be used to cover Army Group North's advance on Leningrad and that also made provision for the thrust of part of Army Group Center, mainly Panzer Group 2, into Ukraine to help Army Group South. Halder badly wanted Hitler to change this directive to assign Moscow priority over Leningrad, although he did not disagree with the führer about the necessity of sending Panzer Group 2 to Ukraine. For this reason, Halder had sent Brauchitsch to Hitler to ask for a clarification of Directive 33. This clarification was ready by July 23, and it did not please Halder. Hitler, however, was adamant, so Directive 33-A was issued, confirming the diversion of Panzer Group 2 to the south and the movement of Panzer Group 3 to the north to aid in the capture of Leningrad. In deference to the generals, Hitler said that the advance on Moscow could be continued later with the support of Panzer Group 3 but only after it could be released from the Leningrad operations.

Although Hitler could not have been more explicit about his wishes, Halder was not a man who could be easily rebuffed, so Halder sent his minion, Brauchitsch, to Keitel, the head of OKW, to see what could be done to save the Moscow project there—an undertaking that the chief of the General Staff must have known would increase his own sense of frustration. But he realized that he could not now move Hitler save through OKW. Brauchitsch, though Halder's superior, was totally under his sway. The two men had personalities that were similar to those of Hindenburg and Ludendorff during the First World War, with Ludendorff-Halder providing the brains and Hindenburg-Brauchitsch providing the representation before the head of state. The reaction that Brauchitsch encountered in Keitel's office was blunt. Keitel told Brauchitsch that he could do nothing for him, suggesting that the army commander in chief himself see Hitler if the matter still needed straightening out. So, for the second time on July 23, Hitler received a representative from OKH who pleaded with him to reverse his decision placing Leningrad ahead of Moscow.

The path that Brauchitsch took in his audience with the führer was less oblique than that chosen by Halder. Whereas the chief of the General Staff had stressed both the need for pressing forward rapidly in the south, thereby striking at Russian economic capacity to make war, and the importance of taking Moscow ahead of Leningrad, Brauchitsch shifted ground somewhat and put all of his emphasis on the importance of taking Moscow. He backed away from Halder's earlier claim that it was necessary to send Panzer Group 2 and part of Second Army to Ukraine. In fact, he even denied that an encirclement of Gomel was necessary. Instead of suggesting, as Halder had done a few hours earlier, that only one panzer group— that is, Panzer Group 3—was needed in the attack on Moscow, Brauchitsch asserted that, to be safe, both panzer groups would be required. He contended that success would be produced only by continuing the tried and proven tactics of using far-reaching panzer thrusts ahead of and on either side of advancing infantry armies.

Hitler was unmoved by Brauchitsch's argument and told him that he believed the Russians apparently did not care whether or not their flanks were endangered by broadly sweeping tank maneuvers. The examples of Bialystok, Minsk, and Smolensk were clear to Hitler— the Russians would not surrender even if German armor cut off their units from the east by wide encirclement operations. Hitler's final comment was that from then on it would be better to plan operations that relied more on the ability of the infantry to close and eliminate the pockets of trapped Russians rather than to use up the striking power of the armored units for this purpose. In the case of Smolensk, he pointed out, the pocket had not been sealed, nor had it been possible to ready the panzer groups of Army Group Center for further operations. The clash of wills between Hitler and OKH had temporarily ended, but Hitler would find that Halder would surrender his principles no more easily than the Russians did their lives.

On July 25 Keitel visited Army Group Center headquarters to elaborate on what Hitler had told the army commander in chief two days before. Hitler thought that the tanks were being used up too quickly by Russian flank assaults and that too great a distance separated the tanks from the infantry. The distance had to be shortened if the pockets of trapped Russians were to be eliminated effectively. The führer's "ideal solution," reported Keitel, would be to finish with the Russians on the southern flank of Army Group Center in the area of Gomel-Mozyr by forming several small pockets, as the scope of previous operations planned by the General Staff had been beyond the limits of the army to execute. It was also Hitler's view that strongly fortified areas such as Mogilev must be taken with the use of more artillery in order to avoid heavy casualties. Finally, Keitel noted, the führer had become convinced that smaller, more tightly planned operations were needed because Göring, the Luftwaffe chief, had reported to him large numbers of Russians escaping from the Smolensk pocket.

Von Bock protested this decision, charging that the Luftwaffe's reports were exaggerated and that the enemy had lost considerable materiel at Smolensk. He also denied that the operation around Smolensk had been carried out on an unmanageable scale, maintaining that the delays in moving Second Army across the Dnepr to relieve the panzer divisions on the flanks of Army Group Center were responsible for the failure to close the gap at Dorogobuzh. It should be remembered, however, that von Bock himself had been responsible for the decision not to allow the XII Army Corps to relieve the XXIV Panzer Corps along the Sozh. For the moment, von Bock was in the same position as OKH, powerless to take any direct action to rectify a decision he considered a fatal mistake. But von Bock, like Halder, was a tenacious man, and he would not forfeit his objective, Moscow, without a fight.

When Guderian was told on July 27 that the next goal for his panzer group might be Gomel, he insisted that his tanks would be unable to carry out such a mission in a southerly direction. Although his reluctance to move south could perhaps be useful to OKH in forcing a delay in the implementation of Directive 33-A, such tactics did not fit well with Halder's longer-range plans at this time, for he still believed that Panzer Group 2 would have to go to Ukraine; it was the departure of Panzer Group 3 to Army Group North that he wanted to prevent. On July 26 von Bock telephoned Brauchitsch to inform him of the results of Keitel's visit the day before, and Brauchitsch used this occasion to ask him to formulate a plan for sending all of Panzer Group 2 to Kiev. On the following day, the army commander in chief flew to Borisov and asked von Bock personally to order Guderian to begin his move toward Gomel as soon as possible. Brauchitsch did not, however, tell him that this idea had the approval of OKH. Halder actually did not want Panzer Group 2 to be used against Gomel—Kiev was his real objective—but he thought it was necessary that Guderian begin his march to the south quickly. Brauchitsch tried to leave von Bock with the false impression that he was merely transmitting Hitler's orders, although his speech to the army group chiefs of staff on July 25 should have tipped off von Bock as to OKH's intentions. Regardless of whether or not von Bock accepted Brauchitsch's explanation of the order to dispatch Panzer Group 2 to Gomel, he relayed this order to Guderian, saying only that it had Hitler's approval. It is unlikely, however, that Guderian was misled by the attempt to blame Hitler alone for the order for his panzer group to move southward. The panzer general had been attuned to the real feelings of OKH ever since the General Staff communique of July 23.

On July 26 Halder again took his plea to Hitler to argue for conducting broad operations around Moscow and Kiev, not just small maneuvers, as had been envisioned around Gomel. On this point Hitler did not yield, and neither did he yield on the question of Army Group Center pressing on to Moscow with infantry alone, although he now altered his previous plan somewhat and no longer spoke of sending Panzer Group 3 all the way to Leningrad. Instead, Hitler came closer to Halder's viewpoint and said that Hoth could concentrate his attack in the direction of the Valdai Hills and cooperate here with the southern wing of Army Group North.

The debacle at Velikie Luki on July 20, the failure to close the Smolensk pocket, the threat facing Panzer Group 2 from the direction of Roslavl, and the danger to the southern flank of the Second Army from the direction of Gomel, as well as the continued unhealthy situation farther south around Mozyr and Korosten, had all taken their toll on Hitler. He now believed that the army groups should strive to effect smaller encirclements than they had in the past, and the areas around Gomel and Lake Ilmen seemed to offer good opportunities for such tactics. Halder did not take this small shift in the wind from Hitler as being significant and lamented that Hitler's proposals ignored the importance of Moscow. Nevertheless, it seemed possible to Halder that a delay in carrying out Directive 33-A might be brought about now that Hitler was insisting on operations of a smaller scope. Since the führer wanted to send Panzer Group 3 no farther north than the Valdai Hills, between Lake Ilmen and Kalinin, an excellent chance existed for retaining Panzer Group 3 close in to the northern flank of Army Group Center for use against Moscow and not to aid the objectives of Army Group North. The chief of the General Staff was soon to receive help for his project from an unexpected source.

On July 26, Paulus, the OQI, or chief quartermaster, of the General Staff paid a visit to Army Group North to collect information firsthand about conditions pertaining to the use of tanks against Leningrad. The panzer generals Hoepner, Manstein, and Rheinhardt all told Paulus that the area between Lake Ilmen and Lake Peipus—that is, the approach to Leningrad from the south—was not suitable for armor in any respect because of rugged terrain, many lakes, and thick forests. Manstein's advice was to turn Army Group North's armored units toward Moscow instead of Leningrad, saying that a further move northward by his LVI Panzer Corps would have to be undertaken with massive infantry support to clear the enemy from the forests in his path. Paulus agreed that the prospects for employing armor against Leningrad appeared bad.

In the absence of certain key parts of Jodl's diary and also of the necessary Wehrmacht operations staff documents, it is impossible to say for certain that Paulus's report to the General Staff was made known to OKW. Jodl's actions on July 27, however, the day following Paulus's visit, would indicate that he had direct knowledge of the conference at Army Group North headquarters. On this day, Jodl met with Hitler and told him that he had now changed his mind about the future course of strategy. He advised the führer to undertake an immediate assault on Moscow after the conclusion of the battles around Smolensk, "not because Moscow is the Soviet capital, but because here will be located the enemy's main force." This alteration of views by Jodl represented a basic deviation from the course of action he had recommended ever since he learned of the Lossberg Study in mid-November 1940. It had been an important element of the Lossberg plan that Army Group Center should be halted east of Smolensk and that armored strength should be diverted from it to the north against the flank and the rear of the Russian armies confronting Army Group North. Jodl had gone on record as early as June 29 that he thought the approaches to Leningrad from the west and south would be difficult for tanks, and by July 27 he had become convinced of the unworkability of this plan, although he was unable effectively to counter Hitler's argument against pushing on to Moscow until the Russian economic base in Ukraine had been removed from enemy control. Hitler in the past had taken Jodl's advice; in fact, it was probably Jodl, with some help from Göring, who persuaded Hitler not to carry out the Leningrad operation without aid from Army Group Center. Jodl had favored a provision in the original Barbarossa Directive of December 18, 1940, that called for turning armor from Army Group Center to Army Group North after Red Army forces in White Russia had been crushed. Now when the chief of the Wehrmacht operations staff shifted ground on this matter, the effect on Hitler was profound.

On July 28 Hitler informed Brauchitsch that he had decided to suspend the Leningrad and Ukraine operations as ordered in Directive 33-A. His feelings about the future were so uncertain that, at this point, he was unprepared to order anything other than that the situation on the southern flank of Army Group Center around Gomel be taken care of as soon as possible. Hitler did not give up entirely the idea of sending Panzer Group 3 to help Army Group North, but now, instead of calling for Panzer Group 3 to participate directly in the encirclement of Leningrad, he believed that the panzer group should only screen the southern flank of Army Group North from the direction of the Valdai Hills and move in a northeasterly direction to cut communications between Moscow and Leningrad. An advance to Moscow, according to Hitler, would still have to wait until the successful conclusion of the Leningrad operation. The OKH had not yet won a complete victory for the cause of Moscow, although the confidence of Hitler and OKW in the feasibility of the original Barbarossa plan, to place Leningrad ahead of the capital in terms of its strategic importance, had been shaken. The uncertainty that existed in Hitler's mind about future strategy was clearly revealed in his Directive 34 issued on July 30. This new directive officially canceled Directive 33-A and postponed the movement by Panzer Group 3 into the Valdai area for at least another ten days. Army Group Center was ordered to go to the defensive along its entire front and prepare only for a further operation against Gomel; the push by Panzer Group 2 into Ukraine was likewise delayed until proper repairs could be made to the armored vehicles. In discussing the meaning of Directive 34 with Halder, Heusinger (the chief of the General Staff operations department) described the new directive as being "in conformity with our views"; he commented also that "this solution delivered us all from the nightmare [that the] führer's stubbornness would ruin the entire eastern operation—finally a point of light!"[2] For his part, Brauchitsch was so afraid that Hitler might reconsider Directive 34 that he declined to make any written comment on it whatsoever lest it fall into the wrong hands. Now that Jodl and OKW seemed to be gradually coming to accept OKH strategy, Halder could sense that Hitler would sooner or later be forced to give in under the pressure from both command organizations. He had at least decided to delay—for the moment— a firm decision about Moscow. This was all that Halder needed to make another attempt to regain control of strategic planning for the General Staff. Hitler had previously shown himself inclined to defer important decisions if they appeared likely to cause disagreement among his advisors. It was this weakness in his character that Halder could use to his advantage.

Hitler's tendency to postpone unpleasant decisions was evident in a conference held at Army Group Center on August 4, with Keitel, Jodl, Schmundt, von Bock, Heusinger, Guderian, and Hoth, in addition to Hitler, all present. The atmosphere surrounding this conference was tense, especially since some officers on von Bock's staff, including his first General Staff officer, Henning von Treschkow, had hatched a plot to kidnap the führer, a plan that was forestalled by tight SS security measures. According to Alan Clark, "The officers privy to this conspiracy were so numerous and occupied positions so close to the army group commander that it is impossible to believe [that] von Bock was unaware of what was going on." A year and a half later, in March 1943, von Treschkow and his cohorts tried unsuccessfully to explode a bomb aboard Hitler's plane. This plot failed only due to a faulty detonator in the device. Halder's role in this conspiracy was more than passive; he had encouraged von Treschkow in his activities since 1939. More than once, Halder carried a loaded revolver into meetings with Hitler and seriously considered assassinating him. After the explosion at the Wolfschanze in July 1944 in which Hitler was wounded, Halder was arrested and put in prison, where he remained until his liberation by the Americans at the end of the war.[3]

True to Hitler's consistent philosophy of divide and rule, each of the participants in the conference was given a private audience with the führer without being able to know what the others had said. In his memoirs Guderian noted that all the generals of Army Group Center advocated resumption of the offensive against Moscow. He further stated that he told Hitler that the number of tank engines the führer had promised Panzer Groups 2 and 3 for replacements was inadequate. In his account of the conversation, Guderian recorded that Hitler offered only 300 engines for the entire Eastern Front, but according to Halder's diary, the führer actually promised 350 Panzer III engines for Army Group Center. There were also two other topics of discussion that Guderian brought up in his interview with Hitler that were not completely or accurately recorded. Regarding the question of Yelnia, as has been mentioned, Guderian advocated holding the salient for reasons of prestige. In regard to the question of resuming the offensive against Moscow, he told Hitler that the Russian front around Roslavl was thin and that he believed his panzer group should press north and east through Spas-Demensk toward Viazma. He also told the führer that his panzer units and infantry corps had succeeded in overrunning the Russian positions around Roslavl with ease. Guderian gave Hitler the impression on August 4 that the Russians had committed their last "proletarian reserves" and that the enemy henceforth would be unable to offer effective resistance. The panzer general was convinced that he had achieved a full breakthrough of the last line of the Russian main defense force and that the way to the east and Moscow was now relatively free and open.

This fanciful commentary by Guderian was reminiscent of Halder's speech of February 3, 1941, when he attempted to persuade Hitler that the Red Army was no worthy opponent for the Wehrmacht and that Moscow could be taken almost with impunity by an assault through White Russia from the west. At that time Hitler refused to believe that the enemy could be rapidly driven out of the Baltic area and Ukraine, so he declined to accept Halder's version of a strategic plan. Guderian's testimony on August 4 meant more to Hitler, however, because the panzer general was a frontline soldier and had seen combat firsthand. Deep down, Hitler mistrusted the sophisticated and highly trained staff officers of OKH, but Guderian was a man of action, a soldier who, in some ways, had experienced the kind of life he himself had known in face-to-face combat with the enemy. A noted historian, Alan Bullock, has written the following words about Hitler:

> The German officer corps was the last stronghold of the old conservative tradition, and Hitler never forgot this. His class resentment was never far below the surface; he knew perfectly well that the officer corps despised him as an upstart, as "the Bohemian Corporal," and he responded with a barely concealed contempt for the "gentlemen" who wrote "von" before their names and had never served as privates in the trenches.[4]

Guderian was aware of this quirk in Hitler's character and was not above using it to his advantage should an opportunity occur. After listening to his report, Hitler thought it possible that the Russians were indeed approaching the limit of their ability to conduct large-scale operations after suffering such heavy losses during the first six weeks of the war. He was still unable to free himself entirely from the conviction that Leningrad and Ukraine should come before Moscow, however. Despite the führer's reservations about Moscow, though, Guderian's representations had brought about a change in his attitude. Toward the end of the conference, Hitler announced that he would again consider the possibility of a further limited advance eastward by Army Group Center. After hearing a final appeal by von Bock about the necessity of destroying the enemy's main force in front of Moscow, Hitler put off a final decision until a later date. The OKH and the generals of Army Group Center could sense imminent victory in their struggle to force Hitler to accept their view, insofar as they all agreed on the importance of Moscow. There would, however, be disagreements among the generals themselves, particularly between Halder and Guderian, about Ukraine.

On August 5, the day following the conference with Hitler at Borisov, Halder, Brauchitsch, Heusinger, and Paulus held a meeting at OKH headquarters. In this discussion Halder's opinion was accepted: that Moscow would have to be reached before the end of the year if German forces were to attain full freedom of maneuver. Along with the important goal of Moscow, Halder considered it vital that the Russian economic base in the south be eliminated: "We must penetrate the oil region with strong forces all the way to Baku." Halder was still pursuing the same course he charted in the communique of July 23 and that Brauchitsch had reemphasized in the chiefs of staff conference on July 25, that is, that the economic and manpower reserves of the Soviet Union made the country too strong to defeat by purely military means, and that the enemy's power to make war must be reduced by depriving Russia of its resources and war industry. In persevering in this line of thought, Halder was placing himself in a position where he would come into a head-on collision with Guderian. Halder and Guderian could agree on Moscow, and Hitler and Halder could agree on Ukraine, but Guderian would not be prepared to sacrifice Moscow for Ukraine, for he was positive that the Soviet capital could not be taken without his tanks riding in the vanguard. In the end, Halder would try to reach a compromise with Hitler and Jodl whereby the problem of Moscow and Ukraine could be solved to everyone's satisfaction except Guderian's. The last compromise on strategy in 1941, however, would be made outside Halder's control and in a way that would come as a crushing blow to him.

Later in the day on August 5, Brauchitsch conferred with Hitler and subsequently reported to Halder on the results of his conversation. He told him that Hitler had come to realize that the present tactics would lead to a stabilization of the front, as had been the case in 1914. The führer now envisioned three alternatives: (1) the capture of the Valdai highlands by a coordinated maneuver of Army Group North and Panzer Group 3; (2) the clearing of the southern flank of Army Group Center, combined with elimination of strong Russian forces around Korosten; and (3) an operation to eliminate all enemy forces west of the Southern Bug River.

In his discussion with Brauchitsch about the second alternative, Hitler left open the question of a further advance by Army Group Center directly toward Moscow. He also maintained that the Korosten operation could lead to a solution of the problems east and south of Mogilev and at Kiev. In his diary Halder put special emphasis on the words "Mogilev-Kiev," and it would be accurate to say that he was excited about the possibility of being able to take Moscow and Ukraine simultaneously. Halder described the joint Moscow-Kiev plan as "a salvation," although he thought that the inclusion of an attack against the enemy forces around Korosten would be too wasteful in tying up strength. Halder did not want to squander time on winning what he described as tactical victories of the kind that Hitler desired at Gomel and Korosten. Instead, he wished to concentrate on broad, grandiose possibilities such as those that were offered around Bialystok-Minsk and at Smolensk. Halder believed that once the Wehrmacht gained freedom of movement and operations again became fluid, Hitler would give up his notions about concentrating on tactical successes.

Guderian, too, wished to continue wide-ranging maneuvers, but not in the same way that Halder envisioned. His stern threat on August 6 to refuse to give up even one panzer division from his command to aid in the Rogachev-Zhlobin operations by Second Army should have shown Halder the mettle of the man he was dealing with, but he continued to underestimate Guderian's resourcefulness until it was too late. For his part, Guderian was content for the moment to mark time at Roslavl and at Gomel and wait for Hitler to make up his mind about Moscow. Guderian's protest against the OKH decision about Rogachev-Zhlobin on August 6 afforded Halder a chance to confront the panzer general and force him to back down and obey orders, but this was not Halder's way.

Instead, Guderian had won a small but important victory over his superiors, and he would not be discouraged from seeking bigger successes in the future.

The sign of approval for the Moscow project that Jodl had hesitantly given on July 27 stimulated Halder to renew his attempt to assert his influence over OKW, an effort he had first made by sending Brauchitsch to visit Keitel on July 23. Halder contacted Jodl on August 7 in order to reinforce the latter's already favorable attitude toward an advance on Moscow and to convince him that Russia's economic base in the south must be eliminated at the same time. Halder told Jodl that the forces already in motion in the direction of Leningrad were sufficient and that Hoth's Panzer Group 3 should not be taken from Army Group Center and given to Army Group North. In the first place, Panzer Group 3 was needed to carry out the assault on Moscow, and second, Halder insisted that there was no danger to the southern flank of Army Group North from the direction of the Valdai Hills. Finally, the chief of the General Staff said that instead of deciding between Moscow or Ukraine, a decision must be made for Moscow *and* Ukraine. "This must be done or else the enemy's productive strength cannot be vanquished before fall."

This conversation on August 7 between Halder and Jodl was of critical importance in influencing the final outcome of events in 1941. In his diary Halder noted: "Overall impression: Jodl is impressed with the correctness of this plan and will move along in this direction." Halder would continue to work on Jodl, who was ever more inclined to accept the OKH view of strategy. By the third week in August, Jodl would play a vital role in Halder's plan to gain influence over Hitler. Halder had done his work well in convincing him that both Moscow and Ukraine had to be taken before the onset of winter in 1941. He now expected Jodl to remain on his side, but Halder's cleverly laid scheme would soon be endangered, for at the end of August conditions would change and Halder would attempt to undo the impression he had made on Jodl about the economic importance of Ukraine. This attempt would fail, and Halder would be forced to take a new tack with Jodl. For a while, however, after August 7, Halder's confidence in his ability to manipulate OKW was great, for now not only had Jodl apparently become a convert to OKH strategy but

Halder also had an important ally within Jodl's own organization, the deputy chief of the Wehrmacht operations staff and head of Department "L" (*Landesverteidung*), Walter Warlimont, a man who had worked diligently on behalf of the Moscow project since the fall of 1940.

On August 10, Warlimont's Department "L" produced a study that called for a resumption of the Moscow offensive at the end of August after first eliminating the immediate threats to the flanks of Army Group Center around Gomel and Velikie Luki–Toropets with the help of Panzer Groups 2 and 3.[5] The study called for using both panzer groups subsequent to the flank operations in a thrust toward Moscow that would "crush the last, inferior, newly formed replacement divisions that the enemy had apparently brought up along the line Rzhev-Viazma-Briansk." After the Rzhev-Viazma-Briansk line had been cracked, Warlimont anticipated that the progress of Army Group Center would take the form of a "pursuit" of the beaten enemy. Thereafter, Army Group Center would be able to send support to help the neighboring army groups to the north and south. In particular, Warlimont stated that the forces for the assault on Moscow should be arranged so that during the pursuit stage of the advance Guderian's Panzer Group 2 would be in a position to move along the Don River to the southeast. This study was tailored to fit closely with the OKH viewpoint as it was presented to Jodl by Halder on August 7, and there can be little doubt that Warlimont was acting in accordance with Halder's wishes in preparing it to influence his superior, Jodl. The impression that Warlimont's study was looked upon with favor by OKH is enhanced by the fact that on August 8, two days before the Department "L" study, Halder issued a General Staff appraisal of the situation confronting the German army. In this report Halder stated that it was clear that the Russians were deploying all of their available strength along the line Lake Ilmen-Rzhev-Viazma-Briansk. The chief of the General Staff compared the position of the Red Army to that of the French in the second phase of the campaign in 1940, when the enemy relied on strong "defense islands" located along a new defense line. Halder believed that the Russian attempt to push back the German front in the Smolensk area by counterattacks was on the verge of complete collapse. In his words:

My old impression is confirmed, Army Group North is strong enough to carry out its mission alone. Army Group Center must concentrate its forces in order to destroy the enemy's main force [in front of Moscow]. Army Group South is strong enough to fulfill its task, but even so Army Group Center can perhaps lend assistance [by sending Panzer Group 2 to the southeast].

In early August Jodl found himself surrounded both within and without OKW by generals who were all giving him the same advice, advice he was prone to accept after he had been made aware of the problems confronting the armored units in the hill and forest region on the approaches to Leningrad. Jodl could not know that the Red Army was far from finished in front of Army Group Center, although the battles raging around the periphery of the Yelnia salient should have convinced him otherwise. He also could not know that the Rzhev-Viazma-Briansk line did not represent the last Russian line of defense in front of Moscow. He could not know that an advance by Army Group Center beyond this line would not take the form of a pursuit and that thus the entire premise of OKH strategy and also of Warlimont's study was wrong. Halder's General Staff appraisal of August 8 listed the relationship of forces in divisions as follows: in front of Army Group North, 23 Russian (including 2 motorized) versus 26 German (including 6 motorized); Army Group Center, 70 Russian (8.5 motorized) versus 60 German (17 motorized); Army Group South, 50.5 Russian (6.5 motorized) versus 50.5 German (9.5 motorized). No more than three days later, on August 11, Halder had to admit that these figures were awry. Instead of the 200 divisions that he believed the Russians had originally deployed, 360 divisions had been identified on the entire Eastern Front. Halder also noted that although the enemy forces were badly armed and badly led, their preparation to meet the German invasion had been good, and the military strength of their economy had been seriously underestimated. Halder remarked pessimistically that the Wehrmacht was moving farther away from its sources of supply while the Red Army was drawing back closer to its own.

On August 12, most probably because of an inquiry from Jodl, now that he had promised Halder that he would work to see the General Staff plan carried through, Hitler issued further instructions, Directive 34-A. Its language was optimistic because Army Group South had just concluded the Uman battle of encirclement southwest of Kiev, netting some 103,000 prisoners. This battle was a spur to Hitler's desire to finish with the Russians in the western Ukraine, seize the Crimea, and occupy the Donets Basin and Kharkov. About the army groups north of the Pripyat, Hitler stated that the primary goal in the immediate future was for Army Group Center to rectify the situation on its flanks by striking the Russian Fifth Army in the south around Mozyr and using armored units to suppress the enemy in the north around Toropets. The führer also ordered the left flank of Army Group Center, that is, Panzer Group 3 and the Ninth Army, to move northward only far enough to secure the southern flank of Army Group North and enable this army group to shift some infantry divisions toward Leningrad. The directive called for concluding the operations against Leningrad before an advance on Moscow was resumed, but Hitler thought that Leningrad could be dealt with in fairly short order.

Halder's first impression of Directive 34-A was unfavorable, for he disliked Hitler's assertion that Leningrad must come ahead of Moscow, and he described the directive as being too restrictive and not allowing OKH the latitude it needed. Two days later, however, he modified his tone somewhat and said that the directive essentially was in agreement with the OKH point of view, namely, that Army Group Center should undertake only two basic tasks. One was to resolve the situation on its flanks and prepare to push on to Moscow, and the second was to make ready to send forces to aid the advance of Army Group South. Halder, a bit late, had come to recognize the subtle change in Hitler's thinking, and he could see how the führer's insistence on effecting smaller encirclement operations could be used to the benefit of his plan.

Now that OKH had gathered new strength by winning over Jodl, and now that Hitler appeared to be on the verge of changing his mind about Leningrad, Halder was emboldened to mount a two-pronged offensive against the führer's negative attitude toward Moscow. This renewed effort by Halder took the form of two studies presented to Hitler on August 18. The first was submitted by Warlimont's Department "L," and the other was delivered by Brauchitsch, the commander in chief of the army. A comparison of these documents leads to the inescapable conclusion that by mid-August the coordination between OKH and Department "L" of the Wehrmacht operations staff had been developed to a high degree.

Warlimont's "Assessment of the Eastern Situation" of August 18, which was probably prepared without Jodl's approval, laid down the goals for the remainder of 1941 as the capture of the Donets Basin, Kharkov, Moscow, and Leningrad.[6] In setting forth the procedure for reaching these objectives, Warlimont deviated from the line most recently espoused by OKH. The chief of Department "L" described the situation of Army Group South after the battle of Uman as healthy enough so that the turn of Panzer Group 2 all the way to Ukraine was no longer essential in order to defeat the Russian Fifth Army. The crossing of the Dnepr would also be likely on both sides of Cherkassy, south of Kiev, by early September after the rapid movement eastward of the German Seventeenth Army. The capture of the Crimea, an objective that would soon loom larger in Halder's plans, was not deemed necessary in the near future; a screening force would suffice in that direction. The key to all subsequent operations, according to Warlimont, was to be Moscow, and the approach to this city by Army Group Center had been made easier by the successful operations at Roslavl, Krichev, Rogachev-Zhlobin, and Gomel, the latter battle then being in its final stages. On the northern flank, the second attack on Velikie Luki was scheduled to begin on August 21, and it, too, Warlimont anticipated, would be brought to a successful conclusion. As a result of the approaching completion of the operations on the flanks of Army Group Center, the resumption of the Moscow offensive was set for early September, this time with the aid of both Panzer Group 2 and Panzer Group 3, not just Panzer Group 3, as Halder had earlier specified.

The reason for the change in plans by the Halder-Warlimont partnership was that Panzer Group 3 had been weakened by the loss of the XXXIX Panzer Corps, which Hoth had been forced to give up to Army Group North. The XXXIX Panzer Corps had been sent northward at Jodl's request on August 15 to help prevent a Russian breakthrough on the southern wing of Army Group North south of Lake Ilmen in the region of Staraia Russa. After the crisis around Staraia Russa had passed, Hitler had used the opportunity to dispatch the panzer corps farther north, despite Halder's wishes to the contrary. Now, on August 18, both OKH and Department "L" staffs had to take cognizance of the fact that after being deprived of two panzer and one motorized division, Panzer Group 3 alone was too weak to spearhead a drive on Moscow from the northwest. Actually, as will be pointed out, the entire panzer group would have been hard pressed to undertake this task, but the loss of the XXXIX Panzer Corps to Army Group North was a major factor in compelling Halder to readjust his strategy.

The new OKH proposal was presented by Brauchitsch to Hitler also on August 18.[7] On July 23, as noted earlier, Halder had told the führer that it was important to seize both Moscow and Ukraine before the onset of winter. At that time he had emphasized the economic necessity of occupying Ukraine, and it was his opinion that this could best be done by sending part of von Kluge's Fourth Panzer Army to the south and east, a group including Panzer Group 2 and part of von Weichs's Second Army. By August 18, however, Halder realized it would be impossible to send all of Panzer Group 2 to Ukraine and take Moscow at the same time. When thus faced with a choice, Moscow or Ukraine, Halder, true to his basic conclusion, chose Moscow. The problem that he now faced was, however, a serious one. Hitler had not really needed any convincing prior to June 22 that the economic war was vital and that the south of the Soviet Union was crucially important for Russia's armaments industry. Halder had agreed with the führer on July 26 that Ukraine must be taken rapidly for economic reasons and had assigned it a priority equal to that of Moscow. Now he would have to backtrack and disassemble the arguments he had made earlier for both objectives.

Halder attempted to accomplish this by continuing to emphasize economic considerations, though weakening his tone in this respect. He now described the capture of the Moscow industrial area as equal in importance to the economic objectives in the Baltic area and in the south in preventing the Russians from rebuilding their shattered armies. Beyond this, Halder repeated the case he had made many times before that the enemy's main force was positioned in front of Moscow and that once these units were destroyed, the Russians would no longer be capable of maintaining a continuous line of defense. To fortify his point further, Halder made use of Hitler's disinclination to carry out any more wide-ranging maneuvers of the kind that had brought less than desirable results in White Russia around Smolensk.

The ability of the armored units to carry out long-range operations was characterized by Halder as limited, even after repairs were completed. As a result of the panzer groups' lessened capability to maneuver, Halder advocated using them to traverse shorter distances than had previously been expected of them. It was, therefore, essential that the armored units be used only for decisive and strategic goals and that their strength not be wasted on nonessential tasks. In his operations plan section of the August 18 proposal, Halder set forth restricted goals for Panzer Groups 2 and 3, which would remain positioned on the flanks of Army Group Center. Guderian would move from the area Roslavl-Briansk toward Kaluga and Medyn, west of Maloyaroslavets, while Hoth would push from southeast of Beloe and Toropets toward Rzhev. We should note here that the first phase of this planned armored thrust would not have gone far enough to crack the main Russian defense lines running through Mozhaisk and Naro-Fominsk. The infantry armies, the middle of Army Group Center's front, were to remain in defensive positions until the enemy began to pull back eastward due to the pressure exerted by the two panzer groups. In any case, Halder called for the infantry in the center of the front to cooperate closely with the armored units in order to achieve maximum results against surrounded pockets of enemy soldiers, for, as he said, "Experience has taught us that infantry alone can perform this task successfully only under exceptional conditions."

In regard to the missions of Army Groups South and North, Halder's new proposal was less clearly defined and objective than his plan for the renewed assault on Moscow. Army Group South was considered by Halder strong enough by itself to force the Dnepr with the Seventeenth Army by September 9, if not, in fact, sooner. After the Dnepr was crossed, Army Group South would be able to speed up its push eastward. As for Army Group North, it would be able to complete the Leningrad encirclement by the end of August and also forge a link with the Finns. Subsequently, Army Group North would be in a position to move into the Valdai Hills and thus protect the northern flank of Army Group Center's drive on Moscow. It was considered possible that Army Group North could send some units of Panzer Group 4 all the way south to Ostashkov, due north of a line from Velikie Luki to Rzhev, and thereby link up directly with the northern flank of Panzer Group 3. The only precondition set forth by the August 18 study for the offensive against Moscow was that the operations around Gomel, then in progress, and around Velikie Luki, which would begin in three days, should be brought to a successful conclusion.

In announcing his conviction that Moscow and Ukraine could be taken simultaneously, Halder was remaining true to the plan that he had agreed upon with Jodl on August 7. At this conference, Halder had said that unless both objectives were taken, "the enemy's productive strength cannot be overcome before fall." The plan that he outlined on July 23 and presented to Hitler on July 26 called for the sending of Panzer Group 2 into Ukraine and, if need be, all the way to Stalingrad. Halder had again, on August 14, expressed approval of the idea of sending Guderian to Ukraine after Hitler, in his Directive 34-A of August 12, said that the southern flank of Army Group Center would have to cooperate with Army Group South in order to eliminate the Russian Fifth Army's stronghold around Mozyr and south of the Pripyat. The proposal of August 18 did not, however, provide for sending any armor from Army Group Center farther south than Novgorod-Severskii, a city on the Desna River south of Briansk in the extreme northern Ukraine. Even so, Halder wanted no more than two divisions from the XXIV Panzer Corps to move so far away from the path of the main drive on Moscow. "All thoughts that the crossing of the Dnepr by Army Group South should be hastened by these armored units [from Army Group Center] must be given up, otherwise Army Group Center will not be able to mount a proper assault [in the direction of Moscow] along its southern flank."

The OKH proposal of August 18 represented an about-face by Halder insofar as it made no provision for Army Group Center to help Army Group South in any substantive way. In conceding that two armored divisions could be sent from the XXIV Panzer Corps into Ukraine, Halder was opening up the possibility that Guderian's Panzer Group 2 could be divided if the need arose. This particular feature of the proposal made not the slightest difference to Halder, but it would to Guderian, a man who would go to any length to prevent armored units from being removed from his command. This was a potential difficulty that Halder should have been aware of, but for one reason or another, he ignored it until it was too late.

The proposal was permeated with optimism that Army Group South could not only effectively handle the enemy on its own front and cross the Dnepr to regain freedom of movement but also play a role in tying down Russian forces that might otherwise be in a position to oppose Army Group Center. The same, or even greater, optimism could be seen in the task assigned to Army Group North. It was not only supposed to complete the encirclement of Leningrad by the end of August, but it was also expected to support actively the northern flank of Army Group Center. It is very difficult to understand what the source of Halder's optimism was, for on August 11, as has been noted, he lamented the fact that the Red Army was much stronger than had previously been believed and that the economic power of the Soviet Union had been seriously underestimated. The OKH proposal was a reversal of practically everything that Halder had preached since the third week in July, and the conclusion is inescapable that the proposal was designed not to fit the facts but rather to mislead Hitler. Once Hitler had removed the XXXIX Panzer Corps from Panzer Group 3, over Halder's objections, and once the chief of the General Staff realized that its remaining strength would be insufficient for Army Group Center to take Moscow, he was prepared in essence to sacrifice the Ukraine project in favor of the assault on the Soviet capital. In order to justify this change in his strategy, Halder was not truthful or straightforward in his arguments. Instead, he tried to cloud the issue and win Hitler over with optimistic arguments that he himself must have known were false. He had used the same technique before, and it was to be no more successful at this point than it had been earlier, although now the war was two months old and Halder should have seen the impending disaster ahead and warned Hitler that the war was going to last a long time.

By the end of August the damage produced by the fundamental contradictions in German strategic planning and the Wehrmacht command structure came to the surface. By then Halder and von Bock had lost control of Guderian after the panzer general managed to gain personal influence with Hitler at the Wolfschanze conference on August 23. The führer went along with Guderian's bad advice and chose not to divide Panzer Group 2 in undertaking the Kiev encirclement in September. Once this decision had been made, it would have been far better for the Germans to abandon any attempt to take Moscow in 1941. Hitler decided in early September, however, that both goals, Kiev and Moscow, were attainable. His greatest strategic mistake of the war was the result of his simultaneous reliance on too many sources of conflicting advice.

Halder had come to realize after mid-July that Moscow could not be taken unless the situation on both the northern and southern flanks of Army Group Center was remedied beforehand. He won Jodl over to this point of view on August 7, and eventually they concluded that it was possible for both Kiev and Moscow to be taken, but only by leaving a substantial part of Panzer Group 2 in the Yelnia area instead of committing it to Ukraine. The question of whether or not this strategy would have worked is an interesting one indeed. It seems unlikely that Army Group Center could have taken Moscow in the fall of 1941 with only one panzer corps on its southern flank. It is highly likely that the Typhoon offensive would have bogged down well before reaching Moscow. Probably the German high command would have chosen to halt the advance along the line Rzhev-Viazma-Briansk-Orel, thus putting Army Group Center beyond the immediate reach of Zhukov's reserves massed north and south of the capital. If this had happened, Army Group Center would have been in much better shape to resume operations against Moscow in the spring of 1942 than it was in fact. This is why the Halder-Jodl plan has been described as a possible salvation. It would not have worked in the way that its authors intended, but it very probably would have saved Army Group Center from catastrophe. Had the front been stabilized in November 1941 and the Wehrmacht been able to withstand the pressures of the Russian reserves, Hitler might not have been bold enough to relieve, or accept the resignations of, Brauchitsch, von Bock, von Leeb, Rundstedt, and Guderian in the next few weeks, thus tightening his grip over the army even further. Without this defeat in the winter of 1941–42, the generals' conspiracy against Hitler and the Nazis would have had more time to succeed. Had Hitler been overthrown, improvements in the Soviet prisoner situation and in the racial policies in general no doubt would have followed, which could have changed the whole complexion of the war on the Eastern Front and perhaps have led to peace talks.

Guderian's coup at the Wolfschanze was, then, a monumental turning point for Germany. After his triumph, Halder may have been prepared to see the Moscow project go down the drain entirely in 1941, judging from his conversation with Jodl on August 31, a discussion that demonstrated Jodl's commitment to Moscow even after the debacle he and Halder suffered on August 23. In the final analysis, it was this commitment by Jodl, plus Göring's promise to neutralize Leningrad with airpower, that finally swayed Hitler in the fall of 1941 to attempt the taking of Moscow. Ultimately, too, Guderian's insistence on the importance of the capture of the Soviet capital for troop morale and his willingness to see the pursuit of the Red Army toward Moscow continued by a drive of his panzer group from the south through Orel and Tula—a desire carefully concealed in his memoirs—had a decisive influence on Hitler. Hitler did not trust Halder and OKH, but he believed that Jodl, Göring, and Guderian were men worth listening to. It was a tragedy for the Germans that Halder was ensnared by such a tangled web of circumstances, but it must be said that he was responsible for creating most of these troubles for himself with his attempts to manipulate Guderian by fashioning an artificial and awkward command structure and to manipulate Jodl through the influence of his deputy, Warlimont. The final element of the equation, Göring, was not subject to Halder's will, and as no record of his private conversations with Hitler exists, the true extent of his role in the strategic blunders of 1941 must be left open to speculation, although the records of Kesselring's discussions with von Bock indicate that Göring's influence in this respect was extensive. This impression is strengthened by Hitler's references to Göring and the Luftwaffe in his answer to Halder's proposal of August 18 and in the Typhoon directive of September 6.

The Blitzkrieg at the Crossroads

On the tactical level, German plans for the conduct of the War in the East in 1941 were as filled with contradictions as was the making and execution of strategy. The insoluble problems that would arise from the attempt to apply tactics designed for use in France and Poland to a country as large as the Soviet Union were apparent at the time of Paulus's study in December 1940, but neither the General Staff nor any other high command organization was able to find new tactical solutions that more closely suited the realities of the campaign in the east. In his excellent study, *The German Economy at War,* Alan Milward points out that Germany was not an economic superpower in 1941 compared with the United States and was also economically inferior to the Soviet Union in certain key military areas. In order to overcome these economic deficiencies, Hitler and his generals were forced to rely on the blitzkrieg concept of war, one that allowed Germany to become a great military power through armament in breadth, not in depth; that is, many different kinds of weapons were produced that were tailored for specific types of warfare, but in insufficient quantities.

In 1939 and 1940, in order to defeat France, German military planners concentrated on the construction of vehicles and armor. After the fall of France, in order to defeat Britain, a switch was made so that the economy could produce more equipment for the Luftwaffe and the navy. Finally, in order to defeat the Soviet Union, a decision was made to increase greatly the size of the army, resulting in a greater output of infantry arms and equipment of all sorts. In retrospect, it seems incredible that Germany was prepared to fight Russia in a life-and-death struggle with only 3,582 tanks and self-propelled guns, but such was the case. Actually, the German war economy was not fully mobilized until after Stalingrad in early 1943, but by then the war was lost.

Thus, the contradictions revealed in the blitzkrieg concept of warfare were reflections of the fundamental contradictions within the

German economic system. The blitzkrieg concept was a means whereby a long war could be avoided, and once a long war ensued, the economic inferiority of Germany would have an increasingly telling effect. This is not to say that the Soviet Union did not have its economic contradictions and weaknesses also, but the misguided Nazi race ideology and its harshness solidified all segments of Soviet society and strengthened the will of the ethnic minorities in the USSR as well as of the oppressed Russian peasant class to repel the invader. The blitzkrieg could triumph in a politically weakened country such as France, but Stalin's Russia was a state of quite different organization. Here blitzkrieg warfare could have worked only had the Nazi leaders been willing and able to exploit the weakest links in the Soviet system, those implicit in the nationalities problem and in the peasant sector.

Had mass surrenders of Red Army units occurred rapidly at Bialystok-Minsk, at Smolensk-Yelnia, and at Kiev, blitzkrieg tactics could have produced the desired results. But mass surrenders occurred only after prolonged resistance. Communist agitators were skillfully able to use Nazi propaganda against itself and were able to stiffen the resolve of the minority peoples and the peasants to fight for Mother Russia, despite the fact that the Stalinist system had much to answer for so far as they were concerned. In order to increase the propaganda effort, the political commissars were reintroduced into the Red Army on July 16, 1941, though the system had been abolished in 1940. Nazi ideology, therefore, carried within itself the seeds of its own destruction. Even had this not been so, the strategy and tactics employed by the Germans on the Eastern Front would have made a total defeat of the Red Army in 1941 extremely unlikely.

In describing the conditions faced by the Wehrmacht in Russia, a German historian has written:

> The troops began to realize by the third day of the offensive that the war in Russia was not going to be the same as it had been in Poland and France. This was not only because the enemy soldier was proving to be tougher than expected, but also because the terrain was a greater problem. Of what use were motorized vehicles when the wheels became stuck in knee-deep sand? Of-

tentimes when roads were indicated on the maps they were, in fact, nothing more than footpaths through the swamps.[8]

In a way, White Russia acted as a gigantic cocoon for Army Group Center, and soon after June 22, the Wehrmacht began to undergo a remarkable metamorphosis. Gradually, the very color of the German uniforms and vehicles changed from gray to earth brown, and after the supply system began to deteriorate, the diet of the soldier began to change as well; even the lowly sunflower was not overlooked as a source of human energy. By the time of the fall rainy season, crudely built Russian horse-drawn *panye* wagons had assumed great importance for German transportation needs. German construction battalions were set to work to fabricate these primitive vehicles in the autumn, despite the fact that earlier they had been the very symbol of the backwardness of the Red Army. During the winter in 1941 the transformation of the German army continued to progress; the western muzhiks found themselves scrambling for Russian padded coats and hats and for the thick and comfortable felt boots that (incidentally) the Red Army issued in only three sizes.

The question of why proper clothing and equipment was not issued to the German troops in time for the onset of winter in 1941 has never been satisfactorily answered. Halder blamed Hitler for this mistake, but Guderian has written that the führer was misinformed, for some unexplained reason, about the issuance of winter clothing by Quartermaster General Wagner. More recently, however, an American historian has charged Brauchitsch with the responsibility for this error.[9]

According to one German general, Fretter-Pico, in his book *Misbrauchte Infanterie:*

> The external appearance of the troops had been fundamentally altered. . . . The marching columns now resembled the campaigns of the Middle Ages, and the uniforms were now almost unrecognizable as such.

The Wehrmacht had become a "Russian" army.

By late summer and early fall of 1941, the War in the East had

taken on a more human character; it was a man-to-man struggle to
a far greater extent than the German planners had anticipated, and
it was at this time that the Wehrmacht began to pay dearly for the
neglect the infantry divisions had suffered since 1939. As Fretter-Pico
says, the infantry was misused because it was (wrongly) no longer considered to be the backbone of the army. "The infantry was more
poorly armed, clothed, and more poorly provided with replacements than any other branch of the military; it was always thought-
lessly overtaxed by the high command during the course of the war."
This general did not deny that the armored units and the Luftwaffe
were also overstrained, but not because their worth was underestimated. "In regard to the armored forces, the overstraining and resulting misuse followed as a result of the wrong value placed on the
infantry divisions."

Observations of this kind were not confined to lower echelon division commanders. In September 1941, Field Marshal von Kluge submitted a critique to Army Group Center that outlined in some detail
his objections to the continued use of blitzkrieg tactics as advocated
by Guderian and von Bock. The field marshal began his remarks by
saying that he realized motorized units were the wave of the future
and their development must be pressed, but, he added, in the Soviet
Union motorized divisions alone could not achieve decisive victories;
the terrain was too difficult and Russian countermeasures too effective. Much was expected of the infantry units, yet their weapons were
not as varied and plentiful as in a panzer or a motorized division, a
factor that made all forms of combat more difficult. The trouble with
the infantry was that it typically did not have the close cooperation
with the Luftwaffe enjoyed by the panzer groups. About the battles
just concluded around the Yelnia salient, von Kluge stated that armor
and self-propelled artillery were invaluable for close support of the
infantry in both offensive and defensive operations. Much blood
could have been saved by utilizing armor to spearhead the main thrust
of an infantry attack or to act as a reserve to blunt enemy assaults
against static defensive positions. Von Kluge believed that it was
wrong to expect infantry divisions to defend 15–40-km. fronts without adequate barriers against coordinated assaults by enemy tanks,
artillery, and infantry in rough country. If the war were to be won, he

felt the infantry would have to be regarded as something more than an unwanted stepchild; its equipment and personnel would have to be upgraded, and the tasks assigned to it would have to be more reasonable. In essence, the program outlined by von Kluge advocated a reorientation of German tactics toward the kind of combined-arms methods employed by the enemy, the efficacy of which had lately been demonstrated at Yelnia. Von Kluge was given a chance to put his ideas into practice when he was assigned the command of Army Group Center in December 1941.

The Kiev encirclement proved to be the last successful mass armored penetration over a long distance that the Wehrmacht would be able to carry out in the Soviet Union. And so with the conclusion of the Kiev operation on September 26, the era of victorious blitzkrieg warfare had ended. After Briansk-Viazma, on October 13, OKH issued orders for an encirclement of Moscow to be undertaken by the 2d and 4th Panzer Groups, but there was little chance that this operation could succeed. The OKH had persuaded itself that the destroyed Russian forces at Briansk-Viazma represented the last main enemy force barring the road to Moscow, a view that did not correspond to reality. After the Moscow debacle in December, neither Hitler nor anyone else in the German high command, including Halder, would ever depend on independent armored thrusts over vast territories to carry the day.

This new attitude was made concrete in Hitler's Directive No. 41 of April 5, 1942, which set forth the goals for the second year's campaign:

> Experience has sufficiently shown that the Russians are not very vulnerable to operational encirclements. It is therefore of decisive importance that, as in the double battle of Viazma-Briansk, individual breaches of the front should take the form of close pincers movements.
>
> We must avoid closing the pincers too late, thus giving the enemy the possibility of avoiding destruction.
>
> It must not happen that, by advancing too quickly and too far, armored and motorized formations lose connection with the infantry following them; or that they lose the opportunity

of supporting the hard-pressed, forward-fighting infantry by direct attacks on the rear of the encircled Russians.

The blunders made in German strategical planning in the summer of 1941 ensured the prolongation of the war despite anything the Wehrmacht might have done in regard to tactics. The use of combined-arms operations sooner, before the post-Moscow period, might have salvaged at least a partial victory for Germany in the spring and summer of 1942. Once the strategic initiative was lost permanently after Kiev, however, the damage done was irreparable. After Kiev, too, many German officers were afflicted with a "Marne psychosis," a fear that everything must be done to win the war in one campaign, or else, as in 1914–18, Germany would be ground down by its enemies.

Significantly, Russian criticisms of German tactics center around their misuse of tanks and artillery and the failure of the German command to recognize the importance of combined-arms operations. In retrospect, most of these criticisms appear to be valid. Only 18 percent of Army Group Center's manpower was organized into mobile units, and it became obvious in the early stages of the war that the German transportation system was inadequate to allow artillery to be moved forward rapidly enough to be used properly.

During the course of the war, the Wehrmacht suffered greatly from a lack of enough motorized infantry to close swiftly the gaps between fast-racing tank columns and the slower foot-bound units. The German army in the east had only a few battalions that could properly be called motorized infantry; many units were given this designation, but most of them were "in fact nothing more than infantry units that did not carry their own packs." The few German battalions with armored vehicles that did operate in close coordination with tanks proved themselves to be extremely valuable, but there were not enough of them to make a decisive impact on the outcome of the war.

When the Russians began to employ large numbers of close assault antitank weapons as a defensive measure, the German panzers were increasingly forced to depend on marching infantry for support, as not enough motorized columns were available. By midsummer 1941, the speed of the German blitzkrieg attack had been slowed to that of a marching man. During the period between June 22 and July 10, 1941, Army Group Center advanced 500 km., or 25–30 km. per day. During the next sixty days the army group moved only 200–300 km., or 4–5 km. per day. Mobile columns could still race ahead rapidly to encircle large groups of Russians, and this was dramatically demonstrated at Briansk-Viazma, but these units were unable to continue their advance until the infantry came up to secure and contain the enemy pockets. This phenomenon was observable in all of the encirclement battles fought by the Germans in 1941. In 1943, 80 percent of the German army in the east was still composed of infantry divisions relying mostly on horse-drawn power for transportation; this figure had not substantially changed since 1941. An attempt to bring about increased mechanization of the infantry was made after Stalingrad, but by then it was too late. Allied bombing would wreak everincreasing havoc with German industry and the Reich transportation network. The Wehrmacht lost the strategic initiative at Kiev and, by resuming the Moscow offensive in the autumn of 1941, fell into the snare that Stalin had so carefully laid. The Red Army would continue to press for definite tactical superiority also, a goal that was reached after the battle of Kursk in the summer of 1943.

German Strategy and Tactics: The Ultimate Question
One other matter remains to be dealt with in regard to German strategy and tactics. The question may be asked: Could Moscow have been taken by the German army in 1941 and would this success have led to a defeat of the Soviet Union? Since the war, a two-fold myth has been perpetrated by former Wehrmacht commanders such as Halder, Guderian, and Blumentritt and by several German military historians. This myth is (1) that Hitler alone was responsible for the blunders in Russia in 1941 that led to Germany's defeat and (2) that had the blitzkrieg campaign culminated in 1941 with the capture of Moscow, the Wehrmacht would have been victorious.

The first part of this historical misconception has already been discussed. If anything, Hitler was, in 1941, unable to direct personally the strategic development of the War in the East. Intrigues and divisiveness at all levels of command had a telling effect on German planning and operational organization. Whenever Hitler was able to make a decision regarding strategy and tactics, he was all too prone to rely on bad advice from individuals such as Göring and Guderian, who were interested in furthering their own causes and not in sacrificing their personal goals for the sake of the common benefit. The führer proved himself time and again to be unable to resist the psychological pressure from those around him who wished to use their influence to change decisions that he had already made. Hitler's answer to Halder's letter of August 18, for example, positively excluded the possibility of a renewed Moscow offensive in 1941, and yet Halder was successful in changing his attitude (with the help of Warlimont and Jodl). Halder was, in turn, frustrated by the abrupt intervention of another pair of influence mongers, Göring and Guderian, who succeeded in altering still further Hitler's supposedly stubborn will.

The second element of the myth must now be considered: How could an assault on Moscow actually have taken place during the first year's campaign, and would the fall of the city have meant a German victory? Regarding a siege of the Soviet capital, a German historian has written as follows:

> Thanks to Hitler's unfortunate Far Eastern policy, the Soviets were able to draw on a major part of the strength which had been pinned down by the Japanese. Stalin and Marshal Zhukov had gained time, utilizing the entire power of a totalitarian state, to transform the capital into what would have been an "earlier Stalingrad." In any case, if Army Group Center had commenced an actual assault on Moscow, the fight would have lasted until the last man and the last bullet were spent. It is very questionable whether this struggle would have ended in favor of Germany.[10]

Other German commentators have remarked that the use of blitzkrieg tactics against Moscow in 1941 would have been very risky. In street fighting, tanks could have been used only singly or in small groups and would have had to be close to infantry teams capable of neutralizing the enemy's close-quarter antitank weapons, which were usually concealed in underground bunkers and cellars. "If the enemy had enough time to prepare the defense of a large city, then his fortress-type constructions could only be overcome through the use of strong air and artillery support." Also, "The main burden of battle in a street fighting situation must be borne by the infantryman or motorized infantryman."[11] On several occasions Hitler expressed his fear of using tanks in battles inside large cities, and Guderian too is on record as saying street fighting was outside the operational capabilities of tanks. In other words, Moscow could not have been taken in 1941 by the panzer groups alone; the Russian forces were too well prepared for such an eventuality. Moscow could have been captured only by a combined armor, artillery, infantry, and Luftwaffe assault, which in turn would have meant that the final phase of the attack could not have occurred before enough time had elapsed for men to march from the Bug River to the Moskva. It is no accident of fate that the final storm of Moscow was not attempted before November; such an event could not have taken place sooner even if the German tanks had been in a position to carry out the assault more quickly. The Russian tactic of forcing the German infantry to grapple with large pockets of surrounded Soviet soldiers behind the advancing panzer groups thus paid handsome dividends in the fall and winter of 1941. It was not until after the conclusion of the battles at Briansk-Viazma, in late October and early November, that the German infantry was in a position to assault Moscow.

Another possibility must be taken into account. What if the German tanks had bypassed Moscow and succeeded in cutting off the city from the interior, leaving the infantry and artillery units to assault the city later? This was the kind of maneuver that the panzer generals favored, and it was, in fact, the tactic set forth in the Operation Typhoon directive for the period following the "highly coordinated and closely encircling operations" at Briansk-Viazma. The encirclement of Moscow could have been accomplished only at one of three times: (1) in late August, as Guderian advocated, without first eliminating the Russian threat to the northern and southern flanks of Army Group Center; (2) in September, as Halder, von Bock, and, temporarily, Jodl advocated, after the conclusion of the Kiev operation; or (3) in November or December 1941, with all of Panzer Group 2 participating but also after the fall of Kiev and the neutralization of Leningrad, as at first Jodl and then Göring advocated. The second possibility offered the advantage that the Kiev encirclement would have been accomplished first by dividing Panzer Group 2 and sending two of its three panzer corps to Ukraine. The rest of the tanks of Army Group Center would be regrouped and refitted for a drive to or around Moscow from the areas of Nevel and Velikie Luki (Panzer Group 3), and from south of Smolensk and near Yelnia (the XLVI Panzer Corps). Under plan three, supposedly Army Groups South and North would have been able to lend support to the final drive around the capital.

Of these three possible courses of action, the second offered the most advantages, but after the third week in August and the settlement in Guderian's favor of the controversy over the division of Panzer Group 2, this plan could not have been carried out. As pointed out earlier, even if plan two had failed, Army Group Center would have been in the best overall posture for defense during the winter of 1941–42. The third choice was, of course, the plan that was actually followed, even though the situation at Leningrad had not been resolved at the time. The failure of this plan was predetermined because the operation had to be carried out too late in the year— during bad weather—and also because the delay had allowed the enemy to mobilize fully and deploy its strategic reserve. Only the first possibility, then, needs to be discussed, especially since the advocates of this plan were so vocal after the war.

The records of the units in Army Group Center, particularly those of the Second Army and Panzer Group 2 on the southern flank of the army group and Panzer Group 3 on the northern flank, prove that Zhukov's operational echelon in the areas Gomel-Mogilev and Velikie Luki was doing an effective job of pinning down the advancing German forces on the approaches to Moscow. The difficulties experienced by Guderian's XXIV Panzer Corps at Propoisk in mid-July were symptomatic of the troubles faced by Army Group Center on its southern flank. Guderian was unable to secure the southern flank of the army group without help from several infantry divisions, but these same divisions were also desperately needed to aid the XLVI Panzer Corps in closing the gap in the Smolensk pocket between Dorogobuzh and Yelnia. Guderian had originally intended for his panzer group to push around Moscow from the south, through Briansk across the Oka in August in coordination with a thrust by Panzer Group 3 around the northern side of the capital. But after the abandonment of Velikie Luki on July 20 and after strong Russian pressure developed from the directions of Roslavl-Krichev and Rogachev-Zhlobin, such a possibility appeared to be ever more remote. Guderian was, of course, willing to do something about the Roslavl-Krichev situation before he advanced toward Moscow, but the unbeaten Russian forces on the extreme southern flank of the army group along the Dnepr and the Russian presence at Gomel would have seriously jeopardized the flank of Panzer Group 2 had a deep thrust to the east been carried out through Briansk in August. Guderian himself realized this threat, and on August 8 he asked von Bock for permission to send the XXIV Panzer Corps all the way to Gomel, if necessary, a request not mentioned in the panzer general's memoirs.

As it was, the Roslavl operation was ended quickly (by August 5) and Krichev was finished by August 12, but Guderian's success here was due primarily to the fact that his panzer group enjoyed the close cooperation of two army corps, a factor not present at Yelnia and Dorogobuzh, where the panzer groups, without infantry help, were unable to close the Smolensk pocket for eleven crucial days after the fall of Smolensk itself.

Given the failure of German panzer groups to forge a tight ring around Bialystok-Minsk and Smolensk without the help of the infantry, it is hard to imagine how the panzers could have sealed off Moscow from the east. In fact, they could have done so only had the Red Army been totally bereft of reserves and had they prepared no defense of Moscow. By mid-August not only was Army Group Center actively engaged with four Red Army groupings—the Western, Reserve, Briansk, and Central Fronts, with a total of fourteen armies—but since mid-July a new line of reserves had been in the process of deployment along the Mozhaisk line of defense, a force that included three armies also set to bar the way to Moscow, although this barrier was still inadequately manned even in October.

It would have been theoretically possible for Panzer Groups 2 and 3 to penetrate to or around Moscow in August. Zhukov admitted that such a danger was present in October at the start of the Typhoon offensive, yet what would have been the results of such a breakthrough?

To accomplish so rapid a push on Moscow, with all of Panzer Group 2's force, as Guderian had wished, the Kiev encirclement would have had to be postponed indefinitely. Zhukov made a judgment on the results of such a rash maneuver:

> As for the temporary suspension of the Moscow offensive and the drawing off of part of the forces to Ukraine, we may assume that without that operation the situation of the German central grouping could have been still worse than it turned out to be. For the General Headquarters reserves, which were used to fill in the gaps in the southwestern sector in September, could have been used to strike at the flank and the rear of the Army Group Center advancing on Moscow.

This thesis has been echoed by other Russian commentators:

> If the Germans had used the entire strength of the Wehrmacht to support the attack on Moscow, then the pressure would have been reduced on the northern and southern parts of the battlefronts. This would have allowed us to pull in more strength from these areas and also would have enabled us to continue to use the industries in the south, which would have been removed from danger of attack.[12]

The best judgment, in light of conditions existing in the summer of 1941, is that the capture of metropolitan Moscow in August or September by the Wehrmacht would have been impossible for two reasons: (1) the inability of armored units alone, aided by the small number of motorized infantry units the Wehrmacht possessed in 1941, to conquer a large defended urban area, and (2) the demonstrated inability of German mobile units without the close cooperation of infantry divisions to seal off effectively large areas controlled by the Red Army. As we have already seen, the Germans threw away any chance for a victory in the war after Operation Typhoon. In our detailed analysis of the events leading up to the near destruction of Army Group Center at Moscow in December 1941, we have shown that the collapse of the German command and control system and the resulting confusion in strategy, coupled with Zhukov's and Timoshenko's skilled exploitation of their enemy's mistakes, determined that Germany would lose the war on the eastern front.

Final Thoughts

Much in this book has been written about sacrifice. From June to December 1941 the Soviet armed forces lost 3,138,000 KIAs, MIAs, and POWs, and another 1,336,000 were lost due to wounds or illness. In the first eight months of the war, 10 million men enlisted and 3 million of these were sent immediately to the fronts. Total military casualties during the war, including those who died in German POW camps, is reckoned at 8.6 million, and another 3.8 million were lost due to wounds or illness. The Russian medical system each year of the war cared for 4 to 5 million servicemen. At the end of the war more than 1 million were still in hospitals. These numbers, of course, do not account for the large numbers of civilian dead and wounded, with many being lost to epidemic and starvation. Leningrad was the worst example, with perhaps 1 million dying from cold and hunger. The total fatal casualty count for the nation at large is grossly calculated at 20 million, of which approximately 2 to 3 million were Jews within the Soviet borders of June 1941 who died in the holocaust. No effort was made to evacuate the vulnerable Jewish populations in the areas most likely to be overrun by the Nazis; this also is a heavy charge that must be laid at Stalin's feet. In contrast, the total of German military and civilian war dead is calculated at about 6.8 million.

The first major military sacrifice was Bialystok; the second was Kiev. Was Stalin correct in his strategic assessment before the war began? Could another scenario have taken place that would have resulted in fewer losses, less surrender of territory, and more powerful blows against the aggressor? The short answer is a qualified "yes," but even now there are too many unknowns to second-guess the decisions that were made at the time, given the information, or lack thereof, that the strategists had at their disposal.

The overpowering picture that emerges is that Stalin's obsessive penchant for secrecy destroyed much of the ability the men in the higher ranks had to forge compromises that might have led to a more rational strategy than the sacrifice at Bialystok. But, realistically speaking, what could have been done? Remember that Pavlov and his cohorts had actively plotted against Stalin. Could they be trusted? Was it not better for the enemy to destroy their forces and then cut them down later? The height of such paranoia can scarcely be imagined, yet it would be foolish to believe that men are not capable of such extreme behavior and that it will not happen again.

Since the end of World War II, or the Great Patriotic War, passions have cooled, borders have changed, alliances have come and gone, and a new sense of purpose has arisen in the lands most affected by the flames of battle. A new spirit of democracy and goodwill toward neighbors has taken root and is likely not a passing phenomenon. Only time will tell, of course, but the signs are all there for a lasting peace. Not totally now, but over time it is likely that peace will triumph.

Finally, on March 14, 1994, the *New York Times* carried an article "Bitter Good-bye: Russian Troops Leave Germany for Uncertain Homecoming." In 1991 there were 546,000 troops in the Group of Soviet Forces Germany; now there are none. Truly, Germany and Russia have closed out an old era and are forging ahead with a new relationship. There is perhaps no better way to bring this book to a close than to repeat here a ballad that was sung by a Russian colonel, Yevgeny Torsukov, on the Russian military broadcast station at Wünsdorf toward the end of the occupation. The verses are Colonel Torsukov's own composition, and he played the plaintive song on his own guitar.

We came as victors to free Europe from fascism,
And now we leave, soldiers of the glorious Russian nation.
Farewell, Germany, remember the Russian soldiers
As we wave good-bye with fond Russian smiles.
Germany, always remember Bismarck's wise advice:
Never, ever make war with Moscow.
Remember the 600,000 sons of Russia who lie beneath your soil.
And keep the peace with Moscow for a thousand years.

Appendix A
DOCUMENTS

G. K. ZHUKOV AT KHALKHIN-GOL

Those having trouble accepting the existence of a Machiavellian strategy to stave off complete disaster for the Soviet Union in 1941 should ponder the ingenious use of disinformation by Zhukov at Khalkhin-Gol, related in the following essay.

In 1939 Zhukov stopped the Japanese attack at Khalkhin-Gol. His plan was to hold the right bank of the Khalkhin-Gol River while simultaneously preparing a counterattack. He reinforced artillery and aviation units and moved three rifle divisions and one tank brigade closer to the combat area.

In June the Japanese concentrated near the river. The Japanese command was so sure of imminent victory that it even invited foreign reporters and military attachés to the combat area. Among the observers were reporters and attachés from Germany and Italy. The balance of forces favored the Japanese. In the vicinity of Mount Bain-Tsaga, for instance, Soviet forces were substantially outnumbered:

	Japanese	Soviet
Tanks	2,000+	1,000+
FA guns	close to 100	50+
AT guns	up to 60	6

Zhukov decided to use his tanks immediately to defeat the Japanese forces while they were still on the march—before they could construct antitank defenses. The enemy discovered the approach of the Soviet tanks and began to organize a defense. Zhukov quickened the pace of the tank advance and attacked the Japanese troops in the open. The battle ended in the defeat of the main body of Japanese troops. They were prevented from crossing the Khalkhin-Gol River. As Zhukov himself later observed, it was a classic case of active defense: "The experience of the battle in the vicinity of Bain-Tsaga showed that tank and mechanized units in coordination with aviation and mobile artillery are a decisive means for conducting rapid combat operations to achieve decisive goals."

The main factor determining the success of the next operation, Zhukov believed, would be operational and tactical surprise that would deny the enemy any opportunity to counter the blow of the attacking Soviet troops. The Japanese had no well-trained tank units or mechanized troops at their disposal and could not quickly redeploy units from secondary directions or the rear in front of Soviet flank attacks aimed at encircling the Japanese Sixth Army.

Zhukov kept the activities of the military council of the army group secret in order to prevent the enemy from discovering plans for operational and tactical deception of the enemy:

- covert deployment and concentration of arriving reinforcements
- secret redeployment of men and materiel while conducting a defense of the Soviet-held bank of the river
- secret crossing of the river while on reconnaissance missions
- tasks of all combat arms conducted with the utmost secrecy
- disinformation to confuse the enemy about Soviet intentions

According to Zhukov, "With these measures, we tried to make the enemy think that we were making no preparations for offensive actions, to show him that we were conducting large-scale defensive—and only defensive—preparations. To this end, we conducted all movements only at night, when enemy air reconnaissance and visual observation were limited." Before August 17–18, 1939, deployment was strictly forbidden in the areas from which attacks were to be launched against the flanks and rear of the enemy. Commanders conducting reconnaissance in those areas did so in the uniforms of soldiers and only in lorries. Because it was known that the enemy was monitoring radio and telephone communication, a program of disinformation was worked out. All discussions on the radio or telephone concerned the construction of a defense system and preparing it for the winter. Exchanges were in an easy-to-decipher code. Several thousand leaflets with instructions for defense were allowed to fall into enemy hands. All movements at night were masked by the noise of aircraft, artillery, mortars, machine guns, and small arms, all strictly coordinated with the movements. Loudspeakers imitated the sounds of construction work, aircraft, tanks, and so on. In order to accustom the enemy to this noise, all of it began twelve to fifteen days before attacking troops began to move. The enemy reacted by firing into the areas in which they heard noise. Either because they had become accustomed to the noise or because they had discovered the real source of it, the enemy stopped paying attention to it, which was a mistake of great importance when the real redeployment and concentration of Soviet forces took place.

On August 20, 1939, Soviet and Mongolian troops began a general offensive to encircle and destroy the Japanese forces. At 0615 Soviet artillery launched a powerful surprise attack on enemy antiaircraft artillery and machine guns. At 0845 Zhukov's forces fired on enemy objectives. At 0900 they attacked. The enemy was defeated both morally and physically. By the end of August 26, all Japanese forces were encircled.

KREMLIN LOGBOOK (EXCERPT)

From Pavel Sudoplatov, *Special Tasks: The Memoirs of an Unwanted Witness; a Soviet Spymaster* (Boston: Little, Brown, 1994), pp. 434–35

This excerpt from Izvestia CC CPSU (News of the Central Committee, Communist Party of the Soviet Union), no. 6, 1990, confirms Sudoplatov's contention that Stalin, contrary to Khrushchev's claims in his memoirs, was not immobilized by panic after the German invasion of the Soviet Union on June 22, 1941, but rather received a steady stream of visitors at his Kremlin study. The translation omits the "T"., which stands for "*Tovarishch*" (comrade) before each name.

The logbooks of J. V. Stalin's visitors from 1927 to 1953 are kept in the CC (Central Committee) CPSU archives (in Moscow). Below are some entries made by the receptionists on duty during eight days—from the evening of June 21 to June 28, 1941 (the next entry is dated July 1, 1941). These records give the visitors' names and the duration of their stay in Stalin's study in the Kremlin. Among the visitors are members of the Politburo of the Central Committee of the Communist Party of the Soviet Union, CC CPSU, other important Communist Party and government members, and top military commanders.

The Logbook Entries of the People received by J. V. Stalin, June 21–22, 1941.

Table 1: Stalin's Visitors on June 21, 1941

1. Molotov	18:27–23:00
2. Voroshilov	19:05–23:00
3. Beria	19:05–23:00
4. Voznesensky	19:05–20:15
5. Malenkov	19:05–22:20
6. Kuznetsov	19:05–20:15
7. Timoshenko	19:05–20:15
8. Safonov	19:05–20:15
9. Timoshenko	20:50–22:20
10. Zhukov	20:50–22:20
11. Budenny	20:50–22:00
12. Mekhlis	21:55–22:20
13. Beria	22:40–23:00
The last ones left	23:00

Table 2: Stalin's Visitors on June 22, 1941

1. Molotov	5:45–12:05
2. Beria	5:45–9:20
3. Timoshenko	5:45–8:30
4. Mekhlis	5:45–8:30
5. Zhukov	5:45–8:30

6. Malenkov	7:30–9:20
7. Mikoyan	7:55–9:30
8. Kaganovich	8:00–9:35
9. Voroshilov	8:00–10:15
10. Vishnevsky	7:30–10:40
11. Kuznetsov	8:15–8:30
12. Dimitrov	8:40–10:40
13. Manuilsky	8:40–10:40
14. Kuznetsov	9:40–10:20
15. Mikoyan	9:50–10:30
16. Molotov	12:25–16:45
17. Voroshilov	11:40–12:05
18. Beria	11:30–12:00
19. Malenkov	11:30–12:00

Note the meeting beginning at 0545 with Molotov, Beria, Timoshenko, Mekhlis, and Zhukov in attendance. It is possible that the security problems associated with the sacrifice of the Bialystok salient and the details of the arrest of Pavlov were discussed at this meeting.

Report on the Antiaircraft Defense of Troops Located on the Southwestern Front. The Central Archives of the Red Army, fund 37972, Article 1022, dated 22 February 1941.

3 copies typed, 2 copies and the draft copy destroyed

1. The setup at 1700, August 8. There are 43 antiaircraft artillery divisions at the disposal of the front with 29 organic to the armies and 14 at the front level to guard strategic assets. Out of the 43 total, 8 divisions are not assigned special missions.

2. The armies have their own means of air defense combined with those of the fronts.

3. The sector of supply for the army and front are covered by:
    Kovel: 1 Art.Div.,
    Lvov: 1 AA.Reg.,
    Tarnopol: 2 Art.Div.
Note: it is absolutely necessary to reinforce the sectors of:
    Kovel: 2 Art.Div.,

Lvov: 3 Art.Div.,
Tarnopol: 2 Art.Div.,
Kotovsk: 1 Art.Div.

The 163d, 164th and 166th, Art.Divs. are incorporated in the armies and have no missions assigned as well as the arriving 139th, 140th, 141st, 126th, 127th Art.Divs.

In addition, there is a necessity to strengthen the antiaircraft defense of the sectors of supply and the railway junctions by assigning (the listed units).

4. The rear of the Southwestern Front has absolutely no means of AA defense. To defend the railway junctions of the front's rear, specifically Sarna, Korosten, Shepetovka, Berdichev, Zhitomir, Fastov, Kazatin, Prosukrov, Zhmerinka, Vapnayarka, Tsvetkovo, Smela, Cherkassy, Snamenka, Razdelnaia, and Ivanov, it is necessary to engage the 30th AAD, which should be demanded from the commander in chief, or to procure the 29th AAD from the armies.

5. To cover the industrial centers and inhabited areas in the front's rear the following is necessary:

Kiev: 3 AA.Regs. and 1 eng. AAD
Krivoi Rog: 3 AA.Regs., and 1 eng. AAD
Odessa: 2 AA.Regs., and 1 eng. AAD
Nikolaev: 2 AA.Regs., and 1 eng. AAD
Khorson: 2 AA.Divs.
TOTAL: 32 AA.Divs. and 4 eng. AA.Divs.

REQUIRES CONFIRMATION   Lieutenant General Kozlov

Top Secret
Extremely Urgent

TO THE PEOPLE'S COMMISSAR OF DEFENSE
COMRADE STALIN

EXPLANATORY NOTE TO THE PLANNING MAP OF THE COUNTEROFFENSIVE OF THE ARMIES OF THE WESTERN FRONT

The offensive begins depending on the time of arrival and concentration of the troops and their armaments: First Strike, Twentieth and Sixteenth Armies and Golikov's Army—since morning Dec. 3–4, Thirtieth Army—Dec. 5–6.

1. Composition of the armies in accordance with the STAVKA directives and separate units engaged in combat at the front in the zones of armies' offensive as is shown on the map.

2. Immediate objective is to destroy the main enemy grouping at the right wing with a strike in the direction of Klin-Solnechnogorsk and Istra and striking in the direction of Uslavaya and Bogoroditsk at the flank and rear of Guderian's group to defeat the enemy at the left flank of the front of the armies of the Western Front.

3. To restrict the enemy forces at the rest of the front and to deprive him of the opportunity of transporting the troops: Fifth, Thirty-third, Forty-third, Forty-ninth, and Fiftieth Armies of the front engage in offensive on December 4–5 with limited mission.

4. The main part of the aviation (3/4) will be directed to coordination with the right strike grouping and the remaining part with the left, that is, the army of Lieutenant General Golikov.

30.11.41   Resolution: Agree. Stalin

PAVLOV

From the archives of the KGB and the office of the main military prosecutor case R-24000: The interrogation of General D. G. Pavlov July 7, 1941—Top Secret

QUESTION: Then how did everything happen?

ANSWER: First, I'll describe the situation when the Germans began their combat against the Red Army. At 0100 on June 22, I was summoned to the front headquarters by an order of the People's Commissar of Defense. I was accompanied there by Commissar Feminyh, a member of the Military Council of the front, and Major General Klimovskikh, the front's Chief of Staff (CoS). I spoke to the People's Commissar (Timoshenko) on the phone. The first thing he asked was, "How is it there? Is everything calm?" He responded to my report by saying, "Be calm. Don't panic. But assemble the staff in case something happens. Something could happen this morning. But beware. Don't give in to provocations. If there are isolated incidents, call me over the phone."

According to the directions of the People's Commissar, I summoned all the army commanders, ordering them to arrive at the headquarters with the CoS and heads of the operational sections. I also proposed that the commanders set the troops in a state of combat readiness and occupy all fortified zones, even those as yet uncompleted. Kuznetsov replied that the troops, in response to previous orders, had already been issued ammunition and had occupied the fortifications.

Fourth Army commander Korobkov reported that his troops were ready for combat. He promised me that he would check the readiness of the Brest garrison. I told Korobkov that the troops should be in the places marked by the plan and that he should fulfill my order immediately. When air force commander Kopets and his deputy, Tayursky, arrived, they reported that the aviation of the district was ready for combat and positioned according to the order of the People's Commissar. This conversation took place at approximately 0200.

At 0300, the People's Commissar, Timoshenko, called me again and asked if there were anything new. I replied that there was nothing new and that communication with the armies had been established and all the necessary orders issued. I also reported that despite the order of commander of the air force, Zhigarev, prohibiting using stored fuel for refueling and replacing their engines with new ones, I had ordered it done. The People's Commissar approved of my order. I promised to talk with him after another round of talks with my commanders.

Having sensed the real danger of the enemy strike from Lithuania, I ordered the commander of the XXI Rifle Corps to occupy the defense positions immediately along the line to the west of Lida. It was important to keep this line to win time and give the 37th and 24th Rifle Divisions the chance to assemble northwest of Lida in order to secure the right flank of the front from the strike from Lithuania. The commander of the XXI Corps was to establish close contact with our Lithuanian units. Such an attempt was undertaken, but no units in the vicinity of Orana were found.

I also gave an important mission to the commander of the Tenth Army, Golubev. He was to destroy advancing mechanized units by inflicting a blow in the direction of Brest with the VI Mechanized Corps. But then there was a surprise directive from STAVKA demanding a strike in the northern direction by a cavalry mechanized army group to restore the situation near Grodno. To accomplish the mission ordered by STAVKA, I appointed General Boldin, who had arrived at that time. Marshal Kulik also arrived. His task was to effect overall control and coordination of our troops. In spite of my order, the VI Mechanized Corps did not accomplish its mission. For reasons unknown to me, the commander of the Tenth Army did not allow it to attack. Under my demand, the corps changed its assembly area and moved to the east of Bialystok, near Valila. I could have done no more as I had no free units at hand.

During the very first day of combat I learned about major mechanized units near Brest, Semyatichi, and Kobenko, and in Lithuania, to the west of Orana. For instance, the Tenth Army was attacked . . . in the direction of . . . Grodno . . . The 6th and 24th Rifle Divisions covering the way to Brest were attacked by three mechanized corps at the same time. This ensured enemy superiority not only in numbers of soldiers but also in weapons and vehicles. The commander of the Fourth Army . . . failed to protect his sector with the forces available to him and finally resorted to the 49th Division. The enemy also attacked the 6th and 42d Divisions with huge forces of bombers. As Korobkov reported, they bombed the positions of our infantry with great effect. Raiding bombers destroyed one gun after another.

The enemy air superiority was overwhelming. Due to the synchronized enemy strike at all airfields at 0400 sharp, most of our fighters were destroyed while still on the ground. On the first day of the war, we lost up to 300 aircraft of all types, including training aircraft. Because it was dark, the pilots failed to take off. I personally failed to control how air force commander Kopets; his deputy, Tayursky, and political deputy Listrov; and the CoS Taranenko fulfilled the order of the People's Commissar of Defense.

QUESTION: Did you have information about enemy aircraft crossing the border?

ANSWER: The information arrived at the same time the bombs did. At the Minsk central post, the information about enemy aircraft crossing the border arrived in four minutes. The airfields near the border received the information much earlier, but our pilots failed to take off because, as I said, they were not qualified to fly the new types of aircraft at night.

Further events developed like this. On June 23, the front headquarters received a telegram from Boldin. It said that the 6th Mechanized Corps had only one-quarter of the necessary fuel. I immediately sent all available fuel to it, 200 tons. The rest of our fuel was in Maikop, as the plan of the general staff had envisioned. But the fuel sent by rail to the corps could not be transported further than Baranovichi because of persistent bombing of the stations and railway . . .

During the second day of hostilities the enemy approached Kobrin, using aviation, tanks, and motorized units. Our units, poorly commanded by Fourth Army commander Korobkov, had to leave the city under the pressure of superior forces. As a result, the left flank of the neighboring Tenth Army was open, and it was in danger of being encircled. That is why I immediately sent to Korobkov my assistant for the problems of military colleges, Khabarov, with the strictest order: Shoot any number of people, but stop the retreat. Concentrate command and control in his hands! At the same time the 121st Rifle Division, which was defending its positions at Slonim well, was sent in the direction of Rozhany to help the Fourth Army. The 155th Division was ordered to be ready to start for the same region . . .

For the whole day the enemy aviation raided the airfield where the 43d Fighter Regiment was located. Because the airfield was completely destroyed along with the training and civil equipment, the air force command moved what was left of the regiment to Slopyanka. The enemy inflicted devastating blows from the air at the railroad junctions at Orsha, Borisov, Bobruisk, and Osipovichi and totally destroyed the artillery ammunition depot in Gainovka . . .

After my report to the STAVKA about the difficult situation in the direction of Brest and the increasing activity of enemy mechanized units in the direction of Belsk, with the apparent aim of cutting off the Tenth Army from the main body of the front, the order was received to relocate it quickly to the Schara River. This order was sent to the army twice over the radio. It was also sent with the help of paratroopers. Commanders of other armies were made known of the planned retreat in the same way. Special groups of delegates were sent to each of them. The group sent to the Tenth Army was to find Marshal Kulik and inform him personally of the decision of the STAVKA. After receiving the order, the army made a well-planned retreat to positions prepared in advance at the Schara River by units of the 155th, 121st, and 143d Divisions. But it then became known that the 55th Division, which was fighting in the Brest direction, had been attacked by no less than two tank divisions supported by many bombers. As a result, the division was cut into two parts on opposite sides of the highway. Thus, just as our troops occupied the Schara front, there was a breach of the same left flank. Then the enemy drove for Slutsk.

I personally . . . assigned the preparation of the defense of Slutsk. I ordered the commander of the army and the CoS for the 55th Division immediately to establish strict order and defend the former state border. At the same time I ordered units of the 143d Division to attack the enemy in the southern direction and cut off the highway in the vicinity of Kartus-Beresa. But I did not find out whether or not this order was carried out. It did become known that the 55th Division was attacked the same day by numerous enemy tanks from the direction of Baranovichi. The attack was repelled by our artillery and soldiers, but I couldn't help but be aware that some enemy troops were in the rear of the . . . 121st, 143d, and 155th divisions. Thanks to energetic measures undertaken by commander of the XVII Mechanized Corps, General Petrov, forty to fifty of the tanks that had broken through were destroyed, and the rest left for the south. And on June 24, units of the Third Army began the retreat to the Schara River, the line determined by the STAVKA.

It remained unclear where the VI Mechanized Corps with the headquarters of the Tenth Army was. According to my order, which was approved by the STAVKA, the corps was to arrive rapidly in front of our infantry and stay at the line of Slonim ready to rebuff enemy attempts to encircle the army from the south . . .

On June 25, according to information from soldiers fleeing from Lithuania, the enemy destroyed our 5th Mechanized Division. The soldiers of the Lithuanian national division simply deserted. Mechanized units of the enemy appeared unexpectedly on the right flank of the XXI Rifle Corps, compelling me to speed the advance of the 24th Division to the corps. Meanwhile, the enemy advanced to Molodechno, bypassing the XXI Corps and not encountering any resistance because there were no troops in that direction and there was nowhere we could get any. The enemy occupied the city and blocked the approach of the 50th Division to the XXI Rifle Corps.

The fall of Molodechno necessitated putting the Minsk and Slutsk consolidated areas into a state of combat readiness. The 64th, 100th, and 108th Divisions advanced as reinforcements. The 100th Division should have defended the northern suburbs of the Bielorussian capital. The 161st Division remained in reserve south of the city . . . At the same time, the headquarters of the Tenth Army was ordered to the Minsk front along the line of Pleschanitsa-Minsk-Slutsk. Thus, we protected the town and gained the strength for a counterstrike if it were necessary to liberate from encirclement the Minsk-Novogrodek and Baranovichi groupings . . .

On June 25, a telegram from the headquarters of the Tenth Army was received: "The units have arrived at the Zelvianka River. The enemy has occupied all the crossings. I request support from the direction of Baranovichi." In response, I ordered the recapture of the crossings or retreat across the Nieman River or, if the situation dictated it, through the forest . . .

At the same time, my deputy for the military colleges, Khabarov, was sent to Petrov's headquarters for coordination with the retreating troops. By this time, the forward tank units had been destroyed in the vicinity of Slonim. On one of the dead German officers, we found a map showing an entire enemy grouping from the Bug River to Baranovichi. The map indicated that the enemy was carrying out an offensive with three mechanized corps. They had attacked the front of our two divisions at the beginning. It was also clear that the enemy had sent a mechanized division of the left flank corps to Volkovysk and Slonim; that in the fighting near Minsk an enemy corps headquarters was completely destroyed. We have captured all the papers.

"Fight for Minsk with complete stubbornness! Fight until encirclement!" Such was the order of the commander of the Thirteenth Army on the basis of directions of the People's Commissar of Defense, which was distributed with the help of Marshal Shaposhnikov, who was among the troops. This order explains to a great extent the steadfastness of the troops, who were fighting against numerous enemy mechanized units. Running short of armor-piercing ammunition, they set German tanks on fire with bottles filled with gasoline. The 100th Division alone destroyed no less than 100 enemy combat vehicles. I had learned this tactic in Khalkhin-Gol and spread it among the troops this winter. . . .

The mechanized units of the enemy still managed to bypass the Minsk consolidated area. The enemy also cut off the Minsk-Borispol highway, landing a major paratrooper force near Smolovichi. As a result, the only way to replenish the defenders was along Minsk-Osipovichi and the Mogilev highway. That is why I ordered that platoons, companies, and battalions should be formed quickly of retreating personnel and positioned along the line of Stary Doroghi. I also warned the Bobruisk Caterpillar School, which was defending its city. We prepared beforehand to blow up all the bridges across the Berezina River. Commander of the 42d Division, Lasarenko, was responsible for blowing them up in case the enemy appeared. He carried out the order during the retreat of our troops. And at about 0200 on June 28, the CoS of the 13th Air Division received an order from me to leave the airfield at dawn in order to avoid complete destruction. In fact, the division left just in time. By dawn the airfield was already occupied by German tanks. . . .

Meanwhile, the enemy continued to try to construct bridges over the Berezina. . . . To facilitate the attempt, the enemy resorted to massive bomber raids and mortar fire. Our aviation bombed the Bobruisk enemy grouping for two days. . . .

Between June 25 and June 28, there was no radio communication with the Third and Tenth Armies. Aircraft with couriers to them were shot down, so we sent couriers in land vehicles, but I don't know whether or not they reached their destinations. . . . The information that arrived from them at the front headquarters was usually outdated. We tried to detect our lost units at any cost. Paratroopers landed in their supposed locations with orders to turn over cyphergrams or just to tell them the direction of retreat. This was most important in the case of the Tenth Army because we had no communication with them. Marshal Kulik was there all the time. On the eve of my arrest, I learned that our cavalry corps were fighting out of the encirclement. We envisaged a free route to the south of Minsk, including Shatsk. The breakout should have been ensured by detachments formed in advance to defend crossings near Borisov, Beresino, and Svislach. They were to let our units cross the Berezina and keep to its left bank, denying the enemy the chance to cross it. . . .

The front's headquarters functioned with full energy. Information had to be obtained in various ways as wire communications were completely inactivated. In the western area, wire communications were disrupted by anti-Soviet elements and by saboteurs landing from the air. CoS general Klimovskikh was so exhausted that he couldn't stand.

The main cause of all our troubles I consider to be the huge enemy superiority in tanks, including the quality of combat vehicles, and aviation. Besides, at the left flank of the Baltic Military District—later the Northwestern Front—were Lithuanian units that didn't want to fight. As soon as the Germans attacked, the Baltic soldiers shot all the commanders and deserted. This made it possible for the Germans to attack me from Vilnius.

QUESTION: Along the entire state border, only at the front that you commanded why did German units manage to penetrate so deeply into Soviet territory? What is this? Was it the result of your betrayal?

ANSWER: I categorically deny this accusation. I didn't commit treason. The breakthrough at my front took place because I didn't have new materiel in amounts at least equal to that in the Kiev Military District.

QUESTION: It is in vain that you try to explain the defeat of your front. The investigation has established that you have been a member of the plot since 1935. Even then you intended to betray the Motherland. The situation at your front confirms our information. Any comments?

ANSWER: I have never taken part in any plots, and I have never had anything to do with any plotters. This accusation is extremely grave . . . and is incorrect from beginning to end. If there is any testimony against me, it is false and belongs to those who would like to somehow slander honest people and cause harm to the state . . .

KULIK

From the Archives of the KGB: Case of Marshal Kulik; Interrogation of Dmitrii Grigoryevich Pavlov, July 21, 1941

QUESTION: What were the specific manifestations of your criminal activity?

ANSWER: In order to protect ourselves from arrest, we decided upon returning home from Spain to stop anti-Soviet activities for the time being, to stay underground, to display only the good features of our service to prove that we had no connection with any plot.

By that time, many commanders had already been arrested, and the arrests were continuing. The arrests added to our rage against the government because our fellow plotters were being repressed. In order to shelter our co-conspirators, we decided to deceive the government. We made the first attempt at deceit at the conference of the Main Military Council in 1938 when, with members of the Politburo present, Savchenko, then commissar of the artillery department, detailed the decline of discipline in the armed forces. It was suggested that Savchenko and I prepare a statement on the problem. The main author of the statement was Kulik. I want to make it clear that before he wrote it, a group of commanders, including Kulik, Savchenko, and . . . me, discussed its contents. Though all of us supported Savchenko's assertion, none of us started work on the statement for two days. Then Kulik took the initiative and suggested that he, Alliluyev, Savchenko, and I write it together. The four of us wrote it in the form of a letter and sent it to Voroshilov. We were soon informed from his office that the People's Commissar had not read the letter and wanted it taken back. Then on one of the days off, Kulik invited us back, and we rewrote the letter and sent it to the General Secretary of the Central Committee, with a second copy going again to Voroshilov.

QUESTION: Summarize the contents of the letter.

ANSWER: In essence, the letter stated that even though the main body of counterrevolutionary forces in the armed forces had been destroyed, arrests of commanders continued and on such a scale that morale was being affected, as soldiers were starting to criticize commanders and political officers, suspecting them to be enemies of the people. We said in conclusion that the combat readiness of the armed forces might be negatively affected and asked for appropriate measures to be taken . . . *

RADIO SPEECH BY THE CHAIRMAN OF THE STATE DEFENSE COMMITTEE, J. V. STALIN, JULY 3, 1941

(Note: this radio address to the nation was the first public communication by Stalin since the German invasion on June 22.)

Comrades! Citizens! Brothers and sisters! Soldiers of our army and navy!

It's me who is addressing you now, my friends!

Since June 22 a perfidious military aggression by Hitler's Germany against our Motherland has been under way. Despite the heroic resistance of the Red Army, despite the fact that the best enemy divisions and aviation units have already been destroyed and that the battlefields are strewn with enemy graves, the enemy continues to thrust forward by sending fresh forces to the front. Hitler's troops have managed to occupy Lithuania, a significant part of Latvia, the western part of Bielorussia, and part of western Ukraine. The Fascist air force is widening the areas of operation of its bombers, bombing Murmansk, Orsha, Mogilev, Smolensk, Kiev, Odessa, and Sebastopol. Our Motherland is seriously endangered.

How has it happened that our glorious Red Army left the Fascists in control of a number of our cities and regions? Are German-Fascist troops indeed invincible as their boastful propaganda repeats time and again?

Certainly not! History shows us that there are no invincible armies and there have never been. Napoleon's army was considered invincible, but it was defeated in turn by Russian, English, and German armies. The German army of Kaiser Wilhelm during the First Imperialist War [World War I] was also considered invincible, but it suf-

---

*This document was provided from KGB archives by A. Y. Nikolayev, Officer of the Central Archive of the Security Department of the Russian Federation, October 2, 1992.

fered several defeats at the hands of Russian and Anglo-French troops and in the end it was destroyed by Anglo-French forces. This same must be said about the present-day German-Fascist army of Hitler. Hitler's army so far has not encountered serious resistance anywhere else on the European continent. Only on our territory has it encountered serious resistance. And since our Red Army has already destroyed the best German divisions, this means that the Fascist army can also be destroyed and it will be destroyed like the armies of Napoleon and Kaiser Wilhelm.

We can explain the fact that part of our territory is occupied by German troops by saying that the war began under conditions favorable for German troops and unfavorable for Soviet troops. The truth is that German forces were already fully mobilized for wartime, since Germany had already been at war. They moved 170 divisions close to the borders of the USSR and were in complete readiness, awaiting only the signal to attack. Soviet troops, on the other hand, had to be mobilized and advanced toward the borders. The fact that Fascist Germany unexpectedly and perfidiously violated the nonaggression pact signed in 1939 by Germany and the USSR, ignoring the fact that it would be recognized by the world as an aggressor, is also of great significance. Our peace-loving country was unwilling to violate the pact and we never would have started a war of aggression.

People might ask: how could it happen that the Soviet government agreed to sign the nonaggression pact with such perfidious people and monsters like Hitler and Ribbentrop? Wasn't it a mistake on the part of the Soviet government? Certainly not! A nonaggression pact is a pact of peace between two states, and this was the pact offered to us by Germany in 1939. Could the Soviet government have rejected such an offer? I think that no peace-loving state can reject a peace agreement with a neighboring power, even if this power is governed by such monsters and cannibals like Hitler and Ribbentrop. And, of course, the nonaggression pact between Germany and the USSR didn't violate either directly or indirectly the territorial integrity, independence, and honor of our peace-loving state. This is well known.

What did we gain by signing the nonaggression pact with Germany? We ensured peace for our country for a year and a half and gained more time to prepare our armed forces for repelling an attack in case Hitler took the risk of invading our country despite the pact. The time we gained is a victory for us and a defeat for Fascist Germany.

What has Fascist Germany won and lost by perfidiously violating the pact and attacking the USSR? It has gained temporary advantages for its troops for a short time, but it has lost politically, having exposed itself in front of the whole world as a bloody aggressor. There can't be any doubt about the fact that the short-term military advantage for Germany is just an episode, and the huge political gain for the USSR is a significant long-term factor, which will ensure the military success of the Red Army in the war with Fascist Germany.

This is why our entire glorious army, our entire glorious navy, all our fighter pilots, all the peoples of our country, all the best people of Europe, America, and Asia, and, in the end, all the best people of Germany condemn the perfidious actions of the German Fascists. They are sympathetic with the Soviet government, approve of the actions of the Soviet government, and see that our course is right; namely, that the enemy will be destroyed. We are destined to win.

As a result of the war imposed on us, our country is now taking part in a deadly battle with a most vicious and cunning enemy—German fascism. Our forces are heroically fighting against the enemy, who is armed to the teeth with tanks and aviation. The Red Army and Red Navy, overcoming numerous difficulties, are selflessly fighting for every inch of Soviet soil. The Red Army's main forces are being engaged, armed with thousands of tanks and aircraft. The bravery of our soldiers has no parallels. Our resistance to the enemy is steadily growing stronger. All Soviet peoples are rising to the defense of the Motherland together with the Red Army.

What is necessary to eliminate the threat to our Motherland and what measures should be taken to destroy the enemy?

First of all it is necessary that our people, Soviet people, realize the gravity of the threat to our country and abandon peacetime habits that were quite understandable before the war but not at the present since the war has drastically changed our situation. The enemy is wicked and inexorable. His goal is to occupy our lands, cultivated with our sweat, and to capture our wheat and our oil, obtained by our labor. His goal is to restore the power of tsarist landlords and destroy the national cultures and identities of Russians, Ukrainians, Bielorussians, Lithuanians, Latvians, Estonians, Uzbeks, Tatars, Moldavians, Armenians, Azerbaijanians, and other free peoples of the Soviet Union and turn them into slaves for German barons. What is at stake is the life and death of the Soviet state, the life and death of the peoples of the USSR, and whether the peoples of the Soviet Union are free or enslaved. It is necessary that Soviet people understand this and mobilize themselves for restructuring their work to conform with the needs of the military and help defeat the enemy.

It is necessary, further, that there be no place in our ranks for whiners and cowards, alarmists and deserters. It is necessary that our people show no fear in the struggle and that they self-denyingly join our patriotic liberating war against the Fascist enslavers. Great Lenin, who created our state, used to say that the main qualities of the Soviet people should be bravery, boldness, fearlessness in war, and readiness to fight to the death against the enemies of our Motherland. It is necessary that Lenin's example became commonplace for the millions of soldiers in our Red Army and Navy and for all the peoples of the Soviet Union.

We should immediately restructure all our work to satisfy the needs of the military, subordinating everything to the interests of the front and the objectives of defeating the enemy. Peoples of the Soviet Union see now that fascism is implacable in its furious rage and hatred toward our Motherland, which has ensured for all toilers freedom of work and welfare. Peoples of the Soviet Union should rise to defend their rights and their land against the enemy.

The Red Army and Navy and all citizens of the Soviet Union should defend every inch of Soviet soil, fight till the last drop of blood for our cities and villages, and display the courage, initiative, and skills that are inherent in our people.

We should organize everything to help the Red Army, to ensure rapid reinforcement of its ranks, to supply it with everything necessary, to organize speedy transportation of troops and military cargo, and to provide needed assistance to the wounded.

We should strengthen the rear of the Red Army, subordinating our entire activity to the interests of our cause. We must ensure intensive work at all factories to produce more rifles, machine guns, artillery, ammunition, and aircraft. We must organize defenses for plants, electric stations, and telephone and telegraph communication lines and organize local antiaircraft defenses.

We should organize a merciless struggle against all kinds of subversives in the rear—deserters, alarmists, rumor mongers, spies, saboteurs, and enemy paratroopers—by rendering quick support to our security battalions. We should keep in mind that the enemy is crafty, cunning, and experienced in deception and in spreading false rumors. One should take all that into consideration and not give in to provocations. All those who interfere with the cause of defense because of their panic and cowardice should be immediately tried by a military court no matter who they are.

Along with the forced retreat of the Red Army units, all rolling stock should be pulled back; not a single locomotive or railway car should be left for the enemy, not a kilogram of bread, not a liter of fuel should be left either. Collective farmers should evacuate cattle and transfer wheat to state collectors so it can be removed to the rear areas. Anything valuable—including nonferrous metals, wheat, and fuel—that can't be evacuated should be unconditionally destroyed.

In the areas occupied by the enemy, guerrilla detachments should be organized and units should be formed to unleash partisan warfare everywhere: to destroy bridges and roads; to disrupt telephone and telegraph communication lines; to set forests, depots, and railway trains on fire. In occupied areas the enemy should be pursued and destroyed everywhere—all of their activities should be disrupted.

War against Fascist Germany can't be viewed as an ordinary war. It is more than a war between two armies. It is a great war of all the Soviet people against German-Fascist aggression. The goal of this national patriotic war against Fascist oppressors is not just to eliminate the danger to our country, but also to help all the peoples of Europe who are now suffering under the yoke of German fascism. We are not alone in this liberation war. In this great war we shall have true allies—the peoples of Europe and America, including the German people enslaved by Hitler's henchmen. Our struggle for freedom of our Motherland will merge with the struggles of the peoples of Europe and America for their independence and for democratic freedoms. This will be the joint front of the peoples, standing for freedom against slavery and the threat of slavery imposed by Hitler and his Fascist armies. In connection with this, Great Britain's prime minister, Churchill, gave a historic speech promising aid to the Soviet Union. There has been also a declaration by the government of the United States about its readiness to render support to our country. There is a feeling of gratitude in the hearts of the peoples of the Soviet Union for this support, and these feelings are quite understandable and demonstrative.

Comrades! Our forces are invincible. The boastful enemy will see that for himself very soon. Together with the Red Army, many thousands of workers, collective farmers, and representatives of intelligentsia are rising to fight against the aggressor. Millions of people will rise up to fight. The toilers of Moscow and Leningrad have already started to create militias of many thousands of people to support the Red Army. In every town endangered by the enemy, people's militias should be organized. All workers should rise to defend their freedom, their honor, their Motherland with their hearts in our patriotic war against German fascism.

To ensure the rapid mobilization of the entire strength of the peoples of the USSR to resist the enemy that has perfidiously attacked our Motherland, a State Defense Committee was set up that now represents all authority in the state. The State Defense Committee has started its work and calls upon all the people to rally around the party of Lenin and Stalin, around the Soviet government for its self-denying support of the Red Army and Red Navy, for the destruction of the enemy, for victory.

Our entire strength—for support of our heroic Red Army, our glorious Red Navy!

The entire strength of the people—for destruction of the enemy!

Forward, for our victory! (*Vpered na pobedu!*)

PLAN FOR THE STRATEGIC DEPLOYMENT OF THE ARMED FORCES OF THE SOVIET UNION, MARCH 11, 1941

Extremely Important, Top Secret, Strictly Personal the Only Copy. To the Central Committee of the Communist Party of the Soviet Union (Bolshevik) to Comrade Stalin and Comrade Molotov

In connection with the major organizational measures undertaken in the Red Army in 1941, I report for your consideration the detailed plan of strategic deployment of the armed forces of the Soviet Union in the west and in the east.

1. Our Probable Enemies

The political situation in Europe makes us pay exceptional attention to defending our western borders. Aggression may be limited to German attack on our western borders, but Japanese attack on our borders in the Far East is possible. Germany might involve Finland, Rumania, Hungary, and other allies in aggression against us. Thus, the Soviet Union should be prepared for war on two fronts: in the west against Germany, supported by Italy, Hungary, Rumania, and Finland, and in the east against Japan, either as an immediate enemy or as an enemy in a stance of armed neutrality that could always turn into open combat.

2. Armed Forces of Probable Enemies

At present Germany has 225 infantry, 20 tank, and 15 motorized divisions deployed, all in all, up to 260 divisions, 20,000 guns of all calibers, 10,000 tanks, and 15,000 aircraft, 9,000 of them combat aircraft. Of the divisions, 76 are concentrated on our borders, and 35 in Rumania and Bulgaria. Of the divisions concentrated on our borders, 6 are tank divisions and 7 motorized. Should the war against Great Britain end, we can assume that of its 260 divisions Germany will leave no less than 35 in occupied countries and 25 on home territory. Therefore, Germany will send 165 of its 260 divisions against us, 20 of them tank divisions and 15 motorized.

3. Probable Enemy Operational Plans

There is no documented information available to the general staff concerning the operational plans of probable enemies in the west and in the east. The most probable strategic deployment is the following. Germany is most likely to deploy its main forces in the southeast, from Sedlets to Hungary, in order to strike at Berdichev and Kiev and occupy Ukraine. This blow will evidently be accompanied by a blow in the north from East Prussia at Dvinsk and Riga or from

Suvalki and Brest with concentric blows at Volkovysk and Baranovichi. If Finland joins the attack, it is possible that its troops will
be joined by 8 to 10 German divisions in an attack on Leningrad from
the northwest. In the south a simultaneous Rumanian assault on
Zhmerinka with German support is probable. In such a scenario, the
following deployment can be expected. From the lower reaches of
the Zapadny Bug River north to the Baltic Sea: 39 or 40 infantry divisions, 3 to 5 tank divisions, 2 to 4 motorized divisions, and up to
3,750 guns and 2,000 tanks. From the Zapadny Bug River south to
the Hungarian border: up to 10 infantry divisions, 14 tank divisions,
10 motorized divisions, up to 11,500 guns, 7,500 tanks, and the major part of enemy aviation. It is not impossible that the Germans
would concentrate the bulk of their forces in East Prussia and in the
direction of Warsaw in order to inflict the main blow across the
Lithuanian Soviet Socialist Republic at Riga, Kovno, and Dvinsk. In
that case, one would expect simultaneous concentric blows from
Lomzha and Brest at Baranovichi and Minsk.

The following is the most likely scenario of the deployment of the
army of Finland. The attacks in the direction of Riga would apparently be combined with a landing on the coast of the Baltic Sea near
Libava with the aim of striking the flank and rear of our armies on
the lower Nieman and the capture of the Moonzund Archipelago
and landing in the Estonian Soviet Socialist Republic with the aim
of an assault on Leningrad. Under this variant, we should expect that
the Germans would assign for their operations in the north up to 130
divisions and the major part of their artillery, tanks, and aviation, leaving 30 to 40 of their infantry divisions and part of their tanks and aviation in the south. Deployment of German troops at our borders will
take ten to fifteen days. We should expect deployment in fifteen to
twenty days of 30 Rumanian infantry divisions at our border with Rumania, with the main grouping of up to 18 infantry divisions in the
area of Botashani and Suchava.

4. Foundations of Our Strategic Deployment

Facing the necessity of our deploying our forces in the west and in
the east, we should deploy our main forces in the west . . . The rest
of our borders should be protected by minimal force. (1) On our

northern coast should remain the 88th Rifle Division, reserve units, and border guards. (2) On the Black Sea from Odessa to Kerch should remain, in addition to the Black Sea Fleet, the 156th Rifle Division, reserve units, coast guards, and border guards. (3) From Kerch to Sukhumi should remain the 157th Rifle Division and border guards. (4) The Transcaucasus has six infantry divisions, four of them mountain divisions, two cavalry divisions, and eleven aviation regiments. (5) The borders in central Asia are protected by two mountain divisions and three cavalry divisions. In total, our northern and southern borders have eleven infantry divisions, seven of them mountain divisions, and five cavalry divisions. For countering Japan in the east, it is necessary to assign the following: twenty-nine infantry divisions, six of them motorized, with three coming from Siberia.

5. Foundations of Our Strategic Deployment in the West

The deployment of the main body of the Red Army in the west, including the major forces grouped against East Prussia in the direction of Warsaw, arouses grave concern that the armed struggle on this front might entail prolonged hostilities. I request that my report on the foundations of our strategic deployment in the west and in the east be analyzed.

People's Commissar of Defense of the USSR, Marshal of the Soviet Union *S. Timoshenko,* Chief of the General Staff, General of the Army *G. Zhukov*

Compiled by Major General Vasilevsky, March 11, 1941 (CADD 16/2951, Vol. 241, pp. 1–15.)

FINAL WARNINGS

Secret Copy 148. INTELLIGENCE REPORT 28: Over the period of October 10–20 1940, Intelligence Department of the Kiev Separate Military District (KOVO)

According to intelligence reports, which still need confirmation, the Western group headquarters moved from Lodz to Lublin later in August. The headquarters is located in the Hitler Platz and is heavily guarded.

According to the same report, which needs confirmation, the headquarters of the 8th, 11th, and 3d Armies are located in the zone of Warsaw-Gubeshov. All in all there are six armies in the territory of the general-governorship of Poland.

Intelligence reports have it that the Germans are expanding their cantonments. They are building wooden barracks in the towns of Krasnostav, Sandomir, and Zamostiye (in Zamostiye, fourteeen barracks have already been built). The barracks are 40 meters long.

There are reports that a military parade of the Warsaw garrison troops was held in Warsaw on October 7. Field Marshal List reviewed the troops.

The same reports make a note of the fact that the German population is being moved from the territory of the Lublin district farther on behind the Vistula River, while the Poles are being moved from behind the Vistula River into the area between the Western Bug and the Vistula.

In the region of Dubetzko, along the western bank of the San River, trenches are being dug.

Artillery positions have been organized on the mountain Chertezhovskaya Golovnya (not far from the village of Trepcha). Iron observation towers are being erected not far off, near the village of Chertezh.

Intelligence reports say ten railroad cars with building materials for antitank barriers arrived at Zhuravitza station (northern Peremyshl) on September 25 and 26. Barbed wire, stone, and cement in large amounts are arriving in the region of Peremyshl. Airfields in Rakovitz (a suburb of Krakow) are being expanded. There are reports, which are to be confirmed yet, saying there is an underground airdrome there with apple trees growing on the surface.

Intelligence reports to be confirmed say camouflaged air grounds and hangars are situated in the Volsky forest (west of Krakow). A large number of dismantled aircraft are being taken there, and entry is forbidden (earlier reports said there were artillery units in the forest).

Intelligence reports say the highway of Peremyshl, Lipovitza, Roketyntza, Pruhnik has been repaired and side gutters have been dug out.

A second highway is being built from Gubeshov up to Milche. The whole length of the highway is being paved with bricks. Up to 3,000 people, Jews, are working at the construction.

Repairs of the highway leading from the border to Gozhitza were started September 25. The work is being done by German soldiers.

Radio intelligence reports confirm the location of aircraft bases in the following points: Radom, Keltze, Warsaw, Tarnow, Lublinetz, Tarnovitze, Dembitza, Novo-Radomsk, and Kotovitze.

Radio intelligence reports say air defense exercises were held in Crakow on October 14 at 2000. Aircraft and searchlight units were involved in the exercise.

TELEGRAPH REPORT

Sent from Belgrade 1000, March 9, 1941. Received by Department 6, 1400, March 10, 1941, by telegraph to the Chief of the Intelligence Department of the General Staff of the Red Army Belgrade, March 9, 1941

The source . . . gave information, coming from a court minister:

The German General Staff has abandoned the plan to attack the British Isles. Its nearest goal is to occupy Ukraine and Baku. The operation is to take place in April–May this year. Preparations are being made in Hungary, Rumania, and Bulgaria.

Intensive transfer of troops to Rumania is under way via Berlin and Hungary . . . reported, the real power in Yugoslavia is in the hands of the General Staff since March 7. The ministerial council doesn't take a single step without consulting the General Staff.

Military Attaché

March 1941: INTELLIGENCE REPORT FROM BERLIN (from the "Corsican")

The senior German officials are seriously discussing the possibility of turning the front to the east, against the Soviet Union. These plans are alleged to be largely substantiated by the acute food problems Germany and the occupied territories are facing (Belgium, for example, is facing famine). Agricultural minister Darre's calculations, that Germany had enough food stores, proved to be incorrect. The situation with food supply is so grave that food rationing was expected to be cut in February.

A civil servant, working with the four-year plan committee, said that several committee employees had got an urgent task to calculate the stock of raw materials and food Germany might obtain as a result of an occupation of the European part of the Soviet Union.

The same informer reports that General Halder, the chief of the General Staff of the army, expects the occupation of the Soviet Union, Ukraine in the first place, to be swift and successful, with the good condition of the roads and railways in Ukraine contributing to the progress of the operation. The same Halder sees the occupation of Baku and its oil fields as an easy mission. He expects the fields could be quickly restored if damaged in the course of military actions. Halder holds that the Red Army will be unable to offer any serious resistance to the rapid advance of the German troops. The Russians will not even have time to destroy their supply stocks.

Presented to: Stalin, Molotov, Beria.

Correct: the Chief of Department 1 of the USSR SSPC, Fitin

Secret Copy 1: INTELLIGENCE SUMMARY: The situation by April 1, 1941

During March, intensive movement of troop units, military cargo, and materials both by railroad and vehicles toward the German eastern borders was observed in the territory of East Prussia and the General-governorship (Poland).

The main items to be transported are: troops, ammunition, fuel, equipment, demolition equipment, pontoons, and medical equipment.

The transport was carried out mainly at night.

There are reports of intensive construction of air bases and storages in the border zones, particularly in the regions of Nosazhevo (Eastern Mlava) and Sedlets. Highways are being repaired and widened, loading grounds are being organized, and railroad stations are being enlarged (east and southeast of Warsaw).

Troops move both along highway and side roads, which are barred from civil transport.

As a result of the arrival of new military units in East Prussia and the General-governorship, the Western Separate Military District (including—to the right—Seiny, Suvalki, Letzen, and Allenstein and—to the left—Voldava, excluding Demblin and Radom) is confronting, by April 1, a group of troops that has increased by two to three infantry divisions, two tank regiments, and one motorcycle battalion, and totals twenty-seven to twenty-eight infantry divisions, more than three tank divisions, one cavalry division and a cavalry brigade, seven cavalry regiments, three air regiments, one railroad regiment, an antiaircraft artillery regiment, and a motorcycle battalion.

Troop buildup is observed mostly in Warsaw and in the Brest direction, in the region of Sokolov, Sedlets, Byala Podlyaska, and Terespol. See the scheme for the location of the units.

According to the information of the Internal Affairs Commissariat of the BSSR (Bielorussia), the whole male population, through the age of fifty-two, has been called up for military service in the territory of the Memel (Klipeda) region and East Prussia.

Deputy Chief of the Intelligence Department of the WSMD (Western Special Military District)

Lieutenant-colonel Ilnitzky, Chief of Unit 3 of the Intelligence Department

Major Samoilovich

Top Secret: A REPORT FROM BERLIN, 30 April 1941 (from the "Sergeant")

The source, working in the German aviation headquarters, informs:

According to the information, given by a communication officer, working in the communication between the Foreign Ministry and the German Gregor at Aviation headquarters, the question of starting an attack against the Soviet Union had been definitely resolved and the attack is expected to start shortly. Ribbentrop, who until recently had not supported an attack against the USSR, changed his position, being well aware of Hitler's firm resolve on the issue. He now sides with the supporters of the invasion.

According to the information, obtained in the aviation headquarters, the cooperation between the German and Finnish General

Staffs has increased over the past few days. They have joined efforts to work out operational plans against the USSR. Finnish-German units are expected to cut across Karelia to leave for themselves the Petsamo nickel mines, to which they attach much importance.

The Rumanian, Hungarian, and Bulgarian headquarters have approached the Germans with a request to swiftly deliver antitank and antiaircraft artillery they would need, should a war with the Soviet Union become a reality.

The reports by the German aviation commission, which returned from its visit to the USSR, and the report by the German air force attaché in Moscow, Herr Aschenbrenner, have produced a depressing impression in the aviation headquarters. However, although the Soviet aviation theoretically is capable of reaching German territory and dealing a serious blow, the German army is expected to rapidly suppress the Soviet troops' resistance by paralyzing major Soviet air bases.

According to the information obtained from Leibrandt, an expert on Russian affairs at the foreign department, Gregor's notification that an attack against the Soviet Union is a settled issue has been reaffirmed.

Presented to: Stalin, Molotov, Beria.

Correct: the Chief of Department 1 of the Soviet State Security People's Commissariat, Fitin.

Top Secret: A REPORT FROM WARSAW: April 30, 1941

Intelligence reports, obtained over the last few days from different sources, say:

The military preparations in Warsaw and in the territory of the General-governorship are being carried on openly. The coming war between Germany and the Soviet Union is being candidly discussed by the German officers and soldiers as if it were a settled matter. The war will allegedly start after the spring crop sowing. Referring to their officers, the German soldiers say that the invasion of Ukraine will succeed due to the effective "fifth column" working in the Soviet territory.

From April 10 to 20, the German troops were moving through Warsaw eastward both day and night. The continuous flow of the troops blocked all traffic in Warsaw. Cargo trains, loaded with heavy artillery, trucks, and aircraft parts, are moving eastward too. Lots of military trucks and Red Cross automobiles have been seen in Warsaw since mid-April.

The German authorities in Warsaw have issued a regulation to put in order all the bombproof shelters, to darken all the windows, to set up medical units in every house, to call up all the previously dismissed Red Cross brigades. All the automobiles, belonging to private owners or civil organizations, including German ones, have been mobilized and taken away for the army.

Starting with April all schools and courses have been closed; the premises have been occupied by military hospitals.

All passenger rail traffic in the General-governorship territory (Poland), except the local line Warsaw-Otwotzk, has been banned.

The information on building a fortified line and separate fortified areas along the Soviet border has been confirmed. The work is carried on by German soldiers and workers under the supervision of the famous creator of the "Siegfried line"—engineer Todt.

Presented to: Stalin, Molotov, Beria.

Correct: the Chief of Department 1 of the Soviet State Security People's Commissariat, Fitin

SPECIAL REPORT: No. 660477, Top Secret: May 5, 1941

On the Group of the German Troops in the East and Southeast by May 5, 1941: By May 5 the total number of the troops built up against the USSR amounts to 103 to 107 divisions, including 6 divisions located in the Danzig and Poznan areas. Out of this amount, 23 or 24 divisions are in East Prussia, 29 divisions against the Western Military District, 31 to 34 divisions against the Kiev Military District; 4 divisions in the Carpathian Ukraine, and 10 or 11 divisions in Moldavia and Northern Dobrudgia. (The information that there were 18 German divisions in Moldavia alone has not been proved and needs confirmation.)

It is important to stress that over the period of time from April 25 to May 5 the strength of the tank force has been increased from 9 to 12 divisions, the motorized force, including the motorized cavalry divisions, to 8 divisions, and the mountain divisions from 2 to 5.

Construction of all kinds is being intensively carried on to prepare the theater of operations. Extra railway tracks along the strategic routes are being laid in Slovakia, the Protectorate (Czech territory), and Rumania, in particular those leading from the east to the west.

Intensive construction of ammunition stores, fuel depots, and other facilities of military support is under way.

The network of airdromes and landing sites is being broadened.

Besides all that, along the entire border, starting from the Baltic Sea to Hungary, the population is being moved from the border zone.

The Rumanian government issued a secret regulation on evacuating institutions and valuables from Moldavia, which has actually gotten under way. Oil companies have an order to build concrete walls around fuel depots.

Air defense training is intense, bombproof shelters are being built, and experimental mobilization operations have been carried out.

German officers are reconnoitering the Soviet border.

Reports from Vienna talk about calling up from the reserve officers who know Hatitzia and Poland.

The chief command reserve group is being set up by using the forces released from Yugoslavia. It will be located in Czech territory; thus the group amounting to ten divisions stationed there before the war with Yugoslavia is being restored.

Conclusion: Over the past two months, the quantity of the German divisions built up against the USSR in the border area has increased by 37 (from 70 to 107). The number of tank divisions has risen from 6 to 12. Together with the Rumanian and Hungarian armies, it will make about 130 divisions.

It is important that we should take into consideration the growth of the German buildup by using the troops released in Yugoslavia and their concentration in the Protectorate and Rumanian territory.

The German buildup is likely to be further strengthened by the troops stationed in Norway. The North Norwegian group may be later used against the USSR via Finland and by sea.

The German force, designed for actions in the Middle East at the moment, is amounting to 40 divisions, 25 of them deployed in Greece and 15 in Bulgaria. Up to 2 parachute divisions are likely to be used in Iraq to serve the same purpose.

The Chief of the Red Army Intelligence Department
(Golikov)

(A) Two copies: No. 4 Top Secret: May 6, 1941; No. 48582 Top Secret

(B) To the Central Committee of the All-Union Communist Party
(C) To Comrade Stalin.

The navy attaché in Berlin, Capt. Idass Vorontzov, is reporting.

A Soviet citizen, Bozer (a Jew and former Lithuanian subject), informed the deputy navy attaché that, according to what a German officer from the Hitler headquarters says, the Germans are preparing to attack the Soviet Union through Finland, the Baltic region, and Rumania by May 14. Powerful air raids are expected to hit Moscow and Leningrad with airborne drops in the border centers. Bozer has declined to specify the source of the information; thus our efforts to know more have failed so far.

I assume this is false information that was deliberately channeled this way to reach our government and to see its reaction.

Admiral Kuznetsov

Appendix B
STRUCTURE AND ORGANIZATION OF THE RED ARMY AND THE GERMAN WEHRMACHT IN 1941

Organization of the Soviet High Command, July 1941

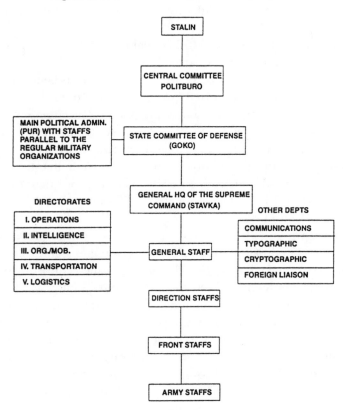

STALIN

CENTRAL COMMITTEE POLITBURO

MAIN POLITICAL ADMIN. (PUR) WITH STAFFS PARALLEL TO THE REGULAR MILITARY ORGANIZATIONS

STATE COMMITTEE OF DEFENSE (GOKO)

GENERAL HQ OF THE SUPREME COMMAND (STAVKA)

DIRECTORATES

I. OPERATIONS
II. INTELLIGENCE
III. ORG./MOB.
IV. TRANSPORTATION
V. LOGISTICS

GENERAL STAFF

OTHER DEPTS

COMMUNICATIONS
TYPOGRAPHIC
CRYPTOGRAPHIC
FOREIGN LIAISON

DIRECTION STAFFS

FRONT STAFFS

ARMY STAFFS

THE ORGANIZATION AND STRUCTURE OF THE RED ARMY
ON THE EVE OF THE WAR

Overall Structure

At the start of the Great Patriotic War, the Soviet Union had a well-developed hierarchical military organization. Under the People's Commissariat for Defense, the country was divided into sixteen military districts, each controlling all army ground and aviation units and installations in its area (except for strategic aviation units). The three special military districts along the western border were better prepared than the rest for rapid mobilization as active field commands (fronts). Each special district controlled several armies and independent corps, along with divisions and smaller units of various branches.

By late 1940 the general staff had elaborated a new strategic deployment plan for the Soviet armed forces. Under the plan, there was a rapid growth in personnel, with many new units being created and old ones being reorganized. An equipment modernization program was also put into place. On September 1, 1939, there were 25 rifle corps, 96 rifle divisions, and 11 motorized rifle divisions. By June 22, 1941, there were 62 rifle corps and 198 rifle divisions.

In June 1941 the armed forces had 5,373,000 men in total. There were more than 67,000 heavy guns and mortars, 1,861 newer model tanks (T-34 and KV), and more than 2,700 newer model aircraft (MiG-3, Il-2, and Pe-2).

In the spring of 1941 the Red Army had 363 divisions. Of these, more than 170 divisions were in the western regions of the country. In addition, a second strategic echelon was formed consisting of the Sixteenth, Seventeenth, Nineteenth, Twentieth, Twenty-first, Twenty-fourth, and Twenty-eighth Armies. Their advance to the Dnepr-Dvina line started in mid-May and was scheduled for completion by July 10. It was these armies, plus other reinforcements, that confronted the Wehrmacht when it reached the upper Dnepr in mid-July.

Rifle troops (the official Soviet term for infantry, coming from the days of the tsars, the term for elite infantry, being used to indicate the supposed superiority of Soviet units) were the backbone of Soviet combat arms. Rifle troops were organized primarily into rifle corps of two or three rifle divisions plus a few support and service units. In frontier armies the rifle corps generally straddled the axes of main advance in the army's sector, with divisions deployed in one echelon. In the interior of military districts were independent rifle corps at a lower state of readiness, deployed in traditional garrison towns. The rifle division was the largest infantry unit with a fixed *shtat*. At the start of the war, three different *shtat*s were actually in use. It should be noted that the "6,000" divisions in the Far Eastern Military District, and at least some divisions on the western border, had a strength of about 7,000 men, intermediate between the two peacetime *shtat* levels.

The Western Special Military District had none of the mountain rifle divisions or rifle brigades. It did include units known as "fortified areas" (UR, or *ukreplennyi raion*), officially considered brigade-sized combined-arms units. A fortified area had variable strength, usually with two to four machine-gun or artillery–machine-gun battalions. These units, which were numbered, occupied a named physical installation, also called a fortified area. The installations were outfitted with obstacles, pillboxes for light artillery and machine guns, and dug-in obsolete tanks. An airborne corps consisted of three airborne brigades plus support and service units. In strength, it was actually like a division, but shortages of transport aircraft made large airborne operations practically impossible. Some cavalry was organized into corps of two to three divisions plus support and service units. The rest, including mountain cavalry divisions, were directly under district or army control. Cavalry divisions were organized to one *shtat*, without a separate level for peacetime.

The armored troops were organized primarily into mechanized corps, each consisting of two tank divisions and one motorized division plus support and service units. This organization was based on that of the German panzer corps and was also used in American armored corps. Although the mechanized corps had a very strong wartime *shtat* (for example, 36,080 men, 1,031 tanks, and 266 armored cars), the actual strength varied widely. Only one corps in the Western Special Military District was at wartime *shtat*; the rest were at about half strength. The total tank strength of the five western border military districts was at 53 percent of *shtat*.

The armored forces were just starting to replace the old light, medium, and heavy tanks (T-28, T-36, BT, T-38, and T-35) with newer models (T-34 and KV). The method of assigning the new tank models made sense, however, only from the viewpoint of the Russian combined-arms doctrine, not from the German model. The new tanks were generally doled out as a battalion of fifty-three T-34s or thirty-one KVs to each tank division, rather than being used to totally reequip a few corps. This policy of parceling out the new tanks was illustrative of the deep divisions within the military hierarchy in 1940 and 1941 about the use of tanks in general. These differences were brought into sharper relief after mid-January 1941 and the continuing arguments between Zhukov and Pavlov over the deployment of tanks in the western regions, particularly within the Bialystok salient. The tank divisions were strong, with 375 tanks by *shtat*, but the variety of tank models in service made it difficult to keep them in operation, especially because spare parts for the older models were no longer being made. The motorized division was to have 275 tanks, attainment of which was complicated by production problems with the new T-34 tank. Additionally, the motorized rifle regiments of both tank and motorized rifle divisions required many trucks that were not available. Anticipating battle with large enemy armored formations, the Russians formed highly innovative antitank artillery brigades of the Supreme Command Reserve (RGK). These brigades were strongly equipped with antitank and antiaircraft guns and were motorized, designed to thwart the advance of a panzer division. At the start of the campaign, most of them were still being formed.

Antiaircraft defense, apart from that in combined-arms units, was in the hands of the Territorial Air Defense (PVO, *Voiska protivovozdushnoi oborony strany*). This branch was organized administratively into PVO zones, each covering the area of a military district. Each consisted of PVO brigades and PVO brigade areas. The administrative and operational distinction between these two types of units is unclear, but their antiaircraft weapons could also serve in antitank and antipersonnel roles. In a few military districts with more important industrial concentrations, the zone controlled PVO corps or divisions. Only the fighter units assigned to the air defense of Moscow, Leningrad, and Baku were directed by the local PVO commander, and they, therefore, occupied a special position. Elsewhere, the PVO fighter aircraft were subordinated to the air force commanders of the military districts.

The air force (VVS, *Voenno-vozdushnye sily*), under control of the Commissariat of Defense, had been reorganized some months before the campaign. Its units were controlled by a deputy commander for aviation within each military district. Directly under his control were several attack, fighter, and bomber air divisions and fighter divisions of the PVO. Each army also had a composite air division. Aviation technical and support functions in each military district were provided by a regional system that controlled air base activities.

The navy was organized into four fleets and several flotillas, the last serving primarily on inland waters. The major operational unit of a fleet was the squadron (*eskadr*), consisting of at least one battleship or cruiser along with smaller surface units. The major permanent operational unit was the brigade, consisting of several ships or smaller vessels of the same type. Each fleet had a naval aviation component that was not part of the army's air force. Among other units, naval aviation still included some brigades, a unit abandoned earlier in the army air force. The navy also included ground branches conducting activities that in other countries would be done by the army or marines. Coast artillery was extensive, organized into area commands containing battalion-sized units. Naval infantry units had the mission of protecting naval bases and conducting small amphibious operations.

The People's Commissariat of Internal Affairs (NKVD) had two types of operational troops trained for combat operations. The border troops guarded the international boundary zone with regiment-sized units. The internal troops had a variety of regiments designed for various internal security activities that could be used for combat emergencies. Some internal troops were organized into divisions. The NKVD also controlled "penal battalions," which were used for especially dangerous work such as clearing minefields in the advance of an offensive.

Political Structure
On August 12, 1940, the Presidium.of the Supreme Soviet issued an order, "Strengthening the Unified Command in the Red Army and Navy." This order replaced the Communist Party commissars, created

in 1937, with deputy political commanders. These commanders were responsible for all activities, including combat as well as political training. They were introduced at all levels of command. In principle, unification of command was to be achieved by the military commander, the political officer, and the Party, all having common goals.

The military-political structure was as follows. At the top of the chain was the Main Political Department of the Red Army. Under it were the political departments of the districts, corps, and divisions. There were also political structures in regiments, battalions, and companies. In the regiments, propagandists were senior officers; sergeants and soldiers with special training performed political work in the lower units. The center of political work was at the company or battery level, where the focus was on training and combat readiness.

The political classes for sergeants and enlisted ranks was, however, largely unrealistic on the eve of the war. There was little emphasis on the practical aspects of combat. Since the pact with Germany in 1939, the political workers were forbidden to talk about the likelihood of a coming German invasion. Instead, in courses such as "The USSR Is the Country of Socialism," "You Swear to Serve in the Red Army," and "Our Socialist State of Workers and Peasants," emphasis was placed on Party history and on Party documents such as the works of Lenin and Stalin. By December 1940, some higher military commanders, Marshal Timoshenko in particular, were warning of the danger of not concentrating on preparation for war with Germany, but Stalin would not relent.

THE ORGANIZATION AND STRUCTURE OF THE GERMAN ARMY ON THE EVE OF THE WAR

In an examination of the organization and structure of the German army in 1941, it is important to keep in mind the distinction between the army (*Das Heer*) and the armed forces (*Die Wehrmacht*). In 1941 much of the army's organizational structure was not at all different from what it had been in World War I. The foundation of the army was the military district (*Wehrkreis*). In 1941 there were twenty-one

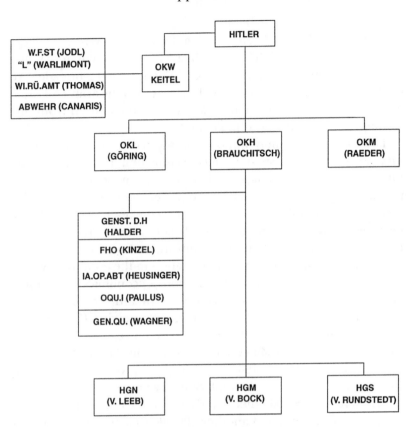

LEGEND:
ABWEHR = OKW INTELLIGENCE/COUNTER INTELLIGENCE
FHQ = GENERAL STAFF INTELLIGENCE DEPARTMENT
GEN.QU. = QUARTERMASTER GENERAL
GENST.D.H. = GENERAL STAFF OF THE ARMY
HGM = ARMY GROUP CENTER
HGN = ARMY GROUP NORTH
HGS = ARMY GROUP SOUTH
IA.OP.ABT. = CHIEF OF OPERATIONS, OPERATIONS STAFF
OKH = ARMY HIGH COMMAND
OKL = AIR FORCE HIGH COMMAND
OKW = ARMED FORCES HIGH COMMAND
OQU.I. = CHIEF QUARTERMASTER
W.F.ST. = OKW OPERATIONS DEPARTMENT
W.F.ST. "L" = DEPUTY CHIEF OKW OPERATIONS DEPARTMENT
WI.RÜ.AMT = OKW ECONOMICS AND ARMAMENTS OFFICE

FIGURE 1-B. STRUCTURE OF THE GERMAN HIGH COMMAND, JUNE 1941

districts in the Greater German Reich. Each district was home base to several divisions and their subordinate regiments. When war mobilization began in 1939, there were 51 divisions and 2 brigades. At the time of the Russian campaign, the strength of the army had risen to 208 divisions; of these about 154 were on the eastern front, including 4 German divisions in Finland.

The German war mobilization plan was based on a two-part *Ersatz*, or replacement system. Each peacetime unit that was already at full combat strength was supposed to have a permanent replacement unit behind it. The purpose of this replacement unit was to handle recruiting and training and also to organize the reservists should they be called up. Replacement divisional headquarters were set up; during peacetime, they had purely administrative functions.

This plan allowed for rapid mobilization in the event of a war or crisis without causing large transportation or economic dislocations. When war occurred, four waves (*Welle*) of infantry could be raised on relatively short notice: (1) active units, (2) reservists, (3) *Landwehr* territorial units, and (4) men nineteen to twenty years old (*Jahrgänge*) who had undergone a short period of training. The 1921 *Jahrgang* was called up in March 1941, and the 1922 group in May. These forces were brought into the replacement army (*Ersatzheer*). In June 1941, there were 80,000 men available as immediate replacements for the eastern front, and another 300,000 to 350,000 were placed in the *Ersatzheer*, mostly in the 20th *Jahrgang*. In 1939 the population of the Greater German Reich was 80.6 million—38.9 million men and 41.7 million women. Of the men, 12 million fell into the age group fifteen to thirty-four; of these, the Wehrmacht could expect to claim 7 million. In 1939 the civilian labor force was reckoned at 24.5 million men and 14.6 million women; 18.1 million men were employed in war-related or critical industries. In June 1941, the German army had 3.8 million men, of which 3.3 million were deployed against the Soviet Union. Of 21 fully equipped panzer divisions, 17 were targeted for Russia, 2 were in OKH reserve destined for Russia, and 2 were in North Africa. The backbone of the German army was, of course, the infantry division. Of the 154 divisions deployed against Russia, including reserves, there were 100 infantry, 19 panzer, 11 motorized, 9 security, 5 Waffen SS, 4 light, 4 mountain, 1 SS police, and 1 cavalry.

A typical infantry division in June 1941 had 17,734 men organized as follows:[1]

Three infantry regiments with staff and communications units; three battalions with three light MG companies, one heavy MG company, one PAK company (mot.), one artillery company; one reconnaissance unit; one Panzerjäger unit with three companies (twelve 3.7cm guns); one artillery regiment; one pioneer battalion; one communications unit; one field replacement battalion; supply, medical, veterinary, mail, and police personnel.

An infantry division was outfitted with the following equipment:

Light machine guns (LMG): 378; heavy machine guns (HMG): 138; antitank rocket launchers (ATL): 90; 50mm mortar (50 Mtr): 93; 81mm mortar (81 Mtr): 54; 20 gun: 12; antitank gun (PAK): 75; 75mm howitzer (75 How.): 20; 105mm howitzer (105 How.): 36; motorized transport vehicles (MT): 1,009; horse-drawn transportation vehicles (HD): 918; horses: 4,842; armored fighting vehicles (AFV): 3

The typical panzer division in 1941 had 15,600 men organized as follows:

One panzer regiment with staff and communications units; two panzer units with two light tank companies, one medium tank company, one repair company; two battalions with three light MG companies, one heavy MG company; one light artillery and PAK company; one infantry artillery company; one reconnaissance unit; one artillery regiment; one Panzerjäger unit; one pioneer battalion; one communications unit; one field surgical battalion; supply, veterinary, mail, and police.

A panzer division was outfitted with the following equipment:

LMG: 850; HMG: 1,067; ATL: 45; 81 Mtr: 30; 20 Gun: 74; PAK: 75; 75 How.: 18; 105 How.: 196; MT: 2,900; Tanks: 165

The typical motorized infantry division in 1941 had 16,400 men organized as follows (in 1943, these units were given extra armor and renamed "Panzer Grenadiers"):
Two infantry regiments with staff and communications units; three battalions with three light MG companies, one heavy MG company; one motorcycle platoon; one artillery company; one PAK company; two motorcycle battalions with three light MG companies, one heavy MG company; one light artillery and PAK company; one reconnaissance unit; one artillery regiment; one Panzerjäger unit; one pioneer battalion; one communications unit; one field-surgical battalion; supply, veterinary, mail, and police.

A motorized infantry division was outfitted with the following equipment:
LMG: 810; HMG: 712; ATL: 63; 50 Mtr: 57; 81 Mtr: 36; 20 Gun: 12; PAK: 63; 75 How.: 14; 105 How.: 48; MT: 2,800; AFV: 82

Note on Sources

The research that went into this book is based heavily on documents found in various archives in Russia and on microfilm copies of the war diaries of German military units located at the National Archives and Records Administration in Washington, D.C. One of us, Mr. Lev Dvoretsky, obtained a special pass permitting access to the following archives in Russia:

- The Central Archives of the Ministry of Defense of the USSR (abbreviated CADD in this book)
- The Central Archives of the Soviet Army
- The Archives of the Chief Intelligence Department
- The KGB Archives
- The Archives of the Central Committee of the Communist Party of the Soviet Union (CPSU)

In addition, Lev Dvoretsky had the opportunity to become acquainted with the personal papers of Marshals Timoshenko and Zhukov.

The authors also have a special arrangement with the *Voenno-istoricheskii zhurnal* (*Military-Historical Journal*) to publish documents relating to the early warnings of the German invasion. The Russian photos in this book were supplied by the Central Museum of the Armed Forces of the USSR. The German photos were supplied by the U.S. Army Military History Institute, Carlisle Barracks, PA.

Throughout this book wherever there are quotes from a primary or secondary source, the source is cited. In general, the quotes from Halder came from his three-volume *Kriegstagebuch* (Stuttgart: W. Kohlhammer Verlag, 1962–1964). The quotes from Guderian came from his book *Panzer Leader* (London: Michael Joseph, 1951), as well as from materials found in various unit war diaries and specifically von Bock's "Tagebuchnotizen Osten I," National Archives Microfilm Publication T-84, roll 271. The Captured German Documents section of the National Archives is staffed with people who are very helpful in introducing researchers to the intricacies of the microfilm indexes. References to directives, orders, and the sizes and movements of units rely on original documents, not on other historians' interpretations of them. It is often the case that historians choose either not to use original sources or elect to examine in detail the records of only one side. A good example of this is *Hitler's Panzers East* by R. H. S. Stolfi (University of Colorado Press, 1991). Stolfi makes the serious mistake of trying to convince his readers that studying Soviet sources is not necessary to interpret the events of 1941: ". . . the Germans controlled events during the summer of 1941 to the degree that most significant points needed for verification can be derived from German sources." It is time for historians to realize that it is wrong to write a one-sided history of the Eastern Front.

It is said that more books have been written about Napoleon than any other historical (nonreligious) character in the world. That being so, it can be added that more books have been written about World War II than any other event in history—so many, in fact, that they could never be counted. Yet, despite this volume of information, the War in the East is still thought of by most westerners as the "Unknown War." Actually, the information needed to open up many of the issues regarding Soviet defense plans has been in print for a number of years, but historians refused to take it seriously.

The problem has been that Soviet history books on the Great Patriotic War, to suit the requirements of the times, contained so much Communist jargon that few could thread their way through the extraneous material and get to the heart of the precious information. Before now the only way anyone could arrive at the true history of the War in the East was to painstakingly examine the German unit records and compare them with available Soviet publications and see where the combatants' accounts differed and, most importantly, coincided. Unfortunately, there have been very few historians who have taken the trouble to go through all of this difficulty. Nearly all of them have chosen to copy from others who claimed to have been given special information by those close to participants in the events. These participants, however, unfortunately had their own views to put forward, which often deliberately distorted the facts, as in the case of Guderian. In Zhukov's case, because of Party discipline in force during the Khrushchev period, he was unable to come forth with the details of the secret defense plan. He did, however, come as close as he could to revealing the true story.

The authors of this book, based on new facts and recently discovered documents, have constructed an alternative interpretation that does not coincide with opinions and publications of other researchers of World War II. The first clue as to what was really going on with Soviet defense planning occurred during an investigation of the reasons why Army Group Center paused in July and August and was unable to pursue the thrust toward Moscow until Operation Typhoon was started at the end of September 1941. This investigation led to a detailed examination of the war diaries of the units directly engaged in combat in the Smolensk-Yelnia area and on the southern flank of Army Group Center. In particular, the diaries of Panzer Group 2, Second Army, IX Army Corps, the 10th Panzer Division, and von Bock all pointed in the same direction—namely that the Soviets were putting such extreme pressure on the Germans that something had to be done to counter them. In other words, the Germans had to bring their own plans to a halt, change their strategy, and take the enemy seriously. To the readers of this book, all of this seems obvious now, but at the time it was a revelation.

The crowning blow to the old interpretation of the War in the East came after a close inspection of Soviet sources was undertaken. As stated above, there were reasons why no one in the West had ever taken these works seriously. The problem was that in many respects the story they had to tell corresponded so closely to what is contained in the German records that it became impossible to deny the truth any longer. This was a problem because the pressure exerted by professional historians and journalists meant that people in the world at large could not be easily convinced of an alternative interpretation. One of the Soviet works that revealed a big part of the truth was written by S. M. Shtemenko, *Generalnye Shtab v gody voiny* (*The General Staff in the War*) (Moscow: Voenn-izdat., 1968). In Shtemenko's book it was revealed that there were two war games in January 1941 and there was ample evidence that these games had a major impact on strategic planning. Another important work was by V. A. Anfilov, *Bessmertnyi podvig: issledovanie kanuna i pervogo etapa Velikoi Otechestvennoi voiny* (*The Immortal Exploit: An Investigation of the Pre-War and*

Early-War Periods) (Moscow: Izdat. "Nauka," 1971). In this book it was revealed for the first time how many Soviet units really were in position at the time to counter the thrust of Army Group Center, not just along the borders but in the depths of the country, particularly south of the Pripyat Marshes. Another important work was edited by V. D. Sokolovskii, *Razgrom nemetsko-fashiskikh voisk pod Moskvoi* (*The Destruction of the German-Facist Army at Moscow*) (Moscow: Voenn-izdat., 1964). From this book it became clear that Zhukov's plan for a Moscow counteroffensive in December 1941 would never have succeeded had not an overall strategy for defense been worked out months earlier, most probably even before the war started.

Additional elements of the puzzle began to fall into place with the publication of successive editions and re-editions of Zhukov's memoirs, the first of which appeared in the West in 1971, *The Memoirs of Marshal Zhukov* (London: Jonathan Cape, 1971). Although constrained by the Khrushchevian interpretation of the beginning of the war, blaming everything on Stalin's refusal to pay heed to the warnings of a German invasion, Zhukov was able to communicate some keen insights as to the working of strategy at the highest levels in the Kremlin. It must be remembered that Zhukov himself was denounced by Khrushchev, and he finally ended his days in internal exile. But, despite the conformity that was forced upon him, Zhukov's memoirs did serve to expand the concept of the real defense strategy. In Zhukov's explanation of the first war game in January, he outlined in clear words the objections he delivered to Stalin regarding the mistake about putting all hopes on fortifications too close to the borders. Zhukov came as close as he could to revealing the truth without actually saying it. He said he expressed his views and that later he received the appointment as chief of the general staff. He did not say that Stalin agreed with him and charged him with developing and implementing a new plan, but that is what he inferred, and it is now known that is what he did. The debate over the now famous May 15, 1941, document, "Considerations on the Plan of Strategic Deployment of the Armed Forces of the Soviet Union in the Event of War with Germany and its Allies," signed by Zhukov and Timoshenko, which purports to show that they advocated a preemptive strike against Germany, has been renewed by the publication of a book by Russian historian Edvard Radzinsky, *Stalin* (New York: Doubleday, 1996). Radzinky's discussion of the document leaves the reader puzzled about what the document really meant. We hope our discussion of this matter provides a satisfactory explanation for why the document came into existence and how it was used.

The path taken in order to arrive at a reinterpretation of the War in the East was nonlinear despite the commentary above, which makes the research process sound scientific and well planned in advance; in truth it was nothing of the sort. The writing of this book was motivated by the idea that a way could be found to present the facts and interpret them to make them comprehensible to the general reader.

Notes

Introduction

1. M. Florinsky, *Russia: A History and an Interpretation* (New York: Macmillan, 1964), vol. I, pp. 215–16.

2. Central Archives of the Soviet Army, File 655, sheet 4.

3. M. V. Frunze, *Collected Works,* (Moscow, 1926), vol. 2, p. 320.

4. A. A. Neznamov, *Modern War* (Petrograd: Voenn-izdat., 1929).

5. G. Isserson, "Razvitie teorii sovetskogo operativnogo iskusstva v 30-e gody" (The Development of Soviet Theories of Operational Art in the 1930s), *Voenno-Istoricheskii Zhurnal,* January 1965, pp. 39–46, March 1965, pp. 44–61.

6. Statement made by Shaposhnikov in a lecture at the Frunze Academy. He was chief of the academy during the period 1932–35. See also his work *Mozg Armiia* (*The brain of the army*) (Moscow: Voennii Vestnik, 1927), pp. 240–41.

7. Classical examples of stereotypical interpretations are: John Erickson, *The Road to Stalingrad: Stalin's War with Germany* (London: Weidenfeld and Nicolson, 1975); Harrison Salisbury, *The 900 Days: The Siege of Leningrad* (New York: Harper and Row, 1969); Paul Carrell, *Hitler Moves East, 1941–43* (New York: Bantam Books, 1966); Gert Buchheit, *Hitler der Feldherr: die Zerstörung einer Legende* (Rastatt: Grote Verlag, 1961); Klaus Reinhardt, *Die Wende vor Moskau: das Scheitern der Strategie Hitlers im Winter 1941/42* (Stuttgart: Deutsche Verlags-Anstalt, 1972). By contrast a more recent book is better balanced about the conflicts between Hitler and his generals and among the generals themselves. See Correlli Barnett, ed., *Hitler's Generals* (New York: Grove Weidenfeld, 1989). Particularly interesting is the essay on Halder by Barry Leach, who agrees with much the present authors have to say, as well as the essay on von Kluge by Richard Lamb. Lamb points out that von Kluge warned about the dangers of a Moscow offensive with tanks unsupported by infantry in the late fall of 1941.

Chapter 1

1. G. Komkov, "Sovetskie organy gosudarstvennoi bezopasnosti v gody Velikoi Otechestvennoi voiny" (The Organs of State Security during the Great Patriotic War), *Voprosy istorii* (Questions of History), May 1965, pp. 25–28.

2. Barry Leach, *German Strategy against Russia, 1939–1941* (Oxford: Clarendon Press, 1973); Andreas Hillgruber, *Hitler's Strategie: Politik und Kriegführung, 1940–1941* (Frankfurt am Main: Bernard und Gräfe Verlag für Wehrwesen, 1965); Otto Jacobsen, *Erich Marcks: Soldat und Gelehrter* (Goettingen: Musterschmidt Verlag, 1971); A. Phillipi, "Das Pripjetproblem," *Wehrwissenschaftliche Rundschau,* supplement, March 1956; A. Phillipi and Ferdinand Heim, *Der Feldzug gegen Sowjetrussland, 1941 bis 1945* (Stuttgart: W. Kohlhammer Verlag, 1962); H. Uhlig, "Das Einwirken Hitlers auf Planung und Führung des Ostfeldzuges," *Das Parlement,* supplement, March 16, 1960.

3. G. K. Zhukov, V*ospominaniia i razmyshleniia* (Memoirs and Reflections) (Moscow: Novosti, 1992), p. 339.

4. *Landscape Atlas of the U.S.S.R.* (West Point, N.Y.: U.S. Military Academy, 1971), p. 44.

5. G. K. Zhukov, *The Memoirs of Marshal Zhukov* (London: Jonathan Cape, 1971), p. 186.

Chapter 2

1. V. I. Lenin, "5-ii Vserosiskii Se'zd Sovetov" (The 5th all-Russian Congress of Soviets) in *Collected Works,* 5th ed., vol. 42, pp. 129–31, 139–40.

2. *Manevrennii i skorostnoi* (Maneuverable and Fast) in Soviet Military Survey, no. 9, 1989, p. 78.

3. Central State Archives of the Soviet Army, Index 40442, Inventory 2, File 170, pp. 13–14.

4. Tukhachevsky, *O Vozmozhnosti pozitsionnikh uslovii borbi* (private correspondence), 1937.

5. A. V. Hrulev, "*Tyl v godi voini*" (The Rear During the War Years) (Tblisi: Newspaper *Lenin's Banner,* September 9, 1962).

6. Central Archives of the Ministry of Defense of the U.S.S.R., Index 138, Inventory 7162, File 10, p. 1.

7. Central State Archives of the Soviet Army, Index 22, Inventory 32, File 4208, pp. 40–47.

8. Central Archives of the Ministry of Defense of the U.S.S.R., Index 2, Inventory 75593, File 14, p. 59.

9. See *Voenno-Istoricheskii Zhurnal,* 1991, no. 3, p. 22.

10. John Erickson, *The Road to Stalingrad: Stalin's War with Germany,* vol. 1.

11. Simonov, "Commentary to Zhukov's Biography. Record of Talks," *Voenno-Istoricheskii Zhurnal,* 1987, no. 6, p. 49.

12. A. Rossi, *Russian-German Alliance, 1939–1941* (Boston: Beacon Press, 1951), pp. 75–76.

13. Adam B. Ulam, *Expansion and Co-Existence: Soviet Foreign Policy, 1917–1973* (New York: Praeger, 1974).

14. "Economic Agreement of February 11, 1940 and Its Evaluation," Archives of the Central Committee of the Communist Party, Index Book 3, Folio 64, File 675-a, pp. 23–26.

15. "Speech at the Conference of Political Agitators" (Tblisi: F. I. Golikov, Newspaper *Lenin's Banner,* April 12, 1961).

Chapter 3

1. CADD, 221/1351, vol. 202, p. 1.

2. Zhukov, *The Memoirs of Marshal Zhukov.*

3. K. K. Rokossovskii, *Na frontakh Velikoi Otechestvennoi Voini* (On the Fronts of the Great Patriotic War), Extracts from Memoirs (Baku: Na Strazhe, 1962), June 22, 1962, p. 24.

Chapter 4

1. H. Krausnick, "The Persecution of the Jews," *Anatomy of the SS State* (London: St. James Place, 1968), p. 64.

Chapter 5

1. Harry Schwartz, *Introduction to the Soviet Economy* (Columbus, Ohio: Charles E. Merrill, 1968); Howard Sherman, *The Soviet Economy* (Boston: Little Brown and Co., 1969).

2. I. Yakubovski, "Nemerknushchii podvig" (Never-forgotten exploits) (Kiev: Newspaper *Lenin's Banner,* August 23, 1966).

3. H. Guderian, *Errinerungen eines Soldaten* (Heidelberg, 1951), pp. 179–180.

4. Alan Clark, *Barbarossa: The Russian-German Conflict, 1941–1945* (New York: William Morrow, 1965), p. 112.

Chapter 6

1. *Istoriia Velikoi Otechestvennoi voiny,* vol. II, p. 104; Zhukov, *Memoirs,* pp. 294–96; A. I. Eremenko, *Na zapadnam napravlenii* (On the Western Front) (Moscow: Voenn-izdat., 1959).

2. A. I. Eremenko, *Gody vozmezdia, 1943–1945* (The years of retribution, 1943–1945) (Moscow: Publishing House "Finance and Statistics," 1985), pp. 305–306.

Chapter 7

1. Franz Halder, *Kriegstagebuch* (Stuttgart: W. Kohlhammer Verlag, 1962–64), vol. III, p. 215.

2. I. S. Konev, "Osen'iu 1941g" (In the Fall of 1941) in *Bitva za Moskvu* (The Battle for Moscow), ed. by the Institute for Party History of the Moscow Committee of the CPSU (Moscow: Izdat. "Moskovskii rabochii," 1968), pp. 35–62.

3. Edgar Rörhricht, *Probleme der Kesselschlacht: dargestellt an Einkreisungs-Operationen im Zweiten Weltkrieg* (Karlsruhe: Condor-Verlag, 1958). See also R. H. S. Stolfi, *Hitler's Panzers East* (Norman, Okla.: University of Oklahoma Press, 1991).

4. *Marshal Zhukov's Greatest Battles,* p. 51.

5. V. D. Sokolovskii, *Razgrom nemetsko-fashistkikh voisk pod Moskvoi* (The destruction of the German-Fascist army at Moscow) (Moscow: Voenn-izdat., 1964). A. M. Vasilevskii, "Nachalo korennogo povorta v khode voiny" (The turn of the tide in the war) in *Bitva za Moskvu,* pp. 11–27.

6. Guderian's Panzer Group 2 had been augmented by two infantry corps and given the unit designation Second Panzer Army for Operation Typhoon. For a good overview of Typhoon, see Albert Seaton, *The Russo-German War* (New York: Praeger, 1970), pp. 192–212.

Chapter 8

1. Heinz Guderian, *Panzer Leader* (London: Michael Joseph, 1952); Franz Halder, *Hitler als Feldherr* (Munich: Münchener Dom Verlag, 1949).

2. Franz Halder, *Kriegstagebuch,* vol. III, p. 134.

3. Peter Hoffmann, *The History of the German Resistance, 1933–1945* (Cambridge: MIT Press, 1977), pp. 128, 265–66, 530.

4. Alan Bullock, *Hitler: A Study in Tyranny* (London: Oldham Press, 1952).

5. Percy Schramm, ed., *Kriegstagebuch des Oberkommandos der Wehrmacht* (Frankfurt am Main: Bernard und Gräfe Verlag für Wehrwesen, 1961–65), vol. I, pp. 1043–44.

6. Percy Schramm, ed., *Kriegstagebuch OKW*, vol. I, pp. 1054–55.

7. Percy Schramm, ed., *Kriegstagebuch OKW*, vol. I, pp. 1055–59.

8. Werner Haupt, *Geschichte der 134. Infanterie-Division* (Tuttlingen: Werner Groll, 1971), p. 27.

9. Leach, *German Strategy*, pp. 118–23.

10. Buchheit, *Hitler der Feldherr: die Zerstörung einer Legende* p. 250.

11. E. Middeldorf, *Taktik im Russlandfeldzug* (Darmstadt: E. S. Mittler und Sohn Verlag, 1956), pp. 189–91.

12. A. I. Eremenko, *Protiv falsifikatsii istorii vtoroi mirovoi voiny* (Against the Falsifications of the History of the Second World War) (Moscow: Izdat. Inostrannoi Literatury, 1958), p. 30.

Appendix B

1. Source: Mueller-H. Hillebrand, Burkhart, *Das Heer, 1938–1945: Entwicklung des organisatorisatorischen Aufbaues* (E. S. Mittler und Sohn, 1977), vols. II and III; *War in the East: The Russo-German Conflict, 1941–1945* (Frankfurt am Main: Simulations Publications, 1977).

Index